Windows® XP For Dummies®

2nd Edition

Cheat Sheet

Knowing Your Windows Desktop

- The Windows desktop serves as the background for running programs and working with files. The taskbar runs along the desktop's bottom edge.
- Click the Start button to reveal the Start menu, where you can run programs (Chapter 5), change settings (Chapter 11), access folders (Chapter 4), and search for files (Chapter 6).

Rest your mouse pointer over any icon for an explanation of what it does.

- The Quick Launch toolbar holds frequently used programs, ready for launch with a single click.
- The taskbar's notification area tells you about events like newly received e-mail or security alerts.
- Confused? Click the Start menu's Help and Support icon to view the Windows XP Help menu (Chapter 20).
- If you accidentally delete a file, double-click the Recycle Bin icon, right-click on the accidentally deleted file, and choose Restore to undelete it, putting it back where it was (Chapter 2).

Mastering Multimedia

Playing Songs and Videos in Media Player (Chapter 15)

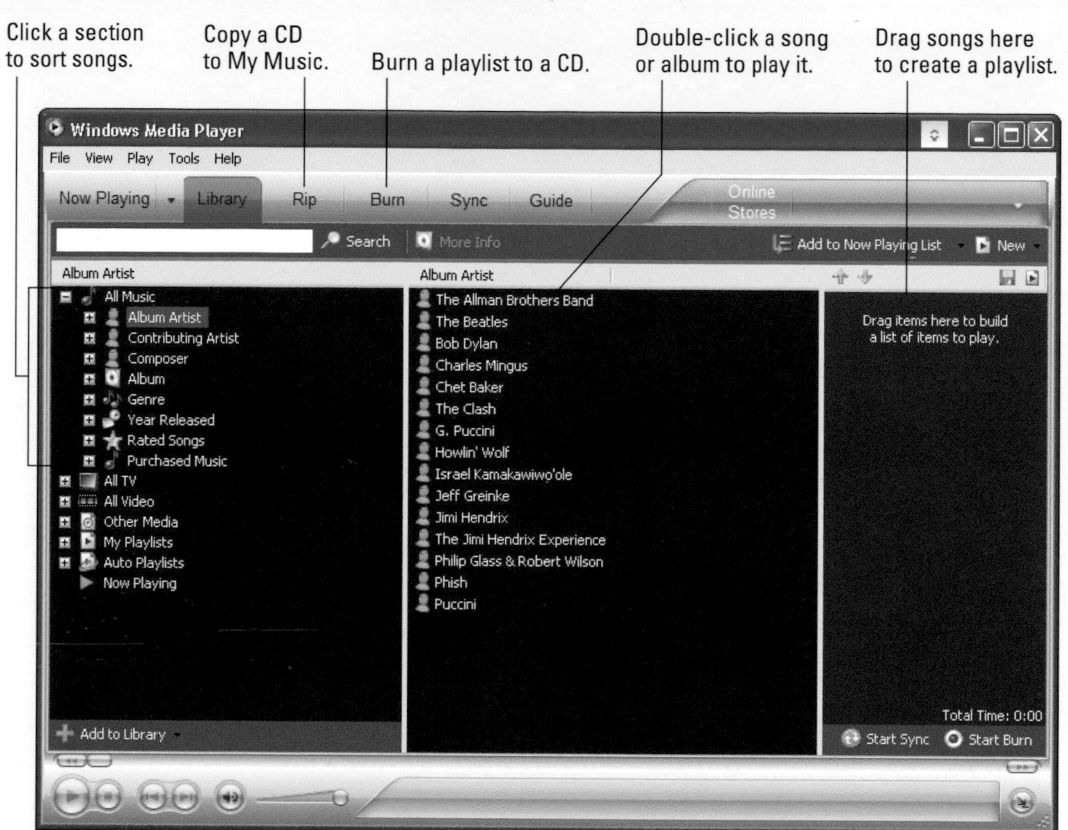

Sorting Through Digital Photos (Chapter 16)

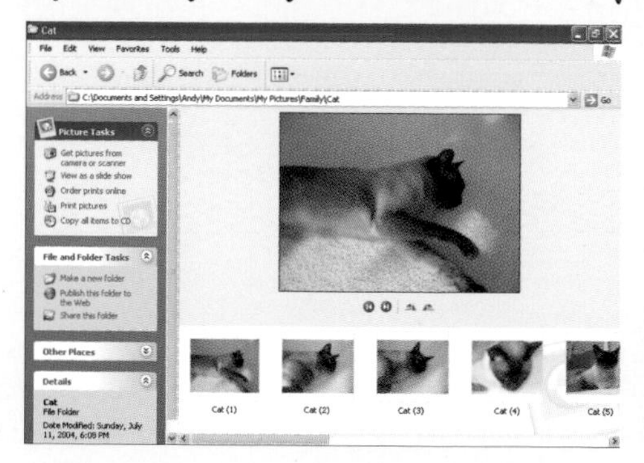

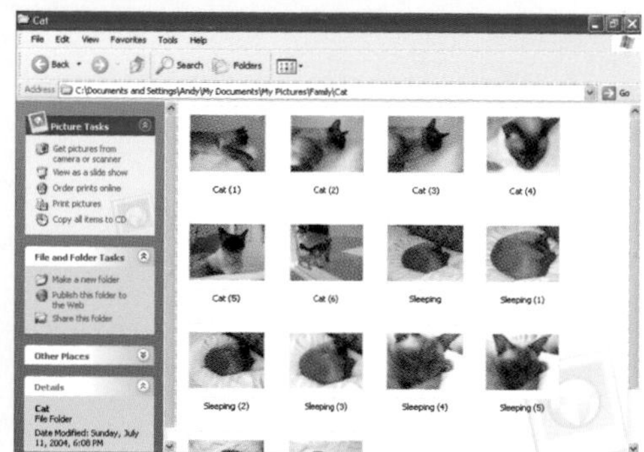

- In My Pictures, choose Thumbnails or Filmstrip from the View menu to display pictures different ways.
- In My Pictures, click View as a Slide Show from the task pane.
- Double-click any photo to see it in a larger window.
- Click any photo and choose E-Mail This File to mail it to a friend.

For Dummies: Bestselling Book Series for Beginners

Windows® XP For Dummies®

2nd Edition

Exploring the Internet

Using Internet Explorer (Chapter 8)

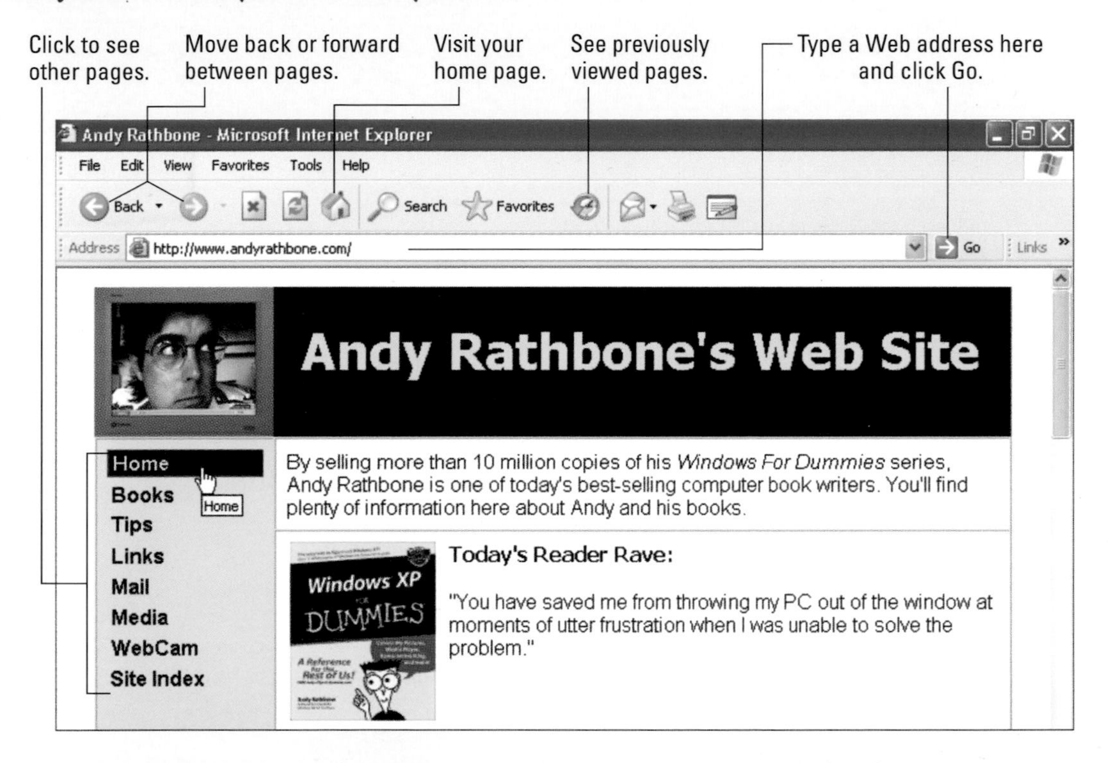

Staying Safe While Online (Chapter 10)

- Choose Security Center from the Start menu's Control Panel area to check your firewall, automatic updates, and virus protection.
- When a defense, such as virus protection, isn't working properly, click the Recommendations button for tips on correcting the problem.
- Click the Internet Options, Automatic Updates, or Windows Firewall icon to adjust settings.

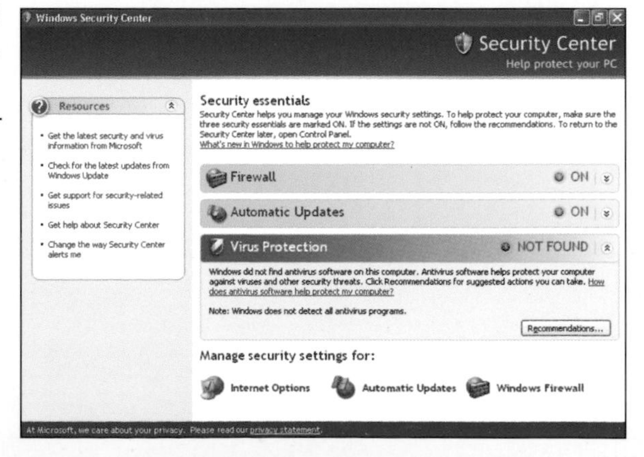

Finding Your Way Around Windows

Saving Time with the Task Panes

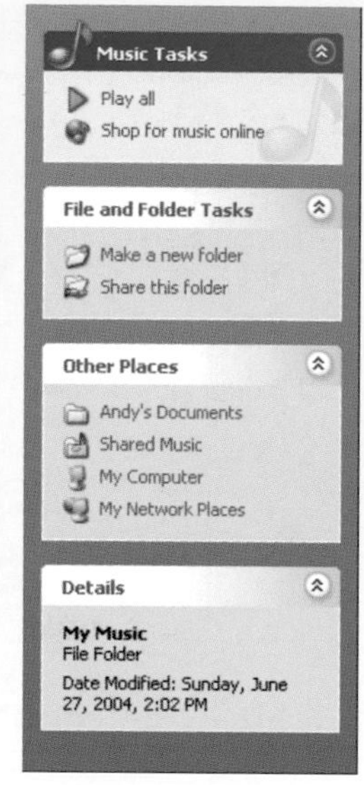

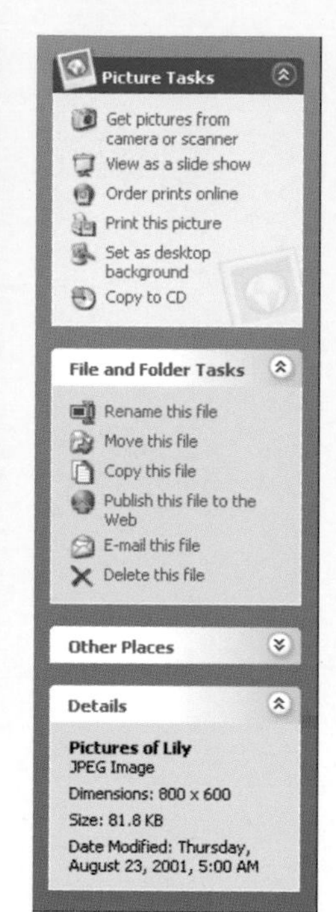

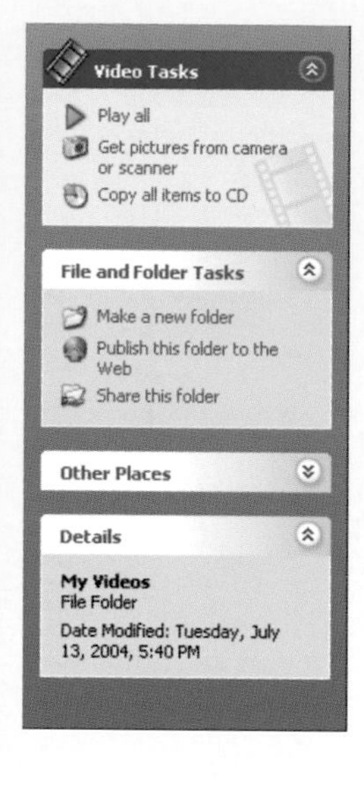

- The task pane, found along a folder's left edge, contains timesaving shortcuts available at a glance. As you open different folders, the shortcuts change to show tasks for your currently viewed folder.

TIP The task pane in your My Pictures folder is particularly handy, providing quick ways to start a slide show, get pictures from a digital camera or scanner, print pictures, or copy all the photos to a CD.

- Click a file's icon in the folder and look in the task pane's Details area to see information about that file's size, contents, and creation date.
- To move quickly from folder to folder, use the shortcuts in the task pane's Other Places area. From there, you can jump to the desktop, My Documents folder, and other commonly accessed places.

Managing Folders and Windows (Chapter 3)

To Do This . . .	*Do This . . .*
See a list of all open windows.	Look at the names on the taskbar along the screen's bottom.
Move from one window to another window.	Press Alt+Tab+Tab or click the window's name on the taskbar.
Cascade the windows across the screen.	Right-click on the taskbar's clock (or a blank part of the taskbar) and then click Cascade.
Shrink all open windows.	Click the little pencil-and-pad icon near the Start button.
Make a window fill the screen.	Double-click the title bar along its top edge.

Windows® XP FOR DUMMIES®

2ND EDITION

by Andy Rathbone

Wiley Publishing, Inc.

Windows® XP For Dummies®, 2nd Edition

Published by
Wiley Publishing, Inc.
111 River Street
Hoboken, NJ 07030-5774
www.wiley.com

Published by Wiley Publishing, Inc., Indianapolis, Indiana

Published simultaneously in Canada

For general information on our other products and services or to obtain technical support, please contact our Customer Care Department within the U.S. at 800-762-2974, outside the U.S. at 317-572-3993, or fax 317-572-4002.

Wiley also publishes its books in a variety of electronic formats. Some content that appears in print may not be available in electronic books.

Library of Congress Control Number: 2004107902

ISBN: 0-7645-7326-8

Manufactured in the United States of America

10 9 8 7 6 5

2B/ST/QZ/QU/IN

About the Author

Andy Rathbone started geeking around with computers in 1985 when he bought a 26-pound portable CP/M Kaypro 2X. Like other budding nerds, he soon began playing with null-modem adapters, dialing up computer bulletin boards, and working part-time at Radio Shack.

When not playing computer games, he served as editor of the *Daily Aztec* newspaper at San Diego State University. Armed with a comparative literature degree, he began writing features for magazines and local newspapers.

He eventually combined his interests in words and computers, and sold articles to a local computer magazine. During the next few years, he started ghostwriting computer books for more-famous computer authors, as well as writing several hundred articles about computers for various techie publications.

In 1992, Andy and *DOS For Dummies* author/legend Dan Gookin teamed up to write *PCs For Dummies*. Andy subsequently wrote the award-winning *Windows For Dummies* series, *Upgrading & Fixing PCs For Dummies, TiVo For Dummies,* and many other *For Dummies* books.

Today, he has more than 15 million copies of his books in print, which have been translated into more than 30 languages.

Andy lives with his most-excellent wife, Tina, and their cat in Southern California. Feel free to drop by his Web site at `www.andyrathbone.com`.

Dedication

To my wife, parents, sister, and cat.

Author's Acknowledgments

Special thanks to Dan Gookin, Matt Wagner, Tina Rathbone, Steve Hayes, Becky Huehls, and Kim Darosett. Thanks also to all the folks I never meet in editorial, sales, marketing, proofreading, layout, graphics, and manufacturing who work hard to bring you this book.

Publisher's Acknowledgments

We're proud of this book; please send us your comments through our online registration form located at www.dummies.com/register/.

Some of the people who helped bring this book to market include the following:

Acquisitions, Editorial, and Media Development

Project Editor: Rebecca Huehls

Senior Acquisitions Editor: Steve Hayes

Senior Copy Editor: Kim Darosett

Technical Editor: Lee Musick

Editorial Manager: Leah Cameron

Media Development Manager: Laura VanWinkle

Media Development Supervisor: Richard Graves

Editorial Assistant: Amanda Foxworth

Cartoons: Rich Tennant, www.the5thwave.com

Composition

Senior Project Coordinator: Nancee Reeves

Layout and Graphics: Lauren Goddard, Denny Hager, Joyce Haughey, Barry Offringa, Jacque Roth, Heather Ryan

Proofreaders: John Greenough, Brian H. Walls

Indexer: TECHBOOKS Production Services

Publishing and Editorial for Technology Dummies

Richard Swadley, Vice President and Executive Group Publisher

Andy Cummings, Vice President and Publisher

Mary Bednarek, Executive Acquisitions Director

Mary C. Corder, Editorial Director

Publishing for Consumer Dummies

Diane Graves Steele, Vice President and Publisher

Joyce Pepple, Acquisitions Director

Composition Services

Gerry Fahey, Vice President of Production Services

Debbie Stailey, Director of Composition Services

Contents at a Glance

Table of Contents

Part IV: Customizing and Upgrading Windows XP.........203

Chapter 11: Customizing Windows XP with the Control Panel 205

Chapter 12: Keeping Windows from Breaking 229

Introduction

Welcome to the second edition of *Windows XP For Dummies,* the world's best-selling book about Windows XP! I've expanded the book to explain all the recent patches, tweaks, fixes, and frustrations that Microsoft has added to Windows XP.

This book's popularity probably boils down to this simple fact: Some people want to be Windows whizzes. They love interacting with dialog boxes. Some randomly press keys in the hope of discovering hidden, undocumented features. A few memorize long strings of computer commands while washing their hair.

And you? Well, you're no dummy, that's for sure. But when it comes to Windows and computers, the fascination just isn't there. You want to get your work done, stop, and move on to something more important. You have no intention of changing, and there's nothing wrong with that.

That's where this book comes in handy. Instead of making you a whiz at Windows, it merely dishes out chunks of useful computing information when you need them. Instead of becoming a Windows XP expert, you'll know just enough to get by quickly, cleanly, and with a minimum of pain so that you can move on to the pleasant things in life.

About This Book

Don't try to read this book in one sitting; there's no need. Instead, treat this book like a dictionary or an encyclopedia. Turn to the page with the information you need and say, "Ah, so that's what they're talking about." Then put down the book and move on.

Don't bother trying to memorize all the Windows XP jargon, such as "Select the menu item from the drop-down list box." Leave that stuff for the computer enthusiasts. In fact, if anything technical comes up in a chapter, a road sign warns you well in advance. Depending on your mood, you can either slow down to read it or speed on around it.

Instead of fancy computer jargon, this book covers subjects like these, all discussed in plain English:

- Keeping your computer safe and secure
- Finding, starting, and closing programs
- Locating the file you saved or downloaded yesterday
- Setting up a computer for the whole family to use
- Copying information to and from a CD
- Working with your digital camera's photos
- Scanning and printing your work
- Fixing Windows XP when it's misbehaving

There's nothing to memorize and nothing to learn. Just turn to the right page, read the brief explanation, and get back to work. Unlike other books, this one enables you to bypass the technical hoopla and still get your work done.

How to Use This Book

Something in Windows XP will eventually leave you scratching your head. No other program brings so many buttons, bars, and babble to the screen. When something in Windows XP has you stumped, use this book as a reference. Look for the troublesome topic in this book's table of contents or index. The table of contents lists chapter and section titles and page numbers. The index lists topics and page numbers. Page through the table of contents or index to the spot that deals with that particular bit of computer obscurity, read only what you have to, close the book, and apply what you've read.

If you're feeling spunky and want to learn something, read a little further. You can find a few completely voluntary extra details or some cross-references to check out. There's no pressure, though. You won't be forced to learn anything that you don't want to or that you simply don't have time for.

If you have to type something into the computer, you'll see easy-to-follow bold text like this:

> Type **Media Player** in the Search box.

In the preceding example, you type the words *Media Player* and then press the keyboard's Enter key. Typing words into a computer can be confusing, so a description of what you're supposed to type usually follows.

Whenever I describe a message or information that you see on-screen or a cryptic Web address, I present it this way:

```
www.vw.com
```

This book doesn't wimp out by saying, "For further information, consult your manual." Windows XP doesn't even *come* with a manual. You won't find information about running specific Windows software packages, such as Microsoft Office. Windows XP is complicated enough on its own! Luckily, other *For Dummies* books mercifully explain most popular software packages.

Don't feel abandoned, though. This book covers Windows in plenty of detail for you to get the job done. Plus, if you have questions or comments about *Windows XP For Dummies,* feel free to drop me a line on my Web site at `www.andyrathbone.com`.

Finally, keep in mind that this book is a *reference.* It's not designed to teach you how to use Windows XP like an expert, heaven forbid. Instead, this book dishes out enough bite-sized chunks of information so that you don't *have* to learn Windows.

And What about You?

Chances are you already own Windows XP or are thinking about upgrading. You know what *you* want to do with your computer. The problem lies in making the *computer* do what you want it to do. You've gotten by one way or another, hopefully with the help of a computer guru — either a friend at the office, somebody down the street, or your fourth-grader.

But if your computer guru isn't around, this book can be a substitute during your times of need. (Keep a doughnut or Pokémon card nearby in case you need a quick bribe.)

How This Book Is Organized

The information in this book has been well sifted. This newly expanded book contains seven parts, and I divided each part into chapters relating to the part's theme. With an even finer knife, I divided each chapter into short sections to help you figure out a bit of Windows XP's weirdness. Sometimes, you may find what you're looking for in a small, boxed sidebar. Other times, you may need to cruise through an entire section or chapter. It's up to you and the particular task at hand.

Here are the categories (the envelope, please):

Part I: Windows XP Stuff Everybody Thinks You Already Know

This part dissects Windows XP's backbone: Its annoying Welcome screen and user name buttons, the mammoth Start button menu that hides all your important stuff, and your computer's desktop — the background where all your programs live. It explains how to move windows around, for instance, and click the right buttons at the right time. It explains the Windows XP stuff that everybody thinks that you already know.

Part II: Working with Programs and Files

Windows XP comes with bunches of free programs. Finding and starting the programs, however, often proves to be a chore. This part of the book shows how to prod programs into action. If an important file or program has vanished from the radar, you discover how to make Windows XP dredge your computer's crowded cupboards and bring it back.

Also, by popular demand, a new chapter explains how to fax, scan, and print your important information.

Part III: Getting Things Done on the Internet

Turn here for a crash course in today's computing playground, the Internet. This part explains how to send e-mail and globetrot across Web sites. Best yet, an entire chapter explains how to do it all safely, without viruses and annoying pop-up ads. (And with the newly strengthened *firewall.*)

An entire section explains Internet Explorer's new security toolbar and how it stops Web parasites from attaching themselves to your board as you Web surf.

Part IV: Customizing and Upgrading Windows XP

When Windows XP needs a jolt, fix it by flipping one of the switches hidden in its Control Panel, described here. Another chapter explains computer maintenance you can easily perform yourself, reducing your repair bills. You discover how to share your computer with several people in a family or shared apartment — without letting anybody peek into anybody else's information.

And when you're ready to add a second computer, head to the networking chapter for quick instructions on linking computers to share an Internet connection as well as files.

Part V: Music, Movies, Memories (And Photos, Too)

Turn here for information on playing music CDs, digital music, and movies. Buy some cheap CDs and create your own greatest hits CDs from your favorite tunes. (Or just copy a CD so your favorite one doesn't get scratched in the car.)

Digital camera owners should visit the chapter on transferring pictures from your camera to your computer, organizing the pictures, and e-mailing them to friends. Bought a camcorder? Head to the section that explains how to edit out the dopey parts and create a movie the relatives will *enjoy* for a change.

Part VI: Help!

Although glass doesn't shatter when Windows XP crashes, it still hurts. In this part, you find some soothing salves for the most painful irritations. Plus, you find ways to unleash the Windows XP program's wise team of Troubleshooting Wizards.

Stuck with the problem of moving your files from an old computer to a new one? You'll find help here, as well, with a walkthrough of Windows XP's Files and Settings Transfer Wizard. (If you're ready to upgrade your old version of Windows to Windows XP, check out the appendix, too, which holds complete instructions.)

Part VII: The Part of Tens

Everybody loves lists (except during tax time). This part contains lists of Windows-related trivia — ten aggravating things about Windows XP (and how to fix them) and ten simple things to keep in mind about Windows. As a bonus (and to help you make conversation with your kids), check out ten things found in the *upcoming* version of Windows.

Icons Used in This Book

It just takes a glance at Windows XP to notice its *icons,* which are little push-button pictures for starting various programs. The icons in this book fit right in. They're even a little easier to figure out:

Watch out! This signpost warns you that pointless technical information is coming around the bend. Swerve away from this icon to stay safe from awful technical drivel.

This icon alerts you about juicy information that makes computing easier: A tried and true method for keeping the cat from sleeping on top of the monitor, for instance.

Don't forget to remember these important points. (Or at least dog-ear the pages so that you can look them up again a few days later.)

The computer won't explode while you're performing the delicate operations associated with this icon. Still, wearing gloves and proceeding with caution is a good idea.

There's a bad corner in every large neighborhood, and the Internet's global reach makes for some very large bad corners. Look here for information about keeping you, your computer, and your information as safe as possible.

Where to Go from Here

Now, you're ready for action. Give the pages a quick flip and scan a section or two that you know you'll need later. Please remember, this is *your* book — your weapon against the computer criminals who've inflicted this whole complicated computer concept on you. Please circle any paragraphs you find useful, highlight key concepts, add your own sticky notes, and doodle in the margins next to the complicated stuff.

The more you mark up your book, the easier it will be for you to find all the good stuff again.

Part I

Windows XP Stuff Everybody Thinks You Already Know

In this part . . .

Most people are dragged into Windows XP without a choice. Their new computers probably came with Windows XP already installed. Or maybe you have Windows XP at the office, where everyone has to learn it except for the boss, who doesn't have a computer. Or perhaps your favorite program's latest version requires Windows XP, so you've had to upgrade.

Whatever your situation, this part gives a refresher on Windows XP basics and buzzwords like dragging and dropping, cutting and pasting, and tugging at mischievous toolbars.

And if you're completely new to computers, the first chapter answers that question you've been afraid to ask around the lunchroom: "Just how do I *use* this thing, anyway?"

Chapter 1

What Is Windows XP?

In This Chapter

- Understanding what Windows XP is and what it does
- Understanding Windows XP's service packs
- Knowing what service pack is on your computer
- Downloading and installing Service Pack 2

Chances are, you've probably heard about Windows. In fact, millions of people all over the world are puzzling over it as you read this. Almost every new computer sold today comes with a copy of Windows XP preinstalled — cheerfully greeting you when first turned on.

This chapter helps you understand why Windows lives inside your computer, and how to keep it alive and well with Microsoft's *service packs.* It explains which service packs you need to keep Windows XP up-to-date and how to deal with the burdens they lay at your feet in the name of increased security.

What Is Windows and Why Are You Using It?

The answer to this one's pretty easy: You're using Microsoft Windows because you don't have much choice. Nearly every computer sold since late 2001 comes with Windows XP preinstalled. A few people escaped Windows by buying Apple computers (those nicer-looking computers that cost more). But chances are, you, your neighbors, your boss, your kids at school, and millions of other people around the world are using Microsoft Windows.

And just what *is* Windows? Sold by a company called Microsoft, Windows isn't like your usual software that lets you write term papers or send angry e-mails to mail-order companies. No, Windows is an *operating system,* meaning it controls the way you work with your computer.

Yes, Microsoft *is* sneaky

Microsoft may tout Windows as your helpful computing companion, always keeping your best interests in mind, but that's not really true. Windows always keeps *Microsoft's* interests in mind. You'll find that out as soon as you call Microsoft for help on making Windows work right. Your first two questions are free if you pick up the long distance charges to Redmond, Washington. The third call (and all the rest) cost $35 apiece.

Microsoft also uses Windows to plug its own products and services. Sometimes you click a menu item that touts something helpful, but Windows simply leads you to a Web site where you can purchase additional items from Microsoft or its business partners.

Simply put, Windows not only controls your computer but also serves as a huge Microsoft advertising vehicle. Most of the offers you see on Windows aren't necessarily the best ones — they're just the ones that make the most money for Microsoft. Many of its offers are simply advertising flyers stuffed inside your computer.

Windows gets its name from all the cute little windows it places on your monitor. Each window shows information, such as a picture, a program that you're running, or a baffling technical reprimand. You can put several windows on-screen at the same time and jump from window to window, visiting different programs. You can also enlarge a window to fill the entire screen.

Like the mother with the whistle in the lunch court, Windows controls every window and each part of your computer. When you turn on your computer, Windows jumps onto the screen and supervises any running programs. Throughout all this action, Windows keeps things running smoothly, even if the programs start throwing food at each other.

In addition to controlling your computer and bossing around your programs, Windows XP comes with a bunch of free programs. Although your computer can run without these programs, they're nice to have. These programs let you do different things, like write and print letters, browse the Internet, play music, and even whittle down your camcorder's vacation footage into a three-minute short — automatically.

- Believe it or not, Windows XP isn't just the newest version of Windows; it's actually the best version so far. (Just ask people who upgraded from previous versions.) Windows XP doesn't crash very often. And if one Windows program crashes, it doesn't drag the entire computer down with it, like earlier versions did.
- Windows XP makes it easier for several people to share a single computer. Each person receives his or her own user account. When users click their names at Windows XP's opening screen, they see their *own* work — just the way they left it.

- Because Windows XP is sturdier and more secure than earlier Windows versions, it's also more difficult to figure out. Computers are pretty dumb, so when a potential security problem arises, they simply make you decide how to handle it. (I cover safe computing in Chapter 10.)

Windows XP's Luggage: Service Packs

Microsoft launched Windows XP in 2001, making it a creaky old-timer in computer years. To keep its old boat afloat until its replacement in 2006, Microsoft has released not one but two chunky add-on programs called *service packs.*

Service packs, given away for free, provide the Microsoft folks a chance to go back and fix the things they messed up when they first released Windows XP. For instance, if Microsoft discovers a programming mistake that keeps Windows XP from working with a certain computer part, the service pack fixes that particular problem.

Most importantly, service packs repair oodles of security problems. Every week, some smart alec figures out a new way to break into Windows XP. Microsoft analyzes the problem and releases software to plug that security hole. Service packs provide all the patches, fixes, and plaster Windows needs to bring your computer up-to-date.

The next section explains how to tell what service packs are on your computer, if any, and how to install Service Pack 2 to make your computer as secure as possible.

- Windows XP Service Pack 1 contains all the patches released during Windows XP's first year of operation. Service Pack 2 contains all the patches in Service Pack 1 and *more.* Installing Service Pack 2 brings your computer up-to-date with all the patches released through mid-2004.
- Although Service Pack 2 includes lots of patches, it doesn't include the newest patches — patches released *after* Service Pack 2. To keep your computer up-to-date, be sure to set Windows Update on Automatic, a simple procedure I discuss in Chapter 10.
- Microsoft doesn't let its service packs install on illegitimate copies of Windows XP. If your copy of Windows XP isn't installed legally, the service pack leaves this message when you try to install it: `The product key used to install Windows is invalid`. If you see that message, contact the person who sold you Windows XP.

What service pack version is on my computer?

Despite the way service packs polish Windows XP and protect it from evil-doers, your computer certainly doesn't shout for joy when it has received one. In fact, the only way to know if you have a service pack installed is to probe your computer's menus. Follow these steps to reveal the service pack that's currently installed on your computer:

1. **Click your Start menu.**
2. **Right-click on the My Computer icon and choose Properties.**

   The System Properties dialog box appears, revealing intimate technical details about your computer.
3. **Look for your service pack version in the System section.**

   You should see the words *Service Pack* as the bottom line of the window's System section. The number after the words Service Pack reveals its version number. For example, the computer shown in Figure 1-1 has Service Pack 2 installed. (The mouse's arrow points to the words.)

- If you don't see the words Service Pack 2 listed, your computer has serious security problems. Jump to the next section to install it as soon as you can.
- If your computer already has Service Pack 2, you don't need to install Service Pack 1. Service Pack 2 includes Service Pack 1.
- If you see the words Service Pack 1 listed, you still need to install Service Pack 2.

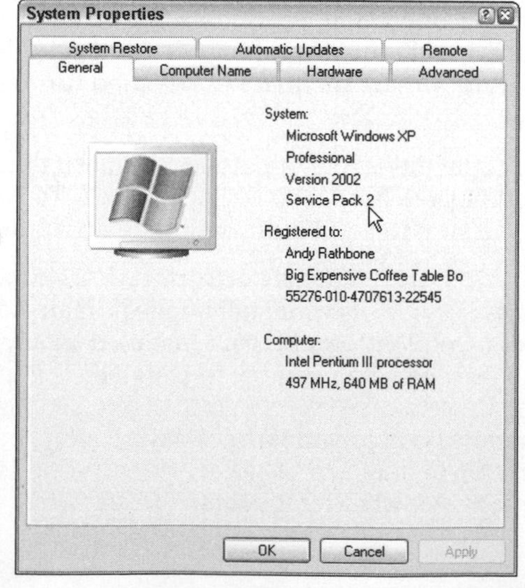

Figure 1-1: Your computer should say the words *Service Pack 2* in the System section.

What's in Service Pack 2?

Installing Service Pack 2 is like receiving an updated version of Windows XP with new features — all for free. Here are some of the tastier tidbits that this huge 100MB program brings to Windows XP:

- Service Pack 2 contains several years' worth of security patches and repairs, making Windows XP much safer and more stable.
- A pop-up ad blocker to Internet Explorer keeps ads from exploding in your face as you visit Web sites.
- Internet Explorer's new Add-On manager lets you know when something's trying to install itself onto Internet Explorer. The manager lets you weed out nasty Web parasites but approve the things you *do* want installed, like helpful toolbars.
- The new, improved firewall not only turns itself on automatically but also protects your computer from intruders.

I cover all these features in Chapter 10. You can find also more information about Service Pack 2 on the Internet at `www.microsoft.com/security`.

Installing Service Pack 2

Microsoft lets people install Service Pack 2 in two different ways depending on how you connect to the Internet, either by dial-up (through the phone lines) or broadband (cable or DSL):

- **Dial-up:** Because Service Pack 2 is such a large download (100MB), dial-up Internet users should probably visit Microsoft's Web site at `support.microsoft.com` and sign up to receive Service Pack 2 on a CD.
- **Broadband:** Internet users with this speedy connection can download Service Pack 2 from Windows Update, found by opening Internet Explorer and choosing Windows Update from the Tools menu. Your computer connects to Microsoft's Windows Update Web site and automatically downloads and installs Service Pack 2.

Even after you install Service Pack 2, you still need to use Windows Update. That keeps you updated with fixes discovered *after* Microsoft released Service Pack 2. I explain how to make Windows Update run automatically in Chapter 10.

Service Pack may make some of your programs behave strangely. If you're having problems with any of them immediately after you install Service Pack 2, visit that program's Web site to see whether it offers a patch.

What's Windows XP Professional?

Windows XP comes in two basic versions: Windows XP *Home* and Windows XP *Professional*. Both versions look and act almost indistinguishably from each other. Chances are, you're using Windows XP Home, the version designed for homes and small businesses. Larger businesses often use Windows XP Professional because that version has a few extra menus tucked away for things like advanced corporate security. Other than those extra menus, the two versions are virtually indistinguishable.

If you're planning on using your computer to connect to the office through a network, ask the person in charge of your office's computer networks which version he or she recommends. Windows XP Home connects to most corporate networks without problem, but only Windows XP Professional can connect to a specialized *Windows server domain.*

I run Windows XP Home on my main computer, but I run Windows XP Professional on another computer just to see what the fuss is about.

Chapter 2

The Desktop, Start Menu, and Other Windows XP Mysteries

In This Chapter

- Starting Windows XP
- Entering a password
- Logging onto Windows XP
- Using the desktop
- Using the taskbar
- Using toolbars
- Logging off Windows XP
- Turning off your computer

This chapter provides a drive-by tour of Windows XP. You'll turn on your computer, start Windows, and spend a few minutes gawking at its various neighborhoods: the desktop, the taskbar, the Start menu, and the environmentally correct (and compassionate) Recycle Bin.

Everybody who's anybody hangs out on the Windows desktop (a fancy word for the Windows background). The taskbar provides a convenient hideaway for leaving the spotlight. When something's missing, the Start menu is the best place to look it up.

Former friends wind up in the Recycle Bin where they either fade away or, if necessary, can be safely revived.

Being Welcomed to the World of Windows XP

Starting Windows XP is as easy as turning on your computer — Windows XP leaps onto the screen automatically with a futuristic flourish. But before you can start working, Windows XP may throw you a fastball with its brilliant blue Welcome screen: Windows wants you to *log on,* as shown in Figure 2-1, by clicking your name.

I've customized my Welcome screen. Yours will look different. If you don't see a user name listed for you on the Welcome screen, then you have three options:

- **If you just bought the computer, use the account named Administrator.** Designed to let give the owner full power over the computer, the administrator account user can set up new accounts for new users, install programs, burn CDs, start an Internet connection, and access all the files on the computer — even those of other users. Windows XP needs at least one person to act as administrator, even if your computer isn't connected to other computers. Hit Chapter 13 if you care about this stuff.
- **Use the Guest account.** Designed for household visitors, this account lets guests like the babysitter or visiting relatives use the computer temporarily. (Some administrators turn off the Guest account to lock out visitors.)

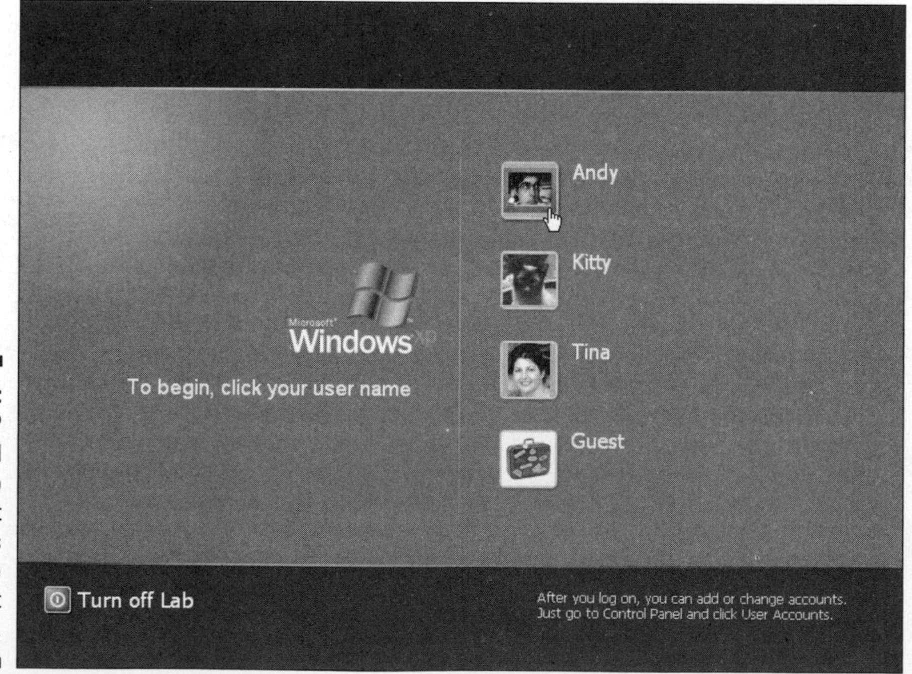

Figure 2-1: Windows XP wants all users to log on so it knows who's using the computer at all times.

Running Windows XP for the first time

If you've just installed Windows XP or you're turning on your computer for the first time, you're treated to a few extra Windows XP spectacles: A hip little box appears on the screen, demonstrating how Windows XP can indeed create cool colors and noises. Then Windows XP leaves you at a box with the following four buttons:

- **Digital Media:** Click here to check out Windows' fun multimedia stuff. It contains tours of Media Player — a program for playing CDs, videos, DVDs, digital music, and much more. You'll also find information about the built-in video editor, Movie Maker, and your official digital photo storage bin called My Pictures.
- **Rich Internet Experience:** Nothing really new here: tours of the Internet Explorer Web browser and the Outlook Express e-mail program. There's also a plug for MSN Messenger, a program for bugging your buddies on the Internet.
- **Home Networking:** On your second or third computer? Perhaps it's time to link them (with or without cables), run Windows XP's built-in Network Setup Wizard software, and add the words *Network Administrator* to your business card. (It's a great pickup tool in Silicon Valley.)
- **Improved User Experience:** These buzzwords merely refer you to the Windows Help program. Yawn.

To take any of the tours, let the mouse pointer hover above the button. Then click either the words Try It or Learn More to head to that particular program. Try It takes you to the program itself; Learn More brings up the program's help menu.

No Guest account *and* no user? Then find out who owns the computer and beg that person to set up a user name for you. (If they don't know how, show them Chapter 13, where I explain how to set up a User Account.)

When first installed, Windows XP dashes back to the Welcome screen whenever you haven't touched the computer for ten minutes. To stop this scurrying, right-click on the desktop and choose Properties. Click the Screen Saver tab and remove the check mark next to the On Resume, Display Welcome Screen option. Then you'll have to log on only when you start up Windows — not throughout the day.

Fiddling around with user accounts

Windows XP allows several people to work on the same computer, yet it keeps everybody's work separate. To do that, it needs to know who's currently sitting in front of the keyboard. When you *log on* — introduce yourself — by clicking your *user name,* as shown in Figure 2-1, Windows XP presents your personalized desktop, ready for you to make your own personalized mess.

When you're through working or just feel like taking a break, log off (explained at this chapter's end) so somebody else can use the computer. Later, when you log back on, your messy desktop will be waiting for you.

Although you may turn your desktop into a mess, it's your *own* mess. When you return to the computer, your letters will be just as you saved them. Jerry hasn't accidentally deleted your files or folders while playing Widget Squash. Tina's desktop contains links to her favorite Web sites. And all of Carrie's Phish MP3s stay in her own personalized My Music folder.

Of course, the big question boils down to this: How do you customize the pictures next to your user name, like my face in Figure 2-1? After you've logged on, open the Start menu (covered in this chapter) and click the little picture at the top. Windows conveniently lets you pick a new one. (For ideas, browse through the digital photos you've saved in your My Pictures folder.)

Keeping your account private with a password

Because Windows XP lets bunches of people use the same computer, how do you stop Rob from reading Diane's love letters to Henry Rollins? How can Josh keep Grace from deleting his *Star Wars* movie trailers? Windows XP's optional *password* solves some of those problems.

By typing in a secret password when logging on, as shown in Figure 2-2, you enable your computer to recognize *you* and nobody else. If you protect your user name with a password, nobody can access your files (except for the computer's administrator, who can peek anywhere — and even delete your account).

Figure 2-2: With a password, nobody else can access your files.

To set up or change your password, follow these steps:

1. **Click the Start button, click Control Panel, and click the User Accounts icon.**

2. **Click your user account's name and choose Create a Password.**
3. **Type in a password that will be easy for you — and nobody else — to remember.**

   Keep your password short and sweet: the name of your favorite vegetable, for example, or your dental floss brand.

4. **In the last box, type a hint that reminds you — and only you — of your password.**
5. **Click the Create Password button, and Windows XP begins asking for your password whenever you log on.**

- Passwords are *case-sensitive. Caviar* and *caviar* are considered two different passwords.
- Forgotten your password *already*? Click the little question mark button in Figure 2-2 that appears whenever you click your user name. Your "hint" appears, hopefully reminding you of your password. Careful, though — anybody can click the question mark and read your hint, so make sure it's something that only makes sense to you.

  Own a laptop? Password protect your account now, before somebody steals your expensive new toy.

- When you create your password, Windows XP offers to make your files and folders *private* to lock out everybody. Before making your account private, remember that private files are *much* more difficult for repair shops to retrieve if something goes wrong with your computer.
- I explain more about user accounts in Chapter 13.

Make Windows stop asking me for a password!

Windows asks for your name and password only when it needs to know who's tapping on its keys. And it needs that information for any of these three reasons:

- Your computer is part of a network, and your identity determines what goodies you can access.
- The computer's owner wants to limit what you can do on the computer.
- You share your computer with other people, and want to keep others from logging on with your name and changing your files and settings.

If these concerns don't apply to you, purge the password by clicking the Control Panel's User Accounts icon and choosing Remove My Password.

Without that password, anybody can now log on using your user account and view (or destroy) your files. If you're working in an office setting, this could be serious trouble. If you've been assigned a password, it's better to simply get used to it.

The Desktop

Normally, people want their desktops to be horizontal, not vertical. Keeping pencils from rolling off a normal desk is hard enough. But in Windows XP, your monitor's screen is known as the Windows *desktop,* and that's where all your work takes place. You can create files and folders right on your new electronic desktop and arrange them all across the screen. Each program runs in its own little *window* on top of the desktop.

Windows XP starts with a freshly scrubbed, empty desktop. After you've been working for a while, your desktop will fill up with *icons* — little push buttons that load your files with a quick double-click of the mouse. Some people leave their desktops strewn with icons for easy access; others organize their work: When they finish working on something, they store it a *folder,* a task covered in Chapter 4.

The desktop boasts three main parts, shown in Figure 2-3. The *taskbar* rests lazily along the desktop's bottom edge and lists the programs and files you're currently working on. The *Start menu,* seen at the taskbar's left edge, lets you locate and run programs. And unlike the office paper shredder, the desktop's *Recycle Bin* lets you safely retrieve accidentally deleted files. Whew!

- You can start new projects directly from your desktop: Right-click on the desktop, choose New, and select the project of your dreams from the pop-up menu. (The menu lists most of your computer's programs for quick 'n' easy access.)

- Are you befuddled about some object's reason for being? Timidly rest the pointer over the mysterious doodad, and Windows will pop up a little box explaining what that thing is or does. Right-click on the object, and ever helpful Windows XP usually tosses up a menu listing nearly everything you can do with that particular object. This trick works on most icons found on your desktop and throughout your programs.

- Everything on your desktop may suddenly disappear, leaving it completely empty. Chances are, Windows XP hid everything in a misguided attempt to be helpful. To bring your work back to life, right-click on your empty desktop and choose Arrange Icons By from the pop-up menu. Finally, choose Show Desktop Icons to make everything reappear with no harm done.

Figure 2-3: The Windows XP desktop, which spreads across your entire computer screen, has three main parts.

Cleaning up a messy desktop

When icons cover your desktop like a year's worth of sticky notes, Windows XP offers several ways to clean up the mess. Many people opt for the Desktop Cleanup Wizard, the built-in robotic housekeeper. Here's how it works:

1. **As shown in Figure 2-4, right-click on a blank part of the desktop, choose Arrange Icons By, and choose Run Desktop Cleanup Wizard.**

   The Desktop Cleanup Wizard carefully examines your clutter and lists every icon's *last used* date.

2. **If you click the OK button, the wizard automatically moves your least-used icons to a new Unused Desktop Shortcuts folder.**

   Quick, simple, and you can always drag 'em back out of the folder if you miss them.

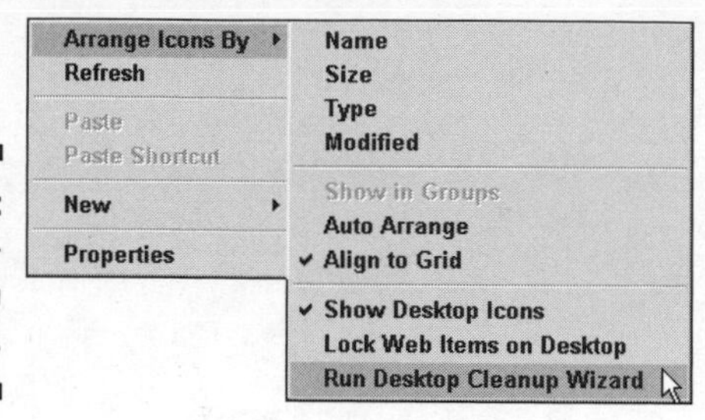

Figure 2-4: Automatically clean up icons.

If you just want your desktop clutter to *look* more organized, try the other Arrange Icons By choices, each discussed in the following list:

Name: Arrange all icons in alphabetical order using neat, vertical rows.

Size: Arrange icons according to their size, placing the smallest ones at the top of the rows.

Type: Line up icons by their *type.* All WordPad files are grouped together, for instance, as are all links to Web sites.

Modified: Arrange icons by the date they were last changed.

Auto Arrange: Automatically arrange everything in vertical rows — even newly dumped icons are swept into rows.

Align to Grid: This option places an invisible grid on the screen, and aligns all icons to the grid to keep them nice and tidy — no matter how hard you try to mess them up.

Show Desktop Icons: *Always keep this option turned on.* When turned off, Windows hides every icon on your desktop. If you can remember in your frustration, click this option again to toggle your icons back on.

Lock Web Items on Desktop: If you've chosen a Web site for your desktop's background (covered in the next section), clicking here locks it in place. (Rarely used.)

Run Desktop Cleanup Wizard: Discussed earlier in this chapter, this cleanup robot automatically drops infrequently used icons in an Unused Icons folder on your desktop.

- These Arrange Icons By options are also available for any of your folders. (You'll find them under a folder's View menu.)
- Every 60 days, the Desktop Cleanup Wizard automatically offers to clean up your desktop. To turn off the wizard's bimonthly offers, right-click on a blank part of the desktop, choose Properties, and click the Desktop tab. Choose Customize Desktop and remove the check mark from the Run Desktop Cleanup Wizard Every 60 Days option.

Jazzing up the desktop's background

To jazz up your desktop, Windows XP covers it with pretty pictures known as a *background.* (Most people refer to the background as *wallpaper.*) Windows XP's background starts as a *Teletubbies*-green hillside.

When you tire of the *Teletubbies* look, choose your own picture — any picture stored on your computer:

1. **Right-click on a blank part of the desktop, choose Properties, and click the Desktop tab.**
2. **Click any of the names listed under Background to slip them onto the little preview screen, shown in Figure 2-5.**

   Found a keeper? Click the OK button to stick it on your desktop. If you're still searching, move to the next step.

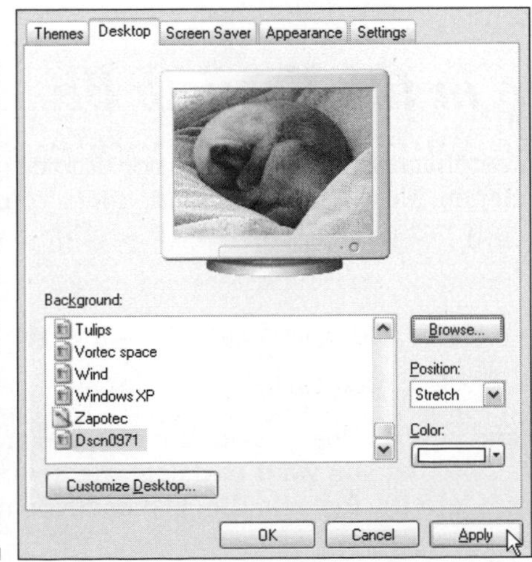

Figure 2-5: Try different backgrounds by clicking their names in the Background list box; click the Browse button to see pictures from different folders.

3. **Click the Browse button and click a file from inside your My Pictures folder.**

   Most people store their digital photos in their My Pictures folder, which lives in the My Documents folder. (I explain browsing folders in Chapter 4.)

4. **Found a good one? Click the photo and click Open to preview it.**
5. **Click OK to close the Display Properties box.**

Here are some tips for sprucing up your desktop:

- As you browse through different pictures, Windows XP automatically decides whether the image should be *tiled* repeatedly across the screen, *centered* directly in the middle, or *stretched* to fill the entire screen. To override Windows' automatic choice, select your own preference from the Position box.
- You can easily borrow any picture on the Internet for a background. Right-click on the Web site's picture and select Set as Background from the pop-up menu. Microsoft sneakily copies the image onto your desktop as its new background.
- To change Windows XP's entire *look,* right-click on the desktop, choose Properties, and click the Themes tab. Aimed at heavy-duty procrastinators, different themes splash different colors across Windows' various buttons, borders, and boxes. I explain more about Themes in Chapter 11. (If you download any themes offered on the Internet, check them with antivirus software, covered in Chapter 10.)

Dumpster diving in the Recycle Bin

The Recycle Bin, that little wastebasket icon in the corner of your desktop, works much like a *real* recycle bin. Shown in the margin, it lets you retrieve Sunday's paper when somebody has pitched the comics section before you had a chance to read it.

You can dump something — a file or folder, for example — into the Windows XP Recycle Bin in one of two ways:

- Simply right-click on it and choose Delete from the menu. Windows XP asks cautiously if you're *sure* that you want to delete the item. Click Yes, and Windows XP dumps it into the Recycle Bin, just as if you'd dragged it there. Whoosh!
- For the ultimate deletion rush, click the unwanted object and poke your keyboard's Delete key.

Want something back? Double-click the Recycle Bin icon to see your deleted items. Right-click the item you want and choose Restore. The handy little Recycle Bin returns your precious item to the same spot where you deleted it. (You can also resuscitate deleted items by dragging them to your desktop or any other folder.)

The Recycle Bin can get pretty crowded. If you're searching frantically for a recently deleted file, tell the Recycle Bin to sort everything by the date and time you deleted it. Click View, point at Arrange Icons By, and choose Date Deleted. (The most recently deleted files are at the list's bottom.)

To delete something *permanently,* just delete it from inside the Recycle Bin. To delete *everything* in the Recycle Bin, right-click on the Recycle Bin and choose Empty Recycle Bin.

To bypass the Recycle Bin completely when deleting files, hold down Shift while pressing Delete. Poof! The deleted object disappears, ne'er to be seen again.

- The Recycle Bin icon changes from an empty wastepaper basket to a full one as soon as it's holding a deleted file. You may have to squint a little to notice the pieces of paper sticking out of the trashcan's top.
- How long does the Recycle Bin hold onto deleted files? It waits until the garbage consumes 10 percent of your hard drive space. Then it begins purging your oldest deleted files to make room for the new. If you're low on hard disk space, shrink the bin's size by right-clicking on the Recycle Bin and choosing Properties. Decrease the percentage to automatically delete files more quickly; increase the percentage, and the Recycle Bin hangs onto them a little longer.

- The Recycle Bin only saves items deleted from your own computer's hard drive. That means it won't save anything deleted from a floppy, CD, memory card, MP3 player, or digital camera.

- If you delete something from somebody else's computer over a network, it can never be retrieved. The Recycle Bin only holds items deleted from your *own* computer, not somebody else's computer. (For some awful reason, the Recycle Bin on the other person's computer doesn't save the item, either.) Be careful.

The Start Button's Reason to Live

The clearly labeled Start button lives in the bottom-left corner of the desktop, where it's always ready for action. By clicking the Start button, you can start programs, adjust Windows XP's settings, find help for sticky situations, or, thankfully, shut down Windows XP and get away from the computer for a while.

The little Start button is so eager to please, in fact, that it starts shooting out menus full of options as soon as you click it. Just click the button once, and the first layer of menus pops out, as shown in Figure 2-6.

Your Start menu will change as you add more programs to your computer. That's why the Start menu on your friend's computer is probably arranged differently than the Start menu on your computer.

- Your My Documents, My Pictures, and My Music folders are always one click away on the Start menu. These folders are specially designed for their contents. The My Pictures folder, for instance, displays little thumbnails of your digital photos. Their biggest perk? Keeping your files in these folders helps you remember where you stored them. I cover file organization in Chapter 4.
- Windows thoughtfully places your most frequently used programs along the left side of the Start menu for easy point 'n' click action.
- See the words All Programs near the Start menu's bottom left? Click there, and yet another menu squirts out to offer more options.

- Spot something confusing on the Start menu? Hover your mouse pointer over the mysterious icon. Windows responds with a helpful explanatory message. Sometimes a hovering mouse pointer summons yet another menu, listing even *more* programs available in that category.
- Strangely enough, you also click the Start button when you want to *stop* using Windows. (You'll click the Turn Off Computer button at the bottom, a decision-wringing process described at this chapter's end.)

Making Windows start programs automatically

Many people sit down at a computer, turn it on, and go through the same mechanical process of loading their oft-used programs. Believe it or not, Windows XP can automate this task. The solution is the StartUp folder, found lurking in the Start button's All Programs menu. When Windows XP wakes up, it peeks inside that StartUp folder. If it finds a program lurking inside, it immediately tosses that program onto the screen.

To make your favorite programs wake up along with Windows XP, follow these steps:

1. **Right-click on the Start menu's Startup icon and choose Open.**

   The Startup icon, which lives in the Start menu's All Programs area, opens as a folder.

2. ***While holding down the Alt key,* drag and drop any of your favorite programs or files into the StartUp folder.**

   You *must* hold down Alt, as that turns your newly dropped items into shortcuts. You *don't* want to drop the actual programs or files.

3. **Close the Startup folder.**

   Now, whenever you start Windows XP from scratch, those programs or files load up right along with it.

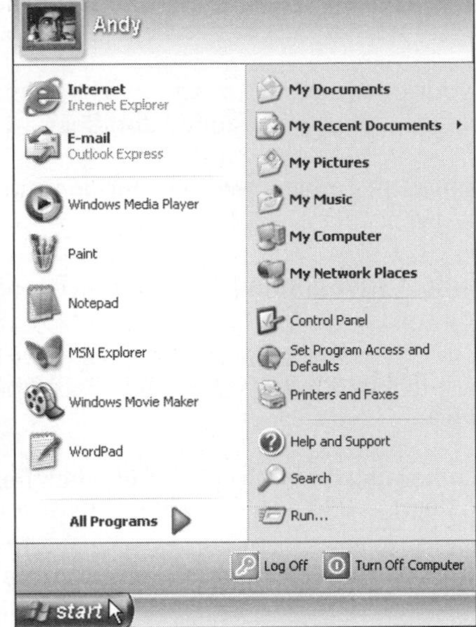

Figure 2-6: The Start button in Windows XP hides dozens of menus for starting programs.

The Start menu's prime real estate

When the Start menu pops up, shown earlier in Figure 2-6, it always shows you the items listed below, from top to bottom. You'll use these things constantly in Windows, so if you're already bored with this Start button section, please feign interest through the following explanations.

If you find Start menus exciting, you'll love the upcoming "Customizing the Start menu" section, which explains how to rearrange your entire Start menu.

Internet Explorer: This lets you visit the Internet, covered in Chapter 8.

Outlook Express: Choose this to send or receive e-mail, covered in Chapter 9.

Recently Used Programs: The Start menu lists your six most frequently used programs' icons above the Start button for easy clicking.

My Documents: Always store your documents in this folder so you'll know where to find them later.

My Pictures: Keep your digital pictures in this folder. Each picture's icon is a tiny thumbnail image of its picture.

My Music: Store your digital music in here so Media Player can find and play it more easily.

My Computer: This displays your computer's storage areas: folders, disk drives, CD drives, digital cameras, and other attached goodies.

My Network Places: If your computer connects with other computers through a network, click here to visit them.

Control Panel: This lets you adjust your computer's oodles of confusing settings, all described in Chapter 11.

Help and Support: Befuddled? Click here for an answer. (Chapter 20 explains the stoic Windows Help system.)

Search: When you can't find something on your computer, click here to make Windows find it. (I explain the Windows Search system in Chapter 6.)

Run: Used mostly by computing veterans, this launches a program if you type in its precise name and location.

Log Off: Click here either to let somebody else use the computer, or to save your work and let the computer rest until others use it.

Turn Off Computer: Click this button to restart the computer, turn it off, or let it sit resting in Standby mode.

Starting a program from the Start menu

This one's easy. Click the Start button, and the Start menu pops out of the button's head. If you see an icon for your desired program, click it, and Windows loads the program.

If your program isn't listed, though, click All Programs, near the bottom of the Start menu. Yet another menu pops up, this one listing the names of programs and folders full of programs. Spot your program? Click the name, and Windows kicks that program to the front of the screen.

If you *still* don't see your program listed, try pointing at the tiny folders listed on the menu. New menus fly out of those folders, as shown in Figure 2-7, listing even more programs.

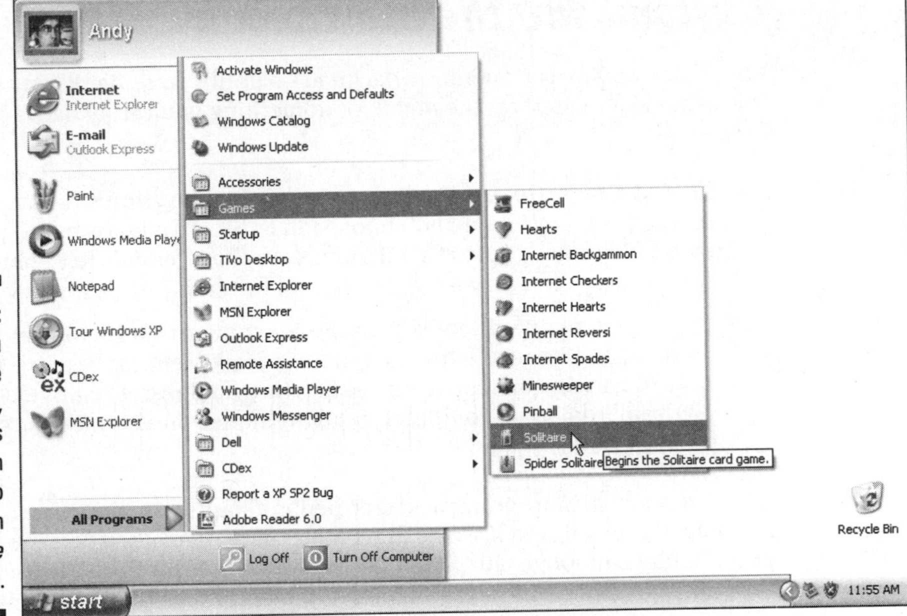

Figure 2-7: As you navigate the Start menu, new menus sprout from the sides to offer even *more* options.

When you finally spot your program's name, just click it. In fact, you never have to actually click the Start menu until you see your desired program's name. The Start menu opens and closes its menus automatically as you move your mouse pointer near them.

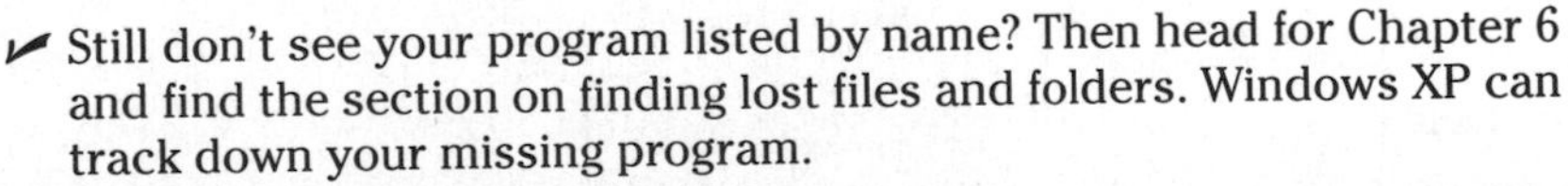

- Still don't see your program listed by name? Then head for Chapter 6 and find the section on finding lost files and folders. Windows XP can track down your missing program.

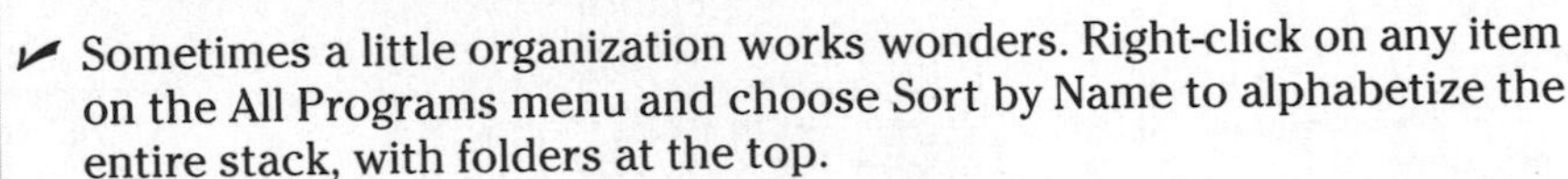

- Sometimes a little organization works wonders. Right-click on any item on the All Programs menu and choose Sort by Name to alphabetize the entire stack, with folders at the top.
- There's another way to load a lost program — if you can find something you created or edited with that program. For instance, if you wrote letters to the tax collector using Microsoft Word, double-click one of your tax letters to bring Microsoft Word to the screen from its hiding place.
- If you don't know how to navigate through your folders, visit Chapter 4. That chapter helps you move gracefully from folder to folder, decreasing the time it takes to stumble across your file.

Customizing the Start menu

The Windows XP Start menu works great — until you're hankering for something that's not listed on the menu, or something you rarely use is just getting in the way.

- **To add a favorite program's icon to the Start button's menu,** right-click on the program's icon and choose Pin to Start Menu from the pop-up menu. Windows copies that icon to your Start menu's left column. (From there, you may drag it to the All Programs area, if you wish.)
- **To purge unwanted icons from the Start menu's left column,** right-click on them and choose either Unpin from Start Menu or Remove from This List. (Removing an icon from the Start menu doesn't remove the actual program from your computer; it just removes one of many push buttons that launch it.)

When you install a program, as described in Chapter 11, the program almost always adds itself to the Start menu *automatically.* Then the program boldly announces its presence, as shown in Figure 2-8. Click All Programs and then follow the highlighted menu items that lead to your newly installed program.

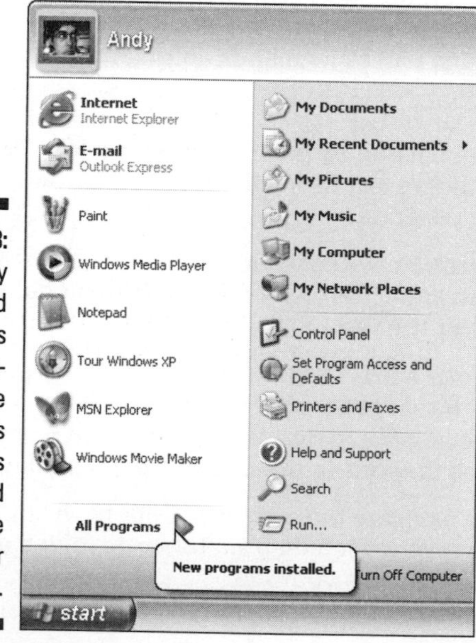

Figure 2-8: Most newly installed programs add themselves to the Start menu's All Programs area and announce their presence.

To stop newly installed programs from announcing their presence, check out Table 2-1.

You can customize the Start menu even more by changing its properties. To start playing, right-click on the Start button, choose Properties, and click the Customize button. See Table 2-1 for the rundown and my recommendations.

Table 2-1 Customizing the Start Menu Properties

Setting	*My Recommendations*
Icon Size	Switching to small icons packs more icons onto the menu, yet keeps them easily recognizable.
Programs	Try increasing the number of frequently used programs to about 15. That lets the Start menu display nearly *all* my frequently used programs with a single click.
Show on Start Menu	The Start menu normally lists Internet Explorer and Outlook along its top. Click here to show other programs, instead.
Advanced tab	Although you can go wild here, I don't change much. I turn off Highlight Newly Installed Programs to stop new programs from sending their annoying announcement pop-ups. Then, under Start menu items, I choose Display as a Menu for the Control Panel. That lets me browse the Control Panel's options directly from the Start menu, saving plenty of time. I leave the rest as is, but feel free to experiment when you're bored at the office.

Here's a dirty little secret: The Start menu isn't really anything special. It's simply one of many folders on your hard drive. In fact, your entire desktop is just a folder, too. Chapter 4 shows how to explore the folders living on your hard drive, so don't be surprised when you discover folders named Desktop and Start Menu in your C drive's Documents and Settings folder.

Bellying Up to the Taskbar

This section introduces one of Windows XP's handiest tricks, so pull in your chair a little closer. Whenever you run more than one window on the desktop, there's a big problem: Programs and windows tend to cover each other up, making them difficult to locate.

Windows XP's solution is the *taskbar* — a special program that keeps track of all your open programs. Shown in Figure 2-9, the taskbar normally lives along the bottom of your screen, although you can move it to any edge you want. (***Hint:*** Just drag it from edge to edge. If it doesn't move, right-click on the taskbar and click Lock the Taskbar to remove the check mark by its name.)

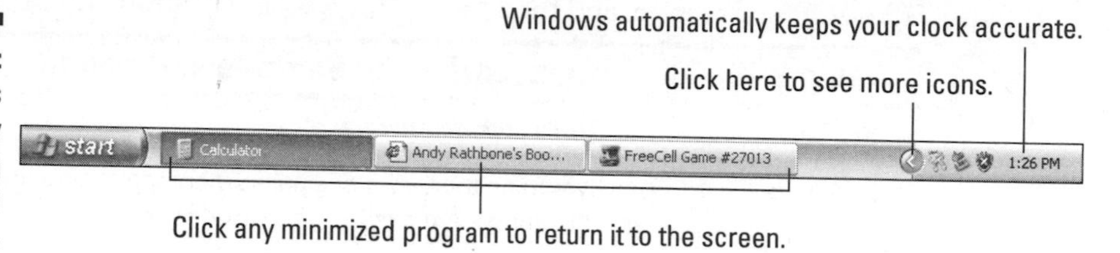

Figure 2-9: Click buttons for currently running programs on the taskbar.

See how the button for Calculator looks *pushed in* in Figure 2-9? That's because Calculator is the currently *active* window on the desktop: It's the program currently accepting your keystrokes. One or more of your taskbar's buttons always look pushed in unless you close or minimize all the windows on your desktop.

From the taskbar, you can perform powerful magic on your open windows, as described in the following list:

- To play with a program listed on the taskbar, click its name. The window rises to the surface and rests atop any other open windows, ready for action.
- To close a window listed on the taskbar, *right-click* on its name and choose Close from the pop-up menu. The program quits, just as if you'd chosen its Exit command from within its own window. (The departing program gives you a chance to save your work before it quits and walks off the screen.)
- Don't see the taskbar? If only the taskbar's top edge peeks up along the screen's bottom, grab the visible part with your mouse and drag it upward until the entire taskbar is visible. (Consider right-clicking on the taskbar and choosing Lock the Taskbar to keep it locked in place.)

- Ever wander inadvertently into a Web site's pop-up window trap, and pop-up ads explode onto your screen? The taskbar stacks all those open Internet Explorer windows onto one button on the taskbar. Right-click on the Internet Explorer button and choose Close Group to close Internet Explorer — including all those renegade pop-ups. (If you're still seeing obnoxious pop-up ads, install Windows XP's second Service Pack, described in Chapter 1. See Chapter 8 for details on blocking pop-ups.

Shrinking windows to the taskbar and retrieving them

Windows spawn windows. You start with one window to write a letter of praise to the local opera house. You open another window to check an address, for example, and then yet another to see whether you've forgotten any upcoming shows. Before you know it, four more windows are crowded across the desktop.

To combat the clutter, Windows XP provides a simple means of window control: You can transform a window from a screen-cluttering square into a tiny button on the *taskbar,* which sits along the bottom of the screen. The solution is the Minimize button.

See the three buttons lurking in just about every window's top-right corner? Click the *Minimize button* — the button with the little line in it, as shown in the margin. Whoosh! The window disappears, represented by its little button on the taskbar at your screen's bottom.

- To make a minimized program on the taskbar revert into a regular, on-screen window, just click its name on the taskbar. Pretty simple, huh?
- Each taskbar button shows the name of the program it represents.
- When you minimize a window, you neither destroy its contents nor close the program. And when you click the window's name on the taskbar, it reopens to the same size you left it, showing its same contents.

- Whenever you load a program, its name automatically appears on the taskbar. If one of your open windows ever gets lost on your desktop, click its name on the taskbar to bring it to the forefront.

Clicking the taskbar's sensitive areas

Like a crafty card player, the taskbar comes with a few tips and tricks. You can see some of them in Figure 2-10. Here's the lowdown:

- **Clock:** Hold the mouse pointer over the clock, and Windows XP shows the current day and date. Or if you want to change the time or date, a double-click on the clock summons the Windows XP time/date change program.
- **Double arrows:** Sometimes the taskbar hides things. Click the little double arrows next to the clock (refer to Figure 2-10), and a few more icons might slide out. (Check out the "Customizing the taskbar" section, later in this chapter, for tips and tricks affecting these icons.)

- **Speaker:** Click the little speaker to adjust the sound card's volume, as shown in Figure 2-11. Or double-click the little speaker to bring up a mixing panel. Mixers let you adjust separate volume levels for your microphone, line inputs, CD and DVD players, and other features.
- **Other icons:** These often appear next to the clock, depending on what Windows XP is up to. If you're printing, for example, a little printer icon appears there. Laptops often show a battery-power-level gauge. As with all the other icons down there, if you double-click the printer or battery gauge, Windows XP brings up information about the printer's or battery's status.

- **Blank part:** This part of the taskbar hides a menu of options. Want to minimize all your desktop's open windows in a hurry? Right-click on a blank part of the taskbar and choose Minimize All Windows from the pop-up menu.

  To organize your open windows, right-click on a blank part of the taskbar and choose one of the tile commands. Windows XP scoops up all your open windows and lays them back down in neat, orderly squares. (I cover tiling in more detail in Chapter 3.)

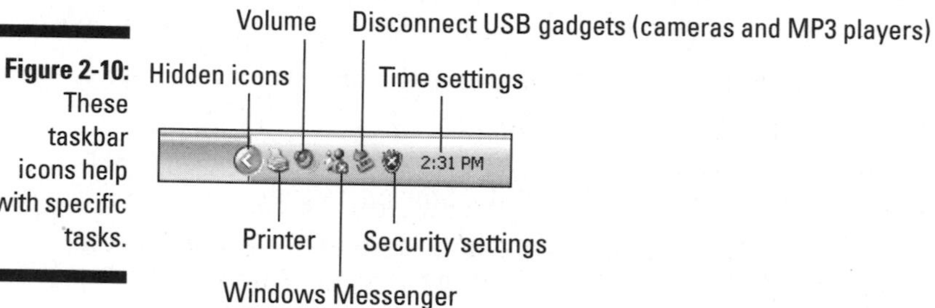

Figure 2-10: These taskbar icons help with specific tasks.

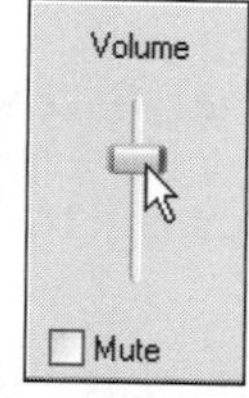

Figure 2-11: Change the volume.

Customizing the taskbar

Windows XP brings a whirlwind of new options for the lowly taskbar, letting you play with it in more ways than a strand of spaghetti and a fork. Right-click on the Start button, choose the Properties option, and click the Taskbar tab to start playing. Table 2-2 explains the options, as well as my recommendations for them. (You need to remove the check mark by Lock the Taskbar before some of these options will work.)

Table 2-2 Customizing the Taskbar

Setting	*My Recommendations*
Lock the Taskbar	Clicking here makes Windows XP lock the taskbar in place, keeping you from changing its look. You can't drag it upward to make it larger, for instance. Lock it, but only after the taskbar is set up the way you like.
Auto-Hide the Taskbar	Selecting this option makes the taskbar *automatically* hide itself when you're not near it. (Point at the taskbar to bring it back up.) I leave this unchecked to keep the taskbar always in view.
Keep the Taskbar on Top of Other Windows	This keeps the taskbar always visible, covering up any windows that may be low on the screen. I leave this checked.
Group Similar Taskbar Buttons	When you open lots of windows and programs, Windows accommodates the crowd by grouping similar windows under one button: All Internet Explorer buttons stack on one button, for instance. This option protects the taskbar from overcrowding, so keep it checked.
Show the Clock	You want to know when it's time to leave work, don't you? Leave this checked.
Hide Inactive Icons	This lets you hide those little icons — like the volume control, printer button, desktop cleanup program, and other goodies — that hang out by your clock. Click the Customize button to choose which icons should stay visible, which should hide, and which should appear only when being used. I click the Restore defaults button and leave 'em alone.

Feel free to experiment with the taskbar, changing its size and position until it looks right for you. It won't break. After you set it up just the way you want, select the Lock the Taskbar check box described in Table 2-2.

The taskbar's crazy toolbars

Your taskbar won't always be a steadfast, unchanging friend. Microsoft lets you customize it even further, often beyond the point of recognition. Some people enjoy this toolbar gadgetry, sculpting extra buttons and bars onto their taskbars. Others accidentally turn on a toolbar and can't figure out how to get rid of the darn thing.

To turn a toolbar on or off, right-click on a blank part of the taskbar (even the clock will do) and choose Toolbars from the pop-up menu. A menu leaps out, offering the options described in the following list:

- **Address:** Choose this, and part of your taskbar becomes a place for typing in Web sites to visit, as shown in Figure 2-12. It's convenient, but so is Internet Explorer, which does the same thing.
- **Windows Media Player:** When turned on, this toolbar turns into a little button panel for controlling your minimized Windows Media Player. (***Tip:*** Click where the arrow points in Figure 2-13 to browse your music.)
- **Links:** This toolbar adds quick access to your favorite Web sites; just click where the arrow points in Figure 2-14. (This toolbar displays all the links in the Links folder of Internet Explorer's Favorites menu.)
- **Desktop:** Shown in Figure 2-15, this places all your desktop icons — plus a miniature My Computer program — onto the taskbar, letting you browse through files by wading up through all the menus.

- **Quick Launch:** The only toolbar I use, this places an arsenal of favorite icons, as shown in Figure 2-16, next to your Start button: Internet Explorer, Outlook Express, Media Player, and the "shrink everything from the desktop" icon shown in the margin. (Add your own icons to the toolbar by dragging and dropping them.)
- **New Toolbar:** Click here and choose *any* folder to add as a toolbar. For instance, choose your My Documents folder (shown in Figure 2-17) for quick browsable access to all its files and folders.

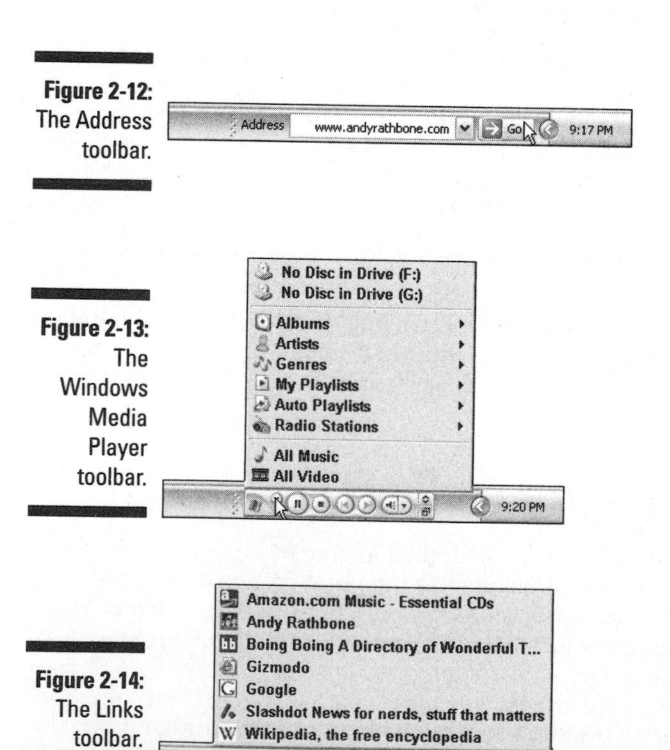

Figure 2-12: The Address toolbar.

Figure 2-13: The Windows Media Player toolbar.

Figure 2-14: The Links toolbar.

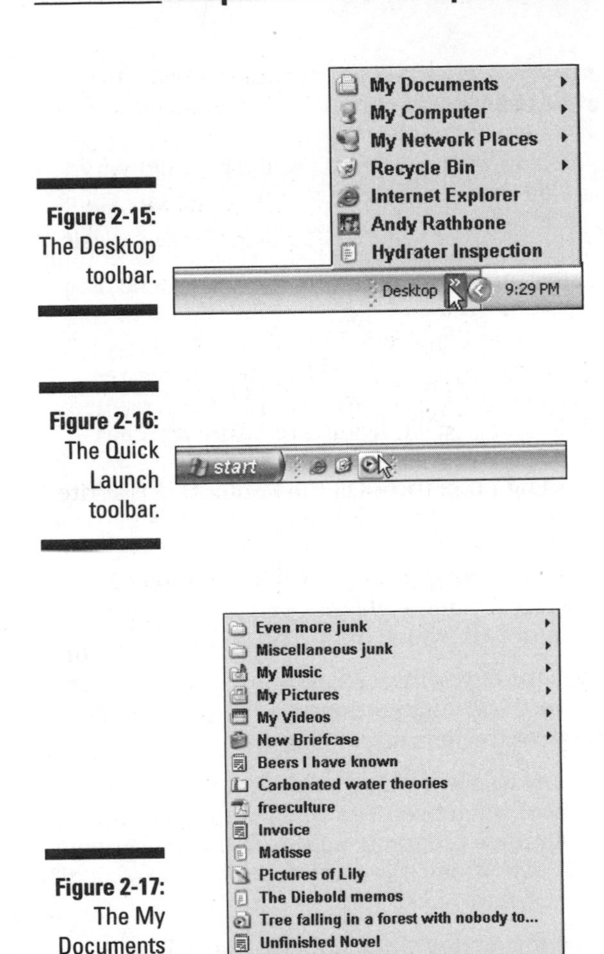

Figure 2-15: The Desktop toolbar.

Figure 2-16: The Quick Launch toolbar.

Figure 2-17: The My Documents toolbar.

The taskbar's tiny toolbars don't leave much room for aiming. For instance, click the ridiculously small arrows next to a toolbar's name (shown in the margin) to view its menu, shown popping up from the toolbars in Figures 2-14, 2-15, and 2-17.

- Toolbars are *supposed* to be dragged around with the mouse. When the taskbar is unlocked, grab the toolbar by its *handle,* a vertical line by the toolbar's name. Drag the handle to the left or right to change a toolbar's size.
- Toolbars can be dragged off the taskbar and dropped anywhere on the desktop. If this happens to you by mistake, drag the toolbar back onto the taskbar; keep trying, the toolbar will eventually stick. Then drag the renegade's handle to the right or left, adjusting it to the right size and position. Finally, right-click on your taskbar and choose Lock the Taskbar to freeze everything in place.

Logging Off from Windows

Ah! The most pleasant thing you'll do with Windows XP all day could very well be to stop using it. And you do that the same way you started: by using the Start button, that friendly little helper you've been using all along. (And if the Start menu is hiding, hold down Ctrl and press Esc to bring it back from behind the trees.) Two options live along the bottom of the Start menu: Log Off and Turn Off Computer.

Be sure to shut down Windows XP through its official Off options before physically turning off your computer. Otherwise, Windows XP can't properly prepare your computer for the dramatic event, leading to future troubles.

From the Start menu, should you Log Off or Turn Off the Computer? Here are the generally accepted guidelines:

- **Log Off:** Choose this when you're through working with Windows XP for the time being. Unable to let go, Windows will toss yet another question in your face, as shown in Figure 2-18. Which option do you choose?
  - **Log Off:** If you're *really* through with the computer, choose Log Off. Windows saves your work and your settings, and returns to the Welcome screen, ready for the next user to log on.
  - **Switch User:** If somebody else just wants to borrow the computer for a few minutes, choose Switch User. The Welcome screen appears, but Windows keeps your open programs waiting in the background. When you switch back, everything's just as you left it. (Personally, I think Logging Off makes more sense.)
- **Turn Off Computer:** Choose this option when nobody else will be using the computer until the next morning. Windows XP saves everything and tells you when it's okay to turn off your computer. (Sometimes it turns it off for you.) When you choose Turn Off Computer, Windows clings like a sleepy cat, tossing up the three options shown in Figure 2-19:
  - **Standby:** Also called Hibernate on some laptops, this option quickly saves all your work and puts the computer in *virtual sleep* — a delicate mode between on and off. Avoid it.
  - **Turn Off:** Choose this option when you're done for the day. Let you — and your computer — get some *real* sleep. When Windows XP leaves the screen, turn off the computer *and* the monitor, if Windows XP doesn't do it automatically.
  - **Restart:** Only choose this option when Windows XP screwed something up: Several programs crashed, or Windows seems to be acting awfully weird. Windows XP turns off and reloads itself, hopefully feeling refreshed.

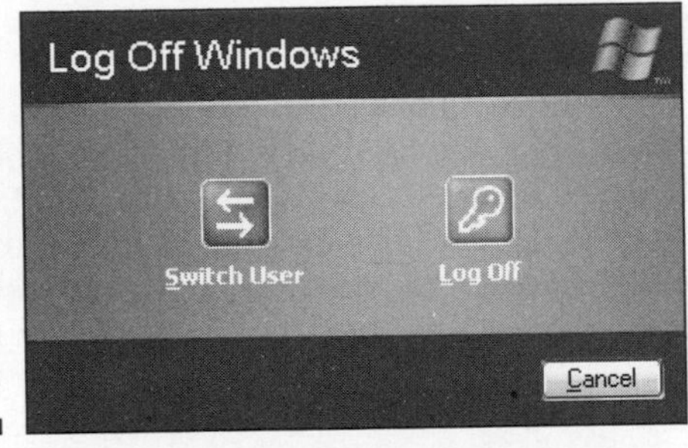

Figure 2-18: You see these options when you Log Off.

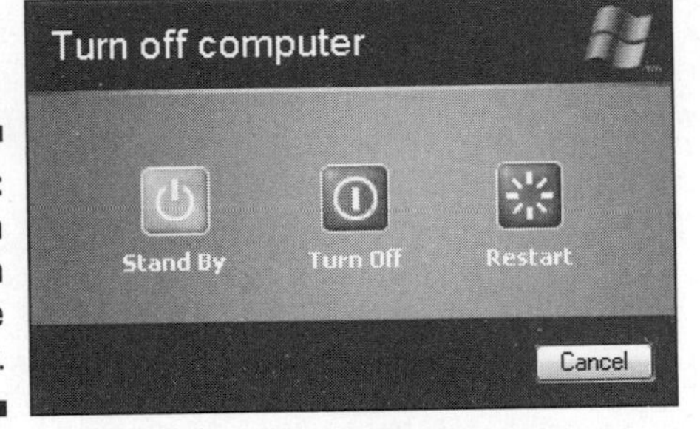

Figure 2-19: Choose Turn Off when you're done for the day.

When you tell Windows XP that you want to quit, it searches through all your open windows to see whether you've saved all your work. If it finds any work you've forgotten to save, it tosses a box your way, letting you click the OK button to save it. Whew!

You don't *have* to shut down Windows XP. In fact, some people leave their computers turned on all the time, saying it's better for their health. Others say their computers are healthier if they're turned off each day. However, *everybody* says to turn off your monitor when you're done working. Monitors definitely enjoy cooling down when not being used.

Chapter 3

Basic Windows Mechanics

In This Chapter

- Understanding a window's parts
- Manipulating buttons, bars, and boxes
- Finding and using menus
- Paging through a document in a window
- Filling out forms
- Moving windows and changing their size

This chapter is for curious Windows anatomy students. You know who you are — you're the ones who see all those buttons, borders, and balloons scattered throughout Windows XP and wonder what would happen if you just clicked that little thing over there.

This rather gruesome chapter tosses an ordinary window (your oft-used My Documents folder, to be precise) onto the dissection table. I've yanked out each part for thorough labeling and explanation. You'll find the theory behind each one and required procedures for making each piece do your bidding.

A standard field guide follows, identifying and explaining the buttons, boxes, windows, bars, lists, and other oddities you may encounter when you're trying to make Windows XP do something useful.

Feel free to don any protective gear you may have lying about, use the margins to scribble notes, and tread forcefully into the world of Windows.

Dissecting a Typical Window

Figure 3-1 places a typical window on the slab, with all its parts labeled. You might recognize it as your My Documents window, that storage tank for most of your work.

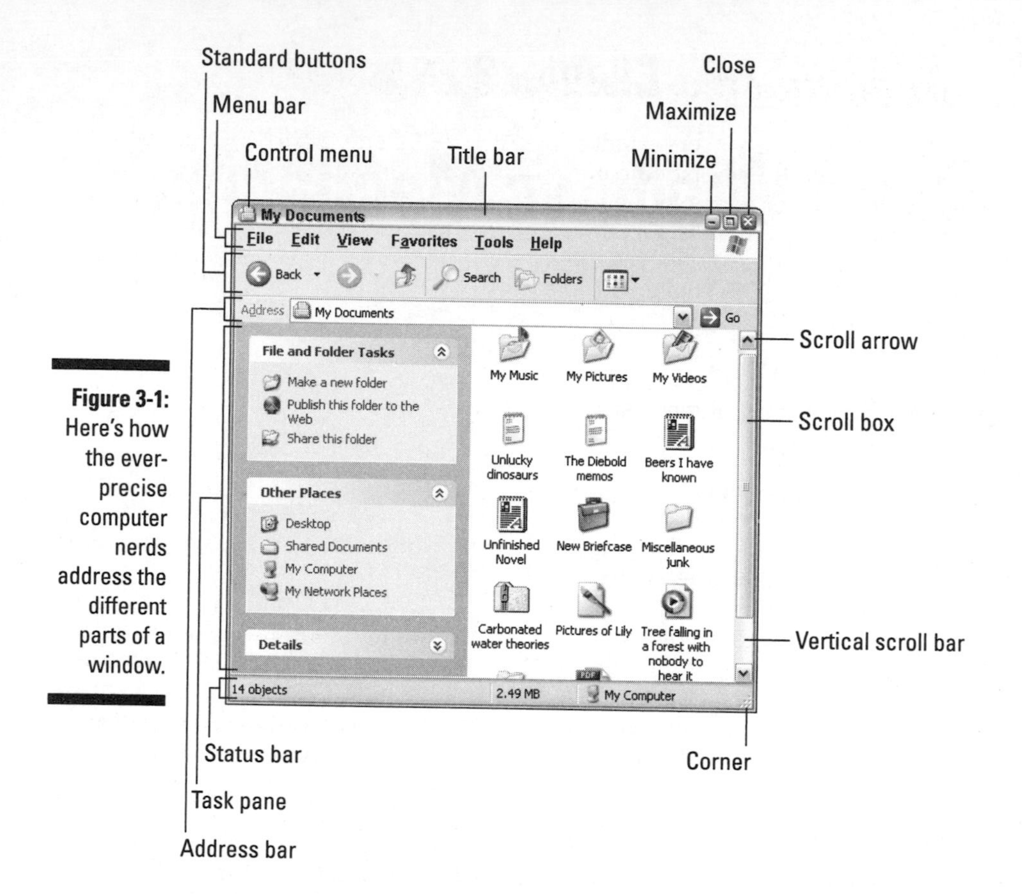

Figure 3-1: Here's how the ever-precise computer nerds address the different parts of a window.

Just as boxers grimace differently depending on where they've been punched, windows behave differently depending on where they've been clicked. The next few sections describe where to click the labeled parts of the window and how Windows jerks in response.

- Windows XP is full of little weird-shaped buttons, borders, and boxes. It's not important to remember all their names. Most items can be dealt with by simply clicking, double-clicking, or right-clicking, a decision explained in the nearby sidebar, "Clicking, double-clicking, and right-clicking strategies." (Spoiler: *When in doubt, always right-click.*)
- After you click a few windows a few times, you realize how easy it is to boss them around. The hard part is finding the right controls for the *first* time, like rummaging for the windshield wipers in a rental car.

Tugging on a window's title bar

Found atop nearly every window (see Figure 3-2 and the top of Figure 3-1), the ho-hum title bar lists the name of the program and the file it's currently working on. For example, Figure 3-2 shows the title bar from Windows XP's Notepad program. It lists an unnamed file because you haven't had a chance to save and name the file yet. (It may be full of notes you've jotted down from an energetic phone conversation with Ed McMahon.)

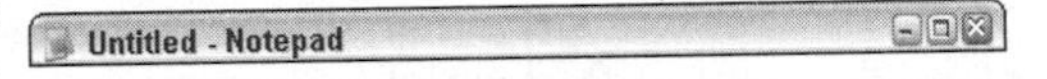

Figure 3-2: A title bar.

Like Peter Parker, the Amazing Spider-man, the boring title bar sports hidden superpowers, described in the following tips:

- Title bars make convenient handles for moving windows around the desktop. Point at the title bar, hold down the mouse button, and move the mouse around: The window follows along as you move your mouse. Found the right location? Let go of the mouse button, and the window sets up camp in its new spot.
- Double-click a title bar to make the window fill the entire screen. Double-click it again to shrink the window back to the first size.
- The window you're currently working with always has a *highlighted* title bar — it's a different color from the title bars of any other open windows. By glancing at all the title bars on the screen, you can quickly tell which window is awake and accepting anything you type.

Barking out orders with the menu bar

Windows XP has more menu items than an Asian restaurant. To keep everybody's minds on computer commands instead of seaweed salad, Windows disguises its menus behind the *menu bar* (see Figure 3-3).

File Edit Format View Help

Figure 3-3: The menu bar.

Clicking, double-clicking, and right-clicking strategies

Clicking or double-clicking your mouse will control nearly everything in Windows, yet Microsoft seems befuddled when defining the difference between the two finger actions. Microsoft says to click when *selecting* something, and double-click when *choosing* something. Huh?

You're *selecting* something when you're highlighting it. For example, you click in a box, on a window, or on a filename to *select* it. That click usually *highlights* the item, preparing it for further action.

Choosing something, by contrast, is much more decisive. An authoritative double-click on a file convinces Windows to open it for you immediately.

Microsoft's theoretical hierarchies bore me, so I almost always take the third option and *right-click* on things. Right-click on nearly anything to see a little menu listing everything it can do. I click the option I want, and Windows does my bidding.

The moral? *When in doubt, right-click.*

Perched on a ledge below the title bar, the menu bar hides a different menu below each word. To reveal the secret options, click any word — *Edit,* for instance. A menu tumbles down, as shown in Figure 3-4, presenting options related to editing a file.

Figure 3-4: Click any menu to see its associated commands.

Just as restaurants sometimes run out of specials, a window sometimes isn't capable of offering all its menu items. Any unavailable options are *grayed out,* like the Undo, Cut, Copy, Paste, Delete, and Go To options in Figure 3-4.

If you accidentally click the wrong word, causing the wrong menu to jump down, simply click the word you *really* wanted. A forgiving soul, Windows retracts the mistaken menu and displays your newly chosen one.

To back out of Menu Land completely, click the mouse pointer back down on your work in the window's *workspace* — the area where you're supposed to be working.

For the convenience of keyboard lovers, previous Windows versions underlined one letter of a menu item. Mouse haters could press the Alt key followed by the underlined letter — the *F* in File, for instance — to make Windows display the File menu. Windows XP removes the underlines, but they quickly reappear when you press Alt. (The underlines disappear again if you press Alt a *second* time, a convenient escape if you find yourself trapped in a sea of menus.)

Playing with a window's Standard Buttons toolbar

In a bizarre effort to blur the difference between Windows XP and the Internet, Microsoft added a strip of buttons (shown in Figure 3-5) beneath each window's menu bar. Officially dubbed the Standard Buttons toolbar, some of the buttons work much like the ones found on Internet Explorer, which I cover in Chapter 8.

Figure 3-5: Standard Buttons toolbar.

Each colorful button performs a common Windows chore — a quick jump to a different folder, for instance. If a button's meaning isn't immediately obvious, hover your mouse over it; a little message explains the button's *raison d'être*. My own translations are in the bullets that follow:

- The large Back and Forward arrows let you navigate through folders the same way you cruise the Internet. When racing through a long string of folders, Windows remembers your path; click the Back or Forward arrows to move backward or forward along your journey, revisiting folders you've previously viewed.

- The folder with the upward escaping arrow (shown in the margin) lets you move *upward* through your folders. For example, when visiting your My Pictures folder (which lives inside your My Documents folder), click this Upward button to visit your My Documents folder upstairs.

- The Search button is simply a shortcut to the Start menu's Search command, which lets you ferret out information from your computer or the Internet. (I cover searching in Chapter 6.)

- Clicking the Folders button whisks away the handy task pane (covered later in this chapter), replacing it with a *tree* view of all your folders. By viewing your folders as branches sprouting from one source, you can easily jump from one branch to another: Leap directly to your CD drive, for instance, your Recycle Bin, a distant folder, or even a different computer on the office network. (Click the Folders button again to bring back the task pane.)

- Easily the most boring button (shown in the margin), the Views button may be the most useful: It makes the window display your files in different ways. Choose Details, for instance, to view everything you wanted to know about a file: its size, creation date, and other minutia. The List view packs as many filenames onto the screen as possible. Taste 'em all and then stick with your favorite. (Windows normally uses the Icons view.)

Moving inside a window with its scroll bar

The scroll bar, which resembles a cutaway of an elevator shaft (see Figure 3-6), rests along the edge of all over-stuffed windows. Inside the shaft, a little elevator (technically, the *scroll box*) rides up and down as you page through your work. In fact, by glancing at the elevator's position in the shaft, you can tell whether you're viewing the top, middle, or bottom of a window's contents.

Figure 3-6: A scroll bar.

You can watch the little box travel up or down as you press the PgUp or PgDn key. (Yes, it's easy to get distracted in Windows XP.) But it's more fun to nudge the elevator around with the mouse. By clicking in various places on the scroll bar, you can quickly move around inside a document. Here's the dirt:

- Clicking in the shaft *above* the elevator shifts your view up one page, just as if you'd pressed the PgUp key. Similarly, clicking *below* the elevator shifts the view down one page.
- To move your view up line by line, click the little arrow (the *scroll arrow*) at the top of the scroll bar. Similarly, clicking the little arrow at the bottom moves your view down one line with each click.

- Scroll bars occasionally hang out along a window's bottom edge. Handy for viewing spreadsheets and other wide documents, scroll bars let you move your view sideways for peeking at the totals in the spreadsheet's last column.
- No little scroll box in the bar? Then you're already seeing all that the window has to offer. No little elevator to play with.
- To move around in a hurry, drag the scroll box up or down the bar. As you drag it up or down, you see the window's contents race past. When you see the spot you want, let go of the mouse button to stay at that viewing position.

- Using a mouse that has a little wheel embedded in the poor critter's back? Spin the wheel, and the list moves up or down, just as if you were playing with the scroll bar.

Quick shortcuts with the Windows XP task pane

To give its users a handy alternative to random guessing, Windows XP's folders now sport a *task pane,* shown in Figure 3-7. Hugging the left side of most folders, the task pane lists common chores customized to what you're viewing. The task pane in your My Pictures folder displays picture-related tasks: Print This Picture, for instance, or View as a Slideshow. Click any listed task, and Windows does your bidding.

Dragging, dropping, and running

Although the term *drag and drop* sounds as if it's straight out of a *Sopranos* episode, it's really a nonviolent mouse trick used in Windows XP. Dragging and dropping is a way of moving something — say, an icon on your desktop — from one place to another.

To *drag,* put the mouse pointer over the icon and *hold down* the left or right mouse button. (I prefer the right mouse button.) As you move the mouse across your desk, the pointer drags the icon across the screen. Place the pointer/icon where you want it and release the mouse button. The icon *drops,* unharmed.

Holding down the *right* mouse button while dragging and dropping makes Windows XP toss up a helpful little menu, asking whether you want to *copy* or *move* the icon.

Helpful Tip Department: Started dragging something and realized midstream that you're dragging the wrong item? Breathe deeply like a yoga instructor and press Esc to cancel the action. Whew! (If you've dragged with your right mouse button and already let go of the button, there's another exit: Choose Cancel from the pop-up menu.)

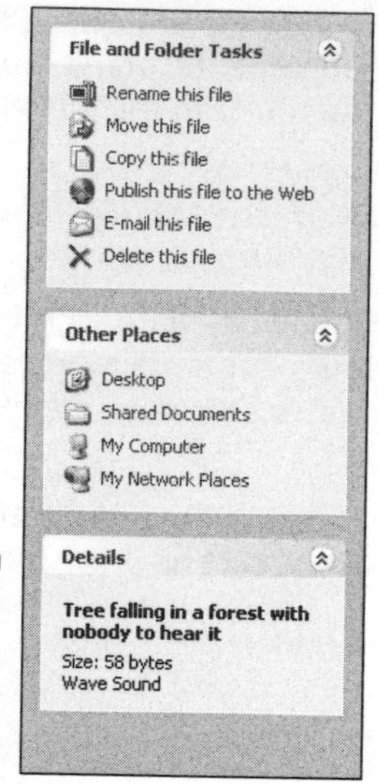

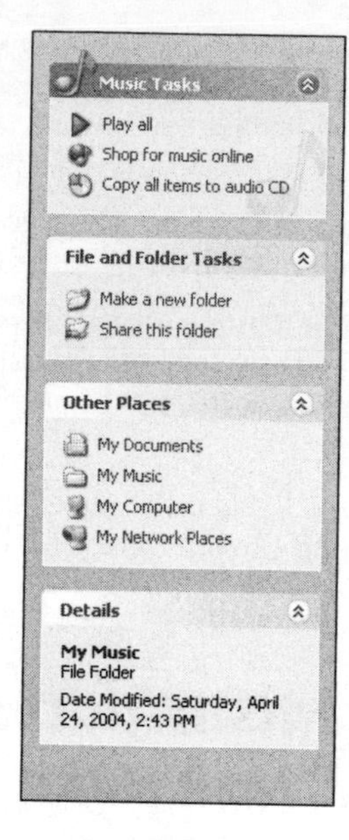

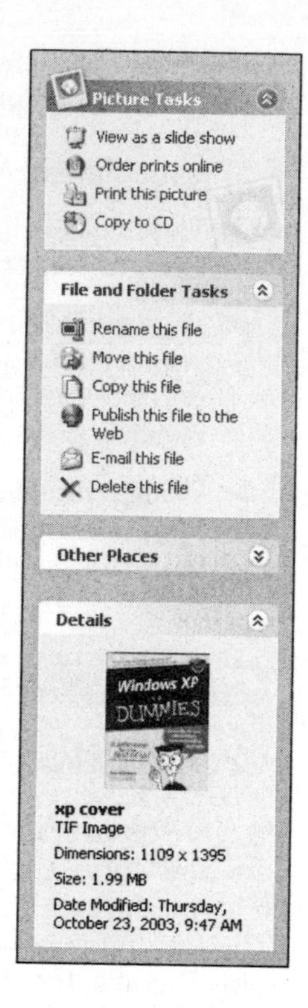

Figure 3-7: The task pane always changes, offering shortcuts that apply to what you're currently viewing.

Clicking an individual file brings the task pane's *Details* area into action. There, at the bottom of the task pane, you'll see your chosen file's size, description, and if you've selected a picture that's not currently displayed, a tiny preview.

- The rather thick and colorful task *pane* has absolutely no relation to the task*bar,* that thin strip along the bottom of your desktop. (I introduce the taskbar in Chapter 2.)

- If the task pane bashfully hides some of its tasks, click the hidden category's little double-arrow thing (shown in the margin). The applicable tasks will spring back into view. (Click it again to hide those tasks, if you wish.)
- Can't find your task pane? Clicking the Folders button along the top of your folder sometimes brings it into view.

- If you think the task pane consumes too much screen space, turn it off: Choose Folder Options from the window's Tools menu, click the General Tab, and choose Use Windows Classic Folders. (Reverse those steps to revive a missing task pane.)

- If Windows shows the *wrong* task pane for your particular folder — it shows the My Pictures task pane in your My Music folder, for instance — fix it this way: Choose Folder Options from the Tools menu, click the View tab, and choose Reset All Folders.

Boring borders

A border is that thin edge surrounding a window. Compared with a bar, it's really tiny.

- To change a window's size, drag the border in or out. (Dragging by the corner gives you even more leeway.)
- Some windows, oddly enough, don't have borders. That means you can't change their size, unfortunately, even if they're way too small.
- Except for tugging on them with the mouse, you won't be using borders much.

Transforming a mere folder into Internet Explorer

Toolbars are optional strips of buttons or controls that live near the top of a window by the menu bar and title bar. Folders come with *three* toolbars, accessed by choosing Toolbars from the folder's View menu. The Standard Buttons toolbar, described in its own section, adds handy push buttons to perform common tasks. But what's the deal with the Address and Links toolbars? Believe it or not, those toolbars let you turn folders into Internet Explorer.

- **Address toolbar:** Clicking the down arrow in Internet Explorer's Address toolbar displays links to sites you've visited. Similarly, clicking that same arrow on a *folder's* Address toolbar lists popular Windows destinations: disk drives, your desktop, frequently used folders, the Control Panel, and more. Click any item — your My Documents folder, for instance — to jump there immediately.
- **Links toolbar:** This toolbar shows your favorite Web links along the top, effectively transforming your folder into Internet Explorer. When you click a link, you jump to that Web page. For a kick, click the Back arrow atop Internet Explorer, and it transforms back into the folder you just left.

To make these toolbars appear, click View from the window's menu bar. Then click Toolbars, and a drop-down menu lists the toolbars that particular window offers. Click the missing bar's name so that a check mark appears next to its name. (Don't like a certain bar? Click that toolbar's name to uncheck it and wipe it from the screen.)

If you're satisfied with the strips of buttons and commands along your window's top, choose Lock the Toolbars (also on the View menu) to lock them in place. That keeps you from accidentally changing a toolbar; they're easy to reposition, especially with an inadvertent drag of the mouse.

Filling Out Bothersome Dialog Boxes

Sooner or later, Windows XP will lapse into surly clerk mode, forcing you to fill out a bothersome form before carrying out your request. To handle this computerized paperwork, Windows XP uses a *dialog box.*

A dialog box is simply a window. But instead of containing a program, it contains a little form or checklist for you to fill out. These forms can have bunches of different parts, all discussed in the following sections. Don't bother trying to remember each part's name. It's much more important to remember how they work.

Poking the correct command button

Command buttons may be the simplest part of a form to figure out — Microsoft labeled them! Command buttons usually require poking after you've filled out a form. Based on the command button you click, Windows either carries out your bidding (rare) or sends you another form (most likely).

Table 3-1 identifies some of the more common command buttons strewn throughout Windows XP.

Table 3-1 Common Windows XP Command Buttons

Command Button	*Description*
OK	A click on the OK button says, "I've finished the form, and I'm ready to move on." Windows XP reads what you've typed and processes your request.
Cancel	If you've somehow loused things up when filling out a form, click the Cancel button. Windows whisks away the form, and everything returns to normal. Whew!
< Back Next >	Boy, would this have come in handy in elementary school! Click the Back button, and Windows returns you to the previous window so that you can change your answer. Click the Next button to move to the next question.
Setup... Settings...	If you encounter a button with dots (. . .) after the word, brace yourself: Clicking that button brings yet *another* form to the screen. From there, you must choose even more settings, options, or toppings.

- Sometimes you'll change a setting that makes things looks weird: For example, a long-loved toolbar will disappear. To bring Windows XP's freshly installed look back to a certain form or program, click the Restore Default button with full force.
- The OK button usually has a slightly darker border than the others, meaning it's *highlighted.* Just pressing Enter automatically chooses the form's highlighted button, sparing you the inconvenience of clicking it. (I usually click it anyways, just to make sure.)

If you've clicked the wrong button but *haven't yet lifted your finger from the mouse button,* stop! There's still hope. Command buttons take effect only *after* you've lifted your finger from the mouse button. Keep holding down the mouse, but scoot the pointer away from the wrong button. When the pointer no longer rests on the button, gently lift your finger. Whew! Try *that* trick on any elevator.

Did you stumble across a box that contains a confusing option? Click the question mark in the box's upper-right corner (it will look like the one in the margin). Then click the confusing command button to see a short explanation of that button's function in life. Sometimes merely resting your mouse pointer over a confusing button makes Windows take pity, sending a helpful caption to explain matters.

Choosing between option buttons

Sometimes, Windows XP gets ornery and forces you to select a single option. For example, you can elect to *eat* your Brussels sprouts or *not* eat your Brussels sprouts. You can't select both, so Windows XP doesn't let you select both of the options.

Windows XP handles this situation with an *option button.* When you select one option, the little dot hops over to it. Select the other option, and the little dot hops over to it, instead. You find option buttons in many dialog boxes, like the one in Figure 3-8.

- If you *can* select more than one option, Windows XP won't present you with option buttons. Instead, it offers the more liberal *check boxes,* which are described in the "Check boxes" section, later in this chapter.
- Some old-time computer engineers refer to option buttons as *radio buttons,* after those push buttons on car radios that switch from station to station, one station at a time.

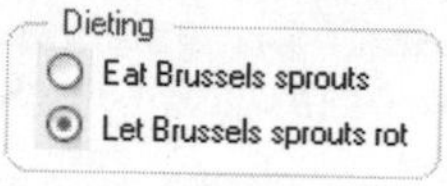

Figure 3-8: Select an option.

Typing into text boxes

A *text box* works like a fill-in-the-blanks test in history class. You can type anything you want into a text box — words, numbers, passwords, or epithets. For example, Figure 3-9 shows a dialog box that pops up when you want to search for some words or characters in some programs. The text box is where you type the words you want to search for.

- When a text box is *active* (that is, ready for you to start typing stuff into it), either the box's current information is highlighted or a cursor is blinking inside it.
- If the text box *isn't* highlighted or there *isn't* a blinking cursor inside it, it's not ready for you to start typing. To announce your presence, click inside it before typing.
- If you need to use a text box that already contains words, remember to delete any text you don't want before you start typing in new information. (Or you can double-click the old information to highlight it; that way, the incoming text automatically replaces the old text.)
- Yes, text boxes have way too many rules.

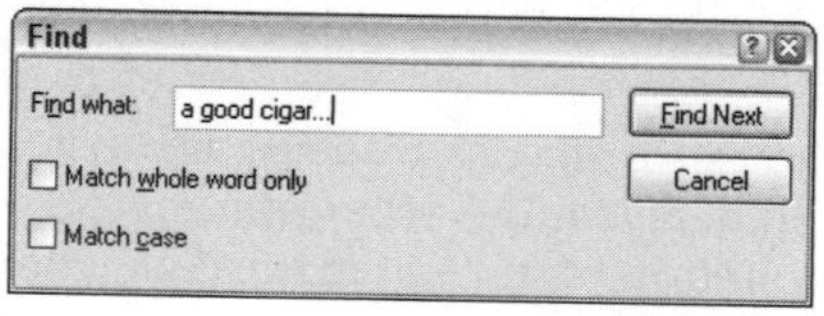

Figure 3-9: This dialog box contains a text box.

Choosing options from list boxes

Some boxes don't let you type *anything* into them. They simply display lists of things, letting you pluck the items you want. Boxes of lists are called, appropriately enough, *list boxes*. For example, some word processors bring up a list box if you're inspired enough to want to change the *font* — the style of the letters (see Figure 3-10).

- See how the Comic Sans MS font is highlighted in Figure 3-10? It's the currently selected item in the list box. Press Enter (or click the OK button), and your program begins using that font when you start typing.

- See the scroll bar along the side of the list box? It works just as it does anywhere else: Click the little scroll arrows (or press the up or down arrow) to move the list up or down, and you can see any names that don't fit in the box.
- Some list boxes have a text box above them. When you click a name in the list box, that name hops into the text box. Sure, you could type the name into the text box yourself, but it wouldn't be nearly as much fun.

- When confronted with zillions of names in a list box or folder, type the first letter of the name you're after. Windows XP immediately hops down the list to the first name beginning with that letter.

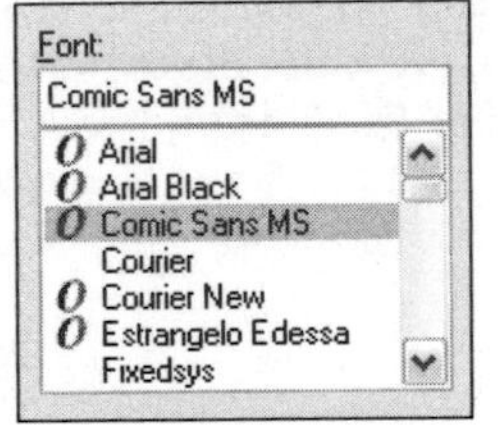

Figure 3-10: Select a font from the list box.

Drop-down list boxes

List boxes are convenient, but they take up a great deal of room. So, Windows XP sometimes hides list boxes, just as it hides pull-down menus. When you click in the right place, the list box appears, ready for your perusal.

So, where's the right place? It's that downward-pointing arrow button, just like the one shown next to the box beside the Font option in Figure 3-11. (The mouse pointer is pointing to it.)

Figure 3-11: Click the arrow next to the Font box to make a drop-down list box display available fonts.

Figure 3-12 shows the drop-down list box, after being clicked by the mouse.

- To scoot around quickly in a long drop-down list box, press the first letter of the item you're after. The first item beginning with that letter is instantly highlighted. You can press the up- or down-arrow keys to see nearby words and phrases.
- Another way to scoot around quickly in a drop-down list box is to click the scroll bar to its right. (Scroll bars are discussed earlier in this chapter, if you need a refresher.)
- You can choose only *one* item from the list of a drop-down list box.

- The program in Figure 3-11 is called Character Map, and it's a handy way for adding characters that don't appear on your keyboard: ½, ©, ¢, and the rest. To play with Character Map, click the Start button and choose the All Programs area. Click System Tools from the Accessories area and then click Character Map.

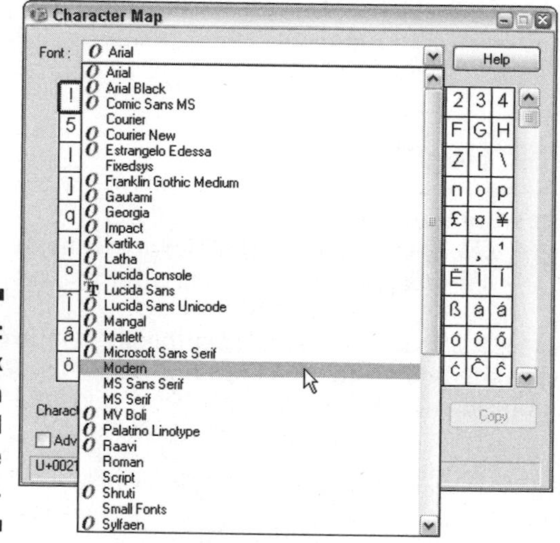

Figure 3-12: A list box drops down to display all the available fonts.

Check boxes

Sometimes you can choose several options in a dialog box simply by clicking in the little square boxes next to their names. For example, the check boxes shown in Figure 3-13 let you pick and choose options in the game FreeCell.

- Clicking in an empty square chooses that option. If the square already has a check mark inside, a click turns off that option, removing the check mark.
- You can click as many check boxes as you want. Option buttons (those similar-looking but round buttons) restrict you to one option from the pack.

Figure 3-13: Click to check a box.

Sliding controls

Rich Microsoft programmers, impressed by track lights and sliding light switches in their luxurious new homes, use sliding controls in Windows XP. These virtual light switches are easy to use and don't wear out nearly as quickly as the real ones do.

When one just isn't enough

Because Windows XP can display only one background on your desktop at a time, you can select only one file from the list box of available backgrounds. Other list boxes, like those in Windows Explorer, let you select a bunch of names simultaneously. Here's how:

- To select more than one item, hold down the Ctrl key and click each item you want. Each item stays highlighted.
- To select a bunch of adjacent items from a list box, click the first item you want. Then hold down Shift and click the last item you want. Windows XP immediately highlights the first item, last item, and every item in between. Pretty sneaky, huh? (To weed out a few unwanted items from the middle, hold down Ctrl and click them; Windows unhighlights them, leaving the rest highlighted.)
- Finally, when grabbing bunches of items, try using the "rubber band" trick: Point at an area of the screen next to one item, and, while holding down the mouse button, move the mouse until you've drawn a lasso around all the items. After you've highlighted the items you want, let go of the mouse button, and they remain highlighted. Fun!

Some levers slide to the left and right; others move up and down. None of them move diagonally, yet. To slide a control in Windows XP — to adjust the volume level, for example — just drag and drop the sliding lever, like the one shown in Figure 3-14.

Sliding works like this: Point at the lever with the mouse and, while holding down the mouse button, move the mouse in the direction you want the sliding lever to move. As you move the mouse, the lever moves, too. When you've moved the lever to a comfortable spot, let go of the mouse button, and Windows XP leaves the lever at its new position.

Figure 3-14: A sliding lever.

Maneuvering Windows around the Desktop

A terrible dealer at the poker table, Windows XP tosses windows around your desktop in a seemingly random way. Programs cover each other or sometimes dangle off the desktop. This section shows you how to gather all your windows into a neat pile, placing your favorite window on the top of the stack. If you prefer, lay them all down like a poker hand. As an added bonus, you can change their size, making them open to any size you want, automatically.

The Alt+Tab trick

Sometimes your desktop becomes so cluttered with windows that you lose track of a particular window. To cycle through every open window, hold down the Alt key while pressing Tab: A little window appears in the middle of the screen, listing every open window by name. Keep pressing Tab until you see the name of the window you're after. Found it? Release both keys, and Windows brings the currently listed window to the forefront.

Moving a window to the top of the pile

Windows XP says the window at the top of the pile getting all the attention is called the *active* window. I won't argue. The active window is also the one that receives any keystrokes you or your cat happen to type.

You can move a window to the top of the pile so that it's active in one of two ways:

- Sometimes you can recognize a tiny portion of the window you're after. If so, you're in luck. Move the mouse pointer until it hovers over any portion of the desired window and click the mouse button. Windows XP immediately makes the clicked-on window active.
- On the taskbar, click the button for the window you want. Chapter 2 explains what the taskbar can do in more detail.

Repeat the process when necessary to bring other windows to the front. (And if you want to put two windows on the screen at the same time, read the "Placing two windows next to each other" section, later in this chapter.)

Moving a window from here to there

Sometimes you want to move a window to a different place on the desktop. Perhaps part of the window hangs off the edge, and you want it centered. Or maybe you want one window closer to another.

In either case, you can move a window by dragging and dropping its *title bar,* that thick bar along its top. (See the sidebar "Dragging, dropping, and running," earlier in this chapter, if you're not sure how dragging and dropping works.) When you *drop* the window in place, the window not only remains where you've dragged and dropped it, but also stays on top of the pile.

Making a window fill the whole screen

Sooner or later, you'll grow tired of all this multiwindow mumbo jumbo. Why can't you just put one huge window on-screen? Well, you can.

To make any window grow as big as it can get, double-click its *title bar,* that topmost bar along the window's top edge. The window leaps up to fill the screen, covering up all the other windows.

To bring the pumped-up window back to its former size, double-click its title bar once again. The window quickly shrinks to its former size, and you can see things that it covered.

- If you're morally opposed to double-clicking a window's title bar to expand it, you can click the little Maximize button. Shown in the margin, it's the middle of the three buttons in the upper-right corner of every window.

- When a window is maximized to fill the screen, the Maximize button turns into a Restore button, shown in the margin. Click the Restore button, and the window returns to its smaller size.

Making a window bigger or smaller

Like big lazy dogs, windows tend to flop on top of one another. To space your windows more evenly, you can resize them by *dragging and dropping* their edges inward or outward. It works like this:

1. **Point at any corner with the mouse arrow. When the arrow turns into a two-headed arrow, pointing in the two directions, you can hold down the mouse button and drag the corner in or out to change the window's size.**
2. **When you're done yanking and the window looks about the right size, let go of the mouse button.**

   As the yoga master says, the window assumes the new position.

Placing two windows next to each other

The longer you use Windows, the more likely you are to want to see two windows side by side. For example, you might want to copy and paste text from one document into another document. By spending a few hours with the mouse, you can drag and drop the windows' corners until they're in perfect juxtaposition.

Or you can simply right-click on a blank part of the taskbar (even the clock will do) and choose Tile Windows Horizontally to place one window directly above the other. Choose Tile Windows Vertically to place the windows side by side, like pillars.

- If you have more than two windows open, minimize the ones you *don't* want tiled. Then use the Tile command to align the two remaining windows.
- To deal all your windows across the desktop like a poker hand, right-click on a blank part of the taskbar and choose Cascade Windows. I haven't found much use for it yet, but it's fun to watch.

Making windows open to the same darn size

Sometimes a window opens to a small square; other times, it opens to fill the entire screen. But windows rarely open to the exact size you want. Until you discover this trick, that is: When you *manually* adjust the size and placement of a window, Windows memorizes that size and always reopens the window to that same size. Follow these three steps to see how it works:

1. **Open your window.**

   The window opens to its usual, unwanted size.

2. **Drag the window's corners until the window is the exact size and in the exact location you want. Let go of the mouse to drop the corner into its new position.**

   Be sure to resize the window *manually* by dragging its corners or edges with the mouse. Simply clicking the Maximize button won't work.

3. **Immediately close the window.**

   Windows memorizes the size and placement of a window at the time it was last closed. When you open that window again, it should open to the same size you last left it. But the changes you make apply only to the program you made them in. For example, changes made to the Internet Explorer window will only be remembered for *Internet Explorer,* not other programs you open.

Chapter 4

Flipping Through Files, Folders, Floppies, and CDs

In This Chapter

- Understanding the My Computer and Explorer programs
- Understanding folders
- Navigating drives and folders
- Creating and naming folders
- Selecting items
- Deleting items
- Copying and moving files and folders
- Writing to CDs, memory cards, and floppies

The My Computer program is where people wake up from Windows' easy-to-use computing dream, clutching a pillow in horror. These people bought a computer to simplify their work — to banish that awful filing cabinet with squeaky drawers.

But click the little My Computer icon from the Start menu, start poking around, and that filing cabinet reappears. Folders, bunches of them, still rule the world. And unless you grasp Windows' folder metaphor, you probably won't be able to find your information very easily.

This chapter explains how to use the My Computer program and its hidden twin Windows Explorer. Along the way, you ingest a big enough dose of Windows file management for you to get your work done. Windows may bring back your dreaded file cabinet, but at least the drawers don't squeak, and files never fall behind the cabinet.

Browsing My Computer's File Cabinets

To keep your programs and files neatly arranged, Windows borrowed the convenient file cabinet metaphor, cleaned it up with light and airy Windows icons, and called it the *My Computer* program. My Computer displays all the files and storage areas inside your computer, allowing you to copy, move, rename, or delete them before the investigators arrive.

Everybody organizes his or her computer differently, and some people don't organize their computers at all. To see how your computer currently organizes your files, click the Start menu and click My Computer (the icon shown in the margin). Although your My Computer window probably looks different from the one shown in Figure 4-1, it has the same basic sections, each described shortly.

In fact, whenever you try to open or store a file or folder, you encounter these same areas. Windows just displays them a little differently depending on what you're up to.

To make your My Computer window look more like the one in Figure 4-1, click the View menu and choose Icons. Then, also from the View menu, choose Arrange Icons by Type, and check the Show in Groups option.

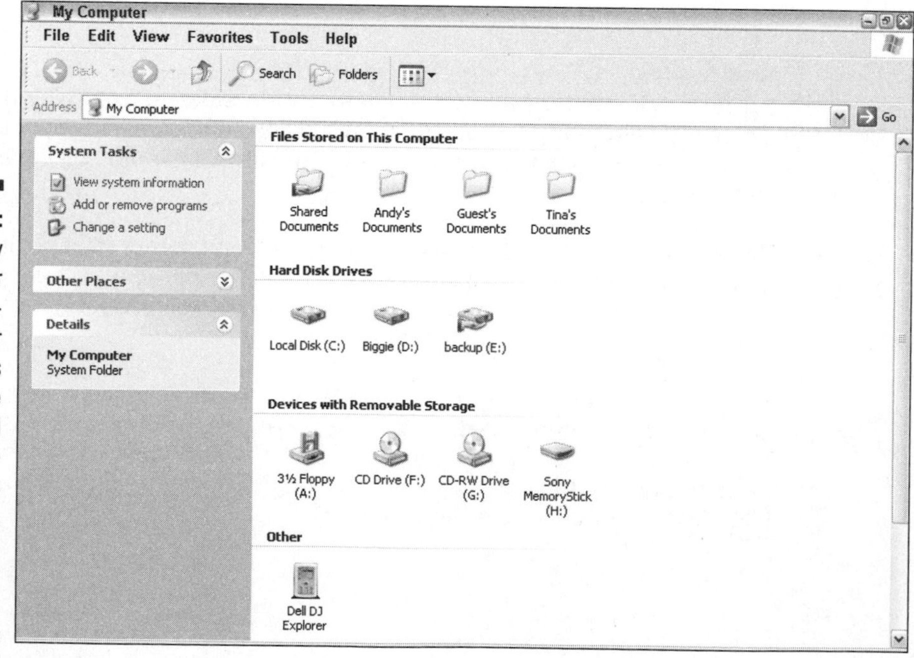

Figure 4-1: The My Computer window displays your computer's storage areas and files, allowing you to copy, rename, move, or delete them.

Files Stored on This Computer: Normally, Windows XP doesn't let different users read each other's files. But when people *want* to share information — party invitations, for instance — the Shared Documents folder (shown in the margin) comes in handy. If one person puts a party invitation in the Shared Documents folder, *everybody* using the computer can read it, making for livelier parties.

Figure 4-1 shows three folders next to the Shared Documents folder: Andy's Documents (which is my My Documents folder), Guest's Documents, and Tina's Documents. What's to stop me from peeking into Tina's folder? Nothing, actually, because I have an almighty *administrator* user account, which lets me peek everywhere. (I explain types of user accounts, and how to keep them private, in Chapter 13.)

Hard Disk Drives: Shown in Figure 4-1, this area lists *hard drives* installed inside your computer. (Every computer has at least one.) Double-clicking a hard drive icon shows its files and folders, but you'll rarely find much useful information. In fact, Windows occasionally sends out a stern warning message to discourage you from peeking. Instead of probing your hard drive, use your Start menu to find and start programs. Use your My Documents folder to store your personal folders and files.

Devices with Removable Storage: This area shows detachable storage gadgetry attached to your computer: CD drives (like the one in the margin), memory card readers (usually from cameras), and even MP3 players, like the Dell DJ Explorer shown in Figure 4-1. (I cover MP3 players in Chapter 15.)

Scanners and Cameras: Although not shown in Figure 4-1, digital cameras and scanners often appear in the My Computer folder. Double-clicking the camera icon lets you grab its pictures; double-clicking the scanner icon lets you scan an item into your computer. (Store both their images in your My Pictures folder.)

Click almost any icon in My Computer, and the task pane's Details area automatically displays information about that object: the date a file was created, for instance, or how much space a folder or drive can hold.

Getting the Lowdown on Folders

This stuff is dreadfully boring, but if you don't read it, you'll be just as lost as your files.

A *folder* is a storage area on a disk, just like a real folder in a file cabinet. Windows XP divides your computer's hard drives into many folders to separate your many projects. That lets you work with a spreadsheet, for example, without having your poems in the way. You can store all your music in your My Music folder and your pictures in your My Pictures folder.

Any type of disk can have folders, but hard drives need folders the most because they contain *thousands* of files. By dividing a hard drive into little folder compartments, you can more easily see where everything sits.

Windows' My Computer program lets you probe into different folders and peek at the files stuffed inside each one. You deal with these main folders in Windows:

My Documents: Please, *please* store all your work inside this folder, and for several reasons. By keeping everything in one place, it's easier to find. Plus, it's something only *you* can find; other people using the computer can't fiddle with it. Create as many new folders inside here as you want. Plus, use its three built-in folders (described next) for storing pictures, music, or movies.

My Pictures: Store all your pictures in here, whether they're from a digital camera, scanner, or the Internet. Covered in Chapter 16, the My Pictures folder lets you view tiny thumbnails of your photos, grab pictures from an attached camera, create slideshows, and have more Foto Fun.

My Music: Keep the digital music in here, so Media Player can quickly locate and play it.

My Videos: Videos downloaded from camcorders and the Internet should stay here.

- Folders used to be called *directories* and *subdirectories.* But some people were getting used to that, so the industry switched to the term *folders.*
- You can ignore folders and dump all your files onto the Windows XP desktop. But that's like tossing everything into the back seat of the car and pawing around to find your tissue box a month later. Organized stuff is much easier to find.
- If you're eager to create a folder or two (and it's pretty easy), page ahead to this chapter's "Creating a New Folder" section.

- Sometimes the befuddled Windows XP displays the My Music or My Pictures task pane for the wrong folders. To fix the switch, open any folder, choose Folder Options from the Tools menu, click the View tab, and click the Reset All Folders button. Windows XP's amnesia clears, and the proper task panes return.

- Just as manila folders come from trees, computer folders use a *tree metaphor* as they branch out from one main folder (a disk drive) to several smaller folders (see Figure 4-2).

- Desktop
  - My Documents
  - My Computer
    - 3½ Floppy (A:)
    - Local Disk (C:)
      - Documents and Settings
        - All Users
        - Guest
        - Owner
        - Tina
          - Cookies
          - Desktop
          - Favorites
          - My Documents
            - My Music
            - My Pictures
          - Start Menu
      - Program Files
      - WINDOWS

Figure 4-2: Windows' folders use a treelike structure, with main folders branching out to smaller folders.

Peering into Your Drives and Folders

Knowing all this folder stuff not only impresses computer store employees, but also helps you find the files you want. Put on your hard hat, go spelunking among your computer's drives and folders, and use this section as your guide.

Seeing the files on a disk drive

Like everything else in Windows XP, disk drives are represented by buttons, or icons. My Computer also shows information stored in other areas, like MP3 players, digital cameras, or scanners. (I explain these icons in "Browsing My Computer's File Cabinets," earlier in this chapter.)

Opening these icons usually lets you access their contents and move files back and forth, just as with any other folders in Windows XP.

- When in doubt as to what you can do with an icon in My Computer, right-click on it. Windows XP presents a menu of all the things you can do to that object.
- Double-click a drive icon in My Computer, and the My Computer window displays the drive's contents. For example, put a CD in your CD drive and double-click My Computer's CD drive icon. After a few gears whirl, My Computer shows what files and folders live on the CD in your CD drive.

- Hold down the Ctrl key while double-clicking a drive icon, and a *second* My Computer window appears, to show the drive's contents. (You might have to rearrange one window's size to see them both.) So what? Well, a second window comes in handy when you want to move or copy files from one folder or drive to another, as discussed in the "Copying or Moving Files and Folders" section, later in this chapter.

- If you click an icon for a CD or floppy drive when no disk is in the drive, Windows XP stops you, gently suggesting that you insert a disk before proceeding further.
- Spot an icon called My Network Places? That's a little doorway for peering into other computers linked to your computer — if there are any. You find more network stuff in Chapter 14.

Seeing what's inside folders

Because folders are really little storage compartments, Windows XP uses a picture of a little folder to stand for each separate place for storing files.

To see what's inside a folder, either in My Computer or on your computer's desktop, just double-click that folder's picture. A new window pops up, showing that folder's contents. Spot another folder inside that folder? Double-click that one to see what's inside. Keep clicking until you find what you want or reach a dead end.

What's all this path stuff?

A *path* is merely the file's address, similar to your own. When mailed to your house, for example, a letter travels to your country, state, city, street, and finally, hopefully, your apartment or house number. A computer path does the same thing. It starts with the letter of the disk drive and ends with the file's name. In between, the path lists all the folders the computer must travel through to reach the file.

For example, look at the My Music folder in Figure 4-2. For Windows XP to find a file stored there, it starts from the computer's C: hard drive, travels through the Documents and Settings folder, and then goes through the Tina folder. From there, it goes into the Tina folder's My Documents folder. And only then does it reach the My Music folder.

Take a deep breath. Exhale slowly. Now add in the computer's ugly grammar: In a path, a disk drive letter is referred to as **C:**. The disk drive letter and colon make up the first part of the path.

All the other folders are inside the big C: folder, so they're listed after the C: part. Windows separates these nested folders with something called a *backslash,* or \. The file's name — *Rivers of Babylon,* for example — comes last.

Put it all together, and you get `C:\Documents and Settings\Tina\ My Documents\My Music\Rivers of Babylon`. That's the official path of the Rivers of Babylon file in Tina's My Music folder.

This stuff can be tricky, so here it is again: The letter for the drive comes first, followed by a colon and a backslash. Then come the names of all the folders, separated by backslashes. Last comes the name of the file itself.

Windows XP automatically puts together the path for you when you click folders. Thankfully. But whenever you click the Browse button to look for a file, you're navigating through folders and showing Windows the path to the file.

Reached a dead end? If you mistakenly end up in the wrong folder, back your way out as if you're browsing the Web. Click the lime-green Back arrow at the window's top-left corner. (It's the same arrow that appears in the margin.) That closes the wrong folder and shows you the folder you just left. If you keep clicking the Back arrow, you end up right where you started.

While burrowing deeply into folders, here's a quick way to jump immediately to any folders you've plowed through: Click the little downward-pointing black arrow next to the green Back arrow in the window's top-left corner. A list drops down, naming the half-dozen folders you've plowed through on your journey. Click any name to jump quickly to that folder.

Here are some more tips for finding your way in and out of folders:

- Want a hint as to what's inside an unopened folder? Rest your mouse pointer over the folder and wait a few seconds. A small pop-up often displays the folder's size and the names of the folder's first few files.
- Sometimes, a folder contains too many files or folders to fit in the window. To see more files, click that window's scroll bars. What's a scroll bar? Time to whip out your field guide, Chapter 3.
- Can't find a file or folder? Instead of aimlessly rummaging through folders, check out the Start button's Search command, which I describe in Chapter 6. Windows can automatically find your lost files and folders.
- When faced with a long list of alphabetically sorted files, click anywhere on the list. Then quickly type the first letter or two of the file's name. Windows immediately jumps up or down the list to the first name beginning with those letters.

Creating a New Folder

To store new information in a file cabinet, you grab a manila folder, scrawl a name across the top, and start stuffing it with information. To store new information in Windows XP — a new batch of letters to the hospital's billing department, for example — you create a new folder, think up a name for the new folder, and start stuffing it with files.

To create a new folder quickly, look at the task pane. Sometimes you can just click the words Make a New Folder, and Windows quickly creates one for you. If your task pane's being surly, here's the manual method:

1. **Right-click inside your folder and choose New.**

   The all-powerful right-click shoots a menu out the side.

2. **Select Folder.**

   Choose Folder, as shown in Figure 4-3, and a new folder appears in the folder, waiting for you to type in a new name.

3. **Type in a new name for the folder.**

   A newly created folder bears the boring name of New Folder. When you begin typing, Windows XP quickly erases the old name and fills in your new name. Done? Either press Enter or click somewhere away from the name you've just typed.

   If you mess up and want to try again, right-click on the folder, choose Rename, and start over.

- You can also create new folders by choosing New from a folder's File menu and selecting Folder.
- Certain symbols are banned from folder (and file) names. The "Using legal folder names and filenames" sidebar spells out the details, but you never have trouble when using plain old letters and numbers for names.

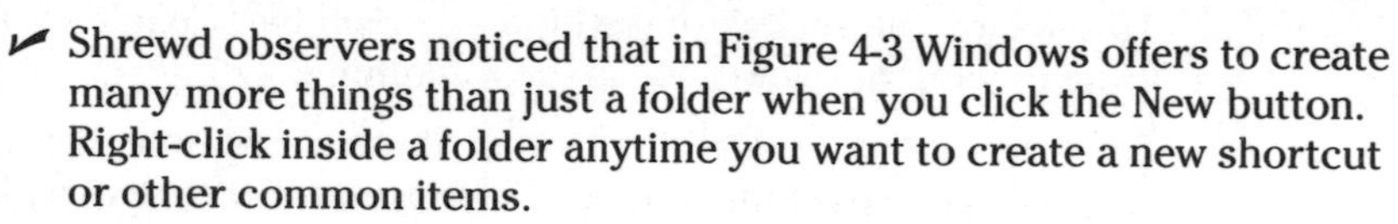

- Shrewd observers noticed that in Figure 4-3 Windows offers to create many more things than just a folder when you click the New button. Right-click inside a folder anytime you want to create a new shortcut or other common items.

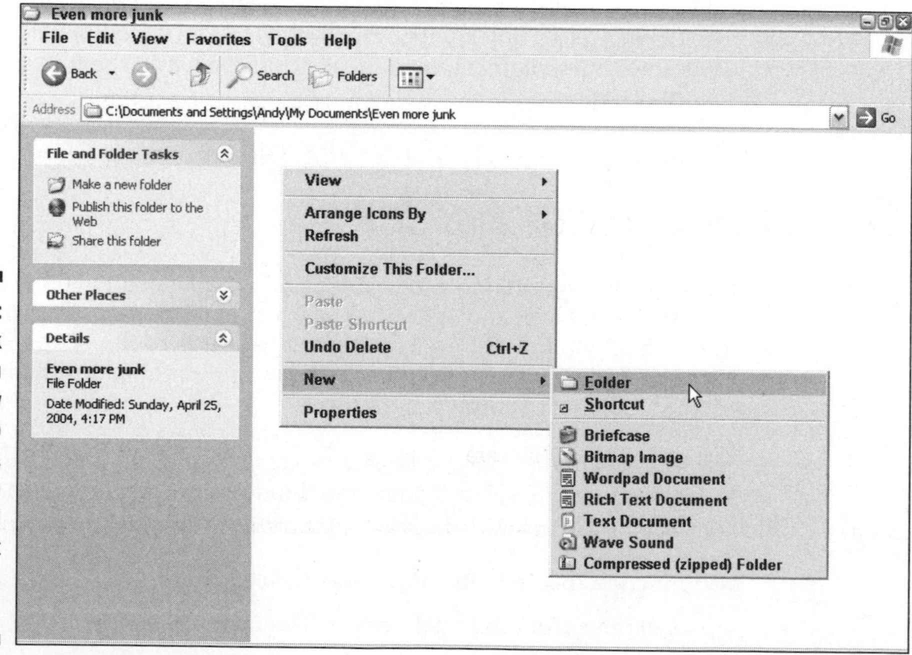

Figure 4-3: Right-click where you want a new folder to appear, choose New, and select Folder from the menu.

Renaming a File or Folder

Sick of a file or folder's name? Then change it. Just right-click on the offending icon and choose Rename from the menu that pops up.

Windows highlights the file's old name, which disappears as you begin typing the new one. Press Enter or click the desktop when you're through, and you're off.

Or you can click the file or folder's name to select it, wait a second, and click the file's name again to change it. Some people click the name and press F2; Windows automatically lets you rename the file or folder.

- When you rename a file, only its name changes. The contents are still the same, it's still the same size, and it's still in the same place.

- To rename large groups of files simultaneously, select them all, right-click on the first one, and choose Rename. Type in the new name and press Enter; Windows XP renames that file. However, it also renames all the *other* files to the new name, adding a number as it goes: `cat`, `cat (1)`, `cat (2)`, `cat (3)`, and so on.
- Renaming some folders confuses Windows, especially if those folders contain programs. And please don't rename these folders: My Documents, My Pictures, or My Music. Windows won't let you rename other folders — like the Recycle Bin.

Using legal folder names and filenames

Windows is pretty picky about what you can and can't name a file or folder. If you stick to plain old letters and numbers, you're fine. But don't try to stick any of the following characters in there:

```
: / \ * | < > ? "
```

If you try to use any of those characters, Windows XP bounces an error message to the screen, and you have to try again. Here are some illegal filenames:

```
1/2 of my Homework
JOB:2
ONE<TWO
He's no "Gentleman"
```

These names are legal:

```
Half of my Term Paper
JOB2
Two is Bigger than One
A #@$%) Scoundrel
```

Selecting Bunches of Files or Folders

Although selecting a file, folder, or other object may seem particularly boring, it swings the doors wide open for further action: deleting, renaming, moving, copying, and other goodies discussed in the rest of this chapter.

To select a single item, just click it. To select a bunch of files and folders, hold down the Ctrl key when you click the names or icons. Each name or icon stays highlighted when you click the next one.

To gather several files or folders sitting next to each other in a list, click the first one. Then hold down the Shift key as you click the last one. Those two items are highlighted, along with every file and folder sitting between them.

Windows XP lets you *lasso* files and folders as well. Point slightly above the first file or folder you want; then, while holding down the mouse button, point at the last file or folder. The mouse creates an invisible lasso to surround your files. Let go of the mouse button, and the lasso disappears, leaving all the surrounded files highlighted.

- You can drag and drop armfuls of files in the same way that you drag a single file.
- You can also simultaneously cut or copy and paste these armfuls into new locations using any of the methods described in the "Copying or Moving Files and Folders" section.
- You can delete these armfuls of goods, too.

- To quickly select all the files in a folder, choose Select All from the folder's Edit menu. (Or press Ctrl+A.) Here's another nifty trick: To grab all but a few files, press Ctrl+A and, while still holding down Ctrl, click the ones you don't want.

Getting Rid of a File or Folder

Sooner or later, you'll want to delete a file that's not important anymore — yesterday's lottery picks, for example, or a particularly embarrassing digital photo. To delete a file or folder, right-click on its name. Then choose Delete from the pop-up menu. This surprisingly simple trick works for files, folders, shortcuts, and just about anything else in Windows.

To delete in a hurry, click the offending object and press the Delete key.

The Delete option deletes entire folders, as well as any files or folders stuffed inside them. Make sure that you select the right folder before you choose Delete.

- After you choose Delete, Windows tosses a box in your face, asking whether you're *sure.* If you're sure, click Yes. If you're tired of Windows' cautious questioning, right-click on the Recycle Bin, choose Properties, and remove the check mark next to Display Delete Confirmation. Windows now deletes any highlighted items whenever you — or an inadvertent brush of your shirt cuff — press the Delete key. See Chapter 2 for more about the Recycle Bin.

- Be extra sure that you know what you're doing when deleting any file that has pictures of little gears in its icon. These files are sometimes sensitive hidden files, and the computer wants you to leave them alone. (Other than that, they're not particularly exciting, despite the action-oriented gears.)

- Icons with little arrows in their corner (like the one in the margin) are *shortcuts* — push buttons that merely load files. (I cover shortcuts in Chapter 5.) Deleting shortcuts deletes only a *button* that loads a file or program. The program itself remains undamaged and still lives inside your computer.
- As soon as you find out how to delete files, trot off to Chapter 2, which explains several ways to *un*delete them. (***Hint for the desperate:*** Open the Recycle Bin, right-click on your file's name, and choose Restore.)

Don't bother reading this hidden technical stuff

You're not the only one creating files on your computer. Programs often store their own information in a *data file.* They may need to store information about the way the computer is set up, for example. To keep people from confusing the files for trash and deleting them, Windows hides them.

You can view the names of these hidden files and folders, however, if you want to play voyeur:

1. **Open My Computer and choose Folder Options from the Tools menu.**
2. **Select the View tab from along the menu's top and click the Show Hidden Files and Folders button under the Hidden Files and Folders option.**
3. **Click the OK button.**

The formerly hidden files appear alongside the other filenames. Be sure not to delete them, however: The programs that created them will gag, possibly damaging them or Windows itself. In fact, please click the View tab's Restore Defaults button to hide that stuff again and return the settings to normal.

Copying or Moving Files and Folders

To copy or move files to different folders on your hard drive, it's sometimes easiest to use your mouse to *drag* them there. For example, here's how to move a file to a different folder on your desktop. In this case, I'm moving the Traveler file from the House folder to the Morocco folder.

1. **Aim the mouse pointer at the file or folder you want to move.**

   In this case, point at the Traveler folder.

2. **While holding down the right mouse button, move the mouse until it points at the destination folder.**

   As you see in Figure 4-4, the Traveler folder is being dragged to the Morocco folder from the House folder. (I describe how to make windows sit neatly next to each other in Chapter 3.)

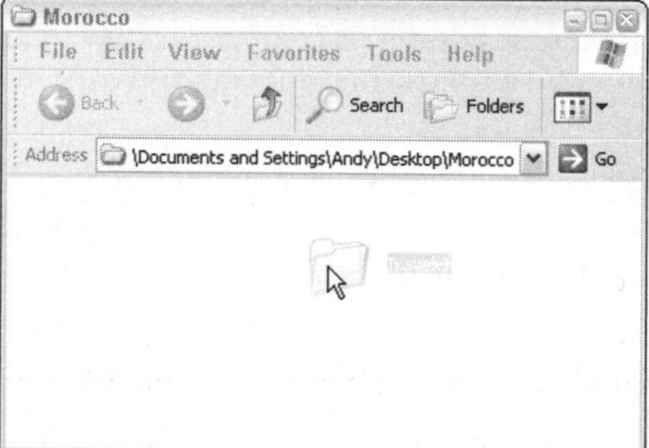

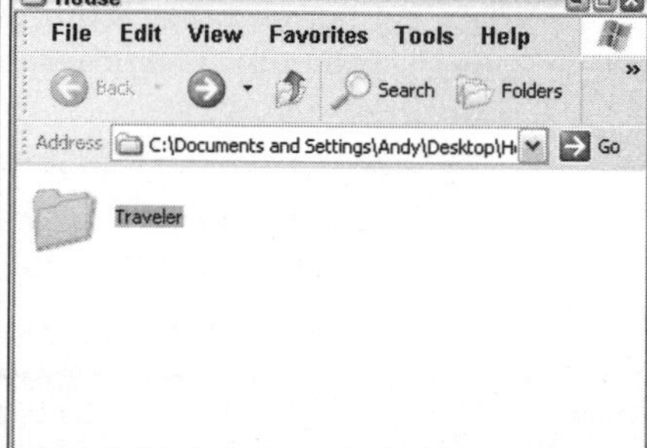

Figure 4-4: To move a folder from one window to another, drag it there.

   Moving the mouse drags the folder along with it. (Be sure to hold down the right mouse button the entire time.)

3. **Release the mouse button and choose Copy, Move, or Create Shortcut from the pop-up menu.**

   Always drag icons while holding down the *right* mouse button. Windows XP is then gracious enough to give you a menu of options when you position the icon, and you can choose to move, copy, or create a shortcut. If you hold down the *left* mouse button, Windows XP sometimes doesn't know whether to copy or move.

Moving a file or folder by dragging it is pretty easy, actually. The hard part is placing both the file and its destination on-screen, especially when one folder is buried deep within your computer.

When dragging and dropping takes too much work, Windows offers a few other ways to copy or move files. Depending on your screen's current layout, some of the following on-screen tools might work more easily:

- **Right-click menus:** Right-click on a file or folder and choose Cut or Copy, depending on whether you want to move or copy it. Then right-click on your destination folder and choose Paste. It's simple, it always works, and you needn't place the item and its destination on-screen simultaneously.
- **Menu bar commands:** Click the file and click Edit from the folder's top menu. Choose Copy to Folder or Move to Folder, and a new window appears, listing all your computer's folders. Click through the folders to reach the destination folder, and Windows carries out the Copy or Move command. A bit cumbersome, this method works if you know the exact location of the destination folder.
- **Windows Explorer:** Described later in this chapter, Windows Explorer lines up all your folders along the window's left side. That makes it easier to see both the object and its destination on the same screen. (For a peek at Windows Explorer, open My Computer and click Folders on the toolbar along the top.)

Don't ever move these folders: My Documents, My Pictures, My Music, Shared Documents, Shared Pictures, or Shared Music. Keep them where they are so they're easy to find.

After you run a program's installation program to put the program on your hard drive, don't ever move that program's folder. Programs wedge themselves into Windows. Moving the program might break it, and you'll have to reinstall it. Feel free to move the program's shortcut, though, if it has one.

Seeing More Information about Files and Folders

Whenever you create a file or folder, Windows XP scrawls a bunch of secret hidden information on it: its size, the date you created it, and even more trivial stuff. Sometimes it even lets you add your own secret information: lyrics and reviews for your music files and folders, or thumbnail pictures for any of your folders.

To see what Windows XP is calling your files and folders behind your back, right-click on the item and choose Properties from the pop-up menu. Choosing Properties on a Jimi Hendrix song, for instance, brings up bunches of details, as shown in Figure 4-5.

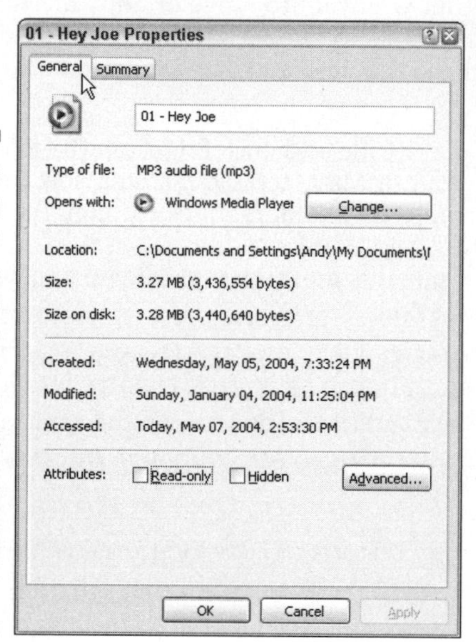

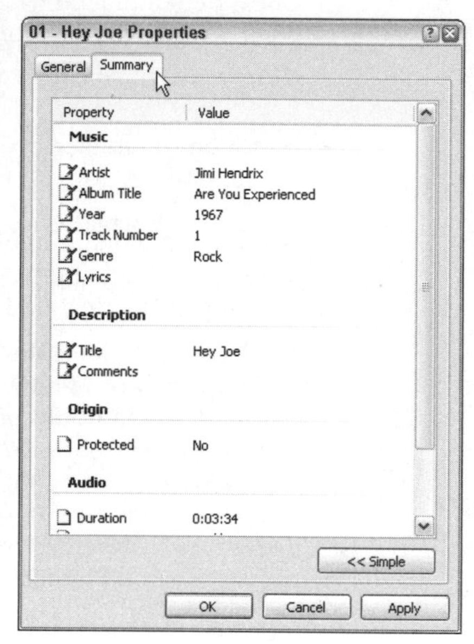

Figure 4-5: When looking at a file's Properties, the General tab shows physical details about the file; the Summary tab shows more varied information.

Click the General tab (shown on the left of Figure 4-5), and Windows shows that the Jimi Hendrix song is an MP3 audio file of the song "Hey Joe." The song is 3.27 MB in size, and it opens with Windows Media Player. (If you want a different MP3 player to play the song, click the Change button to select a different player.)

Click the Summary tab (shown on the right of Figure 4-5) and click the Advanced button for the real fun. Windows displays the song's *ID Tag* information: the Artist, Album Title, Year, Track Number, Genre, Duration, and technical information. (I cover ID Tags in Chapter 15.)

Windows lets you see more information about files as they sit in a folder, too. Choose Details from a folder's View menu, as shown in Figure 4-6. Instead of just displaying icons, Windows displays detailed information about your files.

- To change views, click the square button on the toolbar (shown in the margin.) A drop-down menu appears, listing options for displaying a folder's files: Thumbnails, Tiles, Icons, List, and Details. Try them all to see what they do.

- Is the View menu missing from the top of your folder's window? Put it back by choosing Standard Buttons from the View menu's Toolbars option. The little bar of buttons reappears atop your window like a mantel over a fireplace.

- If you can't remember what those little toolbar buttons do, rest your mouse pointer over a button and pretend it's lost. Windows XP displays a helpful box summing up the button's mission and, occasionally, places a further explanation along the bottom of the window.
- Although some of the additional file information is handy, it can consume a lot of space, limiting the number of files you can see in the window. Displaying only the filename is often a better idea. Then, if you want to see more information about a file or folder, try the following tip.

Folders usually display files sorted alphabetically. To sort them differently, right-click inside the folder and click the Arrange Icons By menu. Choose Sort by Size to place the largest files at the list's top. The Sort by Type option groups together files created by the same program. Choose Sort by Date to keep your most recent files at the list's top.

When the excitement of the Arrange Icons By menu wears off, try clicking the little buttons at the top of each sorted column. Click the Size button, for instance, to quickly place the largest files at the list's top. Click the Date button to quickly sort by date, instead.

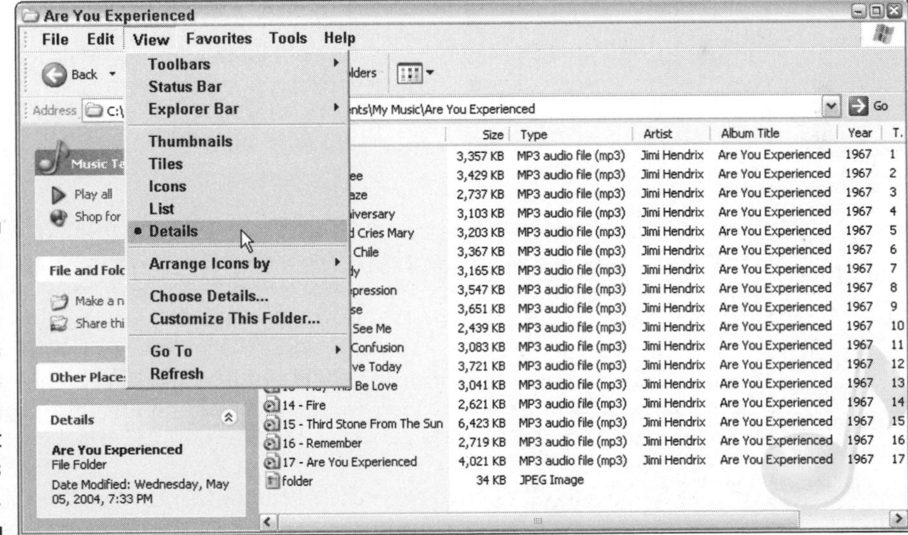

Figure 4-6: Choose Details from a folder's View menu to see more details about a folder's contents.

What's That Windows Explorer Thing?

Windows almost always uses My Computer to display your files and folders, but its twin program — Explorer — can also display your files and folders. What's the difference?

My Computer shows the contents of only one folder at a time. Windows Explorer, on the other hand, lets you see *all* your folders at the same time. Best yet, Explorer is easy to load (and quick to turn off, should you disapprove).

To load Windows Explorer, click the Folders button along the top. A list of folders tacks itself onto your folder's left side, as shown in Figure 4-7, turning the window into Windows Explorer. Windows Explorer displays your files in a "tree" branching off from your hard drive.

See how some folders along that left edge have tiny plus signs next to them? That means more folders hide inside those folders. Click the plus sign, and the folder opens up, displaying the folders living inside. By clicking plus signs, you can worm your way even deeper inside folders.

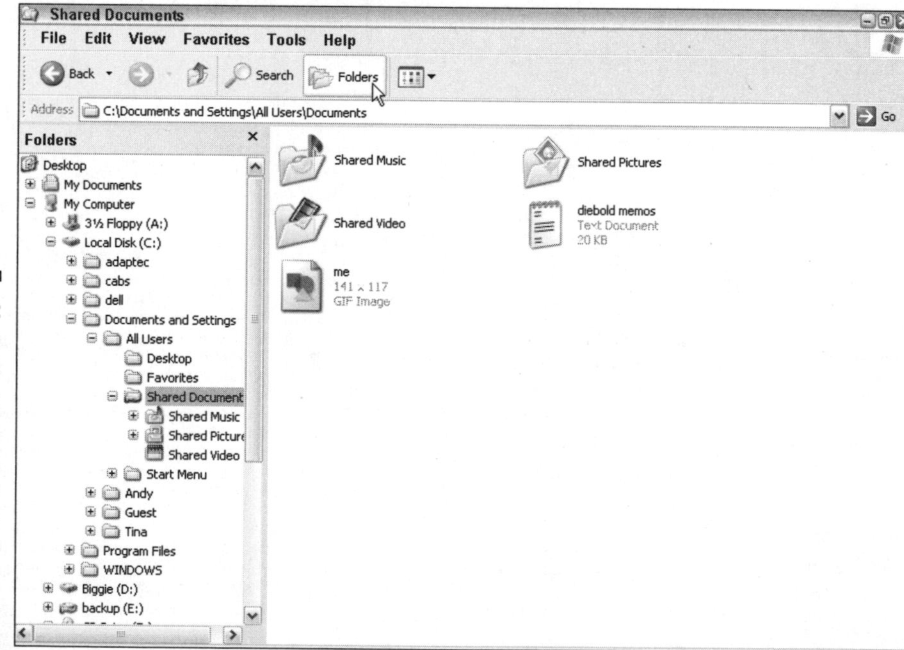

Figure 4-7: Click the Folders button from along a folder's top to see Windows Explorer's view of your folders.

Flipping a file's secret switches

Windows XP gives each file special switches called *attributes*. The computer looks at the way those switches are set before it fiddles with the file. To view a file's attributes, right-click on the file and choose Properties. Here's what you'll probably find:

- **Read Only:** Choosing this attribute allows the file to be read, but not deleted or changed in any way.
- **Hidden:** Setting this attribute makes the file invisible during normal operations.

By clicking the Advanced button, Windows XP presents more switches:

- **File Is Ready for Archiving:** Some backup programs look at this one to see if they've backed up that file or not. When backed up, this attribute changes to reflect its new status.
- **For Fast Searching:** Normally set to on, this setting tells Windows to let its Indexing Service take note of the file and its contents for faster searching.
- **Compress Contents to Save Disk Space:** Only available on computers with special, NTFS drives, this setting lets Windows XP squish the file to save space. That makes the file load more slowly, though.

The Properties box makes it easy — perhaps too easy — to change these attributes. In most cases, you should leave them alone. I just mention them here so that you'll know what computer nerds mean when they tell cranky people, "Boy, somebody must have set your attribute wrong when you got out of bed this morning."

What's the point? Well, Windows Explorer lets you view one folder's contents on the right side of the window, and all of your folder's names on the left. That makes it easier to move to different folders or copy items from one folder to another folder. (See Chapter 5 for details on copying and pasting.)

To get rid of the Windows Explorer view and return to My Computer and its handy task pane, click the Folders button from the toolbar along the top.

Writing to CDs and DVDs

Most computers today can write information to a CD using a flameless approach known as *burning*. To see if you're stuck with an older drive that can't burn CDs, open My Computer and look at the icons for your CD drives. If the drive says RW after its name, you're in luck.

If your disc drive says simply `DVD Drive` or `CD Drive` (like the one in the margin), it can read but not write to CDs. (I explain how to play DVDs in Chapter 15.)

If your disc drive says `CD-RW`, like the one in the margin, it can both read *and* write to CDs. (It can probably play DVDs, too.)

If your drive says `DVD-RW Drive`, like the one in the margin, it can both read and write to CDs as well as DVDs.

- Sometimes a drive claims to be able to write to CDs, but Windows still has trouble with it. Here's a surefire test to see whether Windows XP can write to your drive: Right-click on your drive's icon in My Computer and choose Properties. If you see a Recording tab, Windows XP can write to CDs in that drive. If the Recording tab is missing, Windows XP can't use the drive.
- Lagging Technology Department: Although many people have DVD burners, Windows XP still doesn't know how to write to DVDs. (Microsoft says Windows' *next* version, previewed in Chapter 23, can burn DVDs.) Because Windows XP can't do the job, most DVD burners use a different company's DVD burning software.

Buying the right kind of blank CDs and DVDs for burning

Stores sell two types of CDs: CD-R (short for CD-Recordable) and CD-RW (short for CD-ReWritable). Here's the difference:

Duplicating a CD

Windows XP doesn't have a Duplicate This CD command. It can't even make a copy of a music CD. (That's why so many people buy CD burning programs.) But it can copy all of a CD's files to a blank CD using this two-step process:

1. **Copy a CD's files and folders to your PC.**
2. **Copy those same files and folders back to a blank CD.**

You can try this on a music CD, but it won't work. (I tried.)

CD-R: Most people buy CD-R discs because they're cheap, and they work fine for storing music or files. You can write to them until they fill up; then you can't write to them anymore. But that's no problem, because most people don't want to erase their CDs and start over.

CD-RW: Techies sometimes buy CD-RW discs for making temporary backups of data. You can write information to them, just like CD-Rs. But when a CD-RW disc fills up, you can erase it and start over with a clean slate — something not possible with a CD-R. However, CD-RWs cost more money, so most people stick with CD-Rs.

DVDs: DVDs come in both R and RW formats, just like CDs, so the preceding R and RW rules apply to them, as well. Beyond that, it's chaos: The manufacturers fought over which storage format to use, confusing things for everybody. To buy the right blank DVD, check your DVD burner to see what formats it uses: DVD-R, DVD-RW, DVD+R, DVD+RW, and/or DVD-RAM. (Some new DVD burners can use all of the first four formats, making your choice slightly easier.)

- The disc's "x" speed refers to the speed at which it can accept information. Your drive can write information onto a 40x CD five times faster than onto an 8x CD. Buy CDs with as fast an x rating as your burner can handle.
- You'll often find your CD or DVD burner's format and speed listings printed directly on the drive's face. If the information isn't there, check the receipt for your computer. If you still have no clue, buy reasonably fast discs. Slow burners can still write to speedy discs, but not as quickly as faster burners.
- Blank CDs are cheap; borrow one from a neighbor's kid to see if it works in your drive. If it works fine, buy some of the same type. Blank DVDs, by contrast, are expensive. Most neighbors' kids won't let you have one.
- Although Windows XP can handle simple CD burning tasks, it's extraordinarily awkward at copying music CDs. Most people give up quickly and buy third-party CD burning software from Roxio or Nero. I explain how Windows XP creates music CDs in Chapter 15.

Copying things from or to a CD

Copying *music* to or from a CD isn't easy in Windows XP. Windows XP makes you use its awkward and restrictive Media Player program, which I cover in Chapter 15.

Copying files from a CD works pretty easily, by contrast — just like copying files from one folder to another. Double-click your CD drive to view the CD's contents and then drag and drop the desired files to your My Documents folder. (Or any other folder, actually.)

Writing files to a CD takes a little more work, but remember this tip: When you insert a blank CD into your CD burner, a Windows wizard usually pops up, offering to help. Feel free to take the White Bearded One's assistance as it leads you through the entire process. After you master the process, these steps give you more control over the process:

1. **Select the files you want to copy to a CD, right-click on them, choose Send To, and select your CD burning drive.**

   Feel free to roam through your folders, sending more and more files or folders to your CD drive. Windows keeps track of them all in the background. Whenever you choose Send To from a menu, a window pops up saying `You have files waiting to be written to the CD.` (Figure 4-8 shows an example.)

Figure 4-8: Right-click on any files and folders you want to copy to a CD, choose Send To, and select your CD burning drive.

2. **Double-click your CD burning drive from My Computer.**

   Windows displays a folder containing shortcuts to all the files and folders you sent to your CD burning drive in Step 1. Feel free to make any last-minute changes here, deleting any mistaken items and adding any last-minute items. (Copy and paste additional items into this folder, if you like, or drag and drop them here.)

   Note: This folder is filled with *shortcuts* — not the actual files themselves. Deleting items here won't delete the real files; they're just push buttons tied to those files. (I cover shortcuts in Chapter 5.)

3. **Insert a blank CD and then choose Write These Files to CD from the folder's File menu.**

   If you spot Write These Files to CD on the task pane, clicking that does the same thing.

4. **Create a name for your new CD and click Next.**

   Windows CD-Writing Wizard appears, asking you to name the CD. (Just press Enter to use the current date, or type in something describing your files.)

   Windows slowly mulls over something called a CD image and eventually begins writing your files and folders to the CD.

5. **Click the Finish button.**

   Or, if you want to copy those same files to yet another CD, click the Yes, Write These Files to Another CD box. If you're through, just click Finish.

- You can keep writing more and more files to a CD until Windows complains that the CD is full. Then you need to insert another blank CD.
- If you try to copy a large batch of files to a CD — more than will fit — Windows XP complains immediately. Copy fewer files at a time, perhaps spacing them out over two CDs.
- While copying files to the CD, Windows may display a frantic Confirm Stream Loss message about a mysterious Thumbs file. If so, just click the Skip button and skip that file. The message isn't nearly as important as it sounds.

- Most programs let you save files directly to CD. Choose Save from the File menu and select your CD burner. Put a CD (preferably one that's not already filled) into your CD drive and right-click on the CD drive in My Computer to start the process.

Floppy Disks and Memory Cards

Most people own some gadget that uses memory cards, but few people have a memory card drive. The quick solution is to buy an external USB all-in-one memory card reader and plug it into your computer's USB port. Available at most office supply and electronics stores, these card readers accept most popular memory card formats.

As for transferring information between your computer and a memory card (or floppy disk), there's nothing new to figure out: Windows XP treats your inserted card or floppy just like an ordinary folder. The same "drag and drop" and "cut and paste" rules covered early in this chapter still apply.

- Press the F5 key whenever you stick in a different floppy disk and want to see what files are stored on it. Windows XP then updates the screen to show the *new* floppy's files, not the files from the first disk. (You don't have to do this with memory cards.)

- First, the warning: Formatting a card or disk wipes out all its information. Never format a card or disk unless you don't care about the information it currently holds.
- Now, the procedure: If Windows complains that a newly inserted card or floppy isn't formatted, right-click on its drive and choose Format. (This happens most often with damaged cards or floppies.) Sometimes formatting also helps one gadget use a card designed for a different gadget — your camera might be able to use your MP3 player's card, for instance.

Part II

Working with Programs and Files

"The funny thing is he's spent 9 hours organizing his computer desktop."

In this part . . .

The first part of the book explains how to manipulate Windows, applying strategic sequences of clicks and double-clicks to its sweet spots.

Now you'll find ways to put that knowledge to good use, prodding your programs into doing the right things and hopefully getting your work done in the process.

This part of the book also explains ways to print, scan, and fax your work — before it gets lost. And when some of your files wander (it's unavoidable), Chapter 6 explains how to unleash Windows' robotic search hounds to track them down and bring them within reach.

Chapter 5

Playing with Programs and Documents

In This Chapter

- Opening a program or document
- Changing which program opens which document
- Creating a shortcut
- Cutting or copying and pasting
- Using Windows XP's free programs

In Windows, *programs* are your tools: They let you add numbers, arrange words, and shoot spaceships. *Documents,* by contrast, are the things you create with programs: tax forms, heartfelt apologies, and high scores.

This chapter starts with the basics of opening programs, creating shortcuts, and cutting and pasting information between documents. Along the way, it throws in a few tricks — how to add things like © to your documents, for instance. Finally, it ends with a tour of Windows XP's free programs, showing how to write a letter or take notes that you spice up with special characters and symbols.

Starting a Program

Clicking the Start button presents the Start menu, the launching pad for your programs. The Start menu is strangely intuitive. For instance, if it notices you've been playing lots of FreeCell lately, the Start menu automatically moves FreeCell's icon to its first page for easy access, as shown in Figure 5-1.

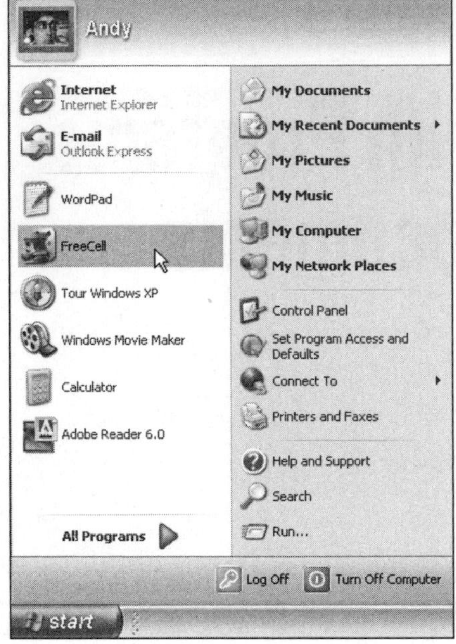

Figure 5-1: Click the Start button and then click the program you want to open.

Don't see your favorite program on the Start menu's first page? Click All Programs along the menu's bottom row. The Start menu squirts an even *larger* list of programs out its right side. Keep moving your mouse toward the menus on the right; some entries sprout even *more* menus. When you spot your program, click its name to haul it onto the desktop.

If you can't find your program on the Start menu, Windows XP offers plenty of other ways to open a program, including these:

- Double-click a *shortcut* to the program. Shortcuts, which often sit on your desktop, are handy, disposable push buttons for launching files and folders. (I explain more about shortcuts later in this chapter.)
- Look for the program's icon on the Windows Quick Launch toolbar — a small strip of icons that often lives next door to the Start button. (I cover the QuickLaunch toolbar, including how to add or remove it, in Chapter 2.)
- Right-click on your desktop, choose New, and select the type of document you want to create. Windows XP loads the appropriate program to handle the matter.
- Open My Computer, open your My Documents folder, and double-click the file you want to work on. The correct program automatically opens.

Windows offers other ways to open a program, but these usually do the job. I cover the Start menu more extensively in Chapter 2.

On its front page, the Start menu creates *shortcuts* — push buttons — for your six most-used programs. Those shortcuts constantly change to reflect the six programs you use the most. Don't want the boss to know you play FreeCell? Right-click on FreeCell's icon and choose Remove from This List. The shortcut disappears, yet FreeCell's "real" icon remains in its normal spot on the Start menu's Games menu.

Opening a Document

Like Tupperware, Windows XP is a big fan of standardization. All Windows programs load their documents — often called *files* — exactly the same way:

1. **Click the word *File* on any program's *menu bar,* that row of staid words along the program's top. When the File menu drops down, click Open.**

   Windows complicates things with the Open box, shown in Figure 5-2. This bothersome box (named after the menu you clicked to reveal it) appears over and over again in Windows XP.

2. **See the list of documents inside the Open box in Figure 5-2? Point at your desired document, click the mouse, and click the Open button.**

   The program opens the file and displays it on the screen.

When programmers fight over file types

When not fighting over fast food, programmers fight over *formats* — ways to pack information into a file. To accommodate the format wars, some programs have a special box that lets you open files stored in several different types of formats.

For instance, the Files of Type drop-down list box in Figure 5-2 lists Word for Windows format. So, the Open box only displays files stored in Word for Windows format. To see files stored in *other* formats, click in the Files of Type box and choose a different format. The Open box quickly updates its list to show files from that new format, instead.

And how can you see a list of *all* the files a program can open, regardless of their content? Unfortunately, there's no easy answer. The Show All Files option works differently in different programs. A sophisticated program shows files in all the formats it *can* open — and filters out the ones it *can't* open. An unsophisticated program such as WordPad shows *all* the files in the folder, even if it *can't* open them.

WordPad lists digital photos in its All Files menu, for instance. But if you try to open a photo, WordPad dutifully displays the photo as a few obscure coding symbols. (If you ever mistakenly open a photo in a program and *don't* see the photo, don't try to save what you've opened. If the program is like WordPad, it will ruin it.)

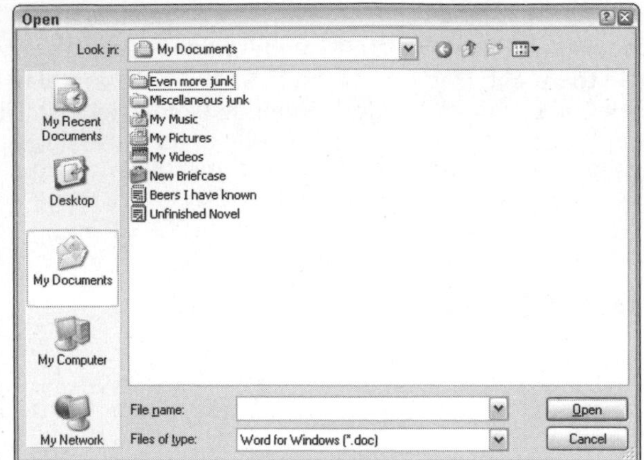

Figure 5-2: Double-click the filename you want to open.

Opening a file works this way in *any* Windows program, whether written by Microsoft, its corporate partners, or the teenager down the street.

- To speed things up, double-click a desired file's name; that opens it immediately, automatically closing the Open box.
- If your file isn't listed by name, start browsing by clicking the buttons along the left of Figure 5-2. Click the My Documents folder, for instance, to see files stored in that folder. Click My Recent Documents to see files you've opened recently; if you spot the one you want, pluck it from the list.
- We puny humans store things in the garage, but computers store their files in neatly labeled compartments called *folders.* (Double-click a folder to see what's stored inside.) If browsing folders gives you trouble, Chapter 4's folders section offers a refresher.
- Whenever you open a file and change it, even by accidentally pressing the spacebar, Windows XP assumes that you've changed the file for the better. If you try to close the file, Windows XP cautiously asks whether you want to save your changes. If you changed the file with masterful wit, click Yes. If you made a mess, click No or Cancel.

- Confused about those little icons along the box's top and side? Rest your mouse pointer over the icons, and a little box announces their occupations.

Saving a Document

Saving means to send the work you've just created to a disk or hard drive for safekeeping. Unless you specifically save your work, your computer thinks that you've just been fiddling around for the past four hours. You must specifically tell the computer to save your work before it will safely store it.

Thanks to Microsoft's snapping leather whips, the same Save command appears in all Windows XP programs, no matter what programmer wrote them. Click File from the top menu, choose Save, and save your document in your My Documents folder for easy retrieval later.

If you're saving something for the first time, Windows XP asks you to think up a name for your document. Type something descriptive using only letters, numbers, and spaces between the words. (If you try to use one of the illegal characters I describe in Chapter 4, the Windows Police step in, politely requesting that you use a different name.)

- Choose descriptive filenames for your work. Windows XP gives you 255 characters to work with, so a file named *June Report on Squeegee Sales* is easier to locate than one named *Stuff.*

- You can save files to any folder, floppy disk, CD, or even a memory card. But files are much easier to find down the road when they stay in the My Documents folder. (Feel free to save a *second* copy onto your floppy or CD as a backup.)
- Most programs can save files directly to a CD. Choose Save from the File menu and click your CD burner from the Save In drop-down menu. Put a CD (preferably one that's not already filled) into your CD-writing drive and right-click on the CD drive in My Computer to start the process.

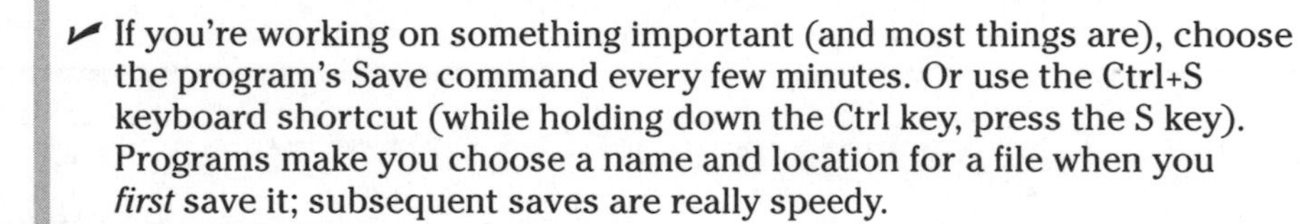

- If you're working on something important (and most things are), choose the program's Save command every few minutes. Or use the Ctrl+S keyboard shortcut (while holding down the Ctrl key, press the S key). Programs make you choose a name and location for a file when you *first* save it; subsequent saves are really speedy.
- Giant clams can reach up to 500 pounds, enough for 571 servings of chowder.

What's the difference between Save and Save As?

Huh? Save as *what?* A chemical compound? Naw, the Save As command just gives you a chance to save your work with a different name and in a different location. Suppose that you open the Ode to Tina file in your My Documents folder and change a few sentences. You want to save your new changes, but you don't want to lose the original words, either. Preserve *both* versions by selecting *Save As* and typing the new name, *Additional Odes to Tina.*

When you're saving something for the *first* time, the Save and Save As commands are identical: Both make you choose a fresh name and location for your work.

Choosing Which Program Opens a File

Most of the time, Windows XP automatically knows which program should open which file. Double-click any file, and Windows tells the correct program to jump in and let you view its contents. But when Windows XP gets confused, the problem lands in *your* lap.

The next two sections explain what to do when the wrong program opens your file or, even worse, *no* program offers to do the job.

If somebody says something about "file associations," feel free to browse the technical sidebar section, which explains that awful subject.

The wrong program loads my file!

Double-clicking a document usually brings up the correct program, usually the same program you used to create that document. But sometimes the wrong program keeps jumping in, hijacking one of your documents. (Different brands of media players constantly fight over the right to play your music or videos, for example.)

The awkward world of file associations

Every Windows program slaps a secret code known as a *file extension* onto the name of every file it creates. The file extension works like a cattle brand: When you double-click the file, Windows XP eyeballs the extension and automatically summons the proper program to open the file. Microsoft Word, for instance, tacks on the three-letter extension .doc to every file it creates. So the .doc extension is associated with Microsoft Word.

Windows XP normally doesn't display these extensions, isolating users from Windows' inner mechanisms for safety reasons. If somebody accidentally changes or removes an extension, they'll no longer be able to open the file.

If you're curious as to what an extension looks like, sneak a peek by following these steps:

1. **Choose Folder Options from a folder's Tools menu and click the View tab.**
2. **Click the Hide File Extensions for Known File Types box to remove the check mark.**
3. **Click the Apply button.**

The files all reveal their extensions. Notice that if you open two different files with the same extension, these files open in the same program. Now that you've peeked, hide the extensions again by putting a check mark back in the Hide File Extensions for Known File Types box.

The moral? Don't *ever* change a file's extension unless you know exactly what you're doing; Windows XP will forget what program to use for opening the file, leaving you holding an empty bag.

When the wrong program suddenly begins opening your documents, here's how to make the *right* program open it instead:

1. **Right-click on your problematic file and select Open With from the pop-up menu.**

   As shown in Figure 5-3, Windows names a few programs you've used to open that file in the past. The top-listed program has *top billing* — it's the program that normally jumps into action when you double-click your file. (Chances are, the wrong program is now sitting in that spot.)

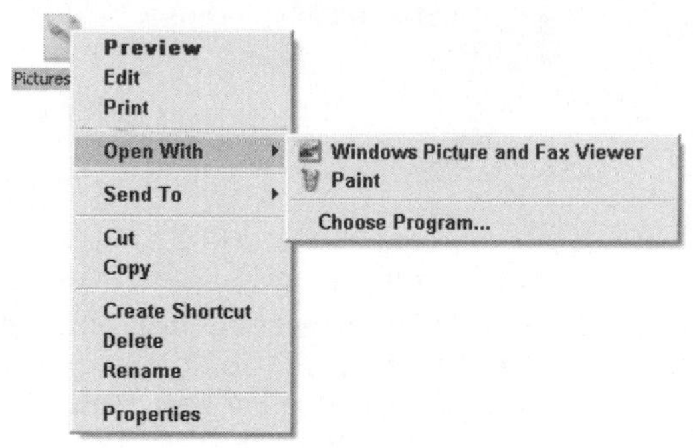

Figure 5-3: Click the program you want to open the file.

2. **Click Choose Program and select the program you want to open the file.**

   The Open With window, shown in Figure 5-4, lists many more programs. If you spot your favorite program, you *could* double-click it to open your file immediately. But that wouldn't prevent the same problem from recurring. The *next* step does that.

   If Windows doesn't list your favorite program anywhere on its list, you have to look for it. Click the Browse button and navigate to the folder containing the program you want. (***Hint:*** Hover your mouse pointer over the folders, and Windows lists the program inside.) You should spot your favorite program's icon sitting in one of those folders.

3. **Click the Always Use the Selected Program to Open This Kind of File check box and click OK.**

   That box makes Windows return top-billing status to your selected program. For instance, choosing Paint Shop Pro (and checking the "Always" box) in Figure 5-4 tells Windows to make Paint Shop Pro open that type of file the next time it's double-clicked.

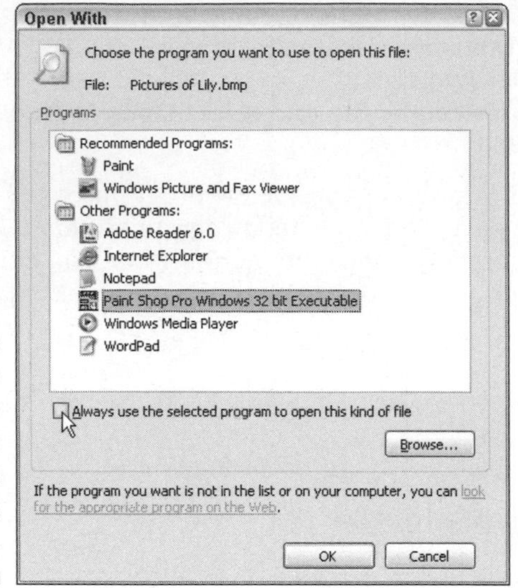

Figure 5-4: Choose the program you want and click the box at the bottom.

- Sometimes you'll want to alternate between two programs when working on the same document. To do that, right-click on the document, choose Open With, and select the program you need at that time.
- Sometimes you can't make your favorite program open a particular file because it simply doesn't know how. For instance, Windows Media Player can usually play videos, *except* when they're stored in QuickTime, a format used by Microsoft's competition. Your only solution, covered in the next section, is to install QuickTime and use it to open that particular video.

No program will open my file!

It's frustrating when several programs fight to open your file. But it's even worse when *no program* ponies up to the task. Double-clicking your file merely summons the cryptic error message shown in Figure 5-5.

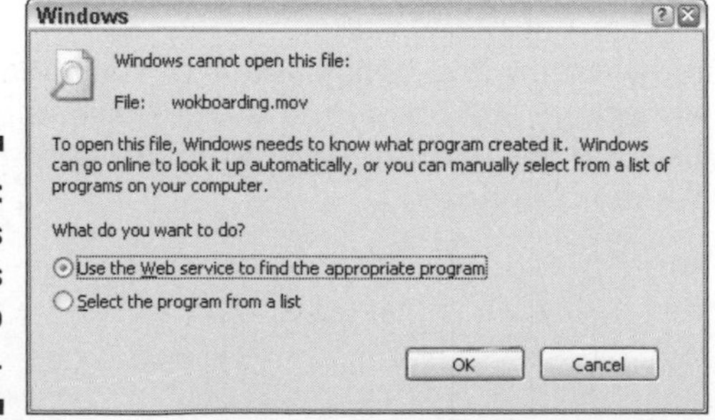

Figure 5-5: Sometimes Windows refuses to open a file.

If you already know the program needed to open your file, choose the second option: Select the program from a list. That summons the familiar window from Figure 5-4, letting you choose your program and click OK to open the file.

But if you have no idea which program should open your mystery file, choose the Use the Web Service to Find the Appropriate Program button and click the OK button. Windows dashes off to the Internet in search of the right program. If you're lucky, Internet Explorer displays a Microsoft Web site like the one in Figure 5-6. There, Microsoft identifies your file, describes its contents, and suggests a Web site for downloading a capable program.

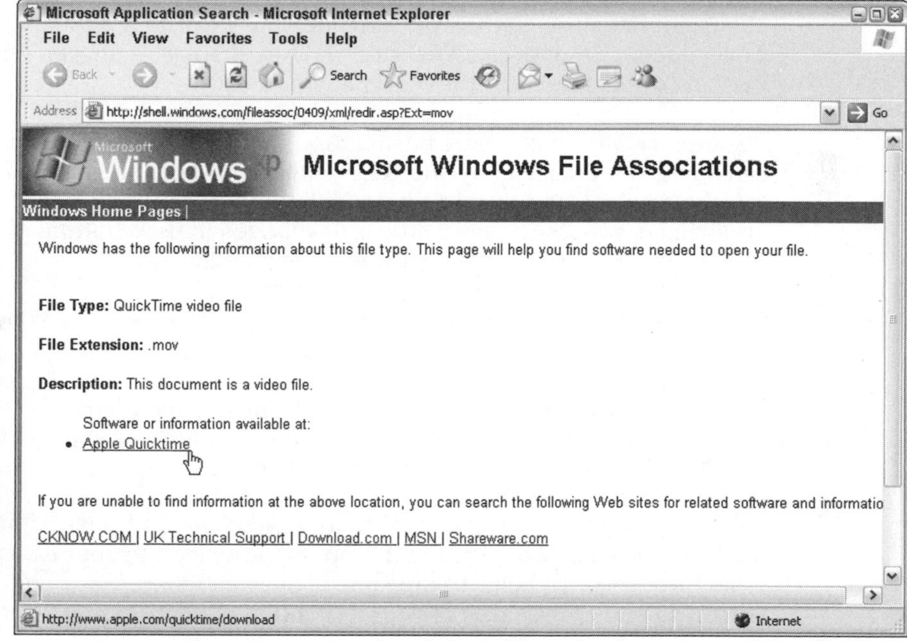

Figure 5-6: Windows sometimes helps you find a program for opening an orphaned file.

Visit the Web site Microsoft suggests, download and install the program (after scanning it with a virus-checking program described in Chapter 10), and you've solved the problem.

- In Figure 5-6, Microsoft identified a *QuickTime video* file. (Microsoft's rival, Apple, created that format to store movies, but Windows' Media Player won't open it.) Luckily, Microsoft provided a link to Apple's QuickTime Web site, where you can download and install Apple's QuickTime Movie Viewer program.
- When you visit a Web site to download a suggested program, you often find *two* versions: Free and Professional (expensive). The free version usually works fine, so try it first.

- If you can't find *any* program that lets you open your file, you're simply stuck. You must contact the people who gave you that file and ask them what program you need to open it. Then, unfortunately, you'll probably have to buy that program.
- The savior of unknown documents, Microsoft's File Associations Web site in Figure 5-6, identified the file's extension as `.mov`.

Taking the Lazy Way with a Shortcut

Some items are buried *way* too deeply inside of your computer. If you're tired of meandering through the woods to find your favorite program, folder, disk drive, document, or even a Web site, create a *shortcut* — an icon push button that takes you directly to the object of your desires.

Because a shortcut is a mere push button that launches something else, you can move, delete, and copy shortcuts without harming the original. They're safe, convenient, and easy to create. And they're easy to tell apart from the original, because they have a little arrow lodged in their bottom-right corner, such as the FreeCell shortcut shown in the margin.

Follow these instructions to create shortcuts to these popular Windows doodads:

Folders or Documents: Right-click on the folder, choose Send To, and select the Desktop (Create Shortcut) option. When the shortcut appears on your desktop, drag and drop it wherever you please.

Web sites: See the little icon in front of the Web site's address in Internet Explorer's Address Bar? Drag and drop that little icon to your desktop — or anyplace else. (It helps to drag one of Internet Explorer's window edges inward so you can see part of your desktop.)

Anything on your Start menu: Right-click on the object and choose Copy. Then right-click where you want the shortcut to appear and choose Create Shortcut.

Nearly anything else: Drag and drop the object to a new place while holding down your right mouse button. When you let go of the mouse button, choose Create Shortcut, and the shortcut appears.

Disk drives: Open My Computer, right-click on the drive, and choose Create Shortcut. Then accept Windows gracious offer to place a shortcut to that drive on your desktop, as shown in Figure 5-7.

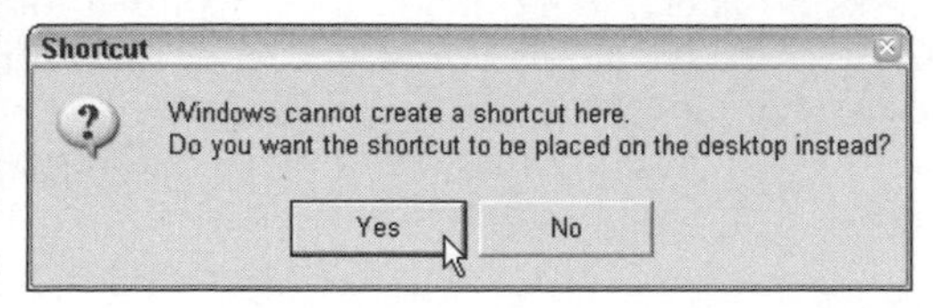

Figure 5-7: Accept Windows' kind offer of placing the shortcut on the desktop.

- For quick CD burning, put a shortcut to your CD burner on your desktop. Burning files to CD becomes as simple as dragging and dropping them onto the CD burner's new shortcut. (Double-click the CD burner's shortcut to begin burning.)

- Feel free to move shortcuts from place to place but *don't* move the items they launch. The shortcut won't be able to find the item, causing Windows to panic, searching (usually vainly) for the moved goods.
- You can often create quick shortcuts by holding down the right mouse button while dragging and dropping an item to a new place. When you let go of the mouse, choose Create Shortcut, and a shortcut appears.
- If you create a shortcut — but the icon *doesn't* have that little arrow in its bottom-left corner — stop. Calmly hold down the Ctrl button and press Z to reverse your action. Then try again.

- Want to see what program a shortcut will launch? Right-click on the shortcut, choose Properties, and click Find Target. The shortcut quickly takes you to its leader.

The Absolutely Essential Guide to Cutting, Copying, and Pasting

Windows XP took a tip from the kindergartners and made *cut and paste* play an integral part of life. You can electronically *cut* or *copy* and then *paste* just about anything somewhere else with little fuss and even less mess.

Windows programs are designed to work together and share information, making it fairly easy to put a scanned map onto your party fliers. You can move files by cutting or copying them from one place and pasting them into another. Or within a program, you can cut and paste paragraphs to different locations.

The beauty of Windows XP is that, with all those windows on-screen at the same time, you can easily grab bits and pieces from any of them and paste all the parts into a new window.

Don't overlook copying and pasting for the small stuff. Copying a name and address from your Address Book is much quicker than typing it into your letter by hand. Or, when somebody e-mails you a Web address, copy and paste it directly into Internet Explorer's Address bar. It's easy to copy items displayed on Web sites, too (much to the dismay of many photographers).

The quick 'n' dirty guide to cut 'n' paste

In compliance with the Don't Bore Me with Details Department, here's a quick guide to the three steps used for cutting, copying, and pasting:

1. **Select the item to cut or copy: a few words, a file, a Web address, or any other item.**
2. **Right-click on your selection and choose Cut or Copy from the menu, depending on your needs.**

   Use *Cut* when you want to *move* something. Use *Copy* when you want to create an exact *copy* of something.

   Keyboard shortcut: Hold down Ctrl and press X to cut or C to copy.
3. **Right-click on the item's destination and choose Paste.**

   You can right-click inside a document, folder, or nearly any other place. Keyboard shortcut: Hold down Ctrl and press V to paste.

The next three sections explain each of these three steps in more detail.

Selecting things to cut or copy

Before you can shuttle pieces of information to new places, you have to tell Windows XP exactly what you want to grab. The easiest way to tell it is to *select* the information with a mouse. In most cases, selecting involves one swift trick with the mouse, which then highlights whatever you've selected:

- **To select text in a document, Web site, or spreadsheet:** Put the mouse arrow or cursor at the beginning of the information you want and hold down the mouse button. Then move the mouse to the end of the information and release the button. That's it! That selects all the stuff lying between where you clicked and released, as shown in Figure 5-8.

  Be careful after you highlight a bunch of text. If you accidentally press the letter *k,* for instance, the program replaces your highlighted text with the letter *k.* To reverse that calamity, choose Undo from the program's Edit menu (or press Ctrl+Z, which is the keyboard shortcut for Undo).

- **To highlight part of a picture or drawing while in Paint, Windows' graphics program:** Click Paint's Select tool — that little button with the dotted lines in a square. (It's shown in the margin.) Then hold down the mouse button and slide the mouse over the desired part of the picture. Missed? Keep trying until you grab it.
- **To select any files or folders:** Simply click a file or folder to select it. To select *several* items, try these tricks:
  - **If all the files are in a row:** Click the first item in the bunch, hold down the Shift key, and then select the last item. Windows highlights the first and last item, as well as everything in between.
  - **If the files *aren't* in a row:** Hold down the Ctrl key while clicking each file or folder you want to select.

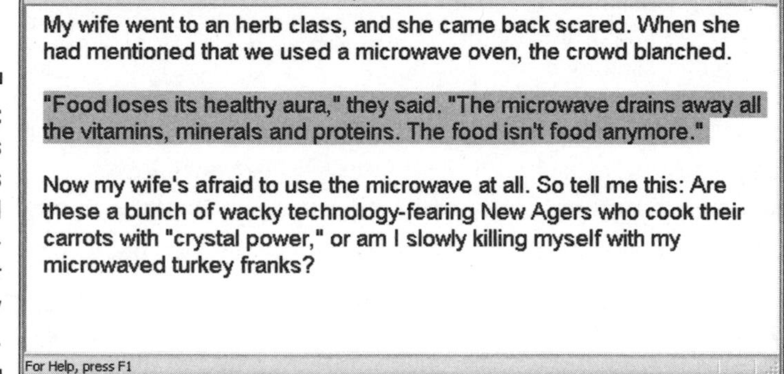

Figure 5-8: Windows highlights the selected text, changing its color for easy visibility.

Now that you've selected the item, the next section explains how to cut or copy it.

- After you've selected something, cut it or copy it *immediately.* If you absentmindedly click the mouse someplace else, your highlighted text or file reverts to its boring self, and you have to start over.
- To delete any selected item, be it a file, paragraph, or picture, press the Delete key.

Cutting or copying your selected goods

After you select some information (which I describe in the preceding section, in case you just arrived), you're ready to start playing with it. You can cut it or copy it. (Or just press Delete to delete it.)

Selecting individual letters, words, paragraphs, and more

When dealing with words in Windows XP, these shortcuts help you quickly select information:

- To select an individual *letter or character,* click in front of the character. Then while holding down the Shift key, press your → key. Keep holding down these two keys to keep selecting text in a line.
- To select a single *word,* point at it with the mouse and double-click. The word turns black, meaning it's highlighted. (In most word processors, you can hold down the button on its second click, and then by moving the mouse around, you can quickly highlight additional text word by word.)
- To select a single *line* of text, click next to it in the left margin. Keep holding down the mouse button and move the mouse up or down to highlight additional text line by line. You can also keep selecting additional lines by holding down the Shift key and pressing the ↓ key or the ↑ key.
- To select a *paragraph,* double-click next to it in the left margin. Keep holding down the mouse button on the second click and move the mouse to highlight additional text paragraph by paragraph.
- To select an entire *document,* hold down Ctrl and press A. (Or choose Select All from the Edit menu.)

This bears repeating. After selecting something, right-click on it. When the menu pops up, choose Cut or Copy, depending on your needs, as shown in Figure 5-9. Then right-click on your destination to choose Paste.

Being Frank - WordPad
File Edit View Insert Format Help
My wife went to an herb class, and she came back scared. When she had mentioned that we used a microwave oven, the crowd blanched.

"Food loses its healthy aura," they said. "The microwave drains away all the vitamins, minerals and p... sn't food anymore."

Now my wife's afraid to use ... ll. So tell me this: Are these a bunch of wacky tec... w Agers who cook their carrots with "crystal power,"... g myself with my microwaved turkey franks?

Cut
Copy
Paste
Font...
Bullet Style
Paragraph...
Object Properties
Object

Cuts the selection and puts it on the Clipboard.

Figure 5-9: Right-click on your selection and choose Cut to move it into another window.

The Cut and Copy options differ drastically. How do you know which one to choose?

- **Choose Cut to move information.** *Cutting* wipes the selected information off the screen, but you haven't lost anything: Windows stores the cut information in a special Windows XP storage tank called the *Clipboard* until you paste it.

  Feel free to cut and paste entire files to different folders in My Computer. When you cut a file in My Computer, the icon turns gray until you paste it. (Making the file disappear would be too scary.) Changed your mind in mid-cut? Press Esc to cancel the cut, and the icon reverts to normal.

- **Choose Copy to make a copy of the information.** Compared with cutting, *copying* information is quite anticlimactic. Whereas cutting removes the item from view, copying the selected item leaves it in the window, seemingly untouched. Copied information also goes to the Clipboard until you paste it.

To copy a picture of your entire Windows XP desktop (the *whole screen*) to the Clipboard, press the Print Screen key, which is sometimes labeled PrtScrn or something similar. (And, no, the Print Screen key doesn't send anything to your printer.) You can then paste the picture into Windows XP's Paint program and print it from there.

Undoing what you've just done

Windows XP offers a zillion different ways for you to do the same thing. Here are four ways to access the Undo option, which unspills your spilled milk:

- Hold down the Ctrl key and press the Z key. The last mistake you made is reversed, sparing you from further shame.
- Hold down the Alt key and press the Backspace key. Nobody but you and the computer know of your now-rectified error.
- Click Edit and then click Undo from the menu that falls down. The last command you made is undone, saving you from any damage.
- Press and release the Alt key, press the letter E (from Edit), and then press the letter U (from Undo). Your last bungle is unbungled, reversing any grievous penalties.

Don't bother learning all four methods. For example, if you can remember the Ctrl+Z key combination, you can forget about the others. Best yet, just write Ctrl+Z on the cover of the book. (The publisher's marketing people wouldn't let me put it there. Or my picture, but that's another story.)

Pasting information to another place

After you cut or copy information to Windows XP's Clipboard, it's ready for travel. You can *paste* that information nearly anyplace else.

Pasting is relatively straightforward:

1. **Open the destination window and move the mouse to the spot where you want the stuff to appear.**
2. **Then right-click the mouse and choose Paste from the pop-up menu.**

   Presto! The item you just cut or copied immediately leaps into its new spot.

Or, if you want to paste a file onto the desktop, right-click on the desktop and choose Paste. The cut or copied file appears where you've right-clicked.

- You can also choose the Paste command from a window's menu bar: Choose the word Edit and then choose the word Paste.
- The Paste command inserts a *copy* of the information that's sitting on the Clipboard. The information stays on the Clipboard, so you can keep pasting the same thing into other places if you want.
- Some programs have toolbars along their tops, offering one-click access to Cut, Copy, and Paste, as shown in Figure 5-10.

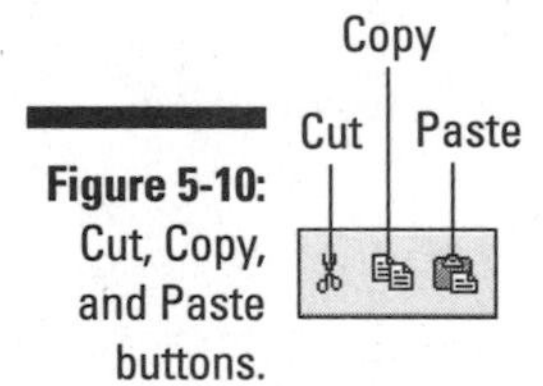

Figure 5-10: Cut, Copy, and Paste buttons.

Windows XP's Free Programs!

Windows XP, the fanciest Windows version yet, comes with oodles of free programs. This makes customers happy and makes the Justice Department members flap their long black robes.

I cover most free programs in other chapters. (Media Player, for example, gets its due in Chapter 15; Outlook Express lives in Chapter 9.) This chapter merely focuses on Windows XP's most useful freebies: its WordPad and Notepad word processors, Character Map, and Paint.

Installing new programs and removing old ones

Because this type of construction takes place in the Windows XP Control Panel, I cover it in Chapter 11. But follow this basic procedure to install a new program or remove an old one:

1. **Create a restore point *before* installing the new program.**

   Covered in Chapter 17, the restore point creates a *snapshot* of your computer's most important settings in case the program messes anything up. Name the restore point *Before Installing the Program.* (Be sure to substitute your own program's name.)

2. **Install the program and create a second restore point.**

   After you install the program with the Control Panel's Add or Remove Programs icon, name your new restore point *After Installing the Program.*

That leaves you two restore points to return to, each with different benefits. If the new program messes things up, return to the first restore point, and Windows forgets the mess. If the new program works fine, then use the *second* restore point when using System Restore in the future. (If you use any older restore points, Windows will forget that you've installed that program.)

To uninstall a program, call up the Control Panel's Add or Remove Programs icon, click the unwanted program's name from the list, and click the Remove button.

Writing letters with WordPad

WordPad is nowhere near as fancy as some of the more expensive word processors on the market. It can't create tables or multiple columns, like the ones in newspapers or newsletters, nor can you double-space your reports. Ferget the spell checker, too.

Shown in Figure 5-11, WordPad is great for quick letters, simple reports, and other basic stuff. You can change the fonts, too. And because all Windows users have WordPad on their computers, anything you create in WordPad can be read by 90 percent of other computer owners.

To give WordPad a whirl, choose All Programs from the Start menu, choose Accessories, and click WordPad.

If you've just ditched your typewriter for Windows, remember this: On an electric typewriter, you have to press the Return key at the end of each line, or else you start typing off the edge of the paper. Computers avoid that. They automatically drop down a line and continue the sentence. (Hip computer nerds call this phenomenon *word wrap.*)

- To change fonts in WordPad, select the words you'd like to change (or select the entire document by choosing Select All from the Edit menu). Then choose Font from the Format menu. Click the name of the font you want; the Sample box offers a preview. Click the OK button, and WordPad displays your changes.
- Quickly insert the current day, date, or time into your document by choosing Date and Time from the Insert menu. Choose the style of date or time you want, and WordPad inserts it into your document.

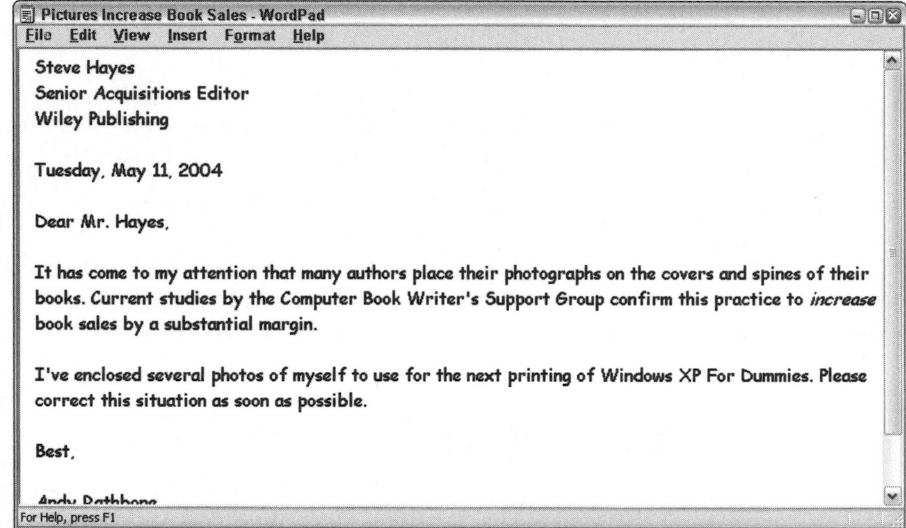
Pictures Increase Book Sales - WordPad
File Edit View Insert Format Help

Steve Hayes
Senior Acquisitions Editor
Wiley Publishing

Tuesday, May 11, 2004

Dear Mr. Hayes,

It has come to my attention that many authors place their photographs on the covers and spines of their books. Current studies by the Computer Book Writer's Support Group confirm this practice to *increase* book sales by a substantial margin.

I've enclosed several photos of myself to use for the next printing of Windows XP For Dummies. Please correct this situation as soon as possible.

Best,

Andy Rathbone

For Help, press F1

Figure 5-11: WordPad lets you write short letters without buying a word processor.

Jotting down notes with Notepad

Use WordPad for letters that you want other people to see. Notepad works best for stuff you're going to keep for yourself. Like its name, it's designed for typing notes to save on the fly.

To nudge Notepad into life, choose All Programs from the Start menu, choose Accessories, and click Notepad.

Unfortunately, Notepad tosses you into instant confusion: When you start typing, the sentences head right off the edge of the window and out of sight. To turn those single-line, runaway sentences into normal paragraphs, choose Word Wrap from the Format menu, as shown in Figure 5-12. Windows XP remembers your preference and *wraps* the lines to fit the page the next time you reach for Notepad.

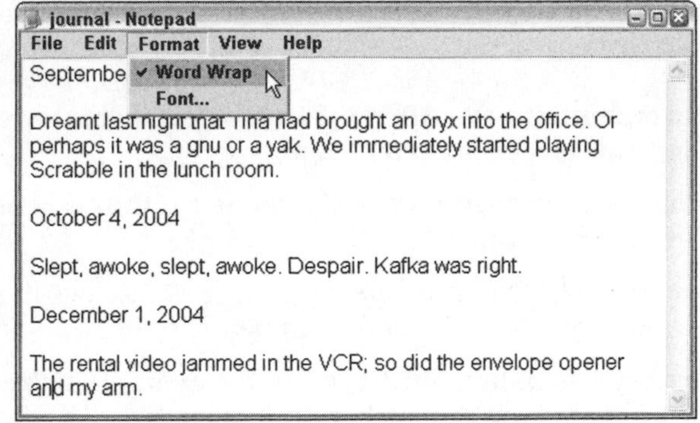

Figure 5-12: If Notepad's lines run off the edge, choose Word Wrap from the Format menu.

Another warning: Unlike most word processors, Notepad doesn't print exactly what you see on-screen. Instead, it prints according to the margins you set in Page Setup from the Format menu. This quirk can lead to unpredictable results. Stick with WordPad for documents you want to print.

Turn Notepad into a logbook by typing **.LOG** as the first sentence of your file. Whenever you open that file, Notepad jumps to the bottom of the file and inserts the current time and date before you start typing.

Finding symbols like © with Character Map

Character Map lets you insert common symbols and foreign characters into your current document, giving your documents that extra *coup de grâce.* The handy little program displays a box like the one shown in Figure 5-13, listing every available character and symbol.

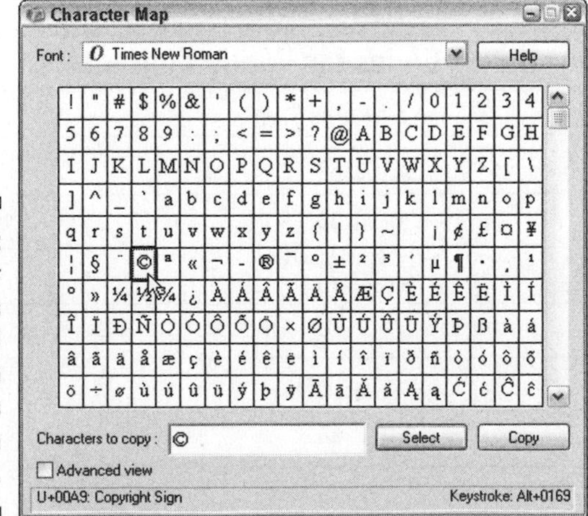

Figure 5-13: Character Map finds symbols and foreign characters to place in your work.

For instance, follow these steps to insert the copyright character — © — somewhere in your work:

1. **Click the Start menu, choose All Programs, select Accessories, choose System Tools, and select Character Map.**
2. **Make sure that your current font — the name for the style of your letters — shows in the Font box.**

   If the font you're using in your document isn't showing, click the Font box's down arrow and click your font when it appears in the drop-down list.
3. **Scan the Character Map box until you see the symbol you're after; then pounce on that character with a double-click.**

   The symbol appears in the Characters to Copy box.
4. **Right-click in the document where you want the symbol to appear and choose Paste.**

   The symbol appears, conveniently using the same font as your document.

- If you use foreign words a lot, place a shortcut to Character Map on your desktop, ready for quick consultation. Right-click on Character Map from the Start menu and choose Copy. Right-click on your desktop and choose Paste as Shortcut. *¡Que conveniencia!*

- Find yourself constantly typing the same foreign character or symbol? Then memorize its shortcut key sequence, the little numbers shown in Character Map's bottom-right corner. See how Figure 5-13 says `Keystroke Alt+0169`? That's the shortcut for the copyright symbol. To paste © into any document any time, hold down Alt and type **0169** using your keyboard's numeric keypad. The copyright symbol appears as you release the Alt key. (Make sure your Num Lock key is turned on.)
- Table 5-1 lists the shortcut keys for some commonly used symbols.

Table 5-1 Handy Codes for Handy Characters

To Insert This . . .	*. . . Press This*
©	Alt+0169
®	Alt+0174
° (as in 75°)	Alt+0176
™	Alt+0153
£	Alt+0163
¢	Alt+0162

Drawing and editing photos with Paint

A very basic graphics program, Paint creates simple drawings. If it's the only graphics program you have, you'll probably use it mostly for cropping photos, which I explain in detail in Chapter 16. Open the Start menu, choose All Programs, and select Accessories to find Paint.

- With such limited capabilities, Paint is better for quick touch-ups than ground-zero creations.
- You can paste anything you create or edit in Paint into almost any other Windows XP program. Paint enables you to add text and numbers to graphics, so you can add street names to maps copied from the Internet, put labels inside your drawings, or add the vintage year to your wine labels.

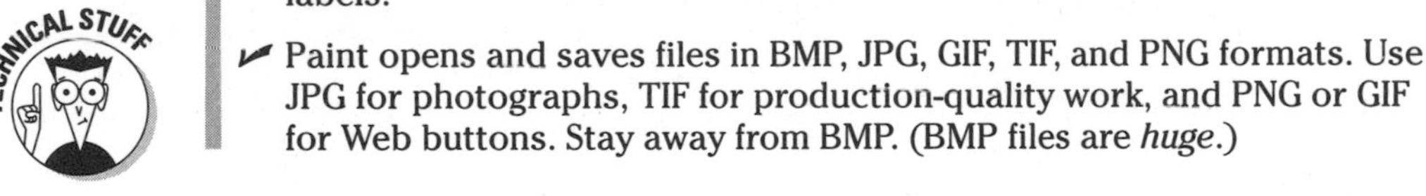

- Paint opens and saves files in BMP, JPG, GIF, TIF, and PNG formats. Use JPG for photographs, TIF for production-quality work, and PNG or GIF for Web buttons. Stay away from BMP. (BMP files are *huge*.)

Chapter 6

I Can't Find It!

In This Chapter

- Finding lost windows
- Finding lost files and downloaded files
- Finding misplaced snippets of information

Sooner or later, Windows XP gives you that head-scratching feeling. "Golly," you say, as you frantically tug on your mouse cord, "that stuff was *right there* a second ago. Where did it go?" When Windows XP starts playing hide-and-seek with your information, this chapter tells you where to search and how to make it stop playing foolish games. Then when you find your missing Solitaire window, you can get back to work.

The Search Companion works fairly well at dredging up items lost inside your computer or network. But it stumbles when asked to search the Internet. To do that, use Goolge instead. Flip to Chapter 8 for details. And to search your e-mail, use Outlook's Find feature, covered in Chapter 9.

Finding Lost Windows on the Desktop

Windows XP works more like a spike memo holder than an actual desktop. Every time you open a new window, you toss another piece of information onto the spike. The window at the top is easy to spot, but what happened to the one just beneath it?

If you can see any part of that window's edge or corner, a well-placed click will fetch it. The second place to look is the taskbar. If you see a button for your missing window there, click it to bring the window to the top. (See Chapter 2 for details about the taskbar.)

But if your window's still missing — or you're not sure if it's even on the desktop anymore — bring in the Windows *Task Manager.* The Task Manager automatically keeps a master list of every open window, making it a cinch to hunt down lost windows. Here's how:

1. **To summon the Windows Task Manager, press the Magic Key Sequence: Simultaneously press the Ctrl, Alt, and Delete keys. (Most people use two hands for this; others contort their right hands only.)**

   The Task Manager appears, as shown in Figure 6-1.

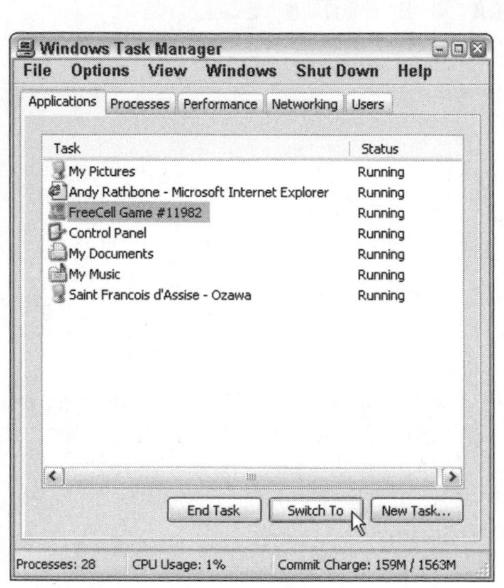

Figure 6-1: Pressing Ctrl, Alt, and Delete simultaneously brings up the Task Manager, which lists all open windows on its Applications tab.

2. **Click the Applications tab, shown at the top of Figure 6-1, and the Task Manager lists all your currently running programs.**

   The Task Manager lists open windows by program name and filename. In Figure 6-1, for instance, Internet Explorer is visiting `www.andyrathbone.com`, and FreeCell is playing game #11982.

   Your missing window is *somewhere* on that list.

3. **When you spot your window, click its name and click the Switch To button along the Task Manager's bottom.**

   The Task Manager pulls your wayward window to the top of the desktop.

   Don't spot your missing window on the list? Then it's no longer running. Restart the program from the Start menu or reopen the document you were working on.

If you're convinced a window is open but still can't find it, tell the Task Manager to tile every open window across the desktop for closer inspection: Choose Tile Horizontally from the Task Manager's Windows menu. It's a last resort, but perhaps you'll pick your missing window from the lineup.

Finding Lost Files, Folders, Music, Photos, Videos, People, or Computers

Windows XP has gotten much better at finding things. And it should because it's the one who lost everything in the first place. When one of your files, folders, or just about anything else disappears into the depths of your computer, tell Windows XP to bring the darn thing back with the Search Companion.

To befriend the Companion, click Windows XP's Start button and choose Search from the menu, as shown in Figure 6-2.

Figure 6-2: Click the Start button and choose Search to look for things on your computer or the Internet.

When you open the Search Companion for the first time, Windows XP asks whether you'd like to search with or without an *animated character.* Cartoon lovers should choose one of several characters: a big-eyed doggy, a gal in a convertible spaceship, a surfing alien, or Merlin the wizard. The character subsequently watches your moves, blinking, barking, or twitching when you click. (That's as helpful as it gets.)

When you tire of the excitement, turn off the animated character by clicking it and choosing Turn Off the Animated Character. (The same page lets you choose a different character during a spat.)

If you want to search a certain place quickly — a single folder, for example — Windows XP obliges with its all-powerful right-click. Right-click on any folder and choose Search from the pop-up menu. The Search Companion leaps into action, presenting its usual menus with one exception: The search is limited to the place you right-clicked, be it a folder, disk drive, or memory card.

Finding any lost files or folders

Following these steps helps the Search Companion locate *any* file that's lost somewhere inside your computer.

For example, suppose that your file called Hydrator Inspection disappeared over the weekend. To make matters worse, you're not even sure you spelled the words *hydrator* or *inspection* correctly when naming the file. You don't remember what program you used to create your file. Word? WordPad? Notepad? Who knows? All you know is that the hydrator was moldy — so the word *moldy* appears somewhere inside the missing file. Even with that little bit of information, Search Companion can probably find your file.

Here's how to scour your computer for any file:

1. **Click the Start button and click Search.**
2. **Click the words All Files and Folders.**

   That tells the Search Companion to search through *every* type of file and folder, as shown in Figure 6-3. Now, you need to tell Windows XP what to search for.

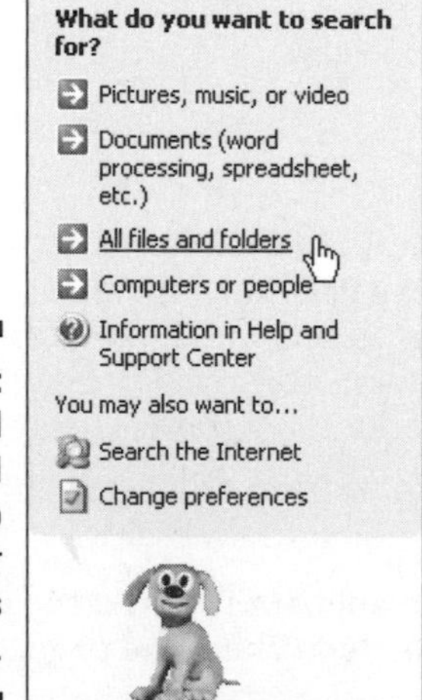

Figure 6-3: Choose All Files and Folders to search for missing files or folders.

3. **In the All or Part of the File Name box, enter any part of your missing file's name.**

   Although not essential for searching, entering any part of the missing file's name speeds up the search. So enter **inspection** in the first box, as shown in Figure 6-4. (Don't know *any* of the file's name? Simply leave it blank.)

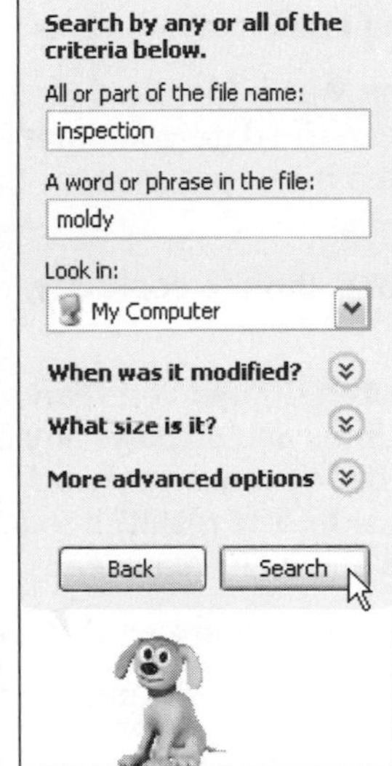

Figure 6-4: Enter part of the file's name — if you know it — or just enter a word or phrase appearing in your missing file.

4. **In the A Word or Phrase in the File box, enter a word that appears in the file.**

   Search for words *least* likely to turn up in other files. For example, I entered the word *moldy* in Figure 6-4 because it's more unique than *like, an,* or *the.*

5. **Tell Windows XP where to search by choosing an option from the Look In drop-down list.**

   My Computer: If you don't know what folder the file is hiding in, My Computer searches your entire computer (including your CD drive). Remove CDs before clicking My Computer for searches because CDs take a long time to search.

   My Documents: Tell the Search Companion to look inside your My Documents folder before searching your entire computer. Many programs automatically save your information into that folder.

   If you remember the name of the folder where you stored the file, click the Browse button to search inside only that folder.

Messed up on any choices? Just click the Back button at the bottom of the menu to fix your mistake. Or keep clicking Back until you arrive at the original menu, where you can start over.

6. **Enter any other clues in the other menus, such as the When Was It Modified menu, by clicking the down arrows next to a menu name.**

   If you told Windows XP to search a specific folder in Step 5, be sure to click the More Advanced Options area and click the Search Subfolders box. The Search will then include any folders living *inside* that folder, as well.

   The Search Companion's question When Was It Modified *really* means When Was It Last Saved. That could mean the date you dumped it into your computer, the date you last changed it in a program, or the date you last changed its name.

7. **When you're satisfied you've made your choices correctly, click the Search button.**

   The little doggy wags its tail, and the Search Companion searches according to your command. In my example, it finds and displays any file or folder on your entire computer witsh a name that contains the word *inspection* as well as the word *moldy* somewhere inside. The result? It found the file even though *hydrator* was misspelled, as shown in Figure 6-5.

8. **Double-click the file or folder to open it and begin working again.**

   To find out where it was hiding, right-click on the file and choose Open Containing Folder.

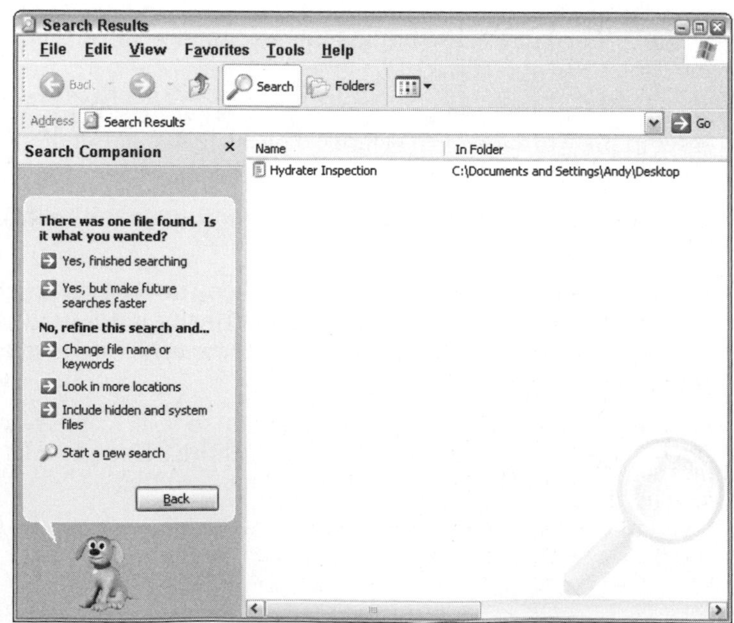

Figure 6-5: The Search Companion searches the entire computer and retrieves any files containing the word you've entered.

Finding lost pictures, music, or video

Can't find the digital pictures you copied from the digital camera yesterday? Where's that MP3 song you downloaded sometime last week? Or perhaps you're missing a short video that a friend e-mailed to you. The Search Companion can easily extract these types of missing files from your computer's digital jowls. Just follow these steps:

1. **Click the Start button and click Search.**
2. **When the menu appears, choose the option marked Pictures, Music, or Video.**
3. **Yet another menu appears, offering three search options: 1) Pictures and Photos, 2) Music and Sound, or 3) Video. Click in the box next to your missing item and type any part of the file's name in the second box.**

   Unfortunately, unless you can help narrow down the search, the overeager Search Companion will find *all* of your pictures, music, or videos.
4. **To increase your odds of a match, click Use More Advanced Options. When that menu appears, add more clues: Where your file is located inside your computer, when it was saved, or its approximate size.**
5. **Click Search, and the Search Companion finds every file meeting your specifications.**

Finding lost documents

Lost an important Word or Excel document? Search Companion's ready to help out here, too. Because you know it was a Word or Excel document, this search is fairly easy:

1. **Click the Start button, click Search, and select Documents (Word, Excel, etc.).**
2. **When the box appears, type in the missing document's name. Click the round button next to the time the file was last changed or saved. Click Search, and the Search Companion ferrets out your file.**

Because the Search Companion knows which program created your files, it limits its search to those files exclusively (Word or Excel files, in this case) speeding up the search considerably.

Finding computers or people

Like a teenager who's watched too many sci-fi flicks, Windows XP lumps computers and people in the same category when searching. Neither type of search is all that exciting, unfortunately, but here goes.The Computer search is only for people working on *networks,* mysteriously bundled bunches of computers, covered in Chapter 14. Don't know if you're on a network? You can still use it. Just follow these steps:

1. **Click the Start button, click Search, and choose the Computers or People option.**
2. **Choose the A Computer on the Network option.**
3. **Enter the name of the networked computer that you want to search for and then click the Search button.**

   But what if you don't know the computer's name? Here's a trick: Just click the Search button. A list of computers connected to your own computer appears. (If just one computer appears, don't get excited. It's probably just your own.)

Don't use this option to search networked computers for files. To do that, fire up the Search Companion and enter your query in the first two boxes. But in the Look In box (refer to Figure 6-4), choose Browse. Browse to the networked computer you'd like to search and click the Search button.

The People search isn't nearly as exciting as it sounds, even for singles. It normally just searches through your Address Book, something easily done from your Address Book itself. (I cover the Address Book in Chapter 9.)

Chapter 7

Printing, Faxing, and Scanning

In This Chapter

- Printing files, envelopes, or Web pages
- Adjusting how your work fits on a page
- Installing fonts
- Troubleshooting printer problems
- Sending and receiving faxes
- Scanning documents

You asked for it — you got it. Readers of the first edition of *Windows XP For Dummies* asked for more information about printers, faxing, and scanners, so I've devoted an entire chapter to the subject in this second edition.

Here you find out how to make that troublesome document fit on a piece of paper without hanging off the right edge. I cover the mysterious *print queue,* a little-known area that lets you cancel documents mistakenly sent to the printer — before they waste all your paper.

When you're ready to spiff up your work with some new fonts, you'll discover how to install them and view them on the screen, before they're even printed.

Another section explains how to turn your computer into a free fax machine by installing the fax program hidden on the Windows XP CD. Now you can delete those junk faxes before they waste your roll of fax paper.

Finally, the last section explains how to scan something with your scanner, choose the right resolution, and fix things if they turn out awful.

Printing Your Masterwork

Windows XP shuttles your work off to the printer in any of a half-dozen different ways. Chances are, you'll be using these three the most:

- Choose Print from your program's File menu.
- Right-click on your document icon and choose Print.
- Drag and drop a document's icon onto the printer icon.

If a dialog box appears, click the OK button; Windows XP immediately begins sending your pages to the printer. Take a minute or so to refresh your coffee. If the printer's turned on (and still has paper), Windows handles everything automatically. If your coffee cup's still full, keep on working or playing FreeCell. Windows prints your work in the background.

If the printed pages don't look quite right — perhaps the information doesn't fit on the paper correctly or it looks faded — then you're ready to fiddle around with the print settings or perhaps change the paper quality, as described in the next sections.

- Stumbled upon a particularly helpful page in the Window Help system? Right-click inside that helpful topic or page and choose Print. Windows prints out a copy for you to tape to your wall or save in this book.
- For quick 'n' easy access to your printer, right-click your printer's icon and choose Create Shortcut. Windows XP puts a shortcut to your printer on your desktop. To print things, just drag and drop their icons onto your printer's new shortcut. (You can find your printer's icon by clicking Printers and Faxes from the Start menu.)
- To print a bunch of documents quickly, select *all* their icons. Then right-click on the selected icons and choose Print. Windows XP quickly shuttles all of them to the printer where they emerge on paper, one after the other.
- Still haven't installed a printer? Flip ahead to Chapter 11, where I explain how to plug one in and make Windows XP embrace it.

Adjusting how your work fits on the page

In theory, Windows *always* displays your work as if it were printed on paper. Microsoft's marketing department calls it *What You See Is What You Get,* forever disgraced with the awful acronym WYSIWYG and its even more awful pronunciation: "wizzy-wig." If what you see on-screen *isn't* what you want to see on paper, a trip to the program's Page Setup dialog box usually sets things straight.

Page Setup, found on nearly any program's File menu, offers several ways to flow your work across a printed page (and subsequently your screen). Page Setup dialog boxes differ among programs, but I've listed the options that you'll find most often and the settings that usually work fine, and explain what happens if you change them anyway. Figure 7-1 shows the Page Setup dialog box from Internet Explorer.

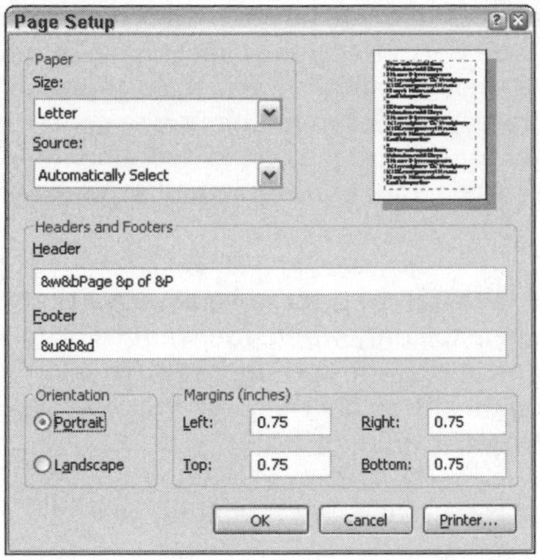

Figure 7-1: Choose Page Setup from a program's File menu to adjust the way your work fits onto a piece of paper.

Size: This lets your program know what size of paper you're currently using. Leave this set to Letter to print on standard, 8.5-x-11-inch sheets of paper. Change this setting if you're using legal size paper (8.5 x 14), envelopes, or other paper sizes. (The nearby sidebar, "Printing envelopes without fuss," contains more information about printing envelopes.)

Source: Choose Automatically unless you're using a fancy printer that accepts paper from more than one printer tray. People with two or more printer trays can select the tray containing the correct paper size. Some printers offer Manual Paper Feed, making the printer wait until you slide in that single sheet of paper.

Peeking at your printed page *before* it hits paper

For many, printing requires a leap of faith: You choose Print from the menu and close your eyes while the thing prints out. If you're blessed, the page looks fine. But if you're cursed, you've wasted another sheet of paper.

The Print Preview option, found on nearly every program's File menu, foretells your printing fate *before* the words hit paper. Print Preview compares your current work with your program's page settings and then displays a detailed picture of the printed page. That makes it easy to spot off-kilter margins, dangling sentences, and other printing fouls.

Different programs use slightly different Print Preview screens, with some offering more insight than others. Microsoft Word's Print Preview, for instance, even lets you make on-the-fly changes by dragging and dropping the margins to change the page's flow. But almost any program's Print Preview screen lets you know whether everything will fit onto the page correctly.

If the preview looks fine, choose Print at the window's top to send the work to the printer. If something looks wrong, however, click Close to return to your work and make any necessary adjustments.

Header/Footer: Type secret codes in these boxes to customize what the printer places along the top and bottom of your pages: page numbers, titles, dates, for instance, as well as their spacing. For example, type **%b%p** in the Footer box of Internet Explorer's Page Setup dialog box to center the current page number at the bottom of each printed page. (The Remember tip that follows explains how to locate and decipher your particular program's secret codes.)

Orientation: Leave this set to Portrait to print normal pages that read vertically like a letter. Choose Landscape only when you want to print sideways; this setting is often used for printing wide spreadsheets. (If you choose Landscape, the printer automatically prints the page that way; you don't need to slide the paper sideways into the printer.)

Margins: You'll rarely change this setting, but if you do, keep the margins equal along the left and right sides.

Printer: If you have more than one printer installed on your computer or network, click this button to choose between them. Click here to change your printer's settings as well, as discussed in the next section.

When you're finished adjusting settings, click the OK button to save your changes. (Click the Print Preview button, if it's offered, to make sure everything looks right.)

Printing envelopes without fuss

Although it's fairly easy to choose Envelopes from a program's Page Setup area, it's extraordinarily difficult to print addresses in the correct spot on the envelope. Some printer models want you to insert envelopes upside down, others prefer right side up. Your best bet is to run several tests, placing the envelope into your printer's tray different ways until you finally stumble on the magic method. (Or you can pull out your printer's manual, if you still have it, and look at the "proper envelope insertion" pictures.)

After you've figured out the correct method, tape a successfully printed envelope above your printer showing the correct way to insert it into the tray.

When you eventually give up on printing envelopes, try using Avery's mailing labels. Buy your preferred size of Avery labels and then download the free Avery Wizard from Avery's Web site (`www.avery.com/us/software/index.jsp`). Compatible with Microsoft Word, the wizard places little boxes on your screen that precisely match the size of your particular Avery labels. Type the addresses into the little boxes and insert the label sheet into your printer, and Word prints everything onto the little stickers. You don't even need to lick them.

Or do like I did: Buy one of those little rubber stamps with your return address. They're much faster than stickers or printers.

Unfortunately, programs don't use the same secret codes for their header and footer. To see your program's codes, click the little question mark in the Page Setup dialog box's top-right corner and then click inside the Header or Footer box. A pop-up box appears, listing the secret codes and their meaning. (To make a handy printout, right-click inside the pop-up box and choose Print Topic.)

Adjusting your printer's settings

When you choose Print from a program's File menu, Windows offers one last chance to spruce up your printed page work. The Print dialog box, shown in Figure 7-2, lets you route your work to any printers installed on your computer or network. While there, you can adjust the printer's settings, choose your paper quality, and select the pages you'd like to print.

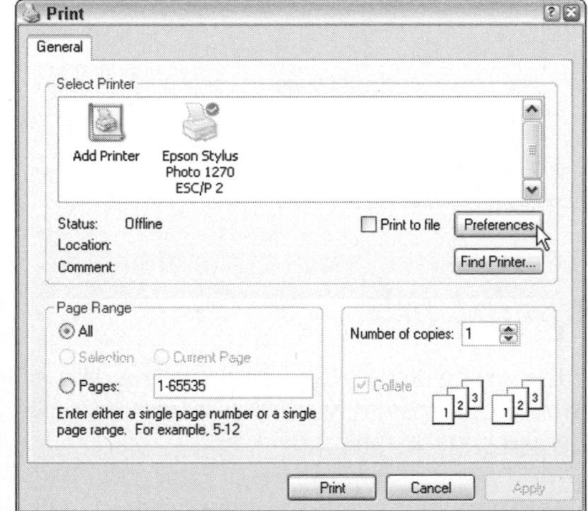

Figure 7-2: The Print dialog box lets you choose your printer and adjust its settings.

Select Printer: Ignore this option if you have only one printer because Windows chooses it automatically. If your computer has access to more than one printer, click the one that should receive the job.

Page Range: Select All to print your entire document. To print just a few of its pages, select the Pages option button and enter the page numbers you want to print.

Number of Copies: Most people leave this set to 1 copy, unless everybody in the boardroom wants their own copy.

Preferences: Click this button to see a dialog box like the one in Figure 7-3, where you can choose options specific to your own printer model. The Preferences area typically lets you choose different types of paper, decide on color or black and white, set the printing quality, and make last-minute corrections to the page layout.

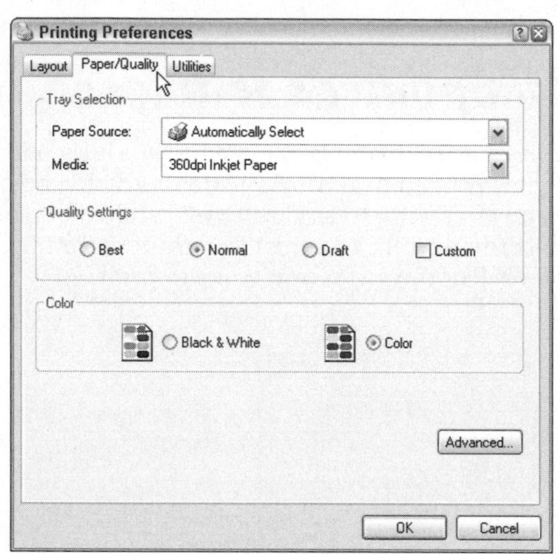

Figure 7-3: The Printing Preferences dialog box lets you change settings specific to your printer, including the paper type and printing quality.

Canceling a print job

Just realized you sent the wrong 26-page document to the printer? Panic and flip the printer's off switch. Unfortunately, most printers automatically pick up where they left off when you turn them back on.

So, to purge your mistake from your printer's memory, double-click your Printer's icon (which sometimes sits by the taskbar's clock) to reveal the *print queue,* shown in Figure 7-4. Right-click on your mistaken document and choose Cancel to end the job. When you turn your printer back on, it won't keep printing that same darn document.

Epson Stylus Photo 1270 ESC/P 2 - Use Printer Offline

Printer Document View Help

Document Name	Status	Owner	Pages	Size	Submitted	Port
Dream Journal - Notepad		Andy	1	1.45 KB	11:41:12 AM 5/17/2004	
The Diebold memos - Notepad		Andy	14	42.6 KB	11:41:21 AM 5/17/2004	
freeculture.pdf	Spooling	Andy	18	16.2 MB	11:41:34 AM 5/17/2004	

3 document(s) in queue

Figure 7-4: Use the print queue to cancel a print job.

- If you can't find your printer's icon, try choosing Control Panel from the Start menu and double-click the Printers and Faxes icon.
- The print queue, also known as the print spooler, lists every document waiting patiently to reach your printer. Feel free to change their printing order by dragging and dropping them up or down the list. (You can't move anything in front of the currently printing document, though.)
- If your printer runs out of paper during a job and stubbornly halts, add more paper. Then to start things flowing again, open the Print Queue, right-click on your document, and choose Restart. (Some printers let you push their Online button to begin printing again.)
- You can send items to the printer even when you're working in the coffee shop with your laptop. When you connect the laptop to your office printer, the print queue notices and begins sending your files. (Beware: When they're in the print queue, documents are formatted for your specific printer model. If you subsequently connect your laptop to a *different* printer model, the print queue's waiting documents won't print out correctly.)

Printing a Web page

Although information-chocked Web pages look awfully tempting, *printing* those Web pages is rarely satisfying because they look so awful on paper. When sent to the printer, Web pages often run off the page's right side, consume zillions of additional pages, or are much too small to read.

To make matters worse, all those colorful advertisements can suck your printer's color cartridges dry fairly quickly. Only three things make for successfully printed Web pages, and I've ranked them in order of success:

Use the Web page's Print This Page option. Some, but not all, Web sites offer a tiny menu option called Print This Page, Text Version, Printer-Friendly Version, or something similar. That option tells the Web site to reformat the page as if it were a simple letter, stripping out all the garbage. This is the most reliable way to print a Web page.

Copy the portions you want and paste into WordPad. Try selecting the desired text from the Web page, copying it, and pasting it into WordPad or another word processor. Delete any unwanted remnants, adjust the margins, and print the portion you want. Chapter 5 explains how to copy and paste.

Copy the entire page and paste it into a word processor. Although it's lots of work, it's an option. Choose Select All from Internet Explorer's Edit menu. Then choose Copy (which is also on the Edit menu) or press Ctrl+C. Next, open Microsoft Word or another full-featured word processor and paste it inside a new document. By hacking away at the unwanted portions, you can sometimes end up with something printable.

- The only surefire way to print a Web page is if the Web page's designer was thoughtful enough to create a Print This Page option. If you spot an E-Mail option but no Print option, e-mail it to yourself. You'll probably have better success printing it as an e-mail message.
- To print just a few paragraphs of a Web page, use the mouse to select the portion you're after. (I cover selecting in Chapter 5.) Choose Print from Internet Explorer's File menu to open the Print dialog box and then click the word Selection in the Page Range box.

- If a Web page's table or photo insists on vanishing off the paper's right edge, try printing the page in Landscape mode rather than Portrait. See the "Adjusting how your work fits on the page" section, earlier in this chapter, for details on Landscape mode.

Installing new fonts

Fonts change the appearance of letters, adding a different *mood* to your document. Windows XP comes with several dozen different fonts, and you can view them all fairly easily.

To see all your currently installed fonts, open the Control Panel from the Start menu, click Switch to Classic View, and double-click the Fonts icon (shown in the margin). Windows XP lists all your fonts by name. Double-click any font — the Impact font icon, for instance — and Windows XP shows how that font looks on the printed page, as shown in Figure 7-5. (Click the Print button to send a sample to your printer.)

Figure 7-5: Double-click any font's name to see what it would look like on paper.

Printing your Outlook Express Address Book

Although it's important to back up your Address Book (which I cover in Chapter 9), it's downright handy to print it — or at least print contact information for the people you'll be meeting that day. Here's how to turn a piece of paper into a personalized, on-the-fly address book:

1. **Open Address Book from Outlook Express and select the people to print.**

   Press Ctrl+A to highlight everybody or just hold down Ctrl and click the names you want.

2. **Choose Print from the File menu, select your printer, and choose your Print Style.**

   In the Print Style section, Outlook Express offers three ways to print your contact sheet:

   Memo: Print *everything* about the contact.

   Business Card: Print standard business card items for that person, including name, phone, address, company, and e-mail address.

   Phone List: Print each contact's name and phone numbers (cell, fax, home, business).

3. **Click Print.**

Outlook Express prints a neatly formatted list according to your specifications. If you've never printed from Address Book, try each option to see the look. It's worth three sheets of paper.

If you're not happy with your current font selection, you can buy or download new ones and install them on your computer. Most fonts sold at stores come with installation programs that spare you the messy details in Windows XP's font installer. But if your new font didn't come with an installation package, here's how to install it:

1. **Place your new font in your My Documents folder.**

   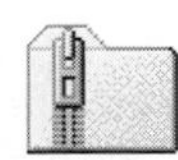

   Many downloaded fonts arrive inside a *compressed* folder, also called a *zipped* folder. (Zipped folders have a little zipper on their icon, shown in the margin.) If your font arrived this way, right-click on its icon, choose Extract All, and let the wizard extract its contents to your My Documents folder.

   If you'll be installing a lot of fonts, create a new folder called Fonts inside your My Documents folder and use it as a dumping ground for fonts.

2. **Open the Control Panel, switch to Classic View, and double-click the Fonts icon.**

   Windows Fonts folder appears on the screen, listing all your currently installed fonts.

3. **Choose Install New Font from the folder's File menu.**
4. **Navigate to the folder containing your new font.**

For some reason, Microsoft never bothered to update its Add Fonts program for Windows XP, so you're stuck with an ugly and confusing holdover from yesteryear. And that holdover, unfortunately, can't automatically find your My Documents folder.

To navigate manually to the font waiting in your My Documents folder, double-click the C:\ drive at the list's top.

Then double-click the Documents and Settings folder, followed by your user name. Finally, double-click the My Documents folder, making the window look like the one in Figure 7-6. The program finally *lists* any fonts contained in your My Documents folder.

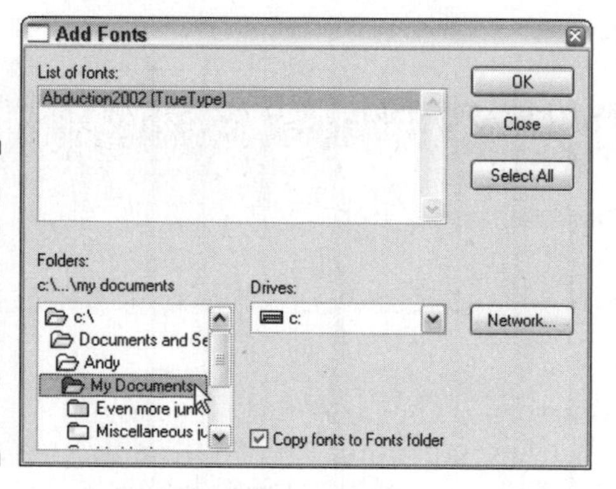

Figure 7-6: Access the fonts you want to install in the Add Fonts dialog box.

5. **Click the name of the font you want to install and click OK.**

   To reward you for all the work, Windows XP quickly installs your font, and its name appears on the font menus of all your programs.

- Don't remove the check mark from the Copy Fonts to Fonts Folder check box, shown in Figure 7-6. Windows must copy your fonts to live with all your other fonts, or programs won't be able to find them. In fact, after you've installed a font, you can delete its installation files. (Better yet, copy the installation files to a CD and save them as a backup.)
- To delete unwanted fonts, right-click on their names in the Fonts folder and choose Delete.

Please don't delete any fonts that came with Windows XP. Just delete fonts *you've* installed. Deleting some of Windows XP's built-in fonts will remove letters from your menus, making Windows XP even *more* difficult to use.

- If you can't resist downloading free fonts from the Internet, remember that Windows XP can handle TrueType fonts, OpenType fonts, and PostScript Type 1 fonts. And if you *really* get into fonts, you'll want to buy a font management program sold at most office supply stores. Finally, always scan downloaded fonts with your virus checker.

- Need to reinstall all the fonts that came with Windows XP? Follow Steps 2 and 3 earlier in the section, but head to the `C:\Windows\Fonts` folder. Select *all* the fonts in that folder and click OK.
- Brave Internet travelers who visit mysterious International Web sites can install foreign fonts that let them view Arabic, Russian, Korean, and other characters. Windows XP usually offers to download them for you the first time you visit a foreign language site, but a quick trip to Windows Update (described in Chapter 10) lets you download them as well. (These fonts don't *translate* the text — they just let you see the words in their native language.)

Troubleshooting your printer

First, are you *sure* that the printer is turned on, plugged in to the wall, full of paper, and connected securely to your computer with a cable?

If so, then try plugging the printer into different outlets, turning it on, and seeing if its power light comes on. If the light stays off, your printer's power supply is probably blown. Printers are almost always cheaper to replace than repair, but if your printer is an expensive one, grab an estimate from a repair shop before discarding it.

If the printer's power light beams brightly, check these things before giving up:

- Make sure that a sheet of paper hasn't jammed itself inside the printer somewhere. (A steady pull usually extricates jammed paper.)

- Does your inkjet printer still have ink in its cartridges? Does your laser printer have toner? Try printing a test page: Right-click on your printer's icon in the Start menu's Printers and Faxes area, choose Properties, and click the Test Page button to see if the computer and printer can talk to each other.
- Before giving up, try updating the printer's *driver,* the little program that helps it talk with Windows XP. Visit the manufacturer's Web site, download the newest driver for your particular printer model, and run its installation program.
- Turn off your printer when you're not using it. Inkjet printers, especially, should be turned off when they're not being used. The heat tends to dry the cartridges, shortening their life.

- Don't unplug your inkjet printer to turn it off. Always use the on/off switch. The switch ensures that the cartridges slide back to their home positions, keeping them from drying out or clogging.

Choosing the right paper for your printer

If you've strolled the aisles at an office supply store lately, you've noticed a bewildering array of paper choices. Sometimes the paper's packaging lists its application: Premium Inkjet Paper, for instance, for high-quality memos. Here's a list of the paper types to keep on hand for different jobs. When printing, be sure to click the Printer's Properties button to select the type of paper you're using for that job.

- **Junk:** Keep some cheap or scrap paper around for testing the printer, printing quick drafts, leaving notes to spouses, and printing other on-the-fly jobs. Botched print jobs work great here; just use the paper's other side.
- **Letter quality:** Bearing the words Premium or Bright White, this paper works fine for letters, memos, and other things designed for showing to others.
- **Photos:** You can print photos on any type of paper, but they only look good on actual Photo-Quality paper — the expensive stuff. Slide the paper carefully into your printer tray so the picture prints on the glossy, shiny side. Some photo paper uses a little cardboard sheet beneath it, which helps glide the paper smoothly through the printer.
- **Labels:** Avery's wizard makes it easy to print any style of Avery labels using Microsoft Word. The wizard handles Avery's preformatted paper in common sizes: mailing labels, greeting cards, business cards, CD labels, and many others.
- **Transparencies:** For powerful PowerPoint presentations, buy special transparent plastic sheets designed to be used with your type of printer.

Before plunking down your money, make sure your paper is designed specifically for your printer type, be it laser or inkjet. Laser printers heat the pages, and not all paper can stand the heat.

Sending and Receiving Faxes in Windows XP

Windows XP Professional comes with a built-in fax program. No more buying rolls of fax paper! Instead of printing your documents and running them through a traditional fax machine, you tell whatever program you're using to print to the built-in fax program. (Windows XP lists the fax program as a printer.) Type in the recipient's phone number, fill out a simple cover page form, push a button, and your document appears on somebody else's fax machine a few minutes later.

When a fax arrives, your computer answers the call, receives the fax, and displays it on your screen. (Feel free to print it out, if necessary.)

You need four things to send or receive faxes with Windows XP:

- A modem with faxing capabilities. (Cable modems and DSL modems can't send faxes; only old-school dial-up modems can.)
- A dial-up phone line. (Cell phones won't work.)
- Installed fax program. Windows XP must have its fax program installed. (It's usually not installed automatically.) You often need to insert a Windows XP CD to install the fax program. (Not all new computers come with a Windows XP CD.)
- A scanner. You need a scanner to send things that aren't already inside your computer: coffee shop menus, for instance. You won't need a scanner if you're sending only those things created by your computer.

The rest of this section explains how to install Windows XP's fax program and send and receive faxes.

If your computer is blessed by the light of the stars, Windows XP's built-in fax program may already be waiting on the Start menu. To see if it's there, choose All Programs from the Start menu, select Accessories, and choose Communications. Finally, choose Fax and look for three programs: Fax Console, Fax Cover Page Editor, and Send a Fax.

Installing Windows XP's fax program

If your computer doesn't have Windows XP's built-in fax program installed (most don't), here's how to pull it out of its hiding place on the CD. These steps always work for Windows XP Professional and sometimes work for Windows XP Home:

1. **Choose Control Panel from the Start menu.**
2. **Choose Add or Remove Programs.**
3. **Click Add/Remove Windows Components to start the Windows Components Wizard.**
4. **In the Components list, select the Fax Services check box and then click Next (see Figure 7-7).**

   The fax program installs. If requested, insert your Microsoft Windows XP CD and click OK.

   Don't have a retail Windows XP CD? Before assuming you're completely out of luck, tell the wizard to look in this folder on your hard drive instead: `C:\windows\i386\`. (Some sneaky manufacturers hide it in there.)

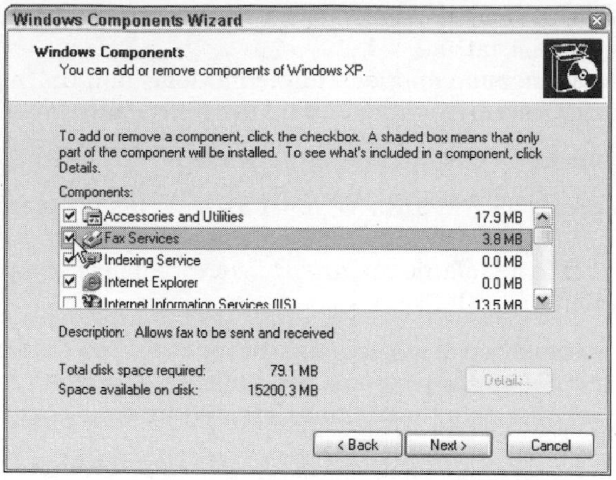

Figure 7-7: Click the Fax Services check box to install Windows XP's fax program.

5. **Click Finish when the installation is through.**
6. **Click OK to close any open windows.**

Setting up your computerized fax machine

Setting up a *real* fax machine starts with the boring stuff: Plugging it in, punching in the current date and your fax number, and telling it when to answer. Windows XP's virtual fax machine starts with a boring set-up ritual as well, which guides you through creating a cover letter, filling out forms, and dealing with other details. I describe the wizard's thunderous steps in the following list:

1. **From the Start menu, choose All Programs, select Accessories, choose Communications, and finally, select Fax Console to summon the Fax Configuration Wizard.**
2. **When the wizard greets you, click the Next button to start the faxing magic.**
3. **Fill out the information to appear on your cover page and then click Next.**

   Unlike real fax machines, Windows XP's fax machine makes you fill out a cover page only *once*. Windows XP fills out all your future cover pages with this information, although you can still add last-minute changes if you want.
4. **Choose your fax modem from the list, click the Enable Send and Enable Receive check boxes, and click Next.**

   Clicking the Enable Send and Enable Receive check boxes lets your computer send *and* receive faxes.

Sharing your fax line with your voice line? Then set the Receive option to Manual Answer. That way, when you pick up the phone and find yourself talking to an incoming fax, rush over to your computer and tell it to pick up the fax, described later in the "Receiving a fax" section, later in this chapter.

5. **Enter your fax number and business name into the TSID box and then click Next.**

   The TSID is that little text identifier running along the top of the faxes you send.

6. **Enter your fax number and business name into the CSID box and then click Next.**

   Containing the same information as your TSID, your CSID is sent to *other* fax machines when they send you faxes. (That lets them know they've reached the right machine.)

7. **Choose your Routing Options and click Next.**

   Feel free to ignore this; the program automatically saves your faxes in its Inbox. Clicking the Print check box automatically sends incoming faxes to your printer. Click the Store a Copy in a Folder check box to store a second copy in a different folder.

8. **Confirm your choices and click Finish.**

   The program lists your choices; when you click Finish, it closes. You've successfully installed your virtual fax machine.

- If you've installed Windows XP's Service Pack 2 (described in Chapter 1), a Security Alert appears when you first load the fax program, asking whether it's okay for this new program to receive information from the Internet or a network. Choose Unblock This Program. (I explain the firewall in Chapter 10.)
- Feel free to change your fax settings at any time. Start the Fax Console program from the Start menu (discussed at this section's beginning) and choose Configure Fax from the Fax Console's Tools menu. The wizard reappears, letting you change any of your settings.
- Unlike printers, Windows XP's fax machine can't be shared on a network.

Sending a fax directly from a program

Think of your new fax program as a printer. Anything you can print can now be faxed: a letter, map, drawing, spreadsheet, or similar item.

1. **Choose Print from the program's File menu.**
2. **When the Print dialog box appears, choose the fax as your printer, as shown in Figure 7-8, and click Print.**

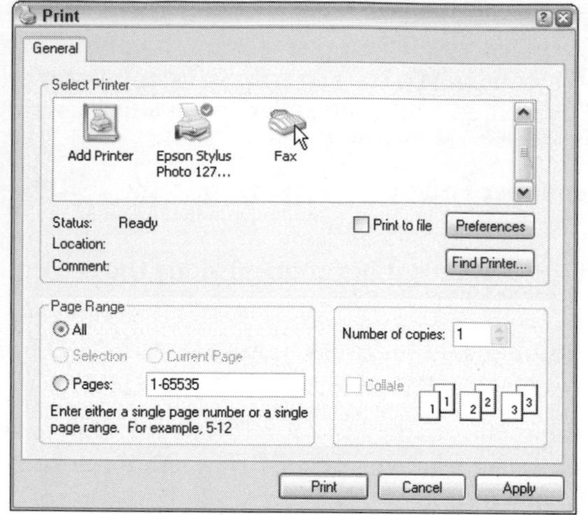

Figure 7-8: To send a fax, pretend you're printing the document but choose the Fax icon as your printer.

3. **Click the Next button on the Welcome to the Send Fax Wizard page.**

   Yes, it's anticlimactic, but the Send Fax Wizard needs a little prodding to get started.

4. **Enter the recipient's name and fax number and then click Next.**

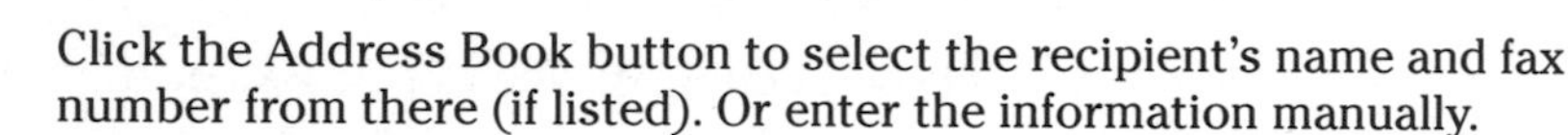

   Click the Address Book button to select the recipient's name and fax number from there (if listed). Or enter the information manually.

   To send a fax to several people, select all their names from the Address Book or enter them manually, clicking the Add button after each name and number.

5. **Prepare the cover page if desired and then click Next.**

   To whip up a quick cover page, as shown in Figure 7-9, click the Select a Cover Page Template check box. Type in your subject line and note, if needed. Click the Sender Information button to view or change your contact information. (You entered that information when you first set up the fax program.)

   To choose among different cover page styles, click the Cover Page Template drop-down list box. (I usually use Generic.) If you're really picky, the awkward Fax Cover Page Editor lets you create your own templates.

6. **Choose a time to send the fax and then click Next.**

   Choose Now to send it immediately. Or, if you're sending something overseas, take advantage of cheaper long distance rates by scheduling a time later in the evening, and make sure to leave your computer turned on. (The priority button doesn't have much effect, so leave it at normal.)

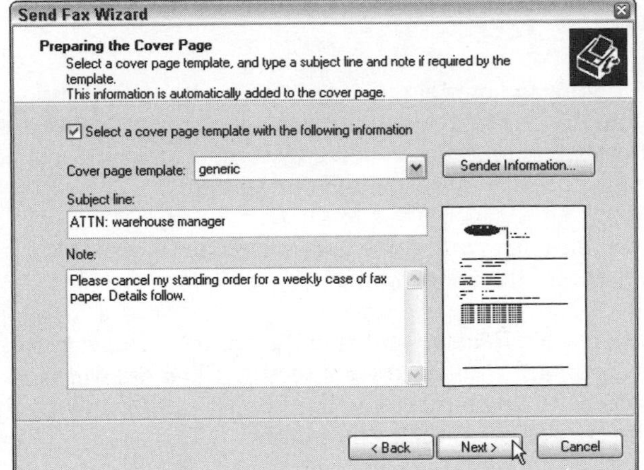

Figure 7-9: Choose a cover page style and then type in your subject and comments on your cover letter.

7. **Confirm your choices, preview your fax if desired, and click Finish to send the fax.**

   Click the Preview button for a glimpse of your cover page and fax. When you click Finish, the wizard either sends your fax immediately or waits until the time you've scheduled in Step 6.

- To immediately cancel a fax, click the Cancel button as it starts to dial.
- To cancel a fax you've scheduled for later in the evening, head for the Fax Console: Choose the Start menu's Add Programs area, select Accessories, choose Communications, and look in the Fax area. The Fax Console resembles Outlook Express; click your Outbox, right-click on your scheduled fax, and choose Delete.

Sending faxes of scanned files

Sometimes you'll want to fax something that didn't begin life inside your computer. You may want to fax some hand-scribbled notes or somebody else's party flyer. For that, you need a scanner, which takes a picture of your notes or flyer and stores it as a file inside your computer. To fax the file, follow these steps:

1. **Open the folder containing the files you'd like to fax and select them.**
2. **Right-click on the selected files, choose Preview, and Windows XP's Photo Printing Wizard appears.**
3. **When the wizard asks you to choose the printer, select your Fax icon. The Photo Printing Wizard kicks the ball to the Send Fax Wizard, which runs with it.**

Receiving a fax

If you hooked up your fax modem to a dedicated phone line and set it to answer automatically during the setup program, receiving a fax is easy. The computer automatically answers, receives your fax, saves it, and heralds its arrival by placing a pop-up message on your screen.

If you share a fax line with your voice line, things are more difficult depending on how you first set up the fax program:

- If you chose Enable Receive and specified *Manual Answer,* an incoming fax brings a pop-up window to your screen. Click Answer Now in the pop-up window to begin receiving the fax. This option works best for people who stay close to their computers.
- If you chose Enable Receive and specified *Automatically Answer,* the program answers *only* after the number of rings you specified. That gives you time to pick up the phone and start your conversation without interruption from the fax machine. If you hear a fax machine instead of a voice, though, hang up. When the fax machine calls back a minute or so later, you'll know not to pick up the phone.
- If you didn't *choose* Enable Receive, your fax program will never answer. To fix it, choose All Programs from the Start menu; select Accessories, choose Communications, and select Fax Console from the Fax area. Finally, choose Configure Fax from the Fax Console's Tools menu to rerun the setup program. This time, choose Enable Receive and select either Manual or Automatic.

If you're expecting an important fax any minute and are waiting by the phone, here's how to turn on your computerized fax machine and receive any incoming faxes:

1. **Choose All Programs from the Start menu.**
2. **Choose Accessories, then Communications, and then Fax.**
3. **Select Fax Console.**
4. **When the phone rings, choose Receive Fax Now from the File menu.**

Scanning a Photo, Letter, Receipt, or Clothing Stain

Most scanners and digital cameras come with their own software — a strange, bulky bundle of commands for you to try and remember. Fortunately, you usually don't have to install or use that software because most cameras and scanners are Windows XP compatible: Windows XP's built-in grabbing wizard performs admirably as a simple way to scan images or grab digital photos. Even if you've been using the software packaged with your scanner or camera, Windows XP's wizard may be all you need.

Scanning with the Scanning and Camera Wizard

After you've hooked up your scanner to Windows XP (right-click on the scanner icon in My Computer, choose Properties, and click the Test Scanner button to check that the scanner is connected correctly), the steps that follow show you how to begin scanning anything: photos, letters, lunch receipts, or even the shirt stain you wanted to e-mail to the restaurant that dropped your wine bottle.

Before scanning, always clean the scanner's glass thoroughly with a lint-free cloth. Even the tiniest dust can show up on the scan. Wipe any dust off the object you're scanning.

1. **Lift your scanner's cover, place the photo or letter on the glass, and close the cover.**

   Place the paper in the top-right corner, pushed up against the edges. If you're scanning a clothing stain, just place the cloth face down on the glass. I explain how to scan only part of an image in Step 4.

   If you don't align your scanned photos or letters against the corner, the resulting scan will tilt to one side, making for weird prints.

2. **Open My Computer and double-click your scanner's icon.**

   No scanner listed? Open the Control Panel, double-click the Scanners and Cameras icon, and look for the scanner icon in there. If it doesn't appear — and you're sure the scanner is plugged into both the wall and your computer (and turned on) — then it's not compatible with Windows XP's built-in software. In this case, you'll have to install the scanner's own software and use it — not Windows XP's built-in software, unfortunately.

3. **Click Next, and the Scanner and Camera Wizard steps forward.**

4. **Choose your Picture type and click Preview.**

   Windows XP offers four choices:

   - **Color:** The usual choice for most scans, it's the obvious choice for anything containing colors.
   - **Grayscale:** Use this setting mostly for scanning black-and-white photos because it picks up different shades of gray. (This sometimes works well for scanning text.)

- **Black and White:** This separates everything into only two colors: black or white. Don't use it for photos (even old black-and-white ones). It's for line drawings, sketches, and other monotone items.
- **Custom:** Stick with the other options until you're used to how they work. Only then should you experiment with the Custom area and its individual settings for resolution, brightness, and contrast. The next section, "Choosing the right scanning resolution," offers helpful tips about resolution.

When you click the Preview button, Windows scans the image and shows the results on the screen, as shown in Figure 7-10.

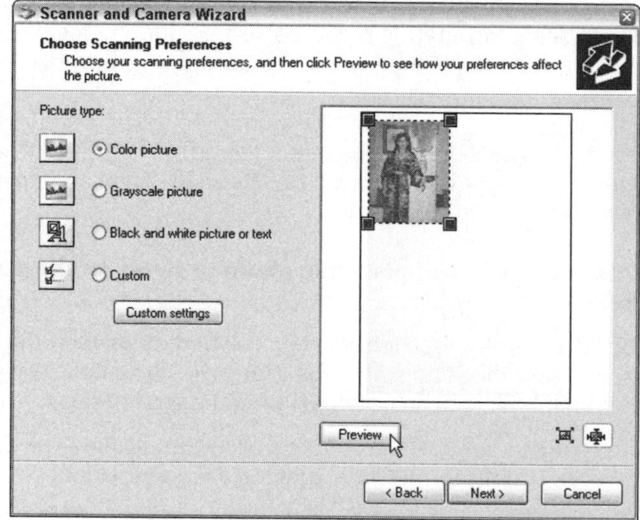

Figure 7-10: Click the Preview button to scan the image and then drag the little boxes to surround the image so the scan crops around the edges.

See the little lines around the picture and the boxes in each corner? Windows surrounds your picture with little lines to crop out everything but your image. If the lines miss the mark — or if you just want to scan *part* of your image (the clothing stain, for instance) — drag the little lines in or out until they surround the portion you want to capture. The handles on each corner make them particularly easy to grab.

Click the Enlarge button (shown in the margin) in the bottom-right corner of Figure 7-10 to see the portion you're about to scan.

Click the Entire Image button (shown in the margin) next to it to return to the previous view.

5. **Click the Next button and then type the file's new name and choose its format and location.**

   When the scanner has cropped your image correctly, click the Next button to chose your image's name and a file format:

- Choose the JPG format for most items, including photos. The JPG format compresses the image to save disk space.
- Choose TIF for a photo or image you'll print or send to a commercial printer. The TIF format doesn't compress the image as much as JPG, resulting in a much larger file. But it saves the highest quality image possible.
- Don't ever choose the BMP format; the images are gargantuan, and TIF does a much better job. Likewise, the PNG format is used mostly for small buttons or artwork on Web sites.

Save all your scanned images in the My Pictures folder so you can find them easily. If you wish, create additional folders inside your My Pictures folder to store related items.

6. **Click Next and then tell the scanner you're finished.**

Windows XP scans your image, as shown in Figure 7-11, stuffs it in the folder you selected in Step 5, and leaves you with three choices:

- Publish the pictures to a Web site. Choosing this option lets you send photos to one of Microsoft's many advertising-driven Web sites, MSN Groups.
- Send the pictures to an online service for printing. Choosing this option lets you send your pictures (and credit card information) to Microsoft's partners: Fujifilm, Shutterfly, or Kodak.
- Nothing. Choose this option to close the program and automatically open your My Pictures folder, letting you ogle your newly scanned image.

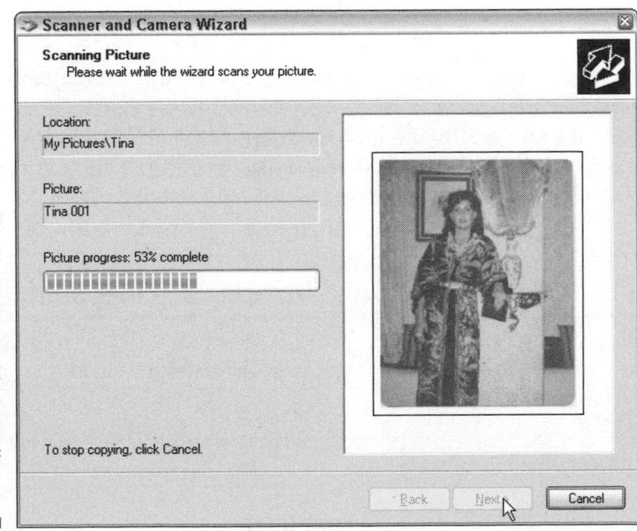

Figure 7-11: Windows XP scans your image and stores it using the name and folder of your choice.

7. **When you've finished working, click the Close button.**

- Unlike printers, scanners can't be shared on a network.
- Always remember to lock a scanner into place before moving it someplace. (Most scanners have a little knob on one side that locks it in place, preventing damage to its internal mechanisms.)

Choosing the right scanning resolution

Today, many people think that a *2400 dpi* scanner must be better than a *1200* or *300 dpi* scanner. After all, it's higher resolution, and it costs more. But that higher resolution costs more than cash — it costs hard drive space and the time your computer spends chugging along to create that scan, too. And many times, you don't even need or want a high-resolution image.

When you scan something at 2400 dpi, you're scanning 2,400 *dots per inch.* Your monitor uses a pixel to display each dot. And very few monitors can display more than 2,000 pixels across their entire screen. The result? When you scan something at 2400 dpi and view it on your screen, you're going to see a huge close-up of only about 1 inch of your image.

There's only one reason to scan at the highest resolution your scanner offers: when you're creating a file to be printed or saved — old family photos for instance. After you've scanned the image, copy the huge file to a CD or DVD for safekeeping or delete it so that the file doesn't take up valuable hard drive space. Store valuable pictures you want to save in a case and lock them in a safe. You may want to print the files on your own color printer, or any professional print shop can make a large high-quality print with a high-resolution image.

Most of the time, a much lower resolution will do the job, as shown in Table 7-1. In fact, for e-mail or Web sites, a lower resolution is better because these lean and mean files take up less space and load faster. (OCR stands for Optical Character Recognition — software that reads a scanned piece of text and converts it to letters and numbers for a word processor.)

Table 7-1 General Guidelines for Scanner Settings

To Scan This . . .	*For This . . .*	*Use This dpi Setting . . .*	*And Save As This*
4-x-6-inch photo	E-mail	75	JPG
4-x-6-inch photo	Web	75	JPG

To Scan This . . .	For This . . .	Use This dpi Setting . . .	And Save As This
Anything	Printing	600	TIF
Letter	Faxing	200	TIF
Text	OCR	300	TIF
Anything	Archive	2400	TIF

Use Table 7-1 as a general guideline; your scanner may not offer these exact resolutions. Try several scans at varying dots per inch to see which looks best to you. Delete the ones that don't look nice, save the ones that do, and remember the setting you used for future reference.

Dealing with scans that look awful

Like nearly everything but eating, scanning requires practice. Okay, maybe eating Dungeness crab from the shell requires a bit of practice, but you get the point. Making practice scans doesn't cost you any money, so experiment with your scanning settings. You can always delete the scans that don't look quite right.

If you'll be scanning lots of things, consider buying some graphics software like Adobe Photoshop Elements. You'll be amazed at how much better a scanned photo looks when touched up.

But if it's just you, Windows XP, and your scanner, these tips will help produce the best scans:

- Never clean your scanner with paper towels because they can leave tiny scratches on the glass. Instead, use standard glass cleaner and a lint-free rag, similar to the one packaged with some computer monitors. Spray the cleaner on the rag, not the glass itself.

- As with most computer parts, scanners rarely come packaged with their latest drivers. To update your scanner's drivers, visit the scanner manufacturer's Web site. Manufacturers constantly update a product's drivers to fix problems as they're discovered by disgruntled users like yourself.
- Before making your first scan, make sure your monitor is displaying all the colors it can. Right-click on a blank part of your desktop, choose Properties, and click the Settings tab. Change the Color Quality setting to the highest available (32-bit, if possible).

Part III
Getting Things Done on the Internet

In this part . . .

The Internet used to be clean, quiet, and helpful, just like a new library. You could find detailed information about nearly anything, read newspapers and magazines around the world, listen to music in the media section, or quietly browse the card catalogs.

Today, our wonderful global library has been bombarded with noisy people who toss ads in front of what you're trying to read. Some won't even let you close that book you inadvertently opened — the book keeps opening back up to the wrong page. Pickpockets and thieves stalk the halls.

This part of the book helps you turn the Internet back into that quiet, helpful library it once was. It shows how to stop pop-up ads, browser hijackers, and spyware. It explains how to send and receive e-mail so you can keep in touch with friends.

Finally, it shows you how to stay safe using Windows XP's firewall, Security Center, and cookie manager and other tricks that help bring back the library we all loved.

Chapter 8

Cruising the Web

In This Chapter

- Understanding the Internet
- Finding out about Internet service providers
- Setting up Internet Explorer the first time
- Navigating the Web
- Finding information on the Internet
- Understanding plug-ins
- Saving information from the Internet
- Troubleshooting Internet Explorer problems

Some people consider an Internet connection to be optional, but Windows XP prefers mandatory, thank you very much. Even when being installed, Windows XP starts reaching for the Internet, eager for any hint of a connection. After checking in with the Internet, for instance, Windows XP kindly nudges your computer's clock to the correct time. Some motives are less pure: Windows XP wants to check with Microsoft to make sure you're not installing a pirated copy.

Before *you* try connecting to the Internet, make sure you install Windows XP's Service Pack 2, which I describe in Chapter 1. That piece of software blocks those annoying pop-up ads in Internet Explorer. (Now if it could just remove all the *other* advertisements, as well.) It also strengthens XP's firewall to thwart predators.

For other ways to keep out the Internet's bad guys, be sure to visit Chapter 10 for a quick primer on safe computing. The Internet's full of back alleys, and that chapter explains how to avoid viruses, spyware, hijackers, and other Internet parasites.

Once your computer's wearing its appropriate helmet and kneepads, however, hop onto the Internet and enjoy the ride.

What Is the Internet?

Today, most people take the Internet for granted, much like a telephone line. Instead of marveling at the Internet's internal gearing, people treat it as a multipurpose tool. After it's connected to the Internet, your computer becomes all of the following:

Library: The Internet is stuffed with educational material: classic books, hourly news updates, foreign language dictionaries, specialized encyclopedias, and more. Visit RefDesk (`www.refdesk.com`) for a detailed list of some of the Internet's best free reference materials.

Store: Although the Internet began as a novelty ten years ago, today the Internet revolves around making money. Nearly anything available in stores (and some things *not* sold in stores) can be purchased on the Internet and shipped to your thatch hut. Amazon (`www.amazon.com`) even lets you listen to song snippets and read reviews before putting that live Jeff Buckley CD on your credit card.

Communicator: Some people treat the Internet as a private postal service for sending messages to friends, coworkers, and even strangers around the world. Unfortunately, unwelcome marketers do the same, filling everybody's inboxes with increasingly desperate sales pitches known as spam. (I cover Outlook Express, Windows XP's e-mail program, in Chapter 9.)

Time waster: When sitting in a waiting room, everybody naturally reaches for the magazine table. The Internet, too, offers zillions of ways to waste time. Jumping from one Web site to another is much like flipping pages in a magazine, but each flip often reveals a completely different yet oddly related magazine, brimming with fascinating information. Or at least it seems so at the time.

Entertainment: The Internet brings not only a movie's show times into your home but also its trailers, cast lists, reviews, and celebrity gossip. If you've already seen the movie, browse for online games, research travel destinations, or look up sporting statistics.

- Just as a television channel surfer flips from channel to channel, sampling the wares, a Web surfer moves from page to page, sampling the vast and esoteric piles of information.
- Almost every government but China loves the Internet. In the United States, the FBI posts pictures of its ten most wanted criminals (`www.fbi.gov`) for public viewing, for example, and the Internal Revenue Service (`www.irs.ustreas.gov`) lets Internet users make free copies of tax forms 24 hours a day.

- Universities and scientists love the network, too, because they can file grant forms more quickly than ever. Worried about the goo coagulating in the crevices of your bromeliads? The Internet's famed botanical site (`www.botany.net`) enables researchers to study everything from Australian acacias to zoosporic fungi.
- Many computer companies support their products on the Internet. Visitors can leave messages to technicians or other users asking why their latest computer doodads aren't working. After posting messages back and forth, visitors can sometimes download a fix or uncover the right series of keystrokes to fix the problem.

What's an ISP and Why Do I Need One?

A first-timer needs four things to connect to the Web: a computer, Web browser software, a modem, and an Internet service provider (ISP). You already have the computer, and Windows XP comes with a built-in Web browser called Internet Explorer. Your computer most likely came with a built-in modem. (If it didn't, you'll find out when you first try to set up your ISP, as I describe in this chapter.)

Most people only need to find an ISP, and you usually find one listed in your local Yellow Pages under *Computers — Online Services & Internet* or *Telecommunications.* Or ask your local computer dealer for names and numbers.

Although signals for television channels come wafting through the air to your TV set for free, you must pay an ISP for the privilege of surfing the Web. You pay the ISP for a password and account name. When your computer's modem connects to your ISP's network, type the information and grab your surfboard: You've entered the Web.

Don't have an ISP? Different ISPs serve different areas. Ask your friends, neighbors, or librarians how they connect and whether they recommend their ISP. Call them up for a rate quote, and choose the cheapest. Most bill on a monthly basis; if you're not happy, you can always switch.

- Although some ISPs charge for each minute you're connected, most charge a flat monthly fee between $15 and $50 for unlimited service. Make sure that you know your rate before hopping aboard, or you may be surprised at the end of the month.
- Most free ISPs went out of business when the bottom fell out of the Internet market. At the time of this writing, you can still find limited Internet access for free from Juno (`www.juno.com`), but you have to peek around the ads to see the screen.

- ISPs let you connect to the Internet in a variety of ways. The slowest ISPs use a dial-up modem and an ordinary phone line. Faster still are special DSL or ISDN lines provided by some phone companies. Some of the fastest connections come from your cable TV company. When shopping for speedy ISPs, your geographic location usually determines your options, unfortunately.
- If you're computer-inclined, some ISPs let you create your *own* Web pages for other Internet members to visit. Show the world pictures of your kids and cats, share your favorite recipes, talk about your favorite car waxes, or swap tips on constructing fishing flies or prom gowns.

Setting Up Internet Explorer the First Time

To guide you smoothly through the turmoil of setting up your ISP account, Microsoft created the New Connection Wizard. After a bit of interrogation, the wizard helps connect your computer to your ISP so you can Web surf like the best of them.

Setting up a network? Then connect one of your computers to the Internet using the New Connection Wizard. When you run the Network Setup Wizard to set up your network (covered in Chapter 14), that wizard helps all your networked computers share that single Internet connection.

To transfer your existing Internet account settings to or from another computer, use Windows XP's Files and Settings Transfer Wizard, covered in Chapter 19. The wizard copies your existing settings onto a floppy. Insert that floppy into your other Windows XP computer, and the wizard automatically installs them.

Here's what you need to get started:

- **Your user name, password, and access phone number.** If you don't have an ISP yet, the wizard finds you one, so grab a pencil and paper. (The wizard's ISP suggestions are a tad pricey, however.) If you're setting up a high-speed connection, you don't need a phone number. High-speed connections use special modems that don't require phone lines.
- **A plugged-in modem.** Most new computers come with a modem lodged in their innards. To see if one's inside of yours, look for telephone jacks on the back of your computer, near where all the other cables protrude. Then connect a standard phone cable between that jack (the computer's jack says *Line,* not *Phone*) and the phone jack in your wall. (Broadband companies usually supply their own modems, and their technicians often set them up for you.)

Whenever your Internet connection gives you log-on problems, head here and run through these steps. The wizard walks you through your current settings, letting you make changes.

Summon the wizard by following these steps:

1. **Click the Start button, click All Programs, choose Accessories, select Communications, and load the New Connection Wizard.**

   Or, just choose Internet Explorer from the Start menu. If you haven't set up an Internet account yet, your PC can't connect, so Windows automatically summons a wizard from the appropriate school.

   Can't find the Start menu's New Connection Wizard? To lure the wizard from its lair, click the Start menu, right-click on the Internet Explorer icon, choose Internet Properties, click the Connections tab, and click the Setup button.

2. **Click Next.**
3. **Choose Connect to the Internet and click Next.**

   Choosing this first option tells Mr. Wizard that yes, you do want to connect to the Internet. (If you want to connect to the Internet through your home or office network, choose Set Up a Home or Small Office Network, and the wizard passes you off to the Network Setup Wizard instead, which I cover in Chapter 14.)

4. **Choose the Set Up My Connection Manually option, as shown in Figure 8-1, and click Next.**

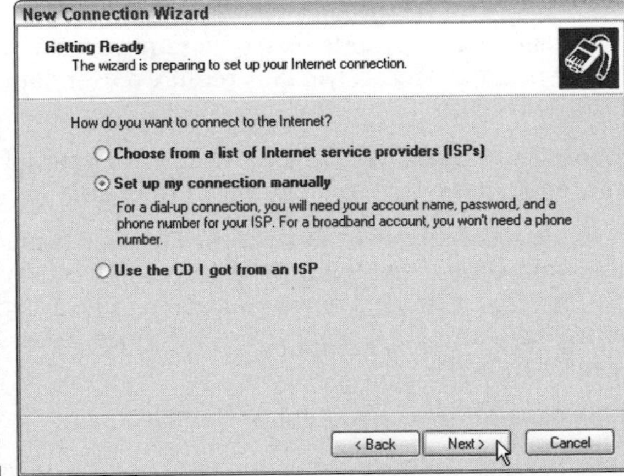

Figure 8-1: The New Connection Wizard helps you connect your computer to the Internet.

Here's what the three options mean:

- **Choose from a List of Internet Service Providers (ISPs).** Choose this option if you don't already have an Internet account and you want to select one from a list provided by Microsoft. If you choose this option, the wizard dials a number to locate Internet service providers in your area and displays their rates and options. The wizard finds providers only with special Microsoft contracts, so it leaves out many providers in your area. (The telephone book is a much better way to find an ISP.)

  If you use this option to choose a provider, the wizard finishes the rest of the setup work by itself.

- **Set Up My Connection Manually.** Chances are, you'll end up choosing this option. This lets you set up an Internet account you've already paid for; you just enter that ISP's settings. After selecting this option, click Next to continue along these steps and introduce your computer to your existing Internet account.

- **Use the CD I Got from an ISP.** Many national ISPs offer free CDs for signing up to their service. You choose this option if you have a CD from America Online, for instance. Choosing this option stops the wizard and lets the ISP's CD take over.

5. **Tell Windows XP how you connect to the Internet and then click Next.**

   The wizard provides three options, as shown in Figure 8-2:

   - **Connect Using a Dial-up Modem.** If your modem plugs into the phone line, choose this option and move to Step 6.

   - **Connect Using a Broadband Connection That Requires a User Name and Password.** Broadband connections are the speedy ones provided by cable or DSL modems. Some require a user name and password for Internet access. (*All* ISPs require a user name and password for e-mail access.)

     If you choose this option, you type in a name for your ISP, your user name, and a password to finish the connection.

   - **Connect Using a Broadband Connection That Is Always On.** Some broadband connections *don't* require a password or user name to access the Internet. (You still enter your user name and password when setting up your e-mail account with Outlook Express, which I describe in Chapter 9.)

6. **Type a name for your Internet provider and click Next.**

   Simply type **My Provider** or the name of company you're paying for Internet service.

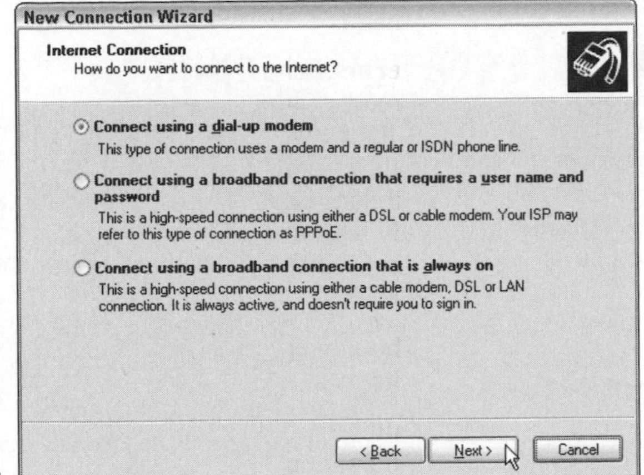

Figure 8-2: Select the type of Internet connection your ISP provides.

7. **Enter the phone number for your Internet service provider and click Next; then enter your user name and password.**

   Your provider gives you these three things. Call your provider if these three magical tidbits of information aren't in your possession. Without them, you can't connect to the Internet.

   Enter the phone number you need to dial to reach the ISP. If you're not sure whether you need to dial an area code or enter "1" for long distance, dial the phone number by hand and listen. When you hear a squealing modem answer, you know you've found the right combination of numbers to enter in this box.

8. **Click the Finish button.**

   You're done. Windows XP automatically leaps into action and uses your settings to call your Internet provider.

If everything goes correctly, a pop-up message appears with your dial-up modem's connection speed. You're logged on to the Internet. Always plugging its own products, Microsoft tosses one of its own Web pages (MSN) onto the Internet Explorer screen, and you're ready to browse. Need a place to go for a quick test? Log on to `www.andyrathbone.com` and see what happens.

All Internet users should upgrade to Windows XP's Service Pack 2, which I describe in Chapter 1. That service pack beefs up the firewall, among other things, keeping Internet scoundrels at bay. You'll certainly enjoy the service pack's new pop-up ad blocker. You can find out how the blocker works in Chapter 10.

Don't be afraid to bug your ISP for help. The best ISPs come with technical support lines. A member of the support staff can talk you through the installation process.

But I want to see some pop-ups!

Early versions of Internet Explorer had no way to stop pop-up advertisements from exploding across your screen. Windows XP's Service Pack 2, covered in Chapter 1, adds a pop-up ad blocker to Internet Explorer that stops 90 percent of them. To make sure it's turned on, choose Pop-up Blocker from Internet Explorer's Tools menu and make sure no check mark appears in the Turn Off Pop-up Blocker box.

If you *want* to see pop-ups on certain sites, that same menu lets you choose Pop-up Blocker Settings. Add the Web site address, and Internet Explorer allows that site's pop-ups to pop unblocked.

If a site tries to send a pop-up ad or message, Internet Explorer places a strip along the top saying `A pop-up was blocked. To see this pop-up or additional options, click here.` Click the strip to see the pop-up, add the site to your pop-ups allowed list, turn off the blocker completely, turn off the informational strip, or change the blocker's settings.

Finally, to stop the informational strip from making that obnoxious pop noise when it stops a pop-up, choose Pop-up Blocker from Internet Explorer's Tools menu, choose Pop-up Blocker Settings, and remove the check mark from the Play a Sound When a Pop-up Is Blocked box.

How Do I Navigate the Web with Microsoft Internet Explorer?

Your Web browser is your Internet surfboard — your transportation between the Internet's thousands of Web sites. Internet Explorer comes free with Windows XP, so many people use it out of convenience. Other people use other browsers published by other software companies, like Netscape Communicator or Opera. People with too much time on their hands switch back and forth between several types of Web browsers.

How do I move from Web page to Web page?

All browsers work basically the same way. Every Web page comes with a specific address, just like houses do. Internet Explorer lets you move from page to page in three different ways:

- By pointing and clicking a button or link that automatically whisks you away to another page
- By typing a complicated string of code words (the Web address) into the Address box of the Web browser and pressing Enter
- By clicking the navigation buttons on the browser's toolbar, which is usually at the top of the screen

Clicking links

The first way is the easiest. Look for *links* — highlighted words or pictures on a page — and click them. See how the mouse pointer turned into a hand (shown in the margin) as it pointed at the word *Books* in Figure 8-3? Click that word to see more information about my books. Most words on this site are links, as well; the mouse pointer becomes a hand when near them, and the words become underlined. Click any of them to view pages dealing with that link's particular subject.

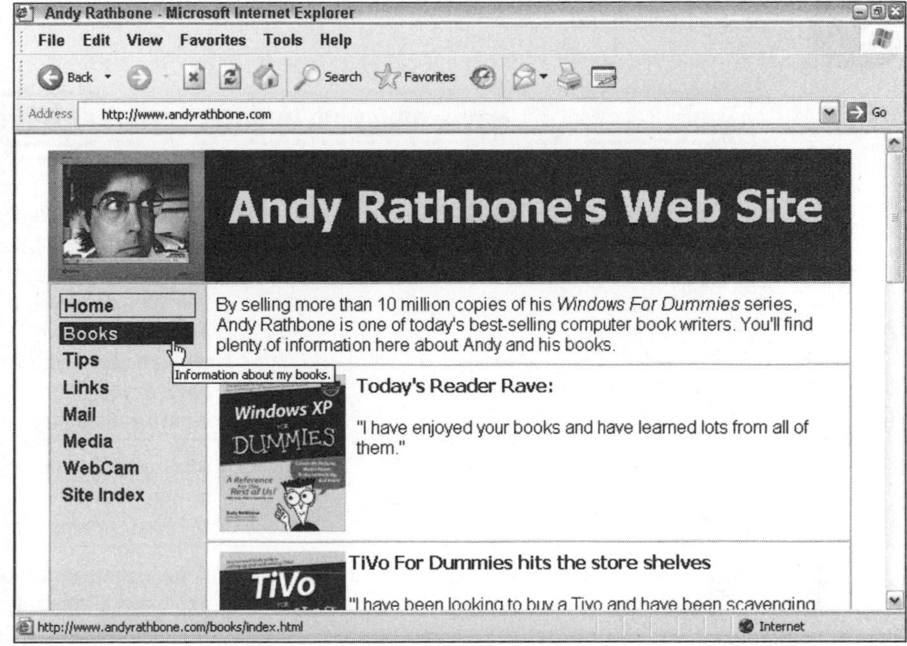

Figure 8-3: When the mouse pointer becomes a hand, click the underlined or highlighted word or picture to see more information about that item.

Web page manufacturers get mighty creative these days, and without the little hand pointer, it's often hard to tell where to point and click. Some buttons look like sturdy elevator buttons; others look more like fuzzy dice or vegetables. But when you click a button, the browser takes you to the page relating to that button. Clicking the fuzzy dice may bring up a betting-odds sheet for local casinos, for example.

Typing Web addresses in the Address box

The second method is the most difficult. If a friend gives you a napkin with a cool Web page's address written on it, you need to type the Web site's address into your browser's Address box yourself. You'll do fine, as long as you don't misspell anything. See the Web site address for my Web site along the top of Figure 8-3? I typed www.andyrathbone.com into the Address box. When I pressed Enter, Internet Explorer scooted me to my Web page. (You don't need to type the http:// part, thank goodness.)

Using Internet Explorer's toolbar

Finally, you can maneuver through the Internet by clicking various buttons on Internet Explorer's toolbar, which sits at the top of the screen. Table 8-1 offers a handy reference of the important navigation buttons.

Hover your mouse pointer over a confusing Internet Explorer button to see its purpose in life.

Table 8-1 Navigating with Internet Explorer's Buttons

This Button	*. . . Is Called This . . .*	*. . . And It Does This*
Back	Back	Pointed and clicked yourself into a dead end? Click the Back button to head for the last Web page you visited. If you click the Back button enough times, you wind up back at your home page, where you began.
	Forward	After you click the Back button, you can click Forward to revisit a page, too.
	Home	If you get stuck as you explore the Internet, click the Home button along the top to move back into familiar territory.
	Favorites	Clicking the Favorites button along the top reveals a folder where you can stash buttons leading to your favorite Web sites.
	History	Click the History button to return to any page that you visited in the past few weeks.

Making Internet Explorer open to your favorite site

Your Web browser automatically displays a Web site when you first log on. That Web site is called your *home page,* and you can tell Internet Explorer to use any site you want for your home page by following these steps:

1. **Visit your favorite Web site.**

   Choose any Web page you want. I use Google News (`news.google.com`) so Internet Explorer always opens with the hour's current headlines.

2. **Choose Internet Options from Internet Explorer's Tools menu.**
3. **Click the General tab and click the Use Current button shown in Figure 8-4.**

   Now, Internet Explorer always opens to the page you're currently viewing.

Figure 8-4: Click the Use Current button, and Internet Explorer always opens to that page.

   Clicking Use Default reverts to Microsoft's MSN site as your home page; click Use Blank for an unappetizing white screen.

4. **Click OK to save your efforts and return to browsing.**

After Internet Explorer loads your chosen home page, you can move around the Internet, searching for topics by looking in indexes or simply pointing and clicking from topic to topic.

- If your home page is suddenly hijacked to a different site and these instructions don't fix it, then it's probably been hijacked by evil forces. Read the spyware section in Chapter 10.
- A home page of a *Web site* is different from your *own* home page. A Web site's home page is its "cover," like the cover of a magazine. Whenever you jump to a Web site, you usually jump to the site's home page.

How can I revisit my favorite places?

Sooner or later, you'll stumble across a Web page that's indescribably delicious. To make sure that you can find it again later, add it to your favorite pages folder by choosing Add to Favorites from the Favorites menu.

Don't choose the Make Available Offline option. (That one tells Windows to automatically download the page's contents once a day or whenever you press a button.) Then click OK to save your efforts.

Whenever you want to return to that page, click the Favorites menu along the top of the screen and then click the name of the link you want to revisit.

Librarian-types like to click the Organize Favorites option when the Favorites menu drops down. By doing so, they can create new folders for storing similar links and move related links from folder to folder.

How do I find things on the Internet?

Just as it is nearly impossible to find a book in a library without a card catalog, it is nearly impossible to find a Web site on the Internet without a good index. Luckily, several exist.

Unfortunately, none exist in Windows XP. Clicking the Search button at the top of the Internet Explorer window brings up Windows' built-in Search function, but that program often stumbles when searching on the Internet. Instead, try this:

1. **Click in Internet Explorer's Address box, type** www.google.com, **and press Enter.**

   That summons Google, the Internet's best search engine.

2. **Type a few key words describing your interest (cornbread recipes, for instance) and click the Google Search button.**

   In less than a second, Google found 95,900 references to cornbread recipes, as shown in Figure 8-5.

Internet Explorer's secret history of your Web visits

Internet Explorer keeps a record of every Web site you visit. For some odd reason, it also keeps track of files you play in Media Player and even some of the files you open. Although Internet Explorer's History list provides a handy record of your computing activities, it's a spy's dream.

To keep tabs on what Internet Explorer is recording, click its History icon on the toolbar at the top of the screen. Internet Explorer lists every Web you've visited in the past 20 days. Feel free to sort the entries: Choose View to list them by date, alphabetically, most visited, or by the order you've visited on that particular day.

To delete a single entry from the history, right-click on it and choose Delete from the menu. To delete the entire list, choose Internet Options from its Tools menu and click the Clear History button. To turn off the history entirely, set the Days to Keep Pages in History setting to 0.

Click any of the sites that Google lists to check out those recipes. Click the Back button to return to Google's search and click a different recipe. Or, right-click on the link and choose Open in New Window. A new copy of Internet Explorer appears, displaying that link, while the other copy keeps displaying your other Google search locations. (That keeps you from losing your place on the search page.)

- If Google finds Web sites in foreign languages, it often translates them into your own language for you.
- Sometimes Google brings up a Web site that's been updated and no longer lists what you're searching for. If that happens, click the word Cached instead of the site's name. That brings up a snapshot of the Web site as it looked when it contained what you're searching for.
- Click Google's I'm Feeling Lucky button, and Google displays the site most likely to contain what you're after. This option works best when searching for common information.
- Although Google is very handy, it's just one way of finding information. The Internet's loaded with other search engines. AltaVista (`www.altavista.com`) and Yahoo! (`www.yahoo.com`) are also popular.

- For many years, people have exchanged messages on a section of the Internet called *Usenet.* Divided into thousands of discussion areas, Usenet lets people type questions about nearly every subject, exchanging information, holding discussions, or simply yelling at each other. It's a fantastic source of computer information from real people, without a corporate filter. To search Usenet in Google, click the word Groups, listed above the entry box.

- Searches usually come up with hundreds or even thousands of hits relating to your subject. If you come up with too many, try again and be more specific with each search.

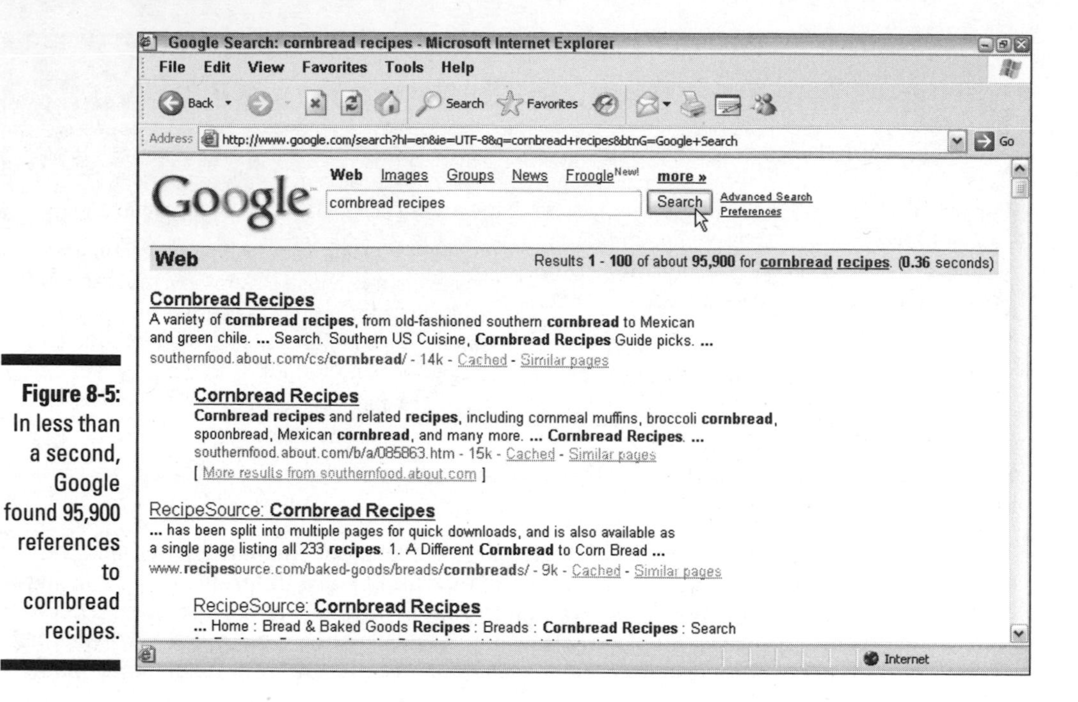

Figure 8-5: In less than a second, Google found 95,900 references to cornbread recipes.

The Web Page Says It Needs a Weird Plug-In Thing!

Computer programmers abandoned their boring old TV sets and turned to their exciting new computers for entertainment. Now, they're trying to turn their computers back into TV sets. They're using fancy programming techniques called Java, Shockwave, RealPlayer, QuickTime, and other goodies to add animation and other gizmos to the Internet.

Programmers are also adding little software tidbits called *plug-ins* that increase your computer's capability to display these gizmos — as well as flashy advertisements along the top of your screen. You'll know when you need one when the Web site sticks a threatening notice in your face, as shown in Figure 8-6.

Internet Explorer - Security Warning
Do you want to install this software?
Name: Macromedia Flash Player 7? This free player is re...
Publisher: Macromedia, Inc.
More options
Install | Don't Install
This type of file can harm your computer. Only install software from publishers you trust. How can I decide what software to install?

Figure 8-6: A site asks to install software.

What's the problem? If your computer says it needs a plug-in or its latest version, click the button that takes you to its download area — *but only if you can trust it.* Although it's often difficult to tell the good programs from the evil ones, I explain in Chapter 10 how to judge a plug-in's trustworthiness. The following plug-ins are both free and safe:

- **QuickTime** (`www.apple.com/quicktime`)**:** The free version of QuickTime plays many video formats that Microsoft's Media Player can't handle, including those required to view most movie trailers.
- **RealPlayer** (`www.real.com`)**:** Although I find this software offensive, sometimes it's the only way to see or view some things on the Internet. Be sure to download the *free* version, no matter now much the Real folks try to hide it behind the pay version on its Web site.
- **Macromedia Flash/Shockwave** (`www.macromedia.com`)**:** Although this free download plays most of the elaborate moving advertisements on Web sites, it also lets you watch funny cartoons and animations.
- **Adobe Acrobat Reader** (`www.adobe.com`)**:** Another popular freebie, Acrobat Reader lets you view documents as if they are printed on paper. (Sometimes it doesn't let you copy parts of them, though, or read them into your word processor.)

Saving Information from the Internet

The Internet places a full-service library inside your house, with no long checkout lines. And just as every library comes with a copy machine, Internet Explorer provides several ways for you to save interesting tidbits of information for your personal use. (Check your country's copyright law for specifics.)

The following sections explain how to copy something from the Internet onto your computer, whether it's an entire Web page, a single picture, a sound or movie, or a program.

I explain how to print a Web page (or information it contains) in Chapter 7.

Saving a Web page

Hankering for a handy Fahrenheit/Centigrade conversion chart? Need that Sushi Identification Chart for dinner? Want to save the itinerary for next month's trip to Russia? When you find a Web page with indispensable information, sometimes you can't resist saving a copy onto your computer for further viewing, perusal, or even printing at a later date.

When you save a Web page, you're saving the page as it *currently exists* on your screen. To see any subsequent changes, you must revisit the actual site.

Saving your currently viewed Web page is easy:

1. **Choose Save As from Internet Explorer's File menu.**

   Internet Explorer enters the Web page's name in the File Name box, as shown in Figure 8-7, and fills out the Encoding box automatically.

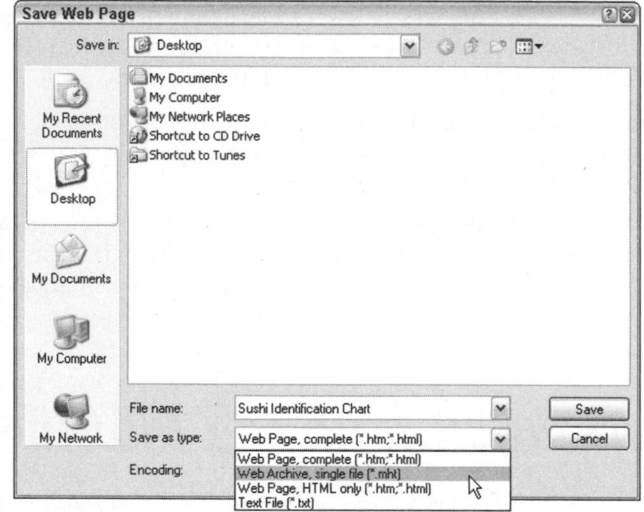

Figure 8-7: Internet Explorer offers four different formats for saving a Web page.

2. **Use the Save In drop-down list to choose where you want to save the file.**

   My Documents or a subfolder that you create in My Documents is usually a good choice.

3. **Choose how you want to save the page in the Save As Type box. Internet Explorer offers *four* different ways to save the Web page:**

   - **Web Page, Complete (*.htm;*.html):** Fast, handy, but a tad awkward, this option tells Internet Explorer to divide the Web page into two parts: a folder containing the page's pictures and graphics, and an adjacent link that tells the computer to display that folder's contents.
   - **Web Archive, Single File (*.mht):** A much tidier option, this also saves an exact copy of the Web page. However, everything's packaged neatly into a single file named after the Web page.
   - **Web Page, HTML Only (*.htm;*.html):** This option saves the page's text and layout but strips away the images. It's handy for stripping pictures and advertisements from tables, charts, and other formatted chunks of text.

- **Text File (*.txt):** This option scrapes all the text off the page and dumps it into a Notepad file, without taking many pains to preserve the formatting. It's handy for saving lists but not much else.

4. **Click the Save button when you're done.**

Saving text

To just save a little of the text, select the text you want to grab, right-click on it, and choose Copy. Open your word processor and paste the text into a new document and save it in your My Documents folder with a descriptive name.

To save *all* the text from a Web site, it's easiest to save the entire Web page, as described in the previous section. But select either the Web Page HTML Only option to preserve the text's formatting (tables, charts, receipts, and similar information work well this way) or select the Text File option to save the words without their formatting (good for lists, for instance.)

Saving a picture

As you browse through Web pages and your mouse pointer rests over a photo or other large image, an annoying box of icons appears, as shown in Figure 8-8.

Figure 8-8: Click the disk icon to save the Web site's picture to your computer.

Those little boxes let you play with the image in different ways. Click the little disk icon, shown in Figure 8-8, to save the image to your My Pictures folder. Click the Printer icon to send the image straight to your printer. A click on the little letter icon e-mails the image through your e-mail program. And clicking the little folder opens your My Pictures folder for browsing.

Saving a sound or movie you've played

Some downright mean Web sites don't let you save movies or sounds you've just played in Media Player. But friendly sites let you choose Save Media As from Media Player's File menu to save the show to your hard drive. But if that option's grayed out or Media Player doesn't automatically fill in the format, you're not allowed to save what you've just watched or heard.

This trick doesn't work for all media (especially for Internet radio stations), and it doesn't always work on different media players like QuickTime or RealPlayer. But it's sometimes worth a try.

Remember the little picture by your name on Windows XP's Welcome screen? Feel free to use any picture from the Internet. Right-click on the new picture and save it to your My Pictures folder. Then use the Control Panel (see Chapter 11) to transform that picture into your new user account picture.

Don't see the little icons pop up when you point at a picture you want? Right-click on the picture and choose Save Picture As. Choose your My Pictures folder, if necessary, and click Save to save the file.

Downloading a program

Sometimes downloading is as easy as clicking a Web site's Click to Download Now button. The Web site asks where to save your file, and you choose your My Documents folder for easy retrieval. The file arrives in a few seconds (if you have a cable modem) or a few minutes to hours (if you have a dial-up modem).

But sometimes downloading becomes a chore, described in the following two-step process:

1. **Right-click on the link pointing to the desired file and choose Save Target As.**

   For instance, to download Cory Doctorow's science fiction novel, *eastern standard tribe,* from his Web site, right-click on its link (the words ASCII text file, in this case). Then choose Save Target As from the pop-up menu, as shown in Figure 8-9.

   When you try to download a program, Windows asks whether you want to Save the File or Run It from Its Current Location. Choose Save the File.

2. **Navigate to your My Documents folder and click the Save button.**

   When the Save As dialog box appears, as shown in Figure 8-10, navigate to your My Documents folder and click the Save button.

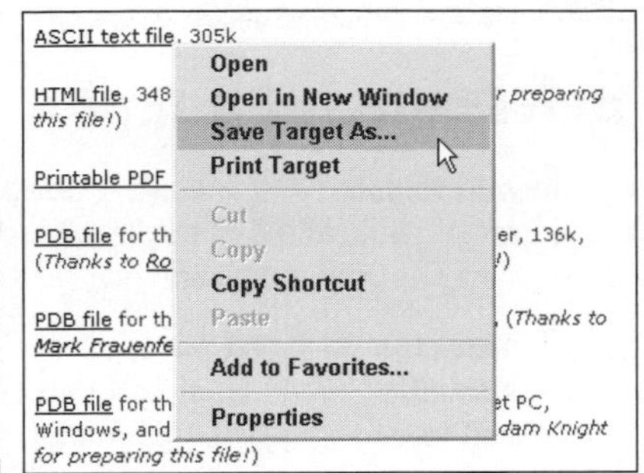

Figure 8-9: Choose Save Target As.

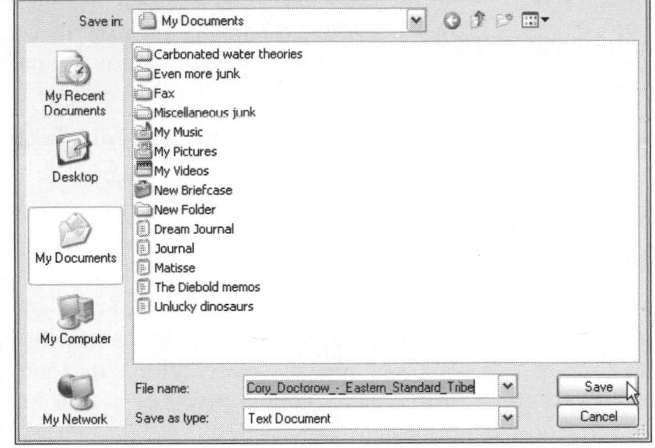

Figure 8-10: Navigate to your My Documents folder and click the Save button.

Windows XP begins copying the file from the Web site to your hard drive. Windows XP tells you when it finishes downloading, and you can click the Open Folder button to open your My Documents folder and see your downloaded file.

- If you download a lot of things, create a file in your My Documents folder called Downloads and save downloaded files in there. That keeps things organized.
- Before running any downloaded programs, screen savers, themes, or other items, be sure to scan them with your antivirus program. Windows XP doesn't come with one built-in, leaving it up to you to purchase one.
- Many downloaded programs come packaged in a tidy folder with a zipper on it, known as a *Zip file.* Windows XP treats them like normal folders; just double-click them to open them. (The files are actually comipressed inside that folder to save download time, if you care about the engineering involved.)

Visiting Web sites in foreign languages

If you travel worldwide on the Internet, you'll eventually come across a Web site you can't read. Actually, Internet Explorer can't *let* you read it because it can't display the Web page's foreign fonts.

Instead of stumbling to the nearest embassy for assistance, Internet Explorer sends a pop-up message, graciously offering to download a Language Pack Installation that lets it display the language's characters correctly.

Click the box's Install button, and Internet Explorer automatically dashes off to the Microsoft Web site, downloads and installs the appropriate language pack, and begins displaying the Web site using its proper characters.

Internet Explorer won't *translate* the Web site, unfortunately, but at least you can see how it looks in its original language. And if you want a free rudimentary translation of the site, copy the Web site's address, visit Google (`www.google.com`), and paste the address into Google's Search box. When Google displays the page, it sometimes offers to translate the Web site into your language, be it English, German, Spanish, French, Italian, or Portuguese.

It Doesn't Work!

Don't feel bad. The Internet's been around for a while, but this whole Web thing is relatively new and complicated. It's not supposed to work smoothly yet, and it isn't something you can figure out overnight. This section explores some of the most common problems and some possible solutions.

The person holding the Administrator account — usually the computer's owner — is the only one who is authorized to make many of the changes you read about in this chapter. If a mean message pops up, waving its finger and mumbling about Administrator restrictions, you're locked out. Better find the computer's owner to proceed.

Here are some general tips that you may want to try before you explore the following sections:

- When a Web site gives you problems, try emptying Internet Explorer's wastebasket. Choose Internet Options from its Tools menu and click the Delete Files button. Click the Delete All Offline Content box and click the OK button. Twiddle your thumbs until it finishes and then revisit the problematic site and try again.
- If your connection settings seem askew, sometimes the New Connection Wizard can set things straight. Described at the beginning of this chapter, it guides you through your current settings, letting you change things that look suspicious.

- If you can't connect to the Internet at all, your best bet is to call your ISP's tech support number and ask for help. (Be sure to call your Internet service provider, not Microsoft.)

- Finally, if a page doesn't seem to display correctly, look for Internet Explorer's warning strip along the page's top. Click the strip and tell Internet Explorer *not* to block what it's trying to block.

The Pages Won't All Fit on My Screen!

Some people (with good eyesight) can afford huge monitors that pack lots of information onto the screen. Other folks have smaller monitors that simply don't have the real estate to display everything. So, how does a Web site reshape itself to fit every screen? It can't.

Some try by fitting squarely onto smaller monitors but leaving white space along the edges of larger monitors. Others try to guess a monitor's size and resize themselves to fit. Others simply fall off your screen's right edge.

The best way to fight back is to experiment with your *screen resolution.* Although I describe the process in Chapter 11, here are the quick-and-dirty steps:

1. **Right-click on a blank part of your desktop and choose Properties.**
2. **Click the Settings tab and slide the bar to adjust your Screen Resolution.**

Sliding the bar to the *right* packs more information onto the screen but makes everything smaller. Sliding to the *left* makes everything larger but sometimes leaves parts of the screen hanging off the edge.

Although the resolution setting of 800 x 600 pixels usually makes a nice combination, many sites now pack their information into a resolution of 1024 x 768 pixels.

Chapter 9

Sending Mail and Instant Messages

In This Chapter

- Using Outlook Express
- Setting up Outlook Express for AOL, Hotmail, or Yahoo! mail
- Sending and receiving e-mail
- Finding lost mail
- Managing your contacts with Address Book
- Using Windows Messenger

Internet Explorer turns the Internet into a multimedia magazine, but Outlook Express turns it into your personalized post office, where you never need fumble for a stamp. A Windows XP freebie, Outlook Express lets you send letters and files to anybody in the world who has an e-mail account. (And that's just about anybody, these days.)

Quite the bargain for a freebie, Outlook Express automatically sorts your incoming mail and stuffs it into the correct folder, juggles several e-mail accounts simultaneously, and adds some security to your e-mail as well.

I wrap up this chapter with another subject requested by readers: Windows Messenger. You find out how to sign up for an account, send instant messages to your friends and coworkers, and uninstall the darn program when all that instant chatter starts grinding on your nerves.

Using Outlook Express

The Outlook Express screen, shown in Figure 9-1, contains three main parts: Folders, which automatically store and sort your e-mail; Contacts, which display names of people in your Address Book; and the work screen, where you tinker with your e-mail.

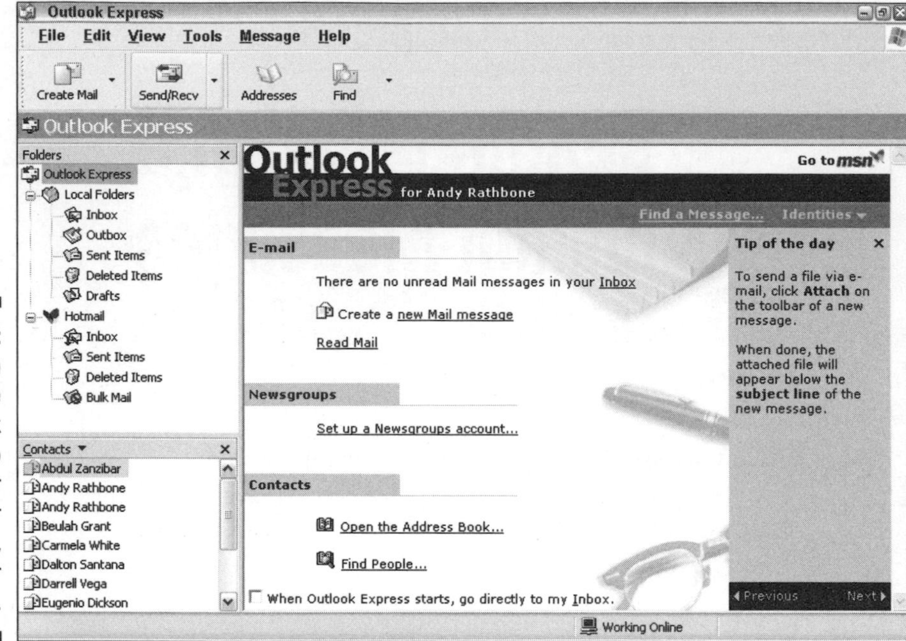

Figure 9-1: You can customize Outlook Express to display your folders, your contacts, and your workspace.

Folders: The folders in Outlook Express work much like in baskets and out baskets for sorting memos. Click any folder's name to peer inside, and you're in for a pleasant surprise. Unlike your own office, Outlook Express automatically sorts your information into the following folders:

- **Inbox:** When you connect to the Internet, Outlook Express grabs any waiting e-mail and places it in your Inbox. (To send and receive any waiting e-mail immediately, click the Send/Recv button along the top of the Outlook Express window.)
- **Outbox:** When you send or reply to a message, it sits in your Outbox, ready to be sent automatically the next time you connect to the Internet. (Clicking the Send/Recv button connects to the Internet, sends your outgoing mail, and fetches any waiting e-mail.)
- **Sent:** *Every* piece of e-mail you've sent stays in here, leaving a permanent record. (Right-click on an offensive e-mail and choose Delete to kill it for good.)
- **Deleted:** The Deleted folder serves as the Outlook Express Recycle Bin. Right-click on anything in here to delete it permanently or move it to a different folder. Or, to keep the Deleted folder empty, choose Options from the Tools menu, click the Maintenance tab, and select the Empty Messages from the 'Deleted Items' Folder on Exit check box.

- **Drafts:** When you're halfway through composing a letter and want to finish it later, choose Save from your e-mail's File menu. The letter moves to your Drafts folder for later retrieval.

Contacts: In the Contacts area, Outlook Express lists the first few names in your Address Book, sorted alphabetically. If you don't see your contacts' names listed like in Figure 9-1, choose Layout from the View menu and click in the Contacts check box. (The Address Book gets its own section later in this chapter.)

- Missing that handy row of buttons along the top of Outlook Express like in Figure 9-1? Choose Layout from the View menu and click to place a check mark in the Toolbar box.
- If your copy of Outlook Express still doesn't look like Figure 9-1, it's time to tweak its layout. Try this trick: Choose Layout from the View menu and make sure that you've selected Folder Bar, Folder List, Status Bar, and Toolbar. (Clicking the Apply button after you select or deselect an option lets you see exactly what that option does to the screen.)
- Want to transfer all your e-mail and contacts from your old computer to a new one? I explain that chore in Chapter 19.

Exactly what do I need to send and receive e-mail?

To send e-mail to a friend or foe with Outlook Express, you need three things:

- **An e-mail account:** The next section describes how to set up Outlook Express to work with your e-mail account. Most ISPs (Internet service providers, covered in Chapter 8) give you a free e-mail address along with your Internet access.
- **Your friend's or foe's e-mail address:** Locate your friends' e-mail addresses by simply asking them. An address consists of a *user name* (which occasionally resembles the user's real name), followed by the @ sign, followed by the name of your friend's Internet service provider. The e-mail address of an America Online user with the user name of Jeff9435 would be `jeff9435@aol.com`.
- **Your message:** Here's where the fun finally starts: typing your letter. After you type in the person's e-mail address and your message, hit the Send button. Outlook Express routes your message in the right direction.

You'll find people's e-mail addresses on business cards, Web sites, and even return addresses: Whenever you reply to e-mail, Outlook Express automatically adds that person's e-mail address to your Address Book.

If you misspell part of an e-mail address, your sent message will bounce back to your own Inbox, with a confusing *undeliverable* message attached. Check the spelling of the address and try again. If it bounces again, humble yourself: Pick up the phone and ask the person if you have the right address.

Setting up your e-mail account

In order to send or receive e-mail in Outlook Express, you need these three things, all available from your ISP: your user name, your password, and a working Internet connection. (You've already used these things if you successfully set up your Internet account, as described in Chapter 8.)

Most people set up more than one e-mail address — a freebie account from both Yahoo! (`www.yahoo.com`), and Hotmail (`www.hotmail.com`), for instance, and separate addresses for each family member. Whether you're setting up your 1st or your 40th e-mail account, follow these six steps:

1. **Set up your Internet account and open Outlook Express.**

   You need to set up your Internet account *first,* as described in Chapter 8, or your e-mail won't have any way to reach the Internet.

   To call up Outlook Express for the first time, open the Start menu and click the Outlook Express icon (shown in the margin). Outlook Express hops onto the screen, ready to be set up to send and receive your e-mail, as shown in Figure 9-2.

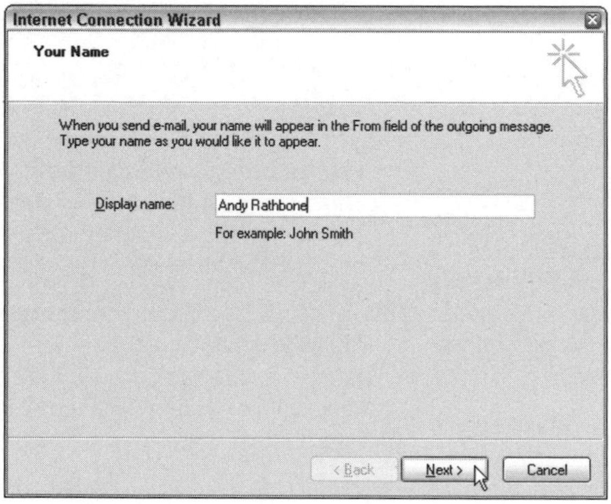

   Figure 9-2: When loaded for the first time, Outlook Express offers to set up your e-mail account.

   If the screen in Figure 9-2 doesn't appear automatically, open Outlook Express and choose Accounts from the Tools menu. Click the Add button and choose Mail to bring up the window in Figure 9-2, ready to add an e-mail account.

2. **Type in your name and click Next.**

   This name will appear in the From box of all your e-mail, so most people simply type in their own name, as shown in Figure 9-2. Names like *DragonSlayer* may come back to haunt you.

3. **Type in your e-mail address and click Next.**

   This is your user name, the @ sign, and your ISP, all information that your ISP must provide you with. For instance, if your user name is *jeff4265* and your ISP's name is *charternet.com,* then type **jeff4265@ charternet.com** into the E-Mail Address box.

   Adding a second e-mail address to Outlook Express? The procedure is the same: Type in the user name for that second account.

4. **Choose your server type and the names for your incoming and outgoing mail servers.**

   Here, you need to know what *type* of e-mail account the service uses. It's a weird word like POP3, IMAP, or HTTP. Most ISPs send you these handy settings and instructions through the post office. If you've lost them, visit your ISP's Web site or call your ISP's tech support folks and ask them for their mail server's *name* and *type.* Table 9-1 lists the information required by some common e-mail services.

Table 9-1 E-Mail Settings for Popular ISPs

Service	*E-Mail Type*	*Incoming Mail Server*	*Outgoing Mail Server*
America Online (AOL) (See the related sidebar for additional settings that AOL accounts need.)	IMAP	`imap.aol.com`	`smtp.aol.com`
Hotmail	HTTP	`http://services.msn.com/svcs/hotmail/httpmail.asp.`	Don't enter anything anything in this area.
Yahoo! (Only paid Yahoo! e-mail accounts can receive mail through Outlook Express.)	POP3	`pop.mail.yahoo`	`smtp.mail.yahoo`

5. **Type in your account name and password and click Next.**

   For your account name, enter the part of your e-mail address before the @ sign. Then type in the password for that account. If you want to log on automatically without entering your password each time, check the Remember Password box.

   (Check the Secure Password Authentication box *only* if your Internet provider requests it.)

Finishing up your AOL account in Outlook Express

Even after finishing Steps 1–6 to set up your AOL account in Outlook Express, your account won't work correctly until you jump through the following hoops:

1. **Choose Accounts from Outlook Express' Tools menu, select Accounts, and click the Mail tab.**
2. **Select the AOL account you created, choose Properties, and click the Servers tab.**
3. **Click the My Server Requires Authentication box and click Apply.**
4. **Click the Advanced tab.**
5. **In the Outgoing Mail (SMTP) box, change the number to 587 and click Apply.**
6. **Click the IMAP tab and click to remove the check from the Store Special Folders on IMAP Server box.**
7. **Click Apply, click OK, and click Close.**

If a message asks you to download folders from the mail server, click Yes.

6. **Click Finish.**

   That's it. You should be able to send and receive e-mail on Outlook Express.

- If the settings don't work or don't look right, they're easy to change. Choose Accounts from the Tools menu, click the Mail tab, and double-click the name of the account that needs tweaking. (This also lets you choose a more descriptive name for it.)
- Some ISPs let you create up to five different e-mail accounts. Feel free to create a "disposable" e-mail account to use when signing up for online offers or filling out forms. When it becomes plagued with spam, simply delete it and create a new one.
- Set up more than one account? Then make your most-used account your *default* account — the one Outlook Express chooses automatically as the From name when you click the Send button. To set your default account, choose Accounts from the Tools menu, click the Mail tab, and click your most-often used account. Finally, click the Set as Default button. (You can always change which account to use before sending a message.)

Composing and sending an e-mail

Ready to send your first e-mail? After you've set up Outlook Express with your e-mail account, follow these steps to compose your letter and drop it in the electronic mailbox, sending it through virtual space to the recipient's computer:

1. **Open Outlook Express and click the Create Mail icon from the program's menu.**

   If you don't see a Create Mail icon along the top (it looks like the one in the margin), click the File menu, select New, and choose Mail Message.

   A New Message window appears, as shown in Figure 9-3.

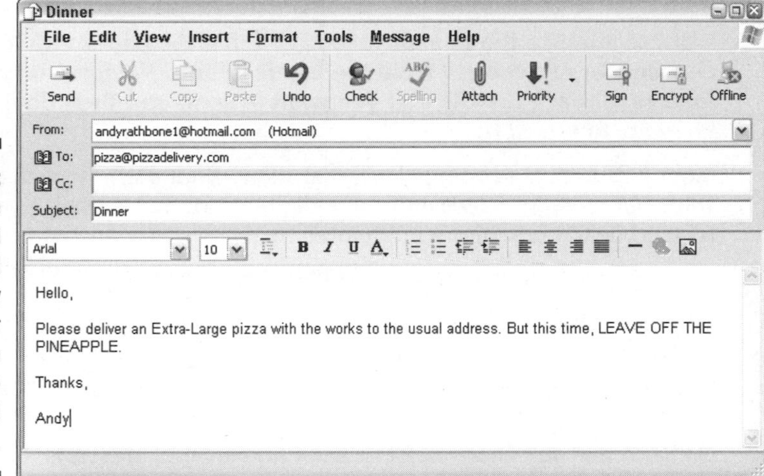

Figure 9-3: Click the Create Mail button, and a window appears for you to compose and send e-mail.

   If you've set up more than one account, described in the previous section, Outlook Express automatically addresses the mail with your default account. To send it from a different e-mail account, click the downward-pointing arrow in the From box and select the other account.

   To send a quick e-mail to somebody in your Address Book, just double-click his or her name. Outlook Express opens an e-mail already addressed to that person, saving you a step.

2. **Type your friend's e-mail address into the To box.**

   Type the person's e-mail address into the To box. Or, if you've e-mailed that person previously, click the word To next to where you type an address: A window appears, listing the names of people you've previously e-mailed. Click your friend's name and click the To button, shown in the margin.

   Sending or forwarding a message to several people? Select their names but click the Bcc button (shown in the margin) instead of the To button. That still sends the same message to them all but hides their e-mail addresses from each other, preserving their privacy.

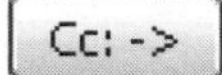

   To let *everybody* see each other's e-mail addresses, select their names and click the Cc button, shown in the margin. (Unless the recipients all know each other, this is considered bad etiquette.)

3. **Fill in the Subject box.**

   Although optional, the Subject line lets your friends know why you're bugging them. That lets them respond right away or file your mail in their "I'll respond when I get around to it" box.

4. **Type your message into the large box at the bottom of the window.**

   Type whatever you want and for as long as you want. There's very little limit on the size of a text file.

5. **Want to attach a file to your message? Click the paper clip icon (or choose File Attachment from the Insert menu). Navigate through the folders to reach the file that you want to send and then double-click its name to attach it.**

   Most ISPs balk at sending files larger than about 4MB, however, which rules out most MP3 files and some digital photos. I explain an easy way to send nearly any photo in Chapter 16.

6. **Click the Send button in the box's top-left corner.**

   Whoosh! Outlook Express dials your modem, if necessary, and whisks your message through the Internet pipelines to your friend's mailbox. Depending on the speed of the Internet connection, mail arrives anywhere within 15 seconds to five days, with a few minutes being the average.

   No Send button? Then click File and choose Send Message.

- Some people like those big buttons along the top of Outlook Express, as shown in Figure 9-3. If your big buttons are missing, and you want 'em back, right-click on a blank part of the Outlook Express menu — an inch to the right of the word Help will do the trick. Choose Toolbar, and the buttons appear. To get rid of 'em, right-click in the same place and choose Toolbar again to toggle them off.
- Not too good of a speler? Then before you send the message, click the Spelling button from the icons along the top. Or choose Spelling from the Tools menu. Or press your F7 key. Or grab a dictionary off the shelf. (Pressing F7 is quicker.) If it doesn't work, read the following warning.

- Microsoft pulled a dirty trick on the spell checker. Outlook Express borrows the spell checker that comes with Microsoft Word, Microsoft Excel, or Microsoft PowerPoint. If you don't have any of those programs, its spell checker won't work. (That's why the Spelling button is grayed out in Figure 9-3.)

Reading a received e-mail

If you keep Outlook Express running while you're connected to the Internet, you'll know when a new letter arrives. Your computer makes a breezy little sound to herald its arrival. You'll also spot a tiny Outlook Express icon in your desktop's bottom-right corner, right next to the clock. Plus, if more than one person uses your PC, the Welcome screen where you log on displays how many e-mails each person has received.

To check for any new mail when Outlook Express isn't running, load the program from the Start menu. When it loads, click the Send/Recv button (or click the Tools menu, choose Send and Receive, and then choose Send and Receive All). Outlook Express logs onto the Internet, sends any outgoing mail you have sitting around, and grabs any incoming mail to place in your Inbox.

Follow these steps to read the letters in your Inbox and either respond or file them away into one of Outlook Express' many folders:

1. **Open Outlook Express and look at your Inbox.**

   Depending on how Outlook Express is set up, you can do this several different ways. If you see an opening screen announcing that you have unread mail in your Inbox, click the words Unread Mail to start reading. Or, if you see folders along the left side of Outlook Express, click the word Inbox.

   Either way, Outlook Express shows you the messages in your Inbox, and they look something like Figure 9-4. Each subject is listed, one by one, with the newest one at the bottom.

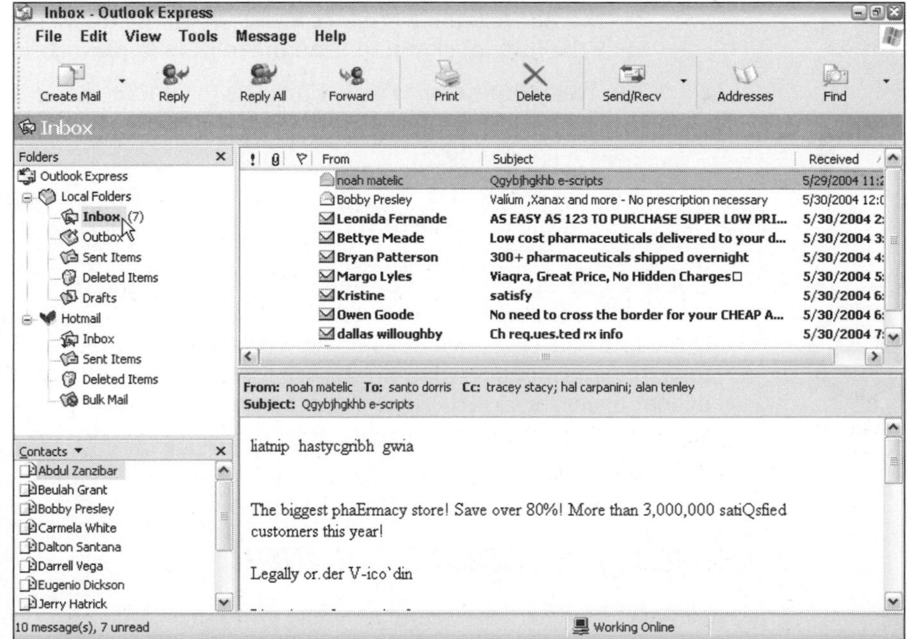

Figure 9-4: Click the Inbox in Outlook Express to see your newly received messages.

Want your newest e-mails to appear at the list's *top?* Then click the word Received at the top of the Received column. Outlook Express resorts everything but now places your newest message at the top. (You can sort mail by name or subject by clicking those column headers, too.)

2. **Click any message's subject to read it.**

   The message's contents then shows in the bottom portion of the screen, as shown in Figure 9-5, ready for you to read. Or, to see the entire message in its own window, double-click it.

3. **From here, Outlook Express leaves you with several options, each described in the following list:**

   - **You can do nothing.** The message simply sets up camp in your Inbox folder until you delete it.

   - **You can respond to the message.** Click the Reply icon along the top of Outlook Express (or choose Reply to Sender from the Message menu), and a new window appears, ready for you to type your response. The window is just like the one that appears when you first compose a message but with a handy difference: This window is preaddressed with the recipient's name and the subject.
   - **You can file the message.** Right-click on the message and choose either Copy to Folder or Move to Folder and then select the desired folder from the pop-up menu. Or drag and drop the message to the desired folder along the left side of your screen. (Don't see the folders there? Click the word Inbox and, when the folders drop down, click the little push pin to keep the folders in place.)
   - **You can print the message.** Click the Print icon along the menu's top, and Outlook Express shoots your message to the printer to make a paper copy.
   - **You can delete the message.** Click the Delete button along the top to send the message to your Deleted items folder.

- Outlook Express can be confusing when you drag and drop a message: As you drag the message over to the folders, the little envelope icon turns into a circle with a diagonal line through it. Don't fret. That menacing circle disappears when the mouse rests over a folder that's able to accept a message.
- To organize your incoming messages, right-click on your Inbox and choose New Folder to create another folder inside. Create as many folders as you need to categorize your spam offers.

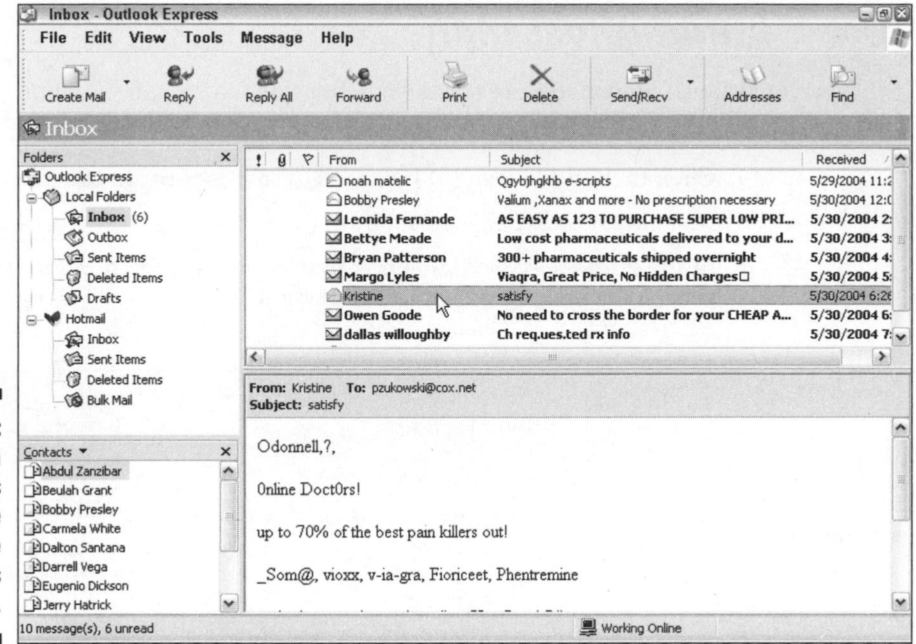

Figure 9-5: Click a message's subject line to see the message's contents.

- When you see a little red *X* in place of a picture or photo on your e-mail, that means Outlook Express is blocking it. It'll appear if you edit, forward, or reply to the message. Or, to make Outlook Express stop blocking it, choose Options from the Tools menu, click the Security Tab, and remove the check mark from the Block Images and Other External Content in HTML E-Mail box.

- If you ever receive a message with an attached file from a friend, *don't open it.* E-mail your friend and ask whether he or she *really* sent it. Evil people have written programs that can mimic other people's e-mail addresses to spread virus and worm programs into other computers. If the worm infects your computer, it sneakily sends copies of itself to everybody in your Address Book.

- To prevent you from opening a virus, Outlook Express refuses to let you open almost *any* attached file. If Outlook Express won't let you open a file you're expecting from a friend, turn off that protection: Choose Options from the Tools menu, click the Security tab, and click to remove the check mark from the Do Not Allow Attachments to Be Saved or Opened That Could Potentially Be a Virus box.

Finding lost mail

Outlook Express retrieves e-mail much faster than a pair of hands. To locate that missing piece of mail anywhere in any folder, follow these steps:

1. **Click the Find button's downward arrow (shown in the margin).**

   No Find button? Choose Find from the Edit menu and select Message.

2. **In the Find Message dialog box that appears, shown in Figure 9-6, search for messages containing certain items.**

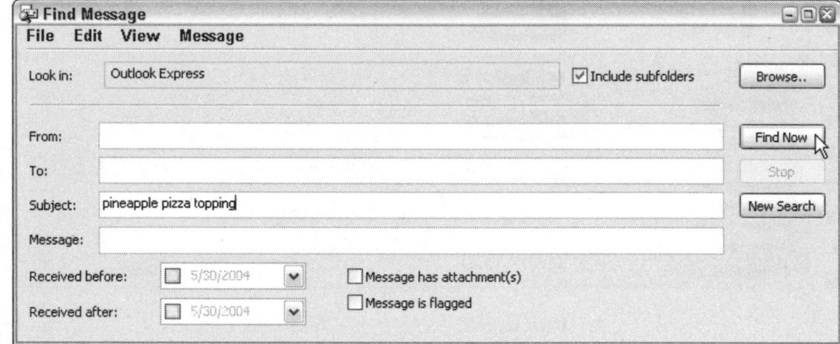

Figure 9-6: Search for a missing message.

   Here are your options:

   - **From:** In here, type the name of somebody who's sent you mail to see all the messages that person has sent you.
   - **To:** Type a person's name here, and Outlook Express shows you every message you've sent to him or her.
   - **Subject:** Type a word that appeared in an e-mail's subject line to locate it.
   - **Message:** Type any word that you *know* appears in the message.

   Usually filling out one box catches your message. Try just entering a few letters of a person's e-mail address or a single word that appeared in the message. If a search turns up too many items, add more and more words to limit the number of matches.

3. **Click Find Now when you're done filling out the boxes.**

Using an Address Book

Just as every office desk needs a business card holder, Outlook Express needs its Address Book (shown in Figure 9-7) to store everybody's contact information. Click the Address Book button in Outlook Express to open it. (You can also click the Start menu, choose All Programs, and open it from the Accessories area.)

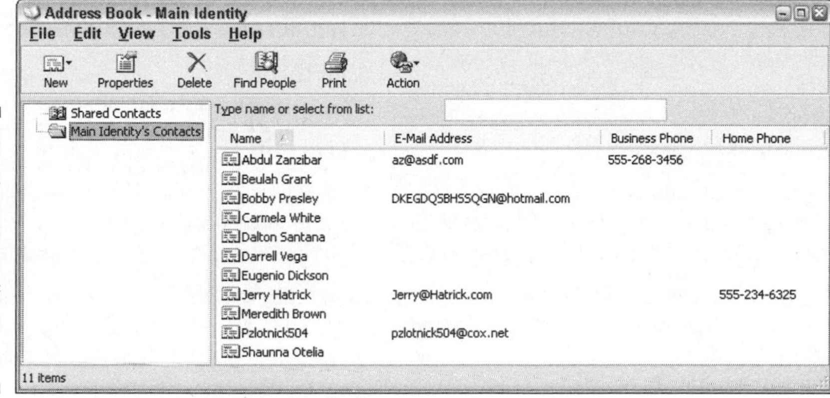

Figure 9-7: The Outlook Express Address Book keeps track of everybody you contact.

You can start beefing up your Address Book several ways:

- **Add contacts manually.** When somebody hands you a business card, you must enter the information by hand: Choose New from the File menu and choose Contact. Start filling out all the boxes on every tab to create a detailed dossier; click OK when you're through.
- **Make Outlook Express do it automatically.** When you respond to an e-mail, Outlook Express will automatically add that person and e-mail address to your Address Book if you do the following: Choose Options from the Tools menu, click the Send tab, and select the Automatically Put People I Reply to in My Address Book check box.
- **Import an old Address Book.** To import an Address Book file from another computer, click the File button and choose Import. Select the Address Book option to import an Address Book from another computer's Outlook Express; select Other Address Book to import a list of addresses created by another program.

Here are some other tasks you might want to know how to do:

- To send a quick message to somebody in the Address Book, double-click that person's name. The Address Book calls up a handy, preaddressed New Message window, ready for you to type your message and click Send.
- I explain how to print an Address Book into handy information sheets in Chapter 7.

Keeping Outlook Express secure, but convenient

Outlook Express automatically turns on many security measures. To see what security switches it has flipped (and to turn them off if they annoy you), choose Options from Outlook Express' Tools menu and click the Security tab.

Virus Protection: Although some of these measures protect you from viruses, they do that by filtering out nearly *everything.* Here's the rundown:

- **Internet Explorer Security Zone:** Ignore this unless you've deliberately set *restricted* security zones in Internet Explorer, as covered in Chapter 10.
- **Warn Me When Other Applications Try to Send Mail as Me:** Leave this on because it's an inoffensive way to keep worms from spreading.
- **Do Not Allow Attachments to Be Saved or Opened That Could Potentially Be a Virus:** Because nearly *any* file can contain a virus these days, this effectively stops you from opening most attachments. Uncheck this box to open your attachments again.

Download Images: Outlook Express simply stops showing any pictures in your e-mail. Remove the check to view them again.

Secure Mail: This is much too complicated to worry about.

- To back up an Address Book, choose Export from the File menu and choose Address Book. Click the Text File (Comma Separated Values) option to create something nearly any program can read. Choose the Microsoft Exchange Personal Address Book option to move your Address Book to another computer using Outlook Express.

Getting rid of all your spam

Unfortunately, you can't get rid of spam. Believe it or not, some people still reply and buy things from spam messages, making them profitable enough for spammers to continue. But although you can't stop spam, you can weed out much of it by following these rules:

- Give your e-mail address only to close friends and relatives. Don't give it to strangers or post it on Web sites.
- Every few months, create a new, *disposable* e-mail account to use when signing up for online offers, filling out online forms, or carrying out any short-term correspondence. If that address becomes plagued with spam, simply delete it and create a new one.
- Never post your real e-mail address in an Internet's chat forum, newsgroup, or other public conversation area. And never respond to a spammer, even if it's to click the unsubscribe link. That merely adds you to the spammer's list of confirmed e-mail addresses.

- See if your ISP offers built-in spam filtering. The filters work so well that many spammers now try to evade the filters by using nonsensical words. If they do make it through, the nonsense in the subject gives it away as being spam.
- If you're seeing pop-up messages titled Messenger Service, head to Chapter 10. Turning on your firewall keeps those messages from entering. (Be sure you've installed Windows XP's service packs, too, as covered in Chapter 1.)
- Although Outlook Express offers some simple filtering rules in its Tools menu, spammers figured out how to fool them long ago. They're no longer handy for filtering spam, but they work fine for routing e-mail from certain people to certain folders.

Bugging Friends with Windows Messenger

When you want to talk with distant friends, you usually call them on the phone and start speaking. A phone conversation is fast, reliable, and efficient. So why do so many people use Windows Messenger, a program that lets people type little messages back and forth to each other? Messenger fans cite several reasons:

- **It's free.** Built in to Windows XP, Windows Messenger lets you communicate with other Windows Messengers users worldwide, with no long distance charges.
- **It's polite.** As Windows Messenger sits in your taskbar, it lists your friends' names and whether they're currently available for conversations. That eliminates playing phone tag and keeps you from bothering people who are busy.
- **It's convenient.** Speaking on the phone requires all your attention. Windows Messenger lets you keep working in the background, simultaneously holding multiple conversations while shuffling papers.
- **It's useful.** In addition to exchanging text messages, users can send files and photos. Windows Messenger can take advantage of attached cameras and microphones to hold videoconferences with your friends.

Windows Messenger is far from problem-free, however. Its far-reaching features make it somewhat complicated to figure out for the first time. And although several companies (Yahoo! and AOL, for instance) offer instant messaging software, they're not always compatible: Windows Messenger can't send messages to AOL's Instant Messenger, for instance.

Also, because people can swap files as easily as banter, instant messaging software provides yet another roadway for traveling viruses. Many corporations ban them at work, fearing that employees are either revealing trade secrets or talking about last night's *Sopranos* episode. Finally, instant message conversations aren't as secure as e-mail.

- Windows Messenger and MSN Messenger are two different programs that do pretty much the same thing. Both Messenger programs can talk to each other. However, it's best to install one or the other, but not both. Uninstall MSN Messenger before using Windows Messenger, for instance.
- Microsoft constantly releases new versions of Windows Messenger. To find out which version you're using, choose About from the program's Help menu. Compare that version number with the latest one available from Microsoft by using Windows Update, and download the newer one if necessary.

Getting started with a .NET Passport

To start flinging messages to people around the world, sign up for what Microsoft dubs a *.NET Passport.* The easiest way is to sign up for a free Hotmail account at `www.hotmail.com`. Fill out the short questionnaire, and Microsoft assigns you a Hotmail e-mail address. Log in to Windows Messenger using that address, and you're set.

It's completely ethical to lie when filling out Microsoft's .NET Passport questionnaire. Your personal information is none of Microsoft's business. Let Microsoft fill its databases from credit card companies, like everybody else does.

Windows Messenger doesn't work!

Can't log on? First, make sure your Hotmail account hasn't expired. (Hotmail accounts disappear if you haven't used them ten days after signing up or if you ignore them for 60 consecutive days.) Visit Hotmail's Web site (`www.hotmail.com`) and see if your account's still valid. Also, visit the .NET Passport site (`www.passport.com`) to see if your passport's still valid.

If you can send messages but not files, your computer's firewall might be causing trouble. (Windows XP's firewall doesn't interfere with Windows Messenger, but some third-party firewalls might.)

If you *can* log on, make sure that Microsoft's computer hasn't crashed: Choose .NET Service Status from Windows Messenger's Help menu to see if Microsoft's network is currently running.

Signing on to Messenger and adding friends

After you have a Hotmail account, you're ready to log on. Windows Messenger almost always sits quietly in your taskbar, next to your clock. (It also tends to pop into action whenever you open Outlook Express.) Can't find it? Then click the Start button, choose All Programs, and click the Windows Messenger icon, shown in the margin, to bring it to life. The program leaps onto the screen, as shown in Figure 9-8.

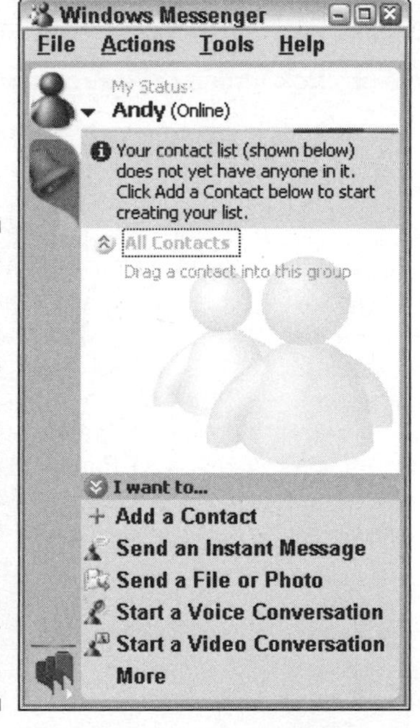

Figure 9-8: When you first open Windows Messenger, you need to start adding the names of friends with Windows Messenger accounts.

When you sign on for the first time, however, there's not much to do. Just as you need a friend's e-mail address in order to send that person an e-mail, you need a friend's Windows Messenger address before you can send him or her an instant message. Ask your friends for their Messenger addresses and then add them as contacts by following these steps:

1. **Click Add a Contact from Windows Messenger.**

   Or you can choose Add a Contact from the Tools menu.

2. **Choose to add the contact by e-mail address or sign-in name and then click Next.**

   Searching by a known e-mail address or sign-in name always works better than searching by name and geographic location. You can also search Microsoft's Web site (`members.msn.com`) for strangers to chat with. (Skip the first few pages to weed out the porn.)

3. **Type your friend's e-mail address and click Next.**

   Make sure you're typing in your friend's Windows Messenger e-mail address, which is often different than his or her e-mail address.

   If you entered the person's correct e-mail address, Microsoft locates your friend and adds his or her name to your Contact list so you can start sending that person messages.

4. **Click Next to add more contacts or click Finish if you're through.**

   Windows Messenger updates itself to display your newly added contacts, as shown in Figure 9-9.

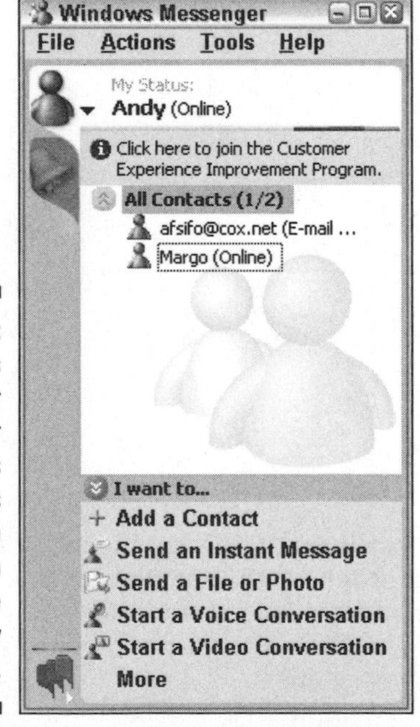

Figure 9-9: Windows Messenger lists your friends as Contacts and lets you see which ones are currently logged on.

- Notice how Figure 9-9 lists Margo as Online? That means Margo is currently logged on to her computer, ready to receive messages.

- Don't want to be disturbed? Then tell Windows Messenger to display your status as unavailable by clicking your name and choosing any of the following options from the drop-down list: Online, Busy, Be Right Back, Away, On the Phone, Out to Lunch, or Appear Offline.
- You can make Windows Messenger automatically list your status as Busy when you begin working. Choose Options from the Tools menu and click the Preferences tab. Then make sure a check mark appears in the Block Alerts and Set Status to "Busy" When Running Full-Screen Programs box.
- Whenever one of your contacts signs in to Windows Messenger, a small window known as an *alert* appears in the bottom-right corner of your screen to let you know they've just fired up Windows Messenger.

Sending and receiving an instant message

If a friend's online, you can contact that person in a variety of ways. Right-click on any contact's name to see your options, shown in Figure 9-10.

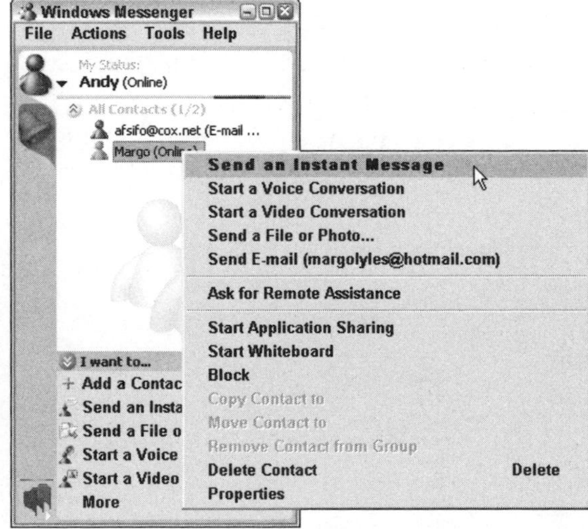

Figure 9-10: Right-click on any contact's name to see how you can contact that person.

Choose Send an Instant Message, for instance, to make a window appear on your friend's screen and display your message. If your computer has a microphone and video camera, you can hold a voice or video conversation. Windows Messenger lets you swap files, too.

Sending instant messages is probably the most foolproof way to communicate, when you follow these steps:

1. **Right-click on your friend's name in Windows Messenger and choose Send an Instant Message.**
2. **Type your message and click the Send button, as shown in Figure 9-11.**

   Your words instantly appear on your friend's Windows Messenger.

   When your friend responds, those words appear in your Windows Messenger window, as shown in Figure 9-12.

- To add little smiley faces and other symbols (known as *emoticons*), click the little smiley face. A menu drops down, listing all the available symbols. Click the one you want, and it appears in your message.
- As Microsoft says, never give out your password or credit card number in an instant message conversation. Instant messages aren't nearly as secure as e-mail.
- After you've started a conversation, it's easy to send or receive a file. Click Send a File or Photo and choose the file or photo from the window that appears. Your friend sees a message asking whether he or she wants the file. If your friend clicks Yes, the file wends its way to his or her computer. If your friend declines to download the file, Windows Messenger tells you that.
- When somebody sends you a file or photo, you'll find it in the My Received Files folder inside your My Documents folder.

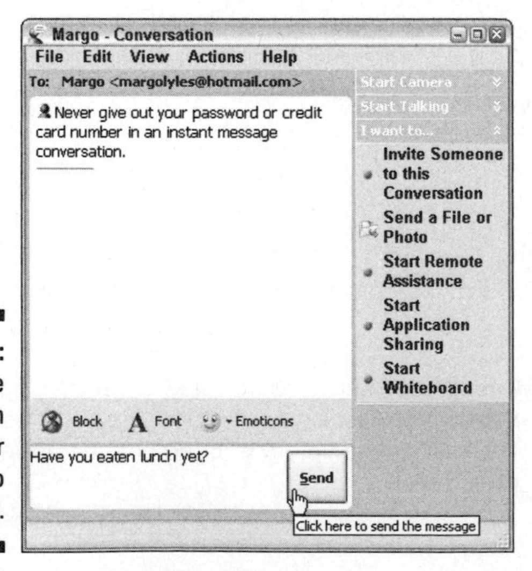

Figure 9-11: Click the Send button to send your message to your friend.

Figure 9-12: Your polite friend responds to your message.

Uninstalling Windows Messenger

Some folks love instant messaging programs like Windows Messenger. They love to be interrupted, and they like to bug their friends. Other folks hate them, and they loathe seeing Windows Messenger's dastardly little icon hogging space next to their computer's system clock.

If your computer's service packs are installed, as described in Chapter 1, removing Windows Messenger is a cinch:

1. **Open the Control Panel from the Start menu.**
2. **Choose Add or Remove Programs.**
3. **Select Add/Remove Windows Components.**
4. **Click to remove the check mark next to Windows Messenger.**
5. **Click the Next button, click the Finish button, and then restart your computer.**

Sometimes simply running Outlook Express revives Windows Messenger from the dead. To keep Windows Messenger from reappearing, choose Options from the Outlook Express' Tools menu and click the General tab. Then click to remove the check mark from the Automatically Log On to Windows Messenger box.

Chapter 10

Safe Computing

In This Chapter

- Assessing your safety with the Security Center
- Changing the Windows Firewall settings
- Automating Windows Update
- Using a virus checker
- Setting Internet Explorer's security zones
- Managing cookies
- Preserving your privacy

Like driving a car, working with Windows is reasonably safe, as long as you steer clear of the wrong neighborhoods, obey traffic signals, and don't steer with your feet while you stick your head out the sunroof.

But in the world of Windows and the Internet, there's no easy way to recognize a bad neighborhood, spot the traffic signals, or even distinguish between your feet, the steering wheel, and the sunroof. Things that look totally innocent — a friend's e-mail or something on the Internet — may be a virus or prank that sneakily rearranges everything on your dashboard or causes a crash.

This chapter helps you recognize the bad streets in Windows' virtual neighborhoods and explains the steps you can take to protect yourself from harm and minimize any damage.

Assessing Your Safety in XP's Security Center

Before reading any further, take a minute to check your safety with Windows XP's new Security Center, installed by Service Pack 2 (described in Chapter 1). Although the Security Center more closely resembles a large panel of On switches than a command post, it lists Windows XP's three main defenses, tells you if they're activated, and lets you flip their On switches, if necessary.

Shown in Figure 10-1, the Security Center shows whether you've turned on Windows Firewall, Microsoft's Automatic Updates feature, and a virus checker. The computer shown in Figure 10-1 passes the firewall test. But it cautions that Windows Update isn't updating automatically, and the virus detector isn't installed or working.

All three of these defenses should be up and running for maximum safety because each protects you against different things.

Whenever the Security Center notices problems like these, it alerts you by placing a red icon (shown in the margin) near your taskbar's clock.

To make sure your computer's three big cannons are loaded and pointing in the right direction, open the Security Center and ogle the settings:

1. **Open the Start menu's Control Panel and choose Security Center.**

   The Security Center hops into action, as shown in Figure 10-1, and displays your computer's current security status.

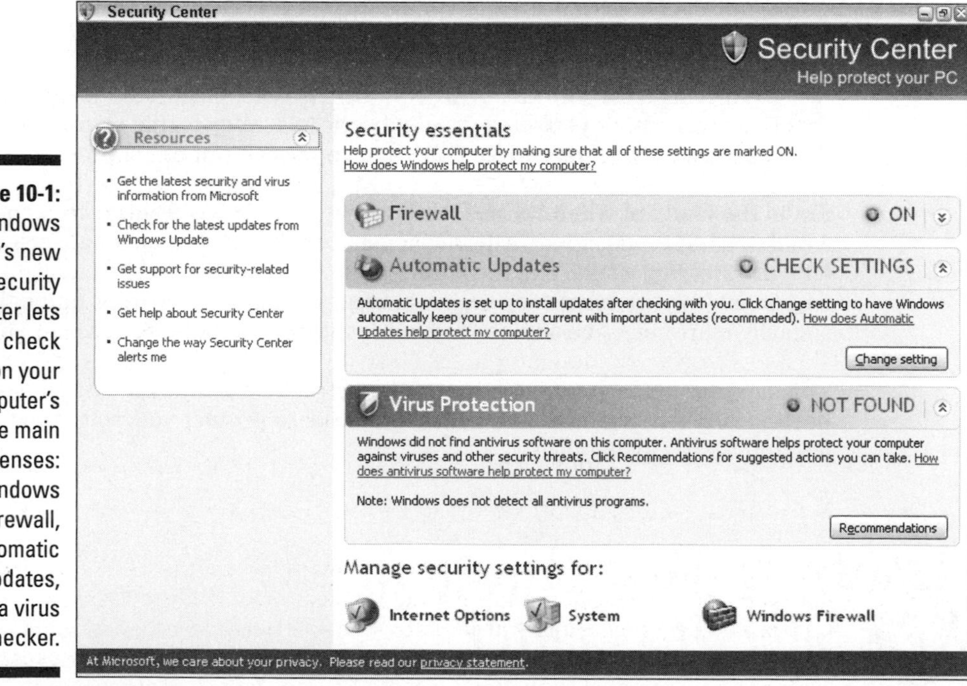

Figure 10-1: Windows XP's new Security Center lets you check on your computer's three main defenses: Windows Firewall, Automatic Updates, and a virus checker.

2. **Turn on the firewall, if necessary.**

   Windows XP's updated, more powerful firewall monitors every connection arriving at your PC. When the firewall notices an unrequested connection trying to enter, it blocks it, stopping potential intruders.

   If the Security Center lists your firewall as being turned off, click the Recommendations button, choose Enable Now, and click OK to turn it on. (Service Pack 2 turns on the firewall by default; the old firewall made you turn it on manually.)

3. **Turn on Automatic Updates, if necessary.**

   When turned on, Windows Update automatically checks in with Microsoft through the Internet, downloads any new safety patches, and installs them, all for free, and all without any effort on your part.

   If the Security Center doesn't show Automatic Updates as being turned on, simply click the Change Setting button to turn it on.

4. **Install virus protection, if necessary.**

   Although Microsoft provides a free firewall and free, automatic patches for your computer, it *doesn't* provide a built-in virus checker. Nearly every computer and office supply store sells virus-checking software, and you can also buy it online.

   After you install the virus checker, the Security Center no longer warns you about it. (If you already have a virus checker installed, make sure it has a valid *subscription* for downloading new virus definitions.)

By following the four preceding steps, your computer will be much safer than under any other version of Microsoft Windows.

The Security Center's three sections only let you flip an On switch. For more detailed diddling, click any of the three icons along the bottom (each one receives its own section later in this chapter):

- Choose the System icon to tweak Windows Update.
- Choose the Windows Firewall icon to adjust the flames of your firewall.
- Choose Internet Options to adjust Internet Explorer's security features.

In addition to using the Security Center, you might want to keep on top of the latest security news. Microsoft lists virus alerts, security bulletins, and other information on the security area of its Web site (`www.microsoft.com/security`). There, you can find out about the latest worms and viruses, as well as some removal tools to fix infected computers (if they're able to reach the Internet).

Changing the firewall settings

Just about everybody has dropped his or her fork to pick up the phone, only to hear a recorded sales pitch. Telemarketers run programs that sequentially dial phone numbers until somebody answers. Computer hackers run similar programs that automatically try to break into every computer that's currently connected to the Internet.

Broadband Internet users are especially vulnerable because their computers are constantly connected to the Internet. That increases the chances that hackers will locate them and try to exploit any available vulnerabilities.

That's where Windows Firewall comes in. The firewall sits between your computer and the Internet, acting as an intelligent doorman. If something tries to connect and you or one of your programs didn't request it, the firewall stops the connection.

Occasionally, however, you'll *want* another computer to interact with your computer over the Internet. You might be playing a multiplayer game, for instance, or using a file-sharing program. To stop the firewall from blocking those programs, add their names to the firewall's exceptions list by following these steps:

1. **Choose Control Panel from the Start menu and click the Security Center icon.**
2. **Click the Windows Firewall icon at the bottom of the Security Center.**
3. **Click the Exceptions tab.**

   Shown in Figure 10-2, Windows Firewall lists every program currently allowed to communicate through its firewall. (Windows XP adds some of its programs automatically, so don't be surprised to see some already listed.)

4. **Click the Add Program button, click Browse to locate and select the program, and click OK.**

   Almost all programs live in the Program Files folder on your C drive; the program's name bears the same icon you see on its Start menu entry.

   The firewall adds your selected program to its exceptions list and begins allowing other computers to connect to it.

In Step 4, make sure a check mark appears in the Display a Notification When Windows Firewall Blocks a Program box, as shown in Figure 10-2. When a program doesn't work correctly, that message lets you know that the firewall may be the culprit. Try adding the program to the exceptions list to see if it begins working.

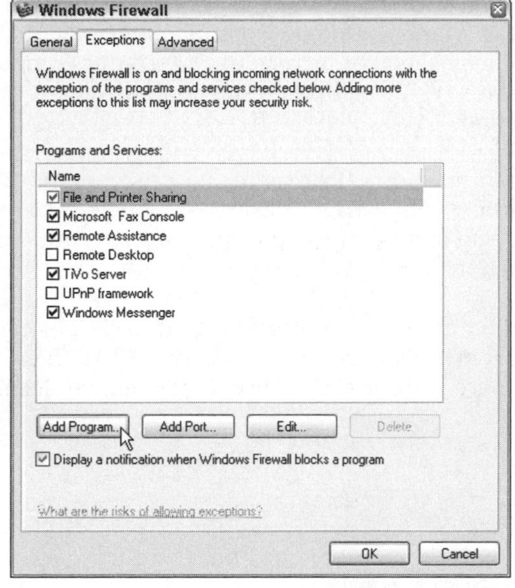

Figure 10-2: If the firewall blocks a program unnecessarily, add the program to the exceptions list.

- Don't add programs to the exceptions list unless you're *sure* the firewall is the problem. Each time you add a program to the list, you're leaving your computer slightly more vulnerable.

- Using a laptop and connecting wirelessly to the Internet in a coffee shop, hotel, or other public place? Click the General tab in Step 3 and choose Don't Allow Exceptions. That temporarily removes *all* your programs from the exceptions list, providing the most security when computing in a public, wireless environment.

- If you think you've messed up the firewall's settings, it's easy to revert to its original settings. Click the Advanced tab in Step 3 and click the Restore Defaults button. Click the OK button, and the firewall removes every change you've made, letting you start from scratch.

Automating Windows Update

Whenever somebody figures out a way to break into Windows, Microsoft releases yet another patch to keep Windows users safe. Unfortunately, the bad folks find holes in Windows as quickly as Microsoft can patch them. The result? Microsoft ends up releasing a river of patches.

In fact, the flow became so strong that many users couldn't keep up. Microsoft's solution is to make Windows Update work *automatically:* Whenever you go online, whether to check e-mail or browse the Web, your computer automatically visits Microsoft's Windows Update site and downloads any new patches in the background.

When your computer's through downloading the new patches, it installs them at 3 a.m. to avoid disturbing your work. Occasionally, you need to restart your computer the next morning to make the patch start working; other times you don't even notice the action taking place.

To make sure your computer's set for Automatic Updates, right-click on My Computer from the Start menu and choose Properties. Click the Automatic Updates tab and make sure you select Automatic (Recommended), as shown in Figure 10-3.

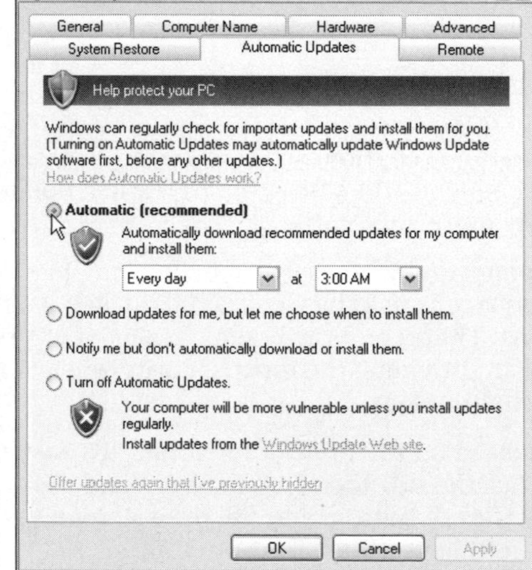

Figure 10-3: Make sure you choose Automatic for Windows Updates.

If you use your computer at 3 a.m. (or an automated backup takes place at that time), the Automatic Updates area in Figure 10-3 lets you change the installation's date or time.

Avoiding viruses

When it comes to viruses, *everything* is suspect. Viruses travel not only in e-mail and programs but also in screen savers, themes, toolbars, and other Windows *add-ons.* Follow these rules to reduce your risk of infection:

- When shopping for a virus program, look for one that automatically scans any program you try to run. If you don't have one, open the Control Panel's Security Center icon and click the Virus Protection section's Recommendations button for free trial offers.
- Tell your virus-checker program to scan everything you download as well as anything that comes in the mail or arrives through a messaging program.
- Only open attachments that you're expecting. If you receive something unexpected from a friend, e-mail or phone to see if he or she *really* sent you something.
- Don't run two virus checkers simultaneously because they often quarrel. If you want to test a different program, first uninstall your existing one with the Control Panel's Add or Remove Programs icon.
- Buying a virus checker isn't enough; you must also buy a subscription to keep it updated. New viruses appear every day, and without the latest virus definitions, virus checkers catch only the older viruses, not the newly discovered ones. (And the newest viruses spread most quickly, causing the most damage.)

If you think you have a virus and you don't have an antivirus program, unplug your modem (or unplug it from the telephone line) before heading to the store and buying an antivirus program. Install and run the antivirus program before connecting your computer back to the Internet. That stops your computer from infecting others before you're able disinfect it.

Staying Safe on the Internet

The Internet is no longer safe. Some people design Web sites specifically to exploit the latest Windows vulnerabilities — the ones Microsoft hasn't yet had time to patch. Installing Service Pack 2 (covered in Chapter 1) provides a good level of protection. This section explains some of the service pack's new features as well as other safe travel tips when navigating the Internet.

Avoiding evil add-ons and hijackers in Internet Explorer

Microsoft designed Internet Explorer to let programmers add extra features through *add-ons.* By installing an add-on program — toolbars, stock tickers, and program launchers, for instance — users could wring a little more work out of Internet Explorer. Similarly, many sites use ActiveX — a fancy word for little programs that add animation and other flashy tricks to a Web site.

Setting Internet Explorer's security zones

Chances are, you don't need to fiddle with Internet Explorer's security zones. They come preset to offer the most protection with the least amount of effort. But if you're curious about Internet Explorer's zones, choose Internet Options from the Tools menu and click the Security tab.

Internet Explorer offers four security zones, each offering different levels of protection. When you add different Web sites to different zones, Internet Explorer treats the sites differently, placing restrictions on some and lifting restrictions for others. Here's the rundown:

- **Internet:** Unless you play with Internet Explorer's zones, Internet Explorer treats every Web site as if it were in this zone. This zone offers medium security, which works very well for most needs.
- **Local Intranet:** This zone is intended for Web sites running on an internal network. (Home users rarely have to deal with these because they're mostly found in corporations and large businesses.) Because internal Web sites are created in-house, this zone removes some restrictions, letting you do more things.
- **Trusted Sites:** Putting sites in here means you trust them *completely.* (I don't trust any Web site completely.)
- **Restricted Sites:** If you don't trust a site at all, place it in here. Internet Explorer lets you visit it but not download from it or use any of its plug-ins. I used to place a few sites in here to strip their pop-up ads, but Internet Explorer's built-in pop-up blocker now eliminates the need.

Outlook Express respects the settings you've used for these zones. Normally, Outlook Express treats all incoming e-mail as if it were a Web site in the Restricted zone. (Many e-mails now come formatted as Web pages.) To change the zone that Outlook Express uses, choose Options from its Tools menu and choose the Security tab. There, you can choose the Internet zone or the safer Restricted zone.

Unfortunately, dastardly programmers began creating add-ons and ActiveX programs that *harm* users. Some of these can spy on your activities, bombard your screen with additional ads, redirect your home page to another site, or make your modem dial long-distance numbers to porn sites. Worst yet, some renegade add-ons can install themselves as soon as you visit a Web site — without asking your permission.

For instance, some sites send a barrage of pop-up windows, like the ones shown in Figure 10-4, to Internet Explorer. As you struggle to close them all, you may accidentally click an OK button, allowing the site to install its evil add-on.

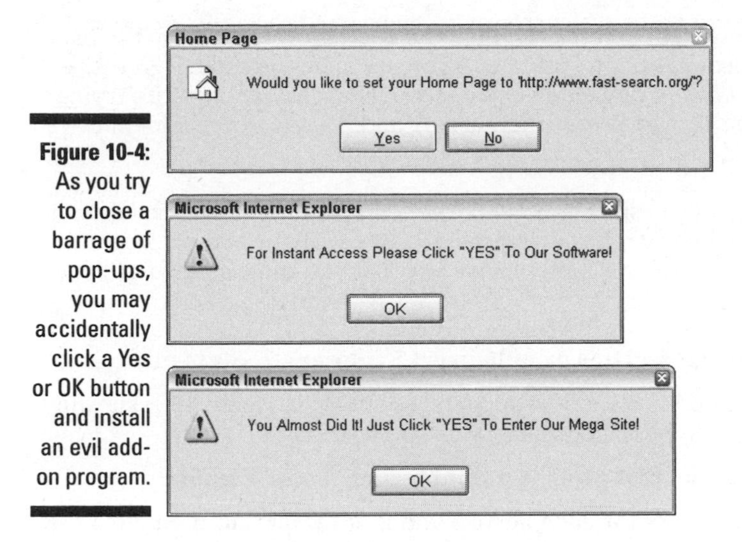

Figure 10-4: As you try to close a barrage of pop-ups, you may accidentally click a Yes or OK button and install an evil add-on program.

Windows XP's Service Pack 2 packs some new guns to combat these trouble-makers. First, if a site tries to sneak a program onto your computer, Internet Explorer quickly blocks it, sending a warning (shown in Figure 10-5) across the top of Internet Explorer's screen. Clicking the warning reveals your options, shown in Figure 10-6.

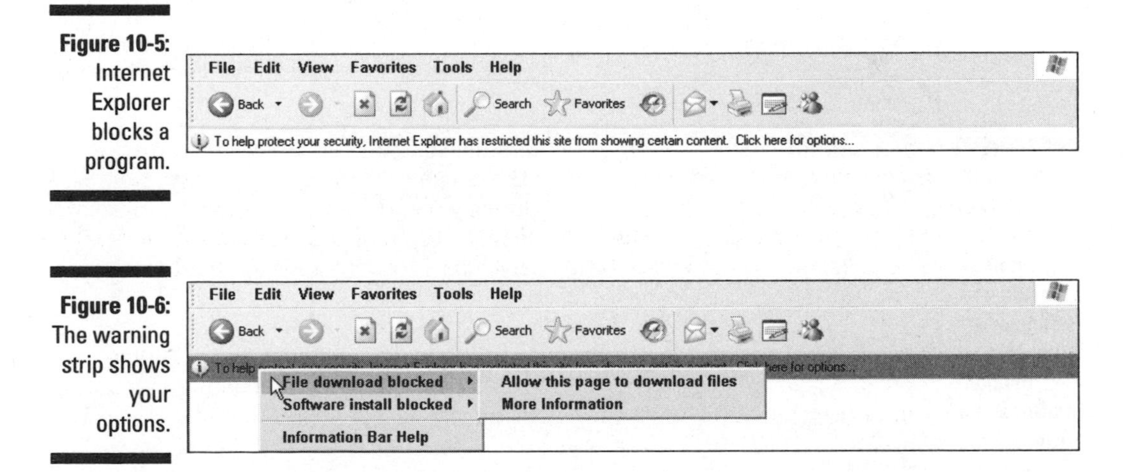

Figure 10-5: Internet Explorer blocks a program.

Figure 10-6: The warning strip shows your options.

Unfortunately, Internet Explorer can't tell the good downloads from the bad, leaving the burden of proof to you. But if you see a message like Figure 10-5 appear and you *haven't* requested a download, chances are the site's trying to harm you: Don't try to thwart the warning and download the add-on or ActiveX program.

If a bad add-on creeps in somehow, you're not completely out of luck. Internet Explorer's Add-on Manager lets you disable it. To see all the add-on programs installed in Internet Explorer (and remove any that you know are bad), follow these steps:

1. **Choose Manage Add-ons from Internet Explorer's Tools menu.**

   The Manage Add-ons window appears, as shown in Figure 10-7, showing all add-ons used by the currently viewed page.

2. **Click the Add-on that gives you trouble and choose Disable.**

3. **Repeat the process for each add-on you don't want and then click the OK button.**

   You probably need to restart Internet Explorer for the change to take effect.

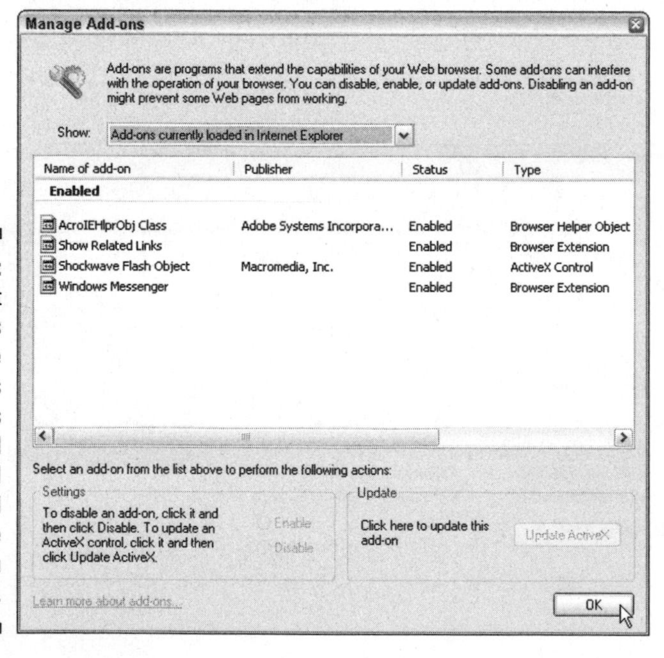

Figure 10-7: Internet Explorer's Manage Add-ons window lets you see all installed add-ons and remove the ones you don't like.

Avoiding and removing spyware and parasites

Spyware and parasites are loosely defined terms for programs that latch onto Internet Explorer without your knowledge. The sneakiest programs may try to change your home page, dial toll numbers with your modem, and do tricky things to keep you from removing them. Many spy on your Web activity, sneaking your surfing habits back to the spyware program's publisher. Most spyware programs admit to being spies — usually on the 43rd page of the 44-page agreement you're supposed to read before installing the program.

With Service Pack 2, Internet Explorer can now stop some spyware from installing itself automatically, but it can't stop programs that you install yourself. (And lots of spyware piggybacks on software that's marketed for a different use.) Virus checkers don't consider spyware to be a virus, so they don't spot it either.

Several anti-spyware programs can scan your computer for spyware, carefully snipping out any pieces that they find. Some of these programs are free in the hopes you'll buy the more full-featured version later. Ad-Aware (`www.lavasoftusa.com`) and Spybot Search & Destroy (`www.safer-networking.org`) are two of the most popular programs.

Not all add-ons are bad. Many good ones let you play movies, hear sounds, or view special content on a Web site. Don't delete an add-on simply because it's listed in the Add-on Manager.

- On the rare instance that disabling an add-on prevents a page from loading, click that add-on's name in Step 2 of the preceding steps and click the Enable button to return it to working order.
- Although Internet Explorer's Add-on Manager disables add-ons fairly easily, it's quite difficult to *remove* them entirely. Look for the add-on's name in your Control Panel's Add or Remove Programs area. If it's listed, you can remove it just like any other program.

- The Manage Add-ons window opens to let you see *currently* loaded add-ons — the ones loaded for the page you're currently viewing. To see add-ons that Internet Explorer has used for other, previously viewed sites, choose the Add-ons That Have Been Loaded in Internet Explorer option from the Show drop-down list at the top of Figure 10-7.

- If you enjoy a particular add-on, but it's not working correctly, the Manage Add-ons window can still help. Locate the add-on in Step 2 and look to see if it's an ActiveX Control, listed in the Type column. If so, click the add-on's name and click the Update ActiveX button to bring it up-to-date.

- How the heck do you tell the good add-ons from the bad? Unfortunately, there's no sure way of telling, although the name listed under Publisher provides one clue. The best way is to avoid being hijacked in the first place, mainly by not installing things Internet Explorer has tried to block.

- When a renegade site starts throwing around pop-ups or opening up new windows, leading to an out-of-control situation, right-click on Internet Explorer from your taskbar and choose Close Group. Because the taskbar *stacks* several open windows onto the single Internet Explorer entry, closing the group is a quick and convenient way to close *all* instances of Internet Explorer.
- Make sure Internet Explorer's defenses are up: Choose Pop-up Blocker from its Tools menu and make sure the Pop-up Blocker isn't listed as turned off. If it is, choose Turn On Pop-up Blocker.

Stopping pop-up ads

Hurrah! After a decade, Microsoft finally added a pop-up blocker to Internet Explorer. That means you no longer see an annoying flurry of pop-up advertisements each time you visit a site. Although the blocker's much appreciated among Web visitors, it's causing a ruckus among sites that integrate pop-ups as part of their design.

If you encounter a site that doesn't work correctly unless you can see the pop-ups, turn the pop-ups back on: Click the message bar that appears across Internet Explorer when a pop-up is blocked, as shown in Figure 10-8.

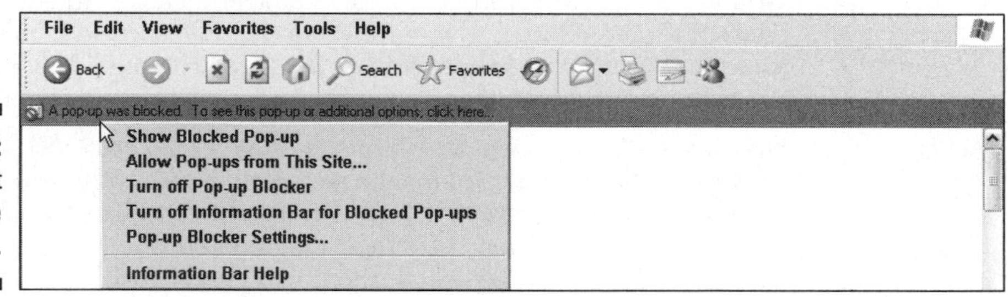

Figure 10-8: You can let a site use pop-ups.

Here's what the settings do:

- **Show Blocked Pop-Up:** Choose this option to see the single pop-up you've missed — and nothing else.
- **Allow Pop-Ups from This Site:** More dangerous, this option allows that particular site to send you all the pop-ups it wants. If you don't trust the site, you could be opening yourself to a deluge.

- **Turn Off Pop-Up Blocker:** If you actually *like* pop-up ads, choose this option to see every pop-up offered by any site.
- **Turn Off Information Bar for Blocked Pop-Ups:** This option makes the pop-up blocker work invisibly, skipping the A Pop-Up Was Blocked information bar.
- **Pop-Up Blocker Settings:** Is a site sending you a *lot* of pop-ups? Click this option to make sure it's not on your list of pop-up allowable sites.

To stop Internet Explorer from making that little bubble-popping noise when it blocks a pop-up, choose Pop-Up Blocker from Internet Explorer's Tools menu. Select Pop-Up Blocker Settings and remove the check mark from the Play a Sound When a Pop-Up Is Blocked box.

If you don't have the pop-up blocker, then you haven't installed Service Pack 2 (see Chapter 1 for directions), or you've somehow turned off the blocker. To turn it back on, choose Pop-Up Blocker from Internet Explorer's Tools menu and click to remove the check mark from the Turn Off Pop-Up Blocker box.

Although the pop-up blocker works better than some of the competing programs I've seen, it's not without flaws. Some pop-ups inevitably sneak through. But it sure stops most pop-ups *and* pop-under windows.

Buying from secure Web sites

Whenever you buy something from a Web site, make sure you're typing in your credit card number onto a *secure* Web site. How can you tell if a site's secure?

- First, you usually see the window shown in Figure 10-9 before you arrive at a secure site.
- Second, before entering your credit card number, check the Web site's address: A secure site begins with the words `https` instead of `http`. This little difference makes a big difference in security.

- Third, glance at the corner of Internet Explorer and look for a little lock icon, like the one shown in the margin. (Don't spot it? Make sure your status bar is turned on by choosing Status Bar from Internet Explorer's View menu.) If you still don't spot that little lock, don't trust the site.
- Finally, double-click the lock icon to see the site's security certificate, like the one issued to Amazon in Figure 10-10. Make sure the current Web site's name is actually listed in the Issued To area and that the dates listed on the Valid From area are still valid.

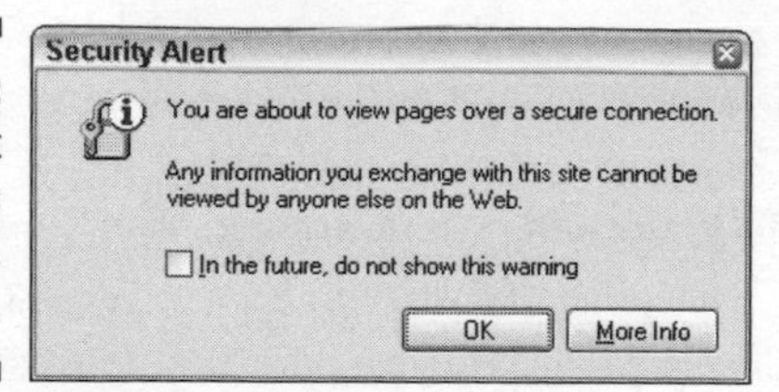

Figure 10-9: This alert indicates a safe, secure site.

Figure 10-10: Before entering a credit card on a site, make sure the site's certificate contains the site's name and that the date is still valid.

If these four things don't look right, don't enter your credit card number. Instead, shop from a different site. Or simply call the company on the phone and place your order by phone. (You usually find phone numbers by clicking the words Contact Us on the site's home page.)

Maintaining Your Privacy in Windows XP

The more computers know about you, the more they can help you. That's why Microsoft designed Windows XP to squirrel away bits and pieces of data you enter in various programs. When you begin to type in a Web site's name, for instance, or fill out a form, Windows XP quickly lists your previous entries, letting you save time by simply clicking them.

Managing cookies on the Internet

Just like grocery store "member shopping cards" create a database of everything you purchase, most Web sites track your activities. Instead of using cards, Web sites track visitors with *cookies* — tiny files stored on your computer's hard drive. If cookies worry you, here's how to delete them.

But before you start deleting cookies in a flurry of indignation, be sure to write down *all* your user names and passwords. After you delete their cookies, your favorite Web sites no longer remember you, and you have to enter that information every time you visit.

Here's how to delete cookies:

1. **Choose Internet Options from the Internet Explorer's Tools menu.**
2. **Click the General tab and click the Delete Cookies button.**

Repeat this process anytime to delete your existing cookies. To go one step further and block any *future* cookies, choose Internet Options from the Tools menu, click the Privacy tab, and click the Advanced button. There, you choose Override Automatic Cookie Handling and click the Block buttons to blocks *all* sites from leaving cookies.

If some sites refuse you entry when you disable the cookies, add the sites' addresses to the exceptions list: Choose Internet Options from the Tools menu, click the Privacy tab, and click the Sites button. Then add the addresses of sites that are allowed to use cookies.

Media Player keeps track of the DVDs you watch and the CDs you play, so it can offer information about them in its Now Playing window. Even Web sites drop little identifiers called *cookies* onto your hard drive, letting them tailor their menus to meet your interests.

Although spreading around your personal information makes computing easier, there's a fine balance between convenience and a comfort level of privacy. This section explains the information Windows XP (and the Internet) gathers from you and how to delete it if you wish.

Removing previously typed words from online drop-down lists

As soon as you begin to type something online — a Web site address in Internet Explorer, for instance, or a name into an online form — Windows XP often races in to help. It sends down a little box, shown in Figure 10-11, listing items you've typed previously.

Figure 10-11: AutoComplete shows words you typed.

r
rathbone
rathboone
rrathbone

A quick point and click lets you retrieve a word or phrase from Windows XP's handy AutoComplete list, sparing you the effort of typing it in yet again.

Some people, however, don't like Windows XP looking over their shoulder as they type. And it's especially annoying when Windows XP keeps listing your typographical errors.

To delete a word or phrase from most AutoComplete drop-down lists, press the down-arrow key to highlight the entry and then press the Delete key. Unfortunately, this trick doesn't delete individual Web addresses you type into Internet Explorer. You must delete Internet Explorer's History to remove those, a process I describe in Chapter 8.

To make Internet Explorer stop listing your previous entries, follow these steps:

1. **Open Internet Explorer and choose Internet Options from the Tools menu.**
2. **Click the Content tab and click the AutoComplete button.**

   The AutoComplete Settings dialog box opens.
3. **Click to remove check marks from these boxes:**
   - **Web Addresses**
   - **Forms**
   - **User Names and Passwords on Forms**
   - **Prompt Me to Save Passwords**

   The AutoComplete Settings dialog box looks like the one in Figure 10-12.
4. **Click the Clear Forms button and the Clear Passwords button and then click OK.**

   Those two final buttons delete previously stored AutoComplete entries.

Turning off Windows' *other* AutoComplete areas

Even after you turn off AutoComplete in Internet Explorer, Windows XP leaves AutoComplete turned on in other programs. Here's the rundown on how to turn it off in other programs:

The Start menu's Search Companion:

1. **Choose Search from the Start menu and choose Change Preferences.**
2. **Choose Turn AutoComplete Off.**

Although that keeps the Search Companion from remembering your newly searched terms, Windows XP doesn't provide a way to remove your existing entries.

Media Player's previously played files:

1. **Choose Options from Media Player's Tools menu.**
2. **Click the Privacy Tab and click the Clear History and Clear CD/DVD buttons.**

These steps work only for Media Player 10; earlier Media Player versions don't have these buttons.

The Start menu's My Recent Documents area:

1. **Right-click on the Start button, choose Properties, and click the Customize button.**
2. **Click the Advanced tab, click the Clear List button, and click the OK button.**

To make Windows XP stop listing your previously opened files, clear the List My Most Recently Opened Documents box in Step 2.

AutoComplete Settings

AutoComplete lists possible matches from entries you've typed before.

Use AutoComplete for

Web addresses

Forms

User names and passwords on forms

Prompt me to save passwords

Clear AutoComplete history

Clear Forms | Clear Passwords

To clear Web address entries, on the General tab in Internet Options, click Clear History.

OK | Cancel

Figure 10-12: Remove the check marks from every box to turn off Internet Explorer's AutoComplete.

It's convenient for Internet Explorer to store the passwords you use for your Web site. But that makes it convenient for anybody who sits at your computer to log on to password-protected sites. Even if you enjoy AutoComplete, consider removing the check mark from the User Names and Passwords on Forms box in Step 3.

Using blind carbon copy when sending e-mail to several people

Ever received a funny e-mail that's been forwarded around the Internet for a few weeks? Some of those e-mails are so stuffed with old e-mail address that it's hard to find the original joke.

And that's the problem. Today, many people like to preserve their privacy (and slow down spammers) by giving out their e-mail to only a few close friends. But when somebody forwards a message to everybody in their Address Book, every recipient sees everybody else's address.

The solution? When you send an e-mail to several people, use Outlook Express' Bcc box (shown in the margin), not the usual To field.

Bcc stands for *blind carbon copy.* Everybody listed in the Bcc box receives the message, but the recipients see only their *own* e-mail address. That not only makes for a less-cluttered e-mail but also preserves everybody's privacy.

Unfortunately, Outlook Express doesn't usually show the Bcc: box as an option when you try to send e-mail. To make Outlook Express show that option, try this:

1. **Click the Create Mail button.**
2. **Choose All Headers from that message's View menu.**

   The Bcc box appears.
3. **Close the message.**

   Now, whenever you try to send or forward a message, you see the Bcc spot, ready for you to add e-mail addresses.

   If, by some twist of Computer Fate, the Bcc area suddenly disappears, repeat these three steps to put it back in place.

Part IV

Customizing and Upgrading Windows XP

"Oh—I like this background much better than the basement."

In this part . . .

When your life changes, you want Windows XP to change with it, and that's where this part of the book comes in. Here's where you discover Windows XP's Control Panel, which lets you change nearly everything but your computer's disposition.

Another chapter describes easy click-through tune-ups you can perform to keep your computer in top shape, backed up, and running smoothly. If you're sharing your computer with others, you'll discover how to dish out user accounts to each of them, with *you* deciding who can do what.

Finally, when you're ready to buy that second (or third, fourth, or fifth) computer, a chapter walks you through linking them all to create a home network, where they can all share the same Internet connection.

Chapter 11

Customizing Windows XP with the Control Panel

In This Chapter

- Opening the Control Panel
- Changing the Control Panel's layout
- Customizing Windows XP's appearance
- Changing video modes
- Installing or removing programs
- Installing new computer parts or printers
- Adjusting your mouse
- Automatically setting the computer's time and date

Anybody who's seen a science fiction movie knows that robots come with secret control panels, the best of which include an emergency Off switch. Windows XP also sports a control panel, although it's not secret or hidden. Called the *Control Panel,* it sits one click away on the Start menu.

Hundreds of switches and options sit inside the Control Panel's two-dozen icons, letting you customize Windows' look, feel, and vibe. This chapter explains the switches and sliders you'll probably want to tweak as well as the ones you should avoid.

Beware, however: These settings can affect your computer so drastically that many can be changed only by the computer's owner — the person holding the almighty Administrator account.

Finding the Right Switch in the Control Panel

Flip open the Start menu's Control Panel, and you can while away an entire workweek opening icons and flipping switches to fine-tune Windows XP's inner workings. Sometimes merely locating the right switch can cause the most aggravation: The Control Panel contains nearly *30* icons, some containing more than two dozen settings.

To save you from searching aimlessly, the Control Panel opens in its Category View, shown in Figure 11-1, which groups the settings into ten neat categories. Open the Appearance and Themes category, for instance, and you see four tasks for changing Windows XP's appearance, including Choose a New Screen Saver and Change Your Desktop's Background. Choose a task, and Windows XP automatically fetches the correct icon, opened to the exact page you need.

Windows XP veterans already well versed in icon mechanics can choose the Control Panel's Classic View, instead. (The mouse points at that option in Figure 11-1.) When in Classic View, the Control Panel dumps the categories/tasks approach and simply displays *all* its icons, as shown in Figure 11-2. (If they look familiar, it's because previous Windows versions used the Classic View.)

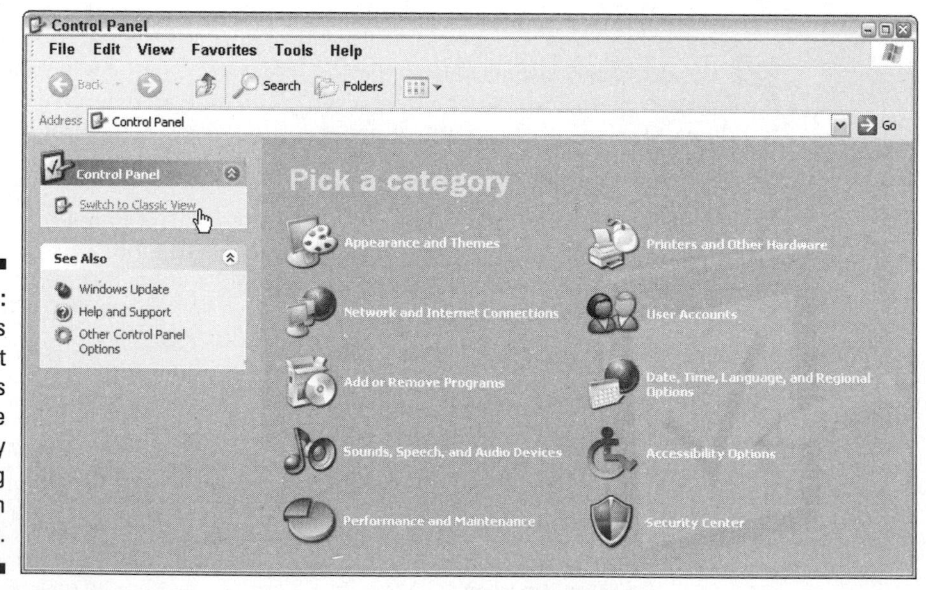

Figure 11-1: Windows XP's default view lets you locate settings by clicking through categories.

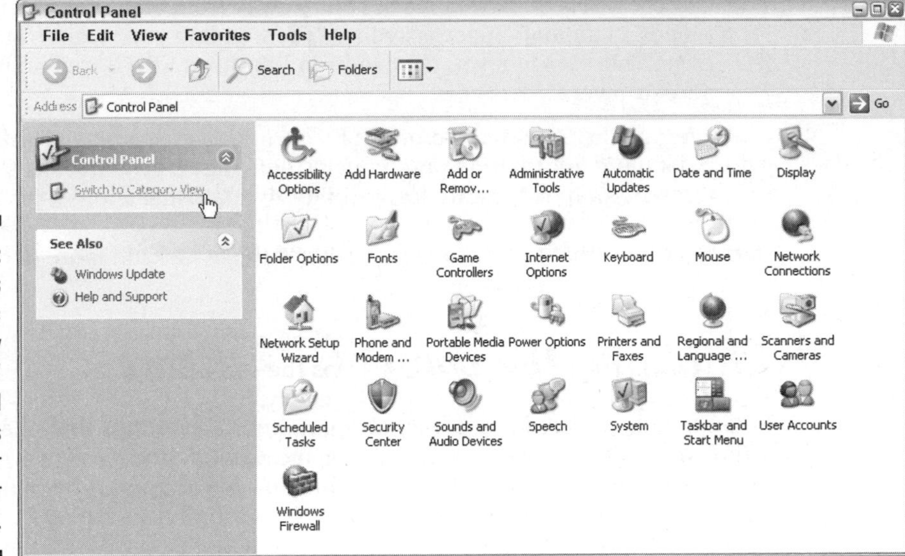

Figure 11-2: Windows XP's Classic View displays *all* the Control Panel's icons for quicker tweaking.

Even when in Classic View, the Control Panel often looks different on different computers. Some brands of monitors add a personalized Control Panel icon, for instance. Sometimes programs add their own icons to the Control Panel, and some computer models sport icons not needed on other brands.

Rest your mouse pointer over any confusing icon, and Windows XP thoughtfully explains its meaning in life.

Changing Windows' Appearance and Themes

Windows XP lumps its decorator items into its Appearance and Themes category and provides access to four common tasks:

- **Change the Computer's Theme:** A *theme* is simply a collection of colors, sound effects, screen savers, and backgrounds for Windows. If you've spent hours tweaking Windows' appearance to match your current mood, save those settings as a single theme for easy access. When your mood changes from dour to dashing, switch to a more upbeat theme to match.
- **Change the Desktop Background:** Head here to splash a new background (also called *wallpaper*) across your desktop, quickly and easily.

- **Choose a Screen Saver:** When you're away from your computer, Windows places an animation across your screen, hiding your work from prying eyes. This area lets you choose from Windows XP's dozen animated screen savers.
- **Change the Screen Resolution:** By shrinking everything slightly, you can pack more information onto your screen. If everything looks too small already, swap real estate for visibility by choosing a lower resolution.

In the sections that follow, I explain each of these tasks in more detail.

Changing the computer's theme

If you haven't created any personalized themes — settings that change Windows' colors, sounds, screen saver, and background — then you won't find much here. Windows XP comes with *very* few themes. Choosing Change the Computer's Theme brings up the Themes tab of the Display Properties dialog box, shown in Figure 11-3.

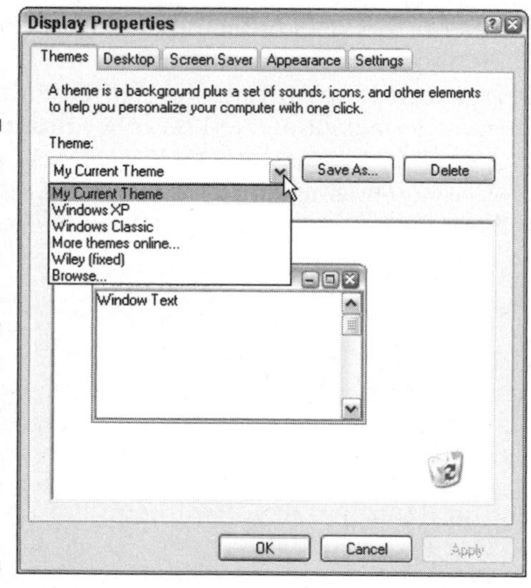

Figure 11-3: Choose a preconfigured theme to change how Windows looks as well as change sounds and icons.

Windows XP lists its three themes:

- **My Current Theme:** If you've somehow messed up Windows XP's appearance settings — but haven't yet saved them — choose this to revert to your last saved theme.

- **Windows XP:** This merely shows the theme Windows XP used when it was first installed.
- **Windows Classic:** Retro users like this because it makes Windows XP look like the venerable Windows 98.

The More Themes Online option whisks you off to Microsoft's Web site, enticing you to purchase more themes packaged in its Microsoft Plus! software.

Choose any of the themes, and Windows XP automatically slips into new clothes. To preview a theme's look, choose it from the drop-down list shown in Figure 11-3. The Sample window offers a sneak preview.

Or, instead of choosing themes, make your own by following these steps:

1. **Click the Appearance tab and adjust Windows' colors, buttons, and fonts.**

   For more options, click the Effects and Advanced buttons.

2. **Click the Desktop tab to change the background (covered in the next section).**

3. **Click the Screen Saver tab to choose a different screen saver.**

4. **Adjust other settings.**

   Make Windows play different sounds by selecting the Control Panel's Sounds, Speech, and Audio Devices category and choosing Change the Sound Scheme. Finally, choose different mouse pointers from the Control Panel's Printers and Other Hardware category. (Click the Mouse icon and click the Pointers tab.)

5. **Save all your new settings as a theme by clicking the Save As button (shown in Figure 11-3) and choosing a name.**

   Windows packs up your changed settings into an easily accessed theme. (Save the theme in your My Documents folder for easy retrieval.)

- Creating themes with Windows XP's basic tools can be tedious and fairly limited. If you're really into creating themes (also called *skinning*) for Windows XP, pick up a third-party program like WindowBlinds (`www.windowblinds.net`) or SkinStudio (`www.skinstudio.net`).
- Before you begin downloading themes from the Web or e-mail attachments, be sure you're using an updated antivirus program. Viruses sometimes masquerade as themes.
- To change themes quickly, right-click on your desktop and choose Properties. Or choose the Control Panel's Display icon. Either brings you directly to the Themes tab of the Display Properties dialog box.

Changing the desktop background

A background, formerly known as wallpaper, is simply the picture covering your desktop. To change it, follow these steps:

1. **Choose the Control Panel's Appearances and Themes category and choose Change the Desktop Background.**

   The Desktop tab of the Display Properties dialog box appears.

2. **Select a file for a new background, and Windows XP shows how it will look on your monitor, as shown in Figure 11-4.**

   Feel free to choose any file listed in the Background list box, or click the Browse button to look for images you've saved on your computer.

   Background files can be BMP, GIF, JPG, JPEG, DIB, or PNG files. That means you can use nearly any photo or art from the Internet or a digital camera.

3. **Windows XP examines your chosen image's size and decides whether it should be *tiled* repeatedly across the screen, *centered* in the middle, or *stretched* to fill the entire screen. To override Windows' choice, set your own preference by selecting it from the Position box.**

4. **When you find a background you like, click OK to close the dialog box and see how it really looks.**

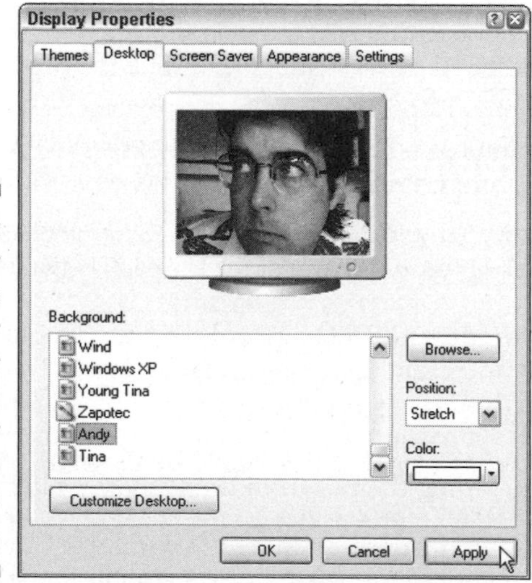

Figure 11-4: Select any picture on your computer to splash across your desktop as the background.

Windows XP has a couple of other ways to customize your desktop:

- Did you happen to spot an eye-catching picture while Web surfing with Internet Explorer? Right-click on that Web site's picture and choose Set as Background. Sneaky Windows copies the picture and splashes it across your desktop as a new background.
- To change your background quickly, right-click on your desktop, choose Properties, and click the Desktop tab. Or open the Control Panel's Display icon and click the Desktop tab.

Choosing a screen saver

In the dinosaur days of computing, computer monitors suffered from *burn-in:* permanent damage when an oft-used program burned its image onto the screen. To prevent this burn-in, people installed a screen saver to jump in with a blank screen or moving lines when a computer hadn't been used for a while. Today's monitors no longer have this problem, but people use screen savers anyway because they look cool.

Windows comes with several built-in screen savers. To try one out, follow these steps:

1. **Open the Control Panel from the Start menu and select the Appearance and Themes category's Choose a Screen Saver task.**

   The Screen Saver tab of the Display Properties dialog box appears.

2. **Then click the downward-pointing arrow in the Screen Saver box and select a screen saver. Click the Preview button to watch the screen saver in action and audition as many screen savers as you like.**

3. **Afraid somebody will sneak into your computer while you're fetching coffee? Add security by selecting the On Resume, Display Welcome Screen check box.**

   With this box checked, when your computer wakes from screen saver mode, Windows displays the user account Welcome screen and asks for a password. (I cover user accounts in Chapter 13.)

4. **Click the up or down arrows next to the Wait box to tell the screen saver when to kick in.**

   If you set the option to 5, for example, Windows XP waits until you haven't touched the mouse or keyboard for five minutes before letting the screen saver out of its cage.

5. **Feel free to click Settings for more options — changing a screen saver's colors or animation speed, for instance.**
6. **When you're done setting up your screen saver, click OK.**

If you *really* want to extend your monitor's life (and save electricity), don't bother with screen savers. Instead, click the Power button on the Screen Savers tab. The resulting Power Options Properties dialog box lets you tell Windows XP to turn off your monitor when you haven't used it for a while — you pick the interval.

Changing the screen resolution

Mostly a holdover from the old days, your screen resolution determines the amount of colors Windows displays on your monitor and the amount of information it packs on your screen. If you run a program (usually a game) that bugs you about screen resolutions or video modes, Windows lets you adjust your screen here.

To adjust your screen resolution, follow these steps:

1. **Choose Change the Screen Resolution from the Control Panel's Appearances and Themes category.**

   The Settings tab of the Display Properties dialog box appears, as shown in Figure 11-5, and your adjusting begins.

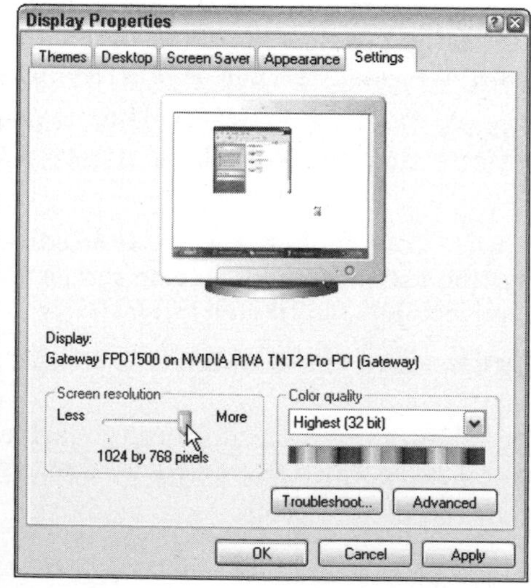

Figure 11-5: Depending on the screen resolution, Windows can squeeze different amounts of information onto your monitor.

2. **To change the number of colors Windows XP displays, click the arrow next to the Color Quality box. Use Highest for most newer computers; if that makes your screen act weird, choose Medium instead.**

To fully experience the sunset in your digital camera photos, make sure Windows XP displays the highest number of colors as possible. Medium (16-bit mode) displays up to 65,000 colors; Highest, or 32-bit mode, slaps up to 16 million colors on the monitor.

3. **To change the screen resolution, use your mouse to slide the little bar in the Screen Resolution area.**

   Watch how the little preview screen changes. The more you slide the bar to the right, the more information Windows XP packs onto the screen. Unfortunately, the information also gets smaller.

4. **After you select a new resolution, click the Apply button to see it in action.**

When Windows XP switches to a new resolution, it usually gives you 15 seconds to click a button approving the change. If your monitor can't handle the new resolution and turns black or blurry, the on-screen button won't be visible. Because you didn't click it, Windows XP automatically reverts to your original resolution. Whew!

5. **Click OK when you're done tweaking the display.**

   After you've chosen the highest color setting and a comfortable screen resolution, you'll probably never return here.

Windows XP may want to restart your computer before making changes. To tell Windows to change the video *without* restarting, click the Advanced button on the bottom of the Settings tab.

If any of the choices seem confusing, click the little question mark in the window's top corner and then click the confusing item. Windows XP explains what will happen should you dare to take that route.

Changing Network and Internet Connections

The Control Panel's Network and Internet Connections category does the grunt work when computers need to talk to each other. It contains four tasks, which are all shortcuts to settings found in other areas:

- **Set Up or Change Your Internet Connection:** Clicking here takes you to the New Connection Wizard, which guides you through setting up an Internet connection. (I guide you through using the New Connection Wizard in Chapter 8.)

- **Create a Connection to the Network at Your Workplace:** Designed for more advanced users, this lets you connect your computer with the one at your office — if your office's network administrator not only grants you permission but also gives you the secret password.
- **Set Up or Change Your Home or Small Office Network:** After you've linked your collection of computers with cables (or a wireless connection), this option lets you introduce Windows XP to the setup. I explain how to use this in Chapter 14.
- **Change Windows Firewall Settings:** If a program needs to peek through Windows Firewall (the one that's been strengthened by Service Pack 2), here's where you can poke the right holes. (I explain Service Pack 2 in Chapter 1 and Windows Firewall in Chapter 10.)

Adding or Removing Programs

Whether you've picked up a new program or you want to purge an old one, the Control Panel's Add or Remove Programs feature handles the job fairly well. It lists your currently installed programs, shown in Figure 11-6, letting you choose any to discard. A convenient list of icons along the left edge lets you handle other program-related chores, all discussed in the sections that follow.

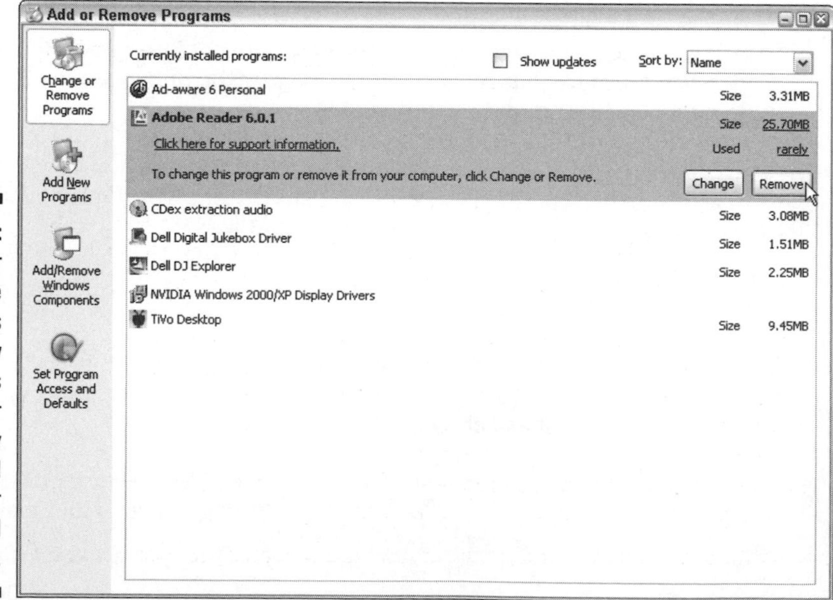

Figure 11-6: The Add or Remove Programs window removes any of your currently installed programs or helps install new ones.

Changing or removing programs

To remove an unwanted or misbehaving program, choose the Control Panel's Add or Remove Programs option. The Add or Remove Programs window appears, shown in Figure 11-6, listing your currently installed programs and some handy statistics: their size, the last time you used them, and how often you use them.

Click the unloved program and then click its Remove button. Windows asks if you're *sure;* if you click Yes, Windows XP summons the program's built-in uninstall program — if it has one — or simply yanks the program off your computer's hard drive.

Be careful, though. After you delete a program, it's gone for good unless you kept its installation CD around. Unlike other deleted items, deleted programs don't linger inside the Recycle Bin.

When a program doesn't have an installation program . . .

Sometimes programs — especially small ones downloaded from the Internet — don't come with an installation program. If you've downloaded one of these low-budget creations to your computer, create a new folder for it and move the downloaded file inside. (Be sure to scan any downloaded file with your antivirus program.) Then try double-clicking the program's file. (It's usually the file with the fanciest icon.) One of two things may happen:

- **The program may simply start running.** That means you're done — the program doesn't need to be installed. (Drag and drop its program icon to your Start button to add it to the Start button.) If you need to uninstall the program, just right-click on it and choose Delete. These types of programs rarely appear on your Add or Remove Programs list.
- **The program may start installing itself.** That means you're also done. The program's installation program takes over, sparing you any more trouble. To uninstall the program, use the Control Panel's Add or Remove Programs area.

But if the program comes in a *zipped* folder — the folder icon bears a little zipper — there's an extra step. Right-click on the zipped folder, choose Extract All, and click Next (several times, usually). Windows automatically *unzips* the folder's contents and places them into a new folder, usually named after the program. From in there, you can either run the program directly or, if it has an installation program, run the installation program.

- Always use the Control Panel's Add or Remove Programs window to uninstall unwanted programs. Simply deleting their folders won't do the trick. In fact, doing so often confuses your computer into sending bothersome error messages.
- Inevitably, some programs continue to be listed *after* you remove them. There's not much you can do at this point, unfortunately. Consider it a cosmetic flaw, and nothing more.
- Although clicking the Remove button nearly always begins removal process, you sometimes spot an adjacent *Change* button, as well. The Change option usually offers to repair a damaged program or change some of its components. It's worth a try for malfunctioning programs.

Adding new programs

Chances are, you'll never have to use this option. Today, most programs install themselves automatically as soon as you slide their CD into the drive. If you're not sure whether a program has installed, click Start and poke around in your All Programs menu. If it's there, the program has installed.

But if a program doesn't automatically leap into your computer, click the Add New Programs button from the left edge of the Control Panel's Add or Remove Programs window. The window quickly offers the following two options:

- **Add a Program from CD-ROM or Floppy Disk:** When a program doesn't install itself automatically, insert the program's CD or first floppy disk and click the CD or Floppy button. Windows locates the program's installation program and installs the program automatically.
- **Add Programs from Microsoft:** This merely tells Windows to visit Windows Update online and download any new patches. Instead of choosing this option, read Chapter 10; there, you can make Windows Update retrieve patches automatically in the background, rendering this choice obsolete.

Here are some other tips that can help you install a pesky program:

- You need an Administrator account to install programs. (Most computer owners automatically have an Administrator account.) That keeps the kids, with their Limited or Guest accounts, from installing programs and messing up the computer. I explain user accounts in Chapter 13.
- Downloaded a program? Then use the Add a Program from CD-ROM or Floppy Disk option described earlier in this section. When Windows can't find the program, it leaves you with a Browse window. Browse to the folder containing your downloaded program. Windows finds its Setup program and installs the program.

- Many eager, newly installed programs want to add a desktop shortcut, Start menu shortcut, and a Quick Launch toolbar shortcut. Say "no" to all but the Start menu. All those extra shortcuts clutter your computer, making programs difficult to find. You can delete these shortcuts if the program adds them without your permission by right-clicking on them and choosing Delete.

- It's always a good idea to create a restore point before installing a new program. (I describe creating restore points in Chapter 12.) If your newly installed program goes haywire, use System Restore to return your computer to the peaceful state of mind it enjoyed before you installed the troublemaker.

Add/remove parts of Windows XP

Here's a secret: Windows XP is so huge that it rarely installs all its parts onto your computer. Windows XP usually leaves off its fax program, for instance. To see what parts of itself Windows XP has left off your computer or to remove unwanted components that Windows XP *has* installed, follow these steps:

1. **Click the Add/Remove Windows Components button from the Add or Remove Programs window.**

   Windows brings up a window listing all its components, as shown in Figure 11-7. The components with check marks by their names are already installed. No check mark? Then that program's not installed. If you see a box that's gray — neither empty nor checked — then double-click the component to see what's installed and what's left out.

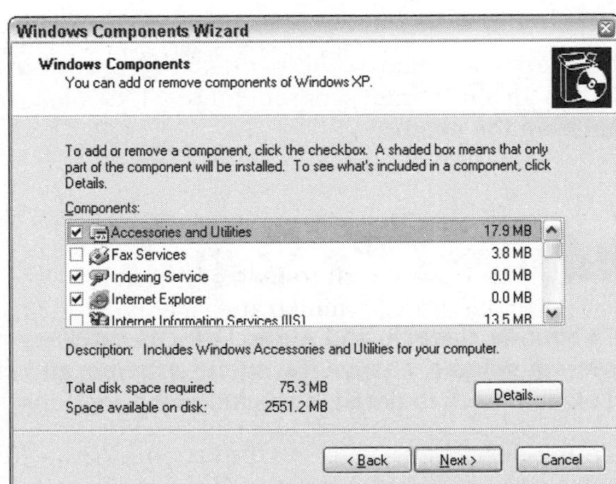

Figure 11-7: The Windows Components Wizard lets you add or remove programs that come with Windows XP.

2. **To add a component like the Fax Services program, click in its empty check box. (To remove an installed component like Windows Messenger, click its check box to uncheck its box.)**
3. **Click the Next button.**

   Windows XP adds the program to your computer. (You may need to insert your Windows XP CD during the process.)

Set program access and defaults

Microsoft lets computer vendors replace Internet Explorer, Media Player, Outlook Express and Windows Messenger with different programs from other companies. Your new computer may come with the Opera Web browser, for instance, instead of Microsoft's Internet Explorer.

To choose between Microsoft's programs or the substitutes installed by your computer vendor, open the Control Panel's Add or Remove Programs icon and choose the Set Program Access and Defaults icon. The window lets you choose between three options:

- **Microsoft Windows:** Choose this option to use Microsoft's programs. If your computer isn't using the Windows programs described in this book, this option makes Windows use them.
- **Non-Microsoft:** Choose this option to hide Microsoft's programs and substitute the alternative programs installed by your computer vendor.
- **Custom:** Choose here for the most control. You may select which programs you'll use — some of Microsoft's and some of the substitutes installed by your computer vendor.

None of these options actually remove Microsoft's programs from your computer. Switching to an alternative program merely hides Microsoft's competing program from the menus.

Adjusting Windows XP's Sounds

The Control Panel's Sounds, Speech, and Audio Devices category offers three tasks: Adjust the system volume, change the sound scheme, and change the speaker settings. I explain each in detail in the following sections.

Adjusting the system volume

Strangely enough, Windows XP doesn't provide easy access to your computer's volume knob. But here's how to fix that:

1. **Click the Control Panel's Sounds, Speech, and Audio Devices category and then choose Adjust the System Volume.**
2. **When the Sounds and Audio Devices Properties dialog box appears, as shown in Figure 11-8, select the Place Volume Icon in the Taskbar check box.**
3. **Click Apply, and a tiny speaker icon appears near your clock. (Check out Figure 11-9.)**

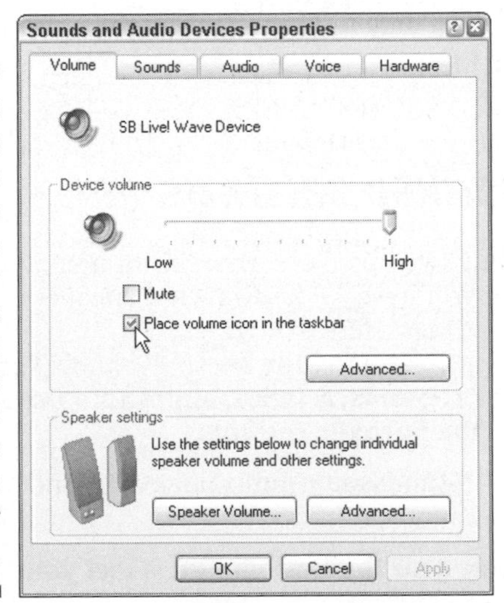

Figure 11-8: Select the Place Volume Icon in the Taskbar check box, and Windows places a volume control icon near your clock.

To mute the sound quickly when the phone rings, click the little speaker icon in Figure 11-9 and click the Mute check box. Click the Mute check box again when the salesperson hangs up, and you're ready to hear your music again. The mute option also comes in handy during late night Web surfing when you stumble across a site that blares *Star Wars* themes.

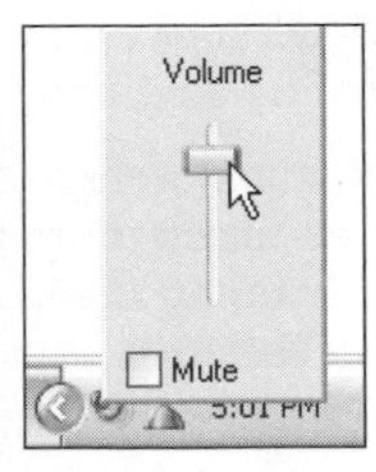

Figure 11-9: Change the volume from the taskbar.

Changing the sound scheme

Windows comes with two built-in *sound schemes* — the collection of sounds played when Windows starts or stops or when you've clicked the wrong thing. To switch between Windows' two schemes, choose the Control Panel's Sounds, Speech, and Audio Devices category and choose Change the Sound Scheme.

Some computers come with Windows XP's default sound scheme turned off. To turn it on and hear Windows XP's full collection of buzzes and beeps, select its Windows Default sound scheme.

Windows XP's only alternative sound scheme, unfortunately, is complete silence. (Microsoft sells Plus! software that adds more sounds to your computer with its collection of themes.)

Windows uses sounds stored in the WAV format, not the MP3 or WMA formats used by most of today's music files.

Changing the speaker settings

If your computer came with only two speakers, there's not much point fiddling in here. But to make sure Windows XP knows what speakers it's using, feel free to test your speaker settings. Here's how:

1. **Choose the Control Panel's Sounds, Speech, and Audio Devices category and choose Change the Speaker Settings.**

   Windows XP brings up the Sounds and Audio Devices Properties dialog box (refer to Figure 11-8).

2. **Click the Advanced button near the bottom and select your type of speakers from the Speaker setup area.**

   Choices range from No Speakers to 7.1 Surround Sound Speakers. (A subwoofer counts as only 0.1 speaker because the speaker numbering committee didn't like booming bass lines.)

3. **Click OK when you're done.**

Performance and Maintenance

Just like a '67 Mustang, Windows XP needs occasional maintenance. In fact, a little bit of maintenance can make Windows XP run so much more smoothly that I've devoted all of Chapter 12 to that subject (including the items listed in the Control Panel's Performance and Maintenance section).

Page ahead to Chapter 12 for more information about your computer's engine, how to speed it up (or slow it down with fancier displays), free up hard drive space, back up your data, make your hard drive run more quickly, or polish its chrome.

Adding Printers and Other Hardware

The Control Panel's Printers and Other Hardware section, shown in Figure 11-10, offers only two tasks: viewing your installed printers (including your fax card, if you have one) and adding a printer (or several) to your computer.

However, you're more likely to use the Control Panel icons shown at the bottom of Figure 11-10 than those two tasks, so I'll cover the two tasks *and* the icons here.

Viewing installed printers or fax printers

The Control Panel's View Installed Printers or Fax Printers task does just what it says: It lets you see the printers (and computerized fax machines) currently hooked up to your printer. Choosing that task on my computer merely reveals two icons: my Epson Stylus Photo 1270 printer and my fax card.

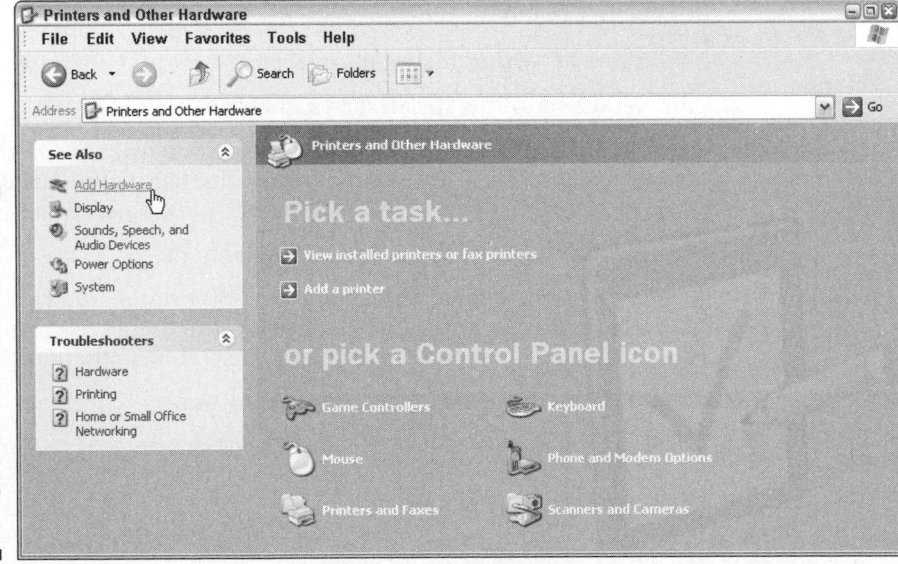

Figure 11-10: Chances are, you'll use the Add Hardware Wizard, shown in the task pane, for more than the two listed tasks.

Click a printer's icon to see its *queue* — a list of documents waiting to be printed. Click the fax icon to see the Fax Console, a list of sent and received faxes. (I cover both printing and faxing in Chapter 7.)

Adding a printer

Troublesome printer manufacturers couldn't agree on how printers should be installed. Usually, adding a printer works in one of two ways:

- Some printer manufacturers say simply to plug in your printer and turn it on. Windows XP automatically recognizes and embraces the printer, which usually plugs in through a little rectangular USB port. Add ink or toner and paper, and you're done.
- Other manufacturers took an uglier approach, saying you must install their bundled software *before* plugging in your printer. And if you don't install the software first, the printer might not work correctly.

The only way to know how your printer should be installed is to check the printer's manual. (Sometimes this information appears on a colorful, one page Installation Cheat Sheet packed in the printer's box.)

If your printer didn't come with installation software, install the cartridges, add paper to the tray, and follow these instructions to put it to work:

1. **Choose Add a Printer from the Control Panel's Printers and Other Hardware category.**

   A Windows XP wizard materializes, ready to set up your new printer.

2. **Click Next and follow the wizard's instructions.**

   Make sure your printer's turned on. Then tell the wizard whether your printer is plugged into *your* computer or whether you're installing a networked printer that's installed on somebody *else's* computer.

3. **Click Next and follow the wizard's instructions.**

   Because you're probably not installing a USB printer, you're almost certainly connecting your printer's cable to your computer's printer port. That's called LTP1: in computer language, so choose that option.

4. **Click Next and follow the wizard's instructions.**

   The Add Printer Wizard box lists the names of printer manufacturers on the left; choose yours from the list. The right side of the box lists that manufacturer's printer models.

5. **Double-click your printer's name when you see it listed. Windows XP may ask you to stick the appropriate set-up CD into a drive.**

   After a moment, you see the new printer listed. If it offers to print a test page, take it up on the offer.

6. **Click the new printer's icon and select the Set as Default Printer option from the window's File menu.**

   That's it. If you're like most people, your printer will work like a charm. If it doesn't, I've stuffed some tips and fix-it tricks in Chapter 7's printing section.

To see your newly installed printer, choose View Installed Printers or Fax Printers, described in the previous section. Your newly installed printer will appear as an icon.

If you have two or more printers attached to your computer, right-click on the icon of your most oft-used printer and select Set as Default Printer from the menu. Windows XP then prints to that printer automatically, unless you tell it otherwise.

- To remove a printer you no longer use, right-click on its name and then choose Delete from the menu. That printer's name no longer appears as an option when you try to print from a program. If it asks to uninstall the printer's drivers and software click Yes, unless you might use the printer again.
- You can change printer options from within many programs. Choose File in a program's menu bar and then choose Print Setup or choose Print. From there, you can often access the same box of printer options as you find in the Control Panel. You can also find ways to change things such as paper sizes, fonts, and types of graphics.
- To share a printer over a network, right-click on its icon and choose Sharing. Select the Share This Printer option and click OK. That printer shows up as an option for all the computers on your network.
- If your printer's software confuses you, try clicking the Help buttons in its dialog boxes. Many buttons are customized for your particular printer model, and they offer advice not found in Windows XP.

Adding new hardware

When you add a new part to your computer, the computer should be turned off, leaving Windows XP fast asleep. (You don't need to turn it off when installing USB devices, though.) When you turn the computer back on and Windows XP returns to life, it may not notice your surgical handiwork.

Here's the good news, however: If you simply tell Windows XP to *look* for the new part, it will probably find it. In fact, Windows XP not only spots the new part but also often recruits a wizard, if needed, to help you set it up. Here's the process:

1. **Choose the Control Panel's Printers and Other Hardware icon and then choose Add Hardware. (It's hidden in the top-left corner of the task pane along the window's left edge; the mouse points to it in Figure 11-10.)**

   When summoned, the Add Hardware Wizard introduces Windows XP to whatever part you've plugged into your computer.

2. **Click the Next button.**

   Windows XP looks for any recognizable Plug and Play devices installed in your computer. Here's where the path branches off:

   - **If Windows XP locates your new part,** click the newly installed part's name from the Windows XP list, click Finish, and follow the rest of the wizard's instructions.
   - **If the wizard *didn't* find your new part,** click Add a New Hardware Device from the Installed Hardware List and then click Next, telling Windows to search for additional devices. Follow the instructions to see whether Windows finds the device. If it does, rejoice — and click the device's name for Windows to install it.

If Windows can't locate your newly installed part automatically, you need to contact the manufacturer of your new part and ask for a Windows XP driver. (Drivers are usually downloadable from the manufacturer's Web site.) Some drivers come bundled with installation software to minimize installation chores.

Installing or adjusting other items

The Add Hardware Wizard lets you install just about anything, passing along the chores to other wizards, when appropriate. Or you can head directly to the correct wizard when installing the following gadgetry. (These icons all appear at the bottom of the Control Panel's Printers and Other Hardware category.)

Game Controllers

Windows XP almost always recognizes a newly plugged-in game controller (a fancy word for joystick, gamepad, flight yoke, rudder control, and similar gaming gear). But if XP doesn't greet your gear, click the Add button and select your model from the list. Feel free to make any necessary adjustments here as well.

Keyboard

If your keyboard is not working or not plugged in, your computer usually tells you as soon as you turn it on. If you see your computer's startled Keyboard Error message — and Windows can't find the keyboard, either — it's time to buy a new one. Plug it in, and Windows XP and your computer should find it automatically.

Use this icon mainly for minor keyboard adjustments like repeat rate and touch sensitivity.

Mouse

Windows XP lets left-handers swap their mouse buttons with a click in this icon's Switch Primary and Secondary Buttons check box. You can also change your double-click speed, mouse pointers, and set options for different mouse models.

Phone and Modem Options

You'll rarely use these phone and modem options unless you're a laptop owner who constantly encounters different area codes. If that's you, click this area's Dialing Rules tab and then click New to add your new location to your area code arsenal. (Windows saves your previously entered area codes. Should you revisit, select your current location from the list, and Windows XP will use that area's area code.)

Printers and Faxes

Clicking this is the same as choosing the task marked View Installed Printers or Fax Printers. As discussed in this section's first part, it simply lists your installed printers and fax printers.

Scanners and Cameras

Click here to see your currently installed (and turned on) scanners and/or cameras. Or, to install *new* scanners or cameras, just plug them in and turn them on. Windows XP almost always recognizes and greets them by name. Windows sometimes doesn't recognize a few older models, though, forcing you to take these extra steps:

1. **Open Printers and Other Hardware from the Control Panel.**
2. **Click the Scanners and Cameras icon.**
3. **Choose Add an Imaging Device (hidden at the top of the window's left side).**

   Windows brings up its Installation Wizard that works amazingly like the Add Printers Wizard.

4. **Choose the manufacturer, model, and port.**

   Click the manufacturer's name on the window's left side and choose the model on the right. Click Next and then choose Automatic Port Detection. If you've turned on your camera or scanner and plugged in its cable correctly, Windows should recognize it and place an icon for it in both your My Computer area and your Control Panel's Scanners and Camera area.

Unfortunately, the installation of cameras and scanners sometimes doesn't work this easily. If Windows doesn't automatically accept your gear, use the scanner or camera's bundled software. The scanner or camera should still work — you just won't be able to use Windows XP's built-in software to grab images.

Chapter 7 has details on using your scanner, and I cover photos in Chapter 16.

Fiddling with User Accounts

Click the Control Panel's User Account category to provide separate accounts for other people to log on to your computer. You can add passwords, add cool pictures to an account's Welcome screen photo, and add security restrictions on certain accounts. (That keeps the kids from installing unapproved programs.) I explain it all in Chapter 13.

Setting the Date, Time, Language, and Regional Options

Microsoft designed this area mostly for laptoppers who frequently travel to different time zones and locations. Otherwise, you touch this information only once — when first setting up your computer. Windows XP subsequently remembers it even if the power goes out. Choosing Date, Time, Language, and Regional Options from the Control Panel offers you these tasks:

- **Change the Date and Time:** Clicking here lets you change your computer's time and date. To make the computer set its clock *automatically,* click the Internet Time tab and choose Automatically Synchronize with an Internet Time Server.
- **Change the Format of Numbers, Dates and Times:** Moved to Italy and need to write to the tailor? Click here first and select Italian, and Windows switches to that country's currency symbols and date format.

- **Add Other Languages:** Bilinguals use this area when working on documents using characters from different languages. (Foreign characters often require installing another font, which is covered in Chapter 7.)

Accessibility Options

Nearly everybody finds Windows XP to be challenging, but some people face special physical challenges, as well. To assist them, the Control Panel's Accessibility Options area makes Windows easier to use for people with a wide variety of physical limitations. Ignore the two listed tasks and click the Accessibility Options icon beneath them to bring up the *real* dialog box, shown in Figure 11-11.

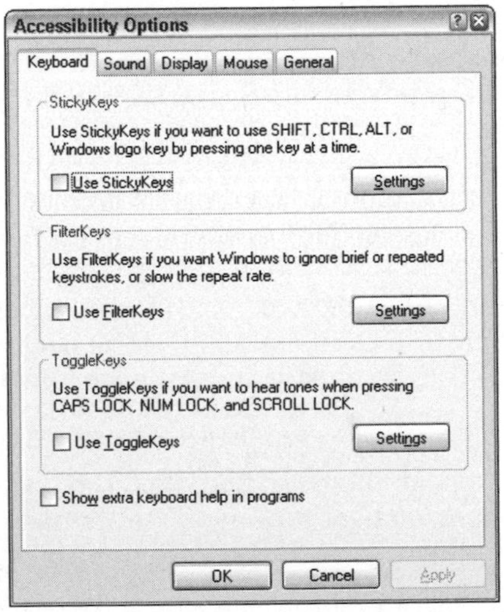

Figure 11-11: The Accessibility Options area contains a wide variety of ways to help users with physical limitations.

The Accessibility Options dialog box offers ways to change the keyboard, sound, display, and mouse to help people use those items:

- **Keyboard:** Options here mostly help people who can't press two keys simultaneously.
- **Sound:** Chose this if you have trouble hearing Windows' sound warnings.
- **Display:** The settings on this tab eliminate most screen colors but help vision-impaired people view the screen and cursor more clearly.

- **Mouse:** This lets you control the mouse pointer with your keyboard's numeric keypad.
- **General:** A catch-all for other settings, this provides different ways to turn the other settings on and off.

Security Center

Choosing this merely brings up the Windows XP Security Center, which I discuss in Chapter 10.

Icons to Avoid

You probably won't come across these icons unless you've chosen the Control Panel's lay-the-cards-on-the-table approach: the Classic View. But if you come across these icons, here's why you shouldn't click them.

Administrative Tools: This icon's a definite no-no. There's nothing here unless you're taking advanced computer classes. This icon is meant for technicians.

Scheduled Tasks: Don't fiddle around in here unless you can't possibly avoid it. Windows XP can perform some tasks automatically in the background, and it lists its scheduled tasks here. They're mostly maintenance jobs that don't need changing.

Speech: Click the Speech icon to hear Microsoft Sam read the text on your screen. Turn him off quickly when you hear how awful he sounds.

Chapter 12

Keeping Windows from Breaking

In This Chapter

- Creating your own restore point
- Freeing up hard disk space
- Making your computer run faster
- Backing up your computer
- Tracking down and installing a new driver
- Cleaning your mouse, keyboard, and monitor

If something in Windows is already broken, hop ahead to Chapter 17 for the fix. But if your computer seems to be running remarkably well, stay right here. This chapter explains how to keep it running that way for the longest time possible.

This chapter is a checklist of sorts, with each section explaining a fairly simple and necessary task to keep Windows running at its best. There's no need to call in a techie because much of this takes place using either Windows' built-in maintenance tools or standard household cleaners. For example, you use XP's built-in Disk Cleanup program to free up space on a crowded hard disk.

This chapter also helps you fix the annoying and ubiquitous "bad driver" problem by explaining how to put a fresh driver behind the wheel.

Finally, you discover a quick way to clean your mouse — a necessary but oft-overlooked task that keeps the pointer on target. (Feel free to grab the vacuum cleaner and suck all the cookies crumbs out of your keyboard during the same cleaning spree.)

In addition to the checklist this chapter offers, make sure Windows Update automatically locates, downloads, and installs Microsoft's latest patches to keep your computer secure. I explain how in Chapter 10.

Creating a Restore Point

When your computer's ailing, System Restore provides a magical way to go back in time to when your computer was feeling better. System Restore works by taking a daily snapshot of your computer's settings as well as an automatic snapshot before you install a new computer part (just in case the newcomer causes problems).

The problem is finding that one, magic restore point that makes everything better. Windows XP simply slaps a date onto its automated System Restore points along with the boring name *System Checkpoint;* it doesn't say, "This restore point is just after you installed Berzerkeroids — and everything still ran fine!"

To maximize System Restore's potential, create your *own* restore points with your *own* labels. Here's how:

1. **When your computer's running especially well, call up System Restore by going to the Start menu's All Programs menu. From there, pop open the Accessories menu and then the System Tools menu, where you find System Restore.**

   The Welcome to System Restore window shown in Figure 12-1 appears.

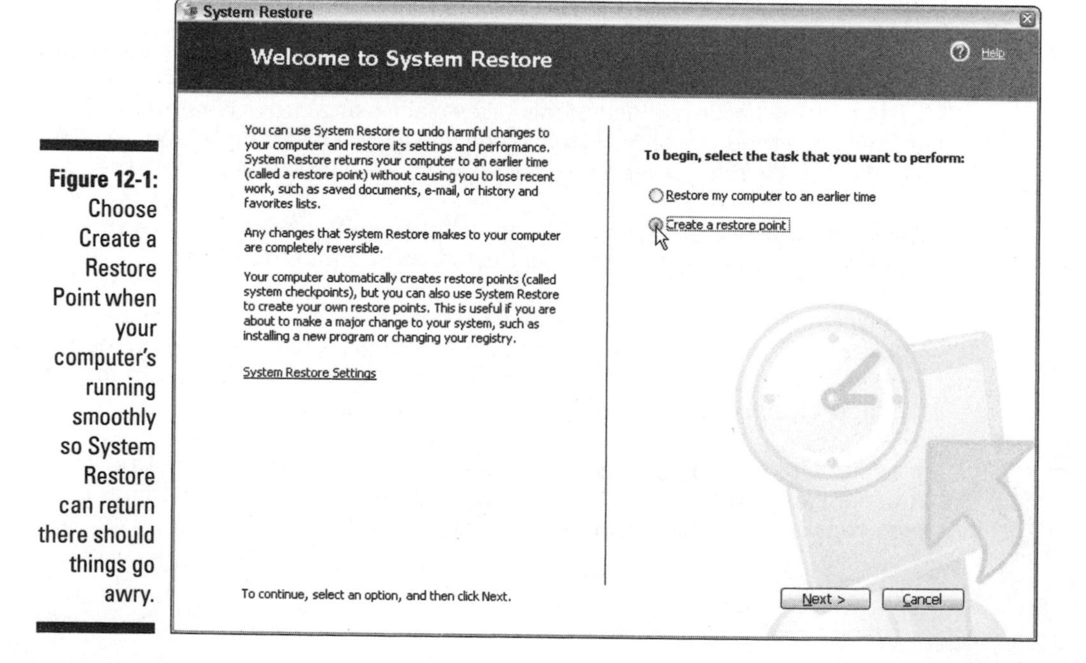

Figure 12-1: Choose Create a Restore Point when your computer's running smoothly so System Restore can return there should things go awry.

2. **Choose Create a Restore Point and then click Next.**
3. **When Windows asks you to describe your new restore point, type in something that helps you remember why you made the restore point.**

   For instance, type in `Nothing has crashed for a week — if only my computer could always run this smoothly!` You needn't add the date in your description because Windows automatically gives it a date stamp.
4. **Click the Create button, and you're done.**

By creating your own restore points on good days, you'll know immediately which ones to use on bad days. I describe how to resuscitate your computer with System Restore in Chapter 17.

Tuning Up Windows XP with Built-In Maintenance Tools

Open Windows XP's Control Panel (it's on the Start menu) and choose the Performance and Maintenance category, and you see a collection of tasks to keep your computer running smoothly. Here's a description of each category:

- **See Basic Information About Your Computer:** Handy mostly when troubleshooting or talking with technical support people, this displays information about Windows, your computer, and its many parts.
- **Adjust Visual Effects:** This describes how to turn off some of Windows XP's visual effects — the little shadows around icons and menus, for instance — to speed up your computer.
- **Free Space on Your Hard Disk:** To free up disk space, this program removes Internet Explorer cache files, empties your Recycle Bin, and deletes temporary files.
- **Back Up Your Data:** Windows XP Professional comes with a backup program. Although quite feeble, it's also free.
- **Rearrange Items on Your Hard Disk to Make Programs Run Faster:** In a process known as defragmenting, Windows rearranges your hard disk's data for faster access.

I describe each category more fully in this chapter's next five sections.

Finding technical information about your computer

If you ever need to look under Windows XP's hood, heaven forbid, open the Control Panel's Performance and Maintenance section and choose See Basic Information About Your Computer. Shown in Figure 12-2, the System Properties dialog box displays oodles of computer information, more than you probably want to know but often just enough for the tech support person on the telephone. Here's the information you find on each of the dialog box's tabs:

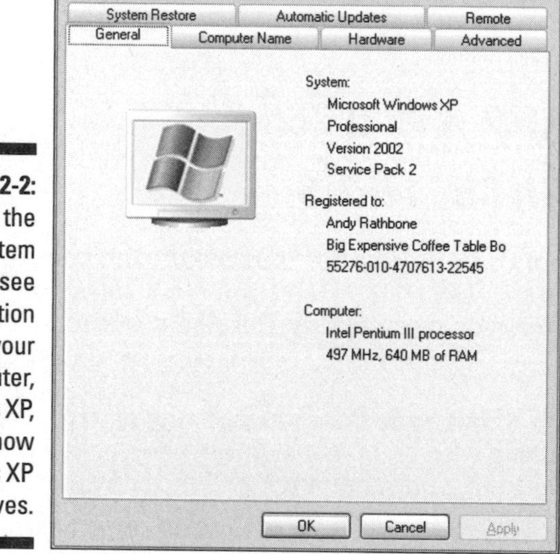

Figure 12-2: Click the System icon to see information about your computer, Windows XP, and how Windows XP behaves.

- **General:** This tab lists your version number of Windows XP, its registered owner, the latest installed service pack, and the horsepower of the CPU inside your computer.
- **Computer Name:** This tab identifies your computer's name on a network (if it's part of one).
- **Hardware:** You'll only use the Device Manager button here, mainly to list all the parts inside your computer. (The parts with exclamation points next to them aren't happy. Double-click them and choose Troubleshoot to diagnose their problem.)
- **Advanced:** Settings, the top button in the Performance category, lets you view and adjust Windows XP's visual effects. (You won't be using the other buttons.)

- **System Restore:** This tab lets you turn off System Restore for some of your hard disks (if your computer has more than one) as well as adjust the amount of hard disk space System Restore consumes. (It normally consumes 12 percent of your hard disk space. Lowering that percentage saves space but reduces your number of restore points.)
- **Automatic Updates:** Leave this set on Automatic. (I cover this and other parts of Windows XP's Security Center in Chapter 10.)
- **Remote:** I cover Remote Assistance in Chapter 17.

Just what *does* Disk Cleanup delete, anyway?

Disk Cleanup doesn't take a random shotgun blast at any files you've created. It doesn't even delete those blurry digital photos that *you* should have deleted long ago. Instead, Disk Cleanup deletes background trash created mostly by your programs as they go about their duties. Here's the rundown:

- **Downloaded Program Files:** If you've seen something flashy on the Internet, chances are, it's been downloaded to your computer — and left there, even after you watched it and moved on to another Web page. This setting deletes those leftovers unless you've specifically asked them to be saved. (Visiting the same page downloads them again.)
- **Temporary Internet Files:** Internet Explorer downloads each Web page you visit and then displays it on your screen. This setting removes that huge stack of old Web pages. (Visit the page to view it again.)
- **Offline Web Pages:** If you've *synchronized* any Web pages, which automatically stores the pages onto your computer for offline reading, this setting removes them. (Click Synchronize from Internet Explorer's Tools menu to put them back.)
- **Recycle Bin:** This empties your Recycle Bin, removing your last chance to undelete any deleted files.
- **Temporary Files:** As they run, many programs create their own work files — temporary storage tanks for crunching numbers. The programs are supposed to delete them when they're through, but they rarely do. This setting deletes any leftovers older than one week.
- **WebClient/Publisher Temporary Files:** More Internet trash, this mysterious option rarely empties completely. Don't worry about it.
- **Compress Old Files:** Windows offers to compress files that you haven't used recently. Although a nice gesture, this means your computer must take time to *decompress* them when you do need them. I don't recommend it.
- **Catalog Files for the Content Indexer:** The Search program (which I cover in Chapter 6) finds files without using an index. Creating an index speeds up your searches but at the expense of disk space. Those huge indexes require so much room Windows XP normally leaves this option turned off. If you turn on indexing, though, this option deletes unneeded files from your old indexes.

Most of the stuff in this area is pretty complicated, so don't mess with it unless you're sure of what you're doing or a technical support person tells you to change a setting. More advanced books cover these features.

Adjusting visual effects to speed up your computer

As it frantically crunches numbers in the background, Windows XP tries to project a navel-gazing image of inner peace. Its menus and windows open and close with a slow fade; aesthetically pleasing shadows surround each menu and the mouse pointer. When a folder opens, Windows automatically chooses its appropriate task pane. Windows also organizes the Control Panel's icons into neat categories instead of presenting one folder crowded with icons.

All these extra visual decisions require extra calculations on Windows's part, however, slowing it down a bit. To change Windows' attitude from peaceful to performance, head for the Control Panel's Performance and Maintenance category and choose Visual Effects, as shown in Figure 12-3.

For fastest action, choose Adjust for Best Performance. Windows quickly strips away all the visuals and reverts to Classic Mode — a faster way of working that mimics earlier, no-frills Windows versions. Choose Adjust for Best Appearance for a prettier, but slower, Windows.

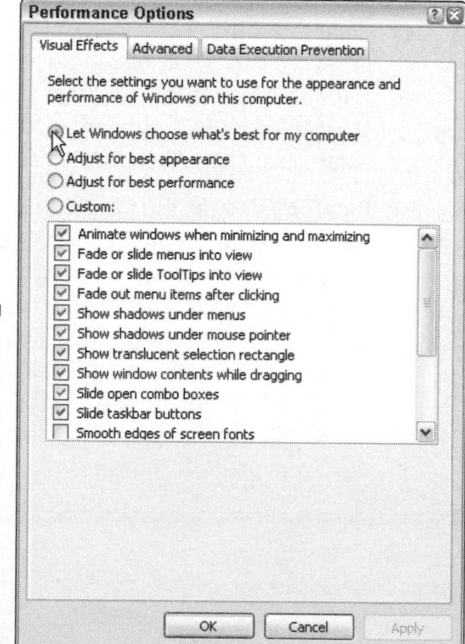

Figure 12-3: Choose Visual Effects to strike a balance between speed and aesthetics.

To let Windows XP examine your computer's processing power and choose a balance between aesthetically pleasing and physically overburdened, select Let Windows Choose What's Best for My Computer.

Bored? Experiment with each visual setting by choosing Custom (refer to Figure 12-3). Choose Apply after making each change; if you notice an unwelcome change in Windows XP's behavior, reverse your change and click Apply again.

Freeing up space on your hard disk

When Windows XP begins whining about running out of room on your hard disk, this solution grants you a short reprieve:

1. **Choose the Control Panel's Performance and Maintenance category and choose Free Up Space on Your Hard Disk.**

   Far from grateful, Windows XP grunts and groans for an eternity and then presents its Disk Cleanup program, shown in Figure 12-4.

2. **Check all the items except the last two: Compress Old Files and Catalog Files for the Content Indexer. Then click the OK button.**

3. **Click Yes when Windows XP asks if you're sure.**

   Windows XP then proceeds to empty your Recycle Bin, destroy leftovers from old Web sites, and remove other hard disk clutter.

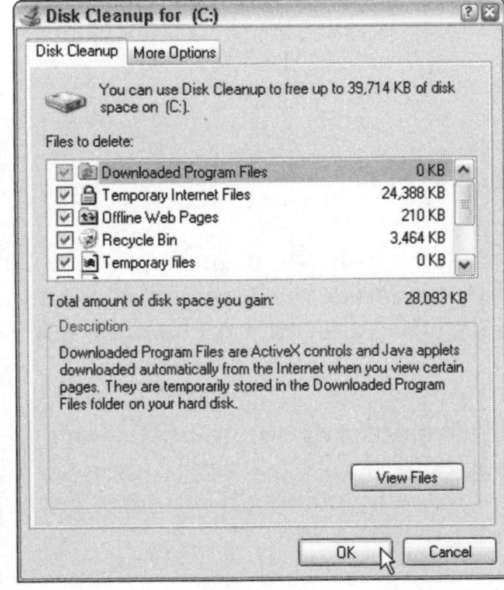

Figure 12-4: The Disk Cleanup tool removes unnecessary files, leaving you more storage space on your hard disk.

Windows XP Home doesn't list my Backup program!

Windows XP Professional conveniently places the Backup program on your Start menu. But Windows XP Home not only leaves it off the Start menu but also doesn't even install it. Instead, the Backup program remains hidden on your Windows XP Upgrade or Full Install CD, and you must install it yourself by following these steps:

1. **While holding down the Shift key, insert the Windows XP Home CD.**

   Holding down Shift keeps Windows XP from trying to install itself again.

2. **Start the installation wizard by double-clicking the `Ntbackup.msi` file in the following folder of the Windows XP Home Edition CD:**

   `D:\VALUEADD\MSFT\NTBACKUP`

   (Replace `D:` with your own drive's letter.)

3. **When the wizard is done, click Finish.**

The wizard then installs the Backup program to your computer and adds it to the Start menu. (You see the little New Program Installed message by your Start button, and the highlights lead you to the actual program.) The Control Panel's Performance and Maintenance category also bear the new Backup option.

Unfortunately, some XP Home users encounter yet another stumbling block: Some computers that come with Windows XP preinstalled don't include a copy of the Windows XP Home CD. Instead, they include a Restore CD. The Restore CD simply restores your computer to the state it was in as it left the factory. It's not an original Windows XP installation CD, and it doesn't contain the Backup program. If you fall into that category, unfortunately, you're completely out of luck.

For a shortcut to Disk Cleanup, call up My Computer on your Start menu, right-click on your hard disk, choose Properties, and click the Disk Cleanup button.

Backing up your data

Windows XP's Backup program offers a rare combination, indeed: It's very basic *and* very difficult to use. But if you have more time than money, here's how to make Windows XP's built-in Backup program back up your important files.

Designed for experienced users, Windows XP's bare-bones Backup program has no frills and offers very little help along the way. To keep your data *really* safe, ask your computer retailer to recommend a third-party backup program that's both more dependable and easier to use.

Before you can use Windows XP's Backup program, you need three things:

- **An external hard drive:** Windows' free Backup program can't write directly to a blank disc, so you need an external hard drive to store your backups. Buy and install one that plugs into your computer's FireWire or USB 2.0 port. (I describe installing an external hard drive — and a FireWire or USB 2.0 port — in *Upgrading & Fixing PCs For Dummies,* 6th Edition [Wiley].)
- **A password-protected Administrator account:** You must be logged on to the computer with an Administrator account, and that account needs a password. I explain passwords and user accounts in Chapter 13.
- **Windows XP's Backup program:** Windows XP Professional comes with the Backup program installed and on the Start menu. Windows XP Home users don't have that luxury — and sometimes they don't even have the Backup program. The nearby sidebar explains the dilemma and discusses options for Windows XP Home users.

When you take care of those three things, follow these steps to make your computer back up your work automatically each night:

1. **Run the Windows XP Backup program and click Next.**

   To find the Backup program, choose the Control Panel's Performance and Maintenance category and choose Backup Your Data. (You'll also find the Backup program listed on the Start menu's System Tools area, found in the Accessories area of All Programs.)

2. **Choose Back Up Files and Settings from the Backup and Restore Wizard and click Next.**

   If you don't see that option, you're in Advanced mode, not Wizard mode. Click the Welcome tab and choose Wizard mode to return to the simpler settings.

3. **Choose My Documents and Settings and click Next.**

   Or, to back up the work of every user account on your computer, select Everyone's Documents and Settings, instead, as shown in Figure 12-5.

4. **Select your external hard drive as the place to save your backup, choose a backup name, and click Next.**

   For instance, if you're backing up your own work, name the file **My Backup Files**. If you're backing up everybody's data, name the file **Everybody's Backup Files**.

5. **Click the Advanced button to automate the process. (To make one backup immediately, click Finish instead.)**

   If you click Finish, you're done. Windows XP immediately begins backing up the files according to your instructions.

   If you click the Advanced button to back up your work on a regular, automatic schedule, move to Step 6.

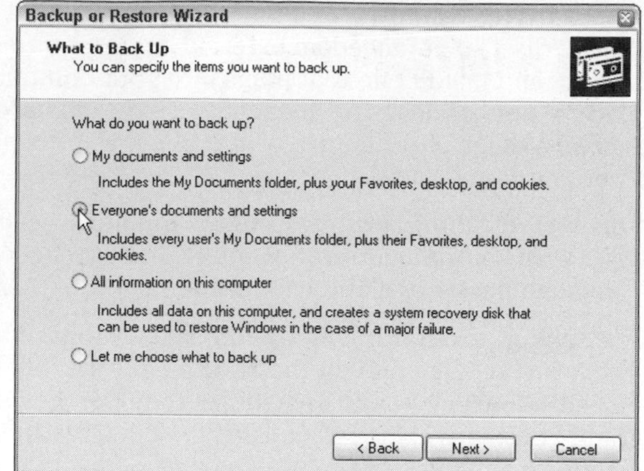

Figure 12-5: Choose what you want to back up.

6. **Choose Normal and click Next.**
7. **Don't choose either option and click Next.**

   You don't need to Verify Data After Backup or Disable Volume Shadow Copy.

8. **Choose Replace the Existing Backups and click Next.**
9. **Choose Later, type a name for the job, and click the Set Schedule button.**

   Name the job **My daily backup** or something similar.

10. **Schedule the task for Daily starting at 4 a.m. and then click OK.**

    Choose a different time if you're still playing computer games at 4 a.m.; otherwise, 4 a.m. usually works well.

11. **Type the password for your Administrator user account and click OK.**

- For your computer to back up automatically each night, you must leave it turned on during the backup time. I leave mine turned on 24 hours a day. (Please turn off your computer's monitor, though.)
- Every day or so, right-click on your backup file, choose Properties, and check the file's Modified date. If you're backing up at 4 a.m., the backup file's Modified date is the current date. If the date's wrong, fire up the Backup program and walk through these steps to figure out the problem.
- To restore a backup — or any of the individual files it contains — follow Step 1 but choose Restore Files and Settings in Step 2. Browse to your backup file and try restoring a few test files to make sure your backups are working and restoring properly.
- Feel free to check out the Backup program's Help utility for the program's more troublesome details.

Checking a hard disk for errors

Today's hard drives rarely have errors, so you probably don't need to check for any. But if you think your hard drive's acting strangely, and defragmenting it doesn't fix the problem, tell Windows XP to check it for errors. Open My Computer, right-click on your hard drive, and choose Properties. Click the Tools tab and click the Check Now button. (Leave the two options blank.) Click the Start button, and you hear your hard drive whirring away as Windows probes it for problems. If it finds any, follow the Windows instructions for making repair attempts. Also start saving your cash and backing up your data — repeated errors mean your hard drive may be on its last legs.

Rearranging items on your hard disk to make programs run faster (defragmenting)

When writing information to your hard disk, Windows isn't the most careful shelf stocker. It often breaks files into pieces, stuffing them into different nooks and crannies. When rummaging around for all the parts, Windows subsequently takes longer to retrieve the files.

To fix the problem, choose the Control Panel's Performance and Maintenance category and select Rearrange Items on Your Hard Disk to Make Programs Run Faster.

When the Disk Defragmenter window appears, click the Analyze button, shown in Figure 12-6. Windows inspects your computer's hard drive and reports back. If it says your hard drive doesn't need defragmentation, click the Close button, close the program, and move on. But if it says you *should* defragment, click the Defragment button.

The Disk Defragmenter does its job in the background as you work, sometimes finishing in a few minutes, other times working through the evening. When it's finished, your computer runs more quickly when opening and closing files.

- Run the Disk Defragmenter once a month or so, especially if your computer seems to be running slowly or you can hear your hard drive making frantic rummaging noises.

- For a shortcut to the Disk Defragmenter, call up My Computer from the Start menu, right-click on your hard drive, and choose Properties. Then click the Tools tab and click the Defragment Now button.

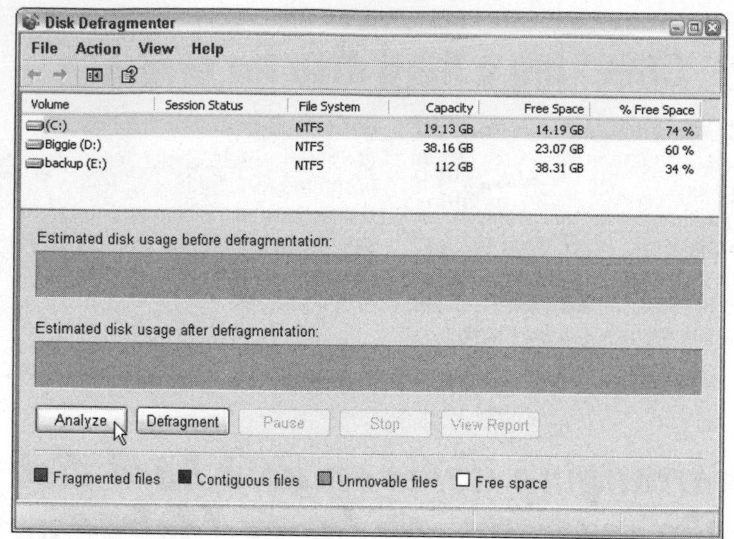

Figure 12-6: The Disk Cleanup tool removes unnecessary files, leaving you more storage space on your hard disk.

Fiddling with Drivers

Windows comes with drivers needed to install almost anything you want to attach to your computer. However, sometimes you want to install something that's either too new for Windows XP to know about or too old for it to remember. In that case, it's up to you to track down and install a Windows XP *driver* for that part. The driver is simply a piece of software that lets Windows communicate with the part.

The best drivers come with an installation program that automatically places the software in the right place. The worst drivers leave all the grunt work up to you.

If Windows XP doesn't automatically recognize and install your newly attached piece of hardware after it's turned on, follow these steps to locate and install a new driver:

1. **Visit the part manufacturer's Web site and download the latest Windows XP driver.**

   You often find the manufacturer's Web site stamped somewhere on the part's box. If you can't find it, try searching for the part manufacturer's name on Google (`www.google.com`) and locate its Web site.

   Look in the Web site's Support or Customer Service area. There, you usually need to enter your part, its model number, and your computer's operating system (Windows XP) before the Web site coughs up the driver.

No Windows XP driver listed? Try downloading a Windows 2000 driver instead because they sometimes work just as well. (Be sure to scan *any* downloaded file with a virus checker.)

2. **Run the driver's installation program.**

   Sometimes clicking your downloaded file makes its installation program jump into action, installing the driver for you. If so, you're through. If not, head to Step 3.

   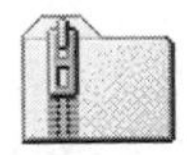

   If the downloaded file has a little zipper on the icon, right-click on it and choose Extract All to *unzip* its contents into a folder. Remember the folder's name and location on your computer because you need it in a later step.

3. **Choose Printers and Other Hardware from the Control Panel.**

4. **Choose the words Add Hardware from the top of the window's left side.**

   The Add Hardware Wizard guides you through the steps of installing your new hardware and, if necessary, installing your new driver.

- Keep your drivers up-to-date. Even the ones packaged in a new part's box are usually old. Visit the manufacturer's Web site and download the latest driver. Chances are, it fixes problems earlier users had with the driver packaged in the box.
- Problems with the new driver? Right-click on My Computer on the Start menu and choose Manage. Double-click Device Manager and double-click your part's name on the window's right side. Click the Driver tab and click the Roll Back Driver button. Windows XP reinstalls the previous driver.

Cleaning Your Computer

Even the best housekeeper or janitor draws the line at cleaning a computer. This chore's up to you, and you'll know when it's necessary. You don't need to turn off your computer for any of this — *except* if you need to remove your keyboard for cleaning.

Cleaning your mouse

If your mouse pointer jumps around on-screen or doesn't move at all, your mouse is probably clogged with desktop gunk. Follow these steps to degunkify it:

1. **Turn the mouse upside down and clean off any dirt stuck to the bottom.**

   Your mouse must lie flat on its pad to work correctly.

2. **Twist off the mouse's little round cover and remove the ball.**
3. **Wipe off any crud from the ball and blow dust out of the hole.**

   A little air blower, sold at office and computer stores, works well here. (It also blows off the dust layers clogging your computer's air vents.)
4. **Pull out any stray hairs, dust, and roller goo.**

   A cotton swab moistened with some alcohol cleans the most persistent goo from the little rollers. (The rollers should be smooth and shiny.) Dirty rollers cause the most mouse problems.
5. **Replace the cleaned ball into the cleaned hole and reinsert the clean little round cover.**

I've had mice last almost ten years. If you get tired of cleaning its innards, pick up an optical mouse. With no moving parts, they rarely need cleaning. (Optical mice don't work well on shiny surfaces, so if your desk is shiny, you need a mouse pad.)

Cleaning your monitor

Don't spray glass cleaner directly onto your monitor because it drips down into the monitor's guts, frightening the circuits. Instead, spray glass cleaner onto a soft rag and wipe the screen. Don't use paper because it can scratch the glass.

For cleaning flat panel monitors, use a soft, lint-free cloth, and a mix of half water and half vinegar. Feel free to clean your monitor's front panels, too, if you're feeling especially hygienic.

Cleaning your keyboard

Keyboards are usually too wide to shake over a wastebasket. The best way to clean them is to shut down Windows, turn off your computer, and unplug the keyboard from the computer. (Never unplug a keyboard from a computer that's turned on.)

Take the keyboard outdoors and shake it vigorously to remove the debris. If you're up to it, spray some household cleaning solution on a rag and remove the grime from around the keyboard' edges and its keycaps.

Plug it back in, turn on your computer, and your computer looks almost new.

Chapter 13

Sharing One Computer with Several People

In This Chapter

- Understanding user accounts
- Setting up, deleting, or changing user accounts
- Logging on at the Welcome screen
- Switching quickly between users
- Understanding passwords

Ten years ago, *everybody* fought over that single, expensive household computer, mostly for the right to play those exciting new computer games.

Today, the Xbox, Playstation, and Nintendo remove that attraction, so instead of adding more entertainment, Microsoft added something much more boring to Windows XP: security. Windows XP allows several people to share one computer securely, without letting anybody peek into anybody else's files.

The secret? Windows XP grants each user his or her own *user account,* which neatly separates that person from other users. When people log on using their own user account, the computer looks tailor-made for them: It displays their personalized desktop background, menu choices, programs, and files — and it forbids them from seeing items belonging to other users.

This chapter explains how to set up a separate user account for everybody in the house, including the computer's owner, family members or roommates, and even occasional visitors who ask to check their e-mail.

Understanding User Accounts

Everyone who uses Windows XP needs a user account. A *user account* is like a cocktail-party name tag that helps Windows recognize who's sitting at the keyboard. Windows XP dishes out three types of user accounts: Administrator, Limited, and Guest. Users log on under their own account when Windows XP first loads, as shown in Figure 13-1.

Who cares? Well, Windows XP allows each type of account to carry out different functions on the computer. If the computer were a huge apartment building, the Administrator account would belong to the manager, each tenant would have a Limited account, and Guest accounts would belong to visitors trying to use the bathroom in the lobby. Here's how the different accounts translate into computer lingo:

- **Administrator:** The administrator controls the entire computer, deciding who gets to use it and what each user can do on it. On a computer running Windows XP, the owner usually holds the almighty Administrator account. He or she then sets up accounts for each household member, changing their accounts when needed, and fixing their lost passwords. Here's the important part: Only administrators can install software and change the computer's hardware.

  More than one person can hold an Administrator account on a computer. In fact, all the users can hold one, if the computer's owner prefers that. That lets anybody install software and change important computer settings. (It also lets all users peek into each other's files, unless they've made their folders "private," covered later in this chapter.)

- **Limited:** Limited accounts can use most of the computer, but they can't make any big changes to it. They can't install programs, for instance, but they can still run them.
- **Guest:** Guests can use the computer, but the computer doesn't recognize them by name. Guest accounts function much like Limited accounts, but with no privacy: Anybody can log on with the Guest account, and the desktop will look the way the last Guest left it.

Here some ways accounts are typically assigned when you're sharing the same computer under one roof:

- In a family, the parents usually hold Administrator accounts, the kids usually have Limited accounts, and the baby sitter logs on using the Guest account.
- In a dorm or shared apartment, the computer's owner holds the Administrator account, and the roommates have either Limited or Guest accounts, depending on their trustworthiness level.

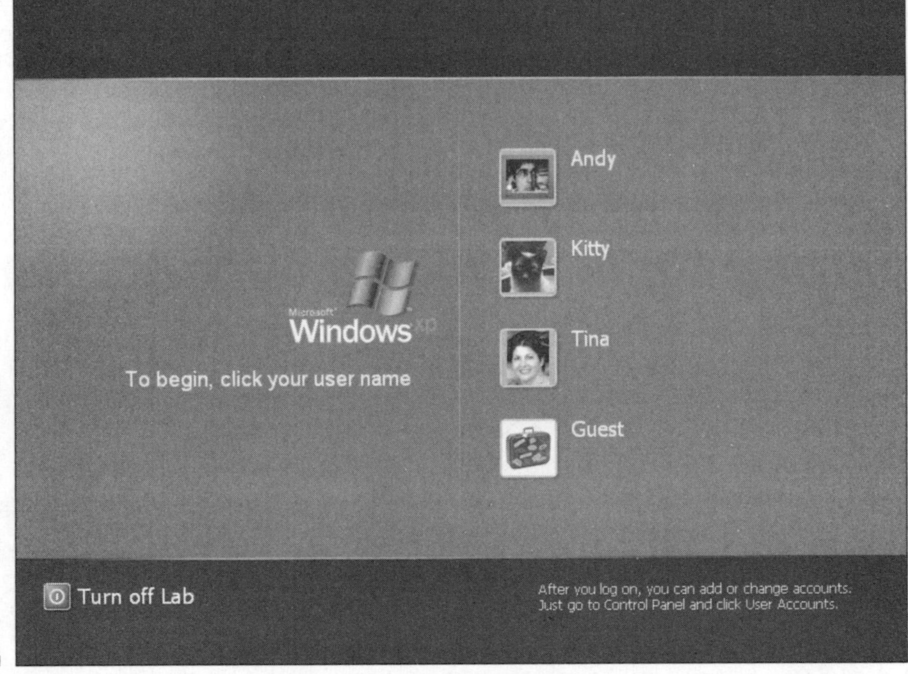

Figure 13-1: When loaded, Windows XP lets users log on under their own accounts.

To keep others from logging on under your user account, you must protect it with a password. (I describe how to choose a password for your account later in this chapter.)

The limitations of the lowly Guest account

People with Administrator or Limited accounts usually have no problem connecting to the Internet through a dial-up modem. But when Guest account users sit down at that same computer and try to connect to the Internet, Windows XP refuses to let them. What gives?

It's a security measure built in to Windows XP, and it works like this: The Guest account can use an *existing* connection to connect to the Internet. But Windows XP's security restrictions forbid Guest account users from starting or disconnecting an Internet connection.

Only computers with dial-up accounts have this problem. If you access the Internet through a cable or other broadband connection, for instance, the Internet connection is always *turned on,* even if it Internet Explorer isn't always running. That lets Guest account users surf the Web without problem.

Guest account users accessing the Internet through a networked computer usually won't have a problem, either. But if you access the Internet through a dial-up modem, your baby sitter won't be able to log on through the Guest account to check for e-mail.

When you're installing Windows XP on your computer, the software automatically grants Administrator status to every account you create. When you're through installing Windows XP, be sure to change those accounts to Limited or Guest status unless you trust those people to handle your computer wisely. After Windows XP is installed, you're given the option of assigning either Administrator or Limited status to the accounts you create.

Setting Up or Changing User Accounts

Limited account users can change their own account's password and picture, but the administrators have the *real* power: They can create or delete entire user accounts, effectively wiping a person off the computer. (That's why you should never upset a computer's administrator.)

Do you want the Microsoft .NET Passport?

In its ever-expanding push toward computer domination, Microsoft launched an evil concept called the *.NET Passport.* (Soon after installation, Windows XP urgently begs you to sign up for one.) In theory, the Passport sounds great: Give Microsoft a user name and password, and you have a Passport. When you visit any Passport-aware Internet sites, you type in your same Passport name and password. You no longer have to remember different user names and passwords for every place that you visit or shop on the Internet.

In fact, when you move from one Passport-enabled site to another, you sometimes don't even need to log on again. With the Passport, your personal data travels with you — your name, your address, and, if you purchased anything, your credit card number. Microsoft says its .NET Passport enables software, Internet services, and computer gadgetry to work together and share information, making the Internet easier for everyone to use.

Think about it, though. No entity should govern your Internet use — except you. The Microsoft Passport contains your Internet identity. With Passport, Microsoft creates a consumer database that's just too powerful. Microsoft can collect information from any Passport-enabled site you visit, so Microsoft knows the stocks you track in Investor.com, the Web pages you view in MSN.com, and where you travel through Expedia.com. When you move from one Passport-enabled site to another, that information could be shared, too.

In concept, Passport sounds great. When computers are working well, they do great things. But everybody knows how terrible computers can be if something goes wrong. Passport, I'm afraid, offers too much opportunity for things to go wrong. Yes, I occasionally use a Passport account when there's no alternative. But I don't enter any personal information into it, and I avoid Passport-enabled sites whenever possible.

If you're an administrator, create a Limited user account for everybody who's going to use your computer. That gives those folks just enough control over the computer to keep them from bugging you all the time, yet it keeps them from accidentally deleting your important files.

To create, change, or delete a user account, click the Start button, choose the Control Panel, and select User Accounts. A window pops up, as shown in Figure 13-2, that's seen only by administrators.

To save time, simply click the picture of the account you want to change, as shown in Figure 13-2. Windows XP brings up that account's settings and lets you change the ones you want. Click the Guest account icon, for instance, and its settings let you turn the account on or off.

Here's a rundown of the different tasks available:

- **Change an Account:** The most encompassing of the options, this lets you change an account's name, password, picture, or type. You can upgrade a user's account to administrator, for instance, if you're tired of handling the computer by yourself. Or, if you're tired of the *user,* here's where you can delete his or her account, as well.
- **Create a New Account:** Click here to create accounts for other computer users. You simply choose the account's name and choose whether to grant the person an Administrator or Limited account.
- **Change the Way Users Log On and Off:** This one's a little more complicated because it brings up two options, described here:
    - **Use the Welcome Screen:** Normally, people log on by clicking their names on the Welcome screen. Removing the check mark in this box turns off the Welcome screen, removing the friendly account names and pictures. Instead, users must type their name and password into a little box. Why? This method is more secure; without the Welcome screen, nobody can tell which people have accounts on the computer. Turning off the Welcome screen also turns off Fast User Switching, described next.
    - **Use Fast User Switching:** Covered in the next section, Windows XP lets users switch between accounts quickly and easily. Instead of logging off, John can simply switch to Carol's account so she can play a quick computer game. When John switches back to his account, his open programs appear just as he left them. Remove this box's check mark to turn off Fast User Switching, forcing users to log off (closing any open programs, as well) normally before letting other users log on.

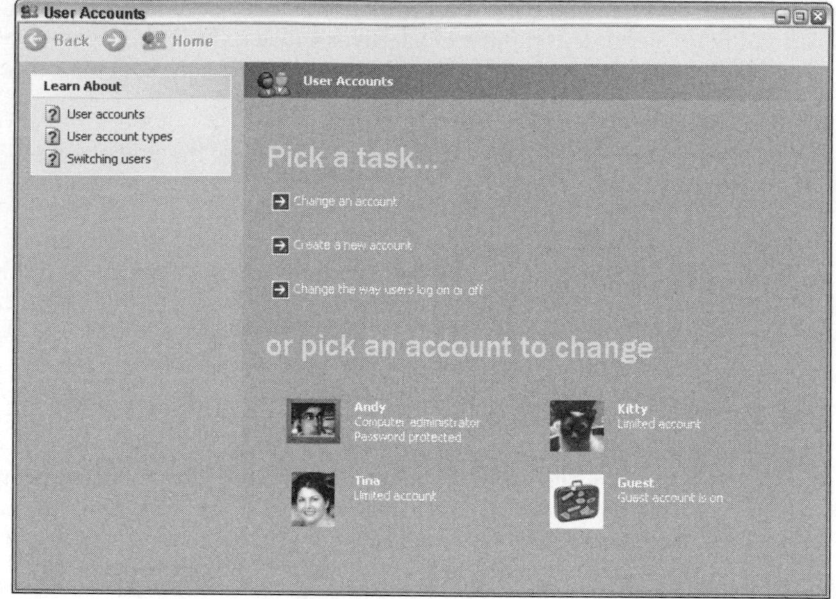

Figure 13-2: Use the User Accounts area to create or change user accounts.

If you've signed up for a Microsoft Passport on the Internet, Windows offers another item on the menu: Change My .NET Passport. This option simply connects you to the Internet, allowing you to update any personal information after typing in your Passport's name and password. (If you don't have a .NET passport, you're not missing much, as explained in the "Do you want the Microsoft .NET Passport?" sidebar.)

Switching Quickly between Users

Windows XP enables an entire family, roommates, or a small office to share a single computer. Because everybody has a user account, Windows keeps track of everybody's settings. The same computer acts like five different computers, each customized to the user's liking.

Best yet, the computer keeps track of everybody's programs while different people use the computer. Mom can be playing chess and then let Jerry log on to check his e-mail. When Mom logs back on a few minutes later, her chess game is right where she left it: deciding between the *en passant* pawn move or sacrificing the queen's bishop.

Known as *Fast User Switching,* the process works quickly and easily. While holding down the Windows key (it's usually between your keyboard's Ctrl and Alt keys), press the letter L. Wham! The Welcome screen pops up, letting another person use the computer for a while.

After that person finishes using the computer, hold down the Windows key and press the letter L. Wham! The Welcome screen pops up again, letting a different user log on.

- You can also switch users quickly by clicking the Start button and clicking Log Off from the bottom of the menu. When the new window appears, click Switch User instead of Log Off. The Welcome screen appears for the other user to log on.
- If Fast User Switching doesn't work on your computer, the administrator may have turned it off, a feat described in the previous section.

- On older computers without a lot of memory, Fast User Switching doesn't work nearly as well as simply logging off. If your computer runs slowly when you've switched between one or more users, turn off the Fast User Switching option and make people simply log on and off normally.

An old problem with Limited accounts

In theory, Limited account users can run just about any software on the computer. In practice, however, some households find themselves upgrading everybody to Administrator accounts for one big reason: Software written for earlier versions of Windows sometimes can't handle Windows XP's new account system.

That means many older games, CD-burning software, and other "pre-XP" programs refuse to run on a Limited account. If that happens to you, try coaxing the program into action by following these steps:

1. **Right-click on the temperamental program's filename or shortcut.**
2. **Click Advanced, click Run with Different Credentials, and then click OK.**
3. **Start the program and wait for a window to appear.**
4. **Enter an administrative user ID and password into the window.**

This isn't much of a workaround because it requires you to be home before the kids can play their cranky old computer games. (Simply giving the kids your administrator ID and password would defeat the purpose of giving them Limited accounts.) But it might be better than Microsoft's solution: Buy a new, Windows XP–compatible version of the troublesome program.

Changing a User Account's Picture

Okay, now the important stuff: changing the dorky picture Windows automatically assigns to your user account. For every newly created user account, Windows XP dips into its image bag and adds a random picture of butterflies, fish, or soccer balls, or some similarly boring image. Feel free to change the picture to something more reflective of the Real You: You can use pictures taken with a digital camera as well as any pictures or graphics found on the Internet.

To change your user account's picture, click the Start button and double-click your picture at the top. A new window appears, as shown in Figure 13-3. Click an appealing picture and click the Change Picture button. Done!

To assign a picture that's *not* currently shown, select Browse for More Pictures. A new window appears, this time showing the contents of your My Pictures folder. (Your digital camera usually stores its pictures in that folder.) Click a desired picture from the folder, choose Open, and click Change Picture. That's it!

FAT, NTFS, security, and you

Microsoft recommends that a Windows XP computer's hard drive be formatted using the newer, more powerful NTFS than the older FAT or FAT32 systems. If you're upgrading your computer to Windows XP, simply select the NTFS option while installing.

Unfortunately, some computer manufacturers ship with Windows XP preinstalled on a drive that hasn't been formatted with NTFS. What does this mean to you? Well, if your computer's hard drive isn't formatted with NTFS, your user accounts aren't secure. Users can peek into each other's users files if they know where to look. People with Limited or Guest accounts can still install programs and delete important files.

To see how your hard drive is formatted, open My Computer, right-click on your hard drive icon, and choose Properties. If you see the word NTFS next to File System, you're safe. But if you see FAT or FAT32 next to File System, your computer isn't as secure as you might think.

To ensure that your user accounts function the way they're described in this book, convert your FAT or FAT32 hard drive to NTFS by using the Windows XP Convert command. The procedure involves the following steps:

1. **Choose Run from the Start menu.**
2. **Type** CMD **and click the OK button.**
3. **Type this into the command prompt and press the Enter key:**

```
convert C: /fs:ntfs
```

Follow the instructions, if any, and Windows XP converts your hard drive from FAT to NTFS, letting you take full advantage of the new system's security. You may have to restart your computer before the change takes place.

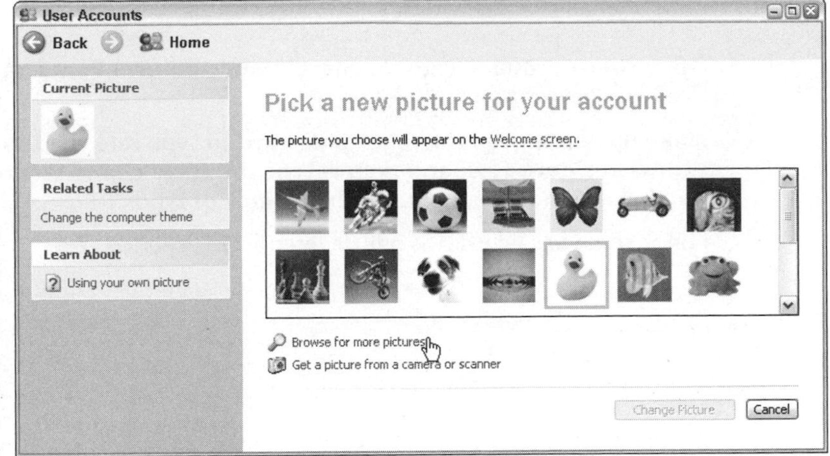

Figure 13-3: Windows XP lets each user choose an account picture.

Want a picture that's stored on your digital camera or sitting on a scanner? Make sure the camera or scanner is connected to your computer, turn on the device, and choose Get a Picture from a Camera or Scanner. Windows XP peeks into the camera or scanner and lets you select the picture you want.

- You can also grab any picture off the Internet and use it for your user account picture. (I explain how to copy a picture off the Internet in Chapter 8.)
- Don't worry about choosing a picture that's too big or too small. Windows XP automatically shrinks or expands the image to fit the postage-stamp-sized space.
- All users may change their pictures — Administrators, Limited, and Guest accounts. (Pictures are about the only thing that guests *are* allowed to change.)

Setting Up Passwords and Security

There's not much point to having a user account if you don't have a password. Without one, Charles from the next cubicle can click your account on the Welcome screen, giving him free reign to snoop through your files.

Administrators, especially, should have passwords. Anybody who logs on with an Administrator account can peek into other user's files or completely sabotage the computer.

To create or change a password, follow these steps:

1. **Open User Accounts from the Start menu's Control Panel and choose Create a Password.**
2. **Make up an easy-to-remember password to type into the first box, shown in Figure 13-4, and then retype the same characters into the box below it. (That eliminates the chance of typos.)**

   I offer some password tips a little later in this section.

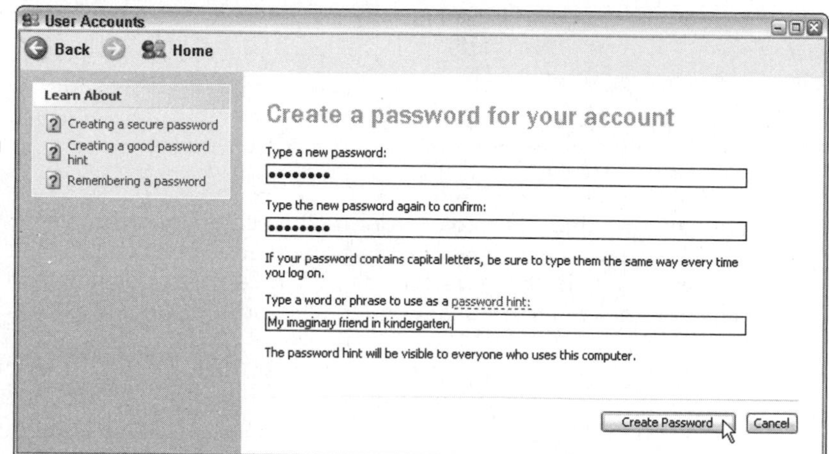

Figure 13-4: Type in a hint that helps you — and only you — remember your password should you forget it.

3. **In the third box, type in a clue that helps you remember your forgotten password.**

   Make sure the clue works only for you. Don't choose "My hair color," for instance. If you're at work, choose "My cat's favorite food" or "The actor on my favorite TV show." If you're at home, choose something only you know — and not the kids. And don't be afraid to change your password every once in a while, too. You can find more about passwords in Chapter 2.

4. **Finally, create a Password Reset Disk by choosing Prevent a Forgotten Password from the task pane along the left side of the User Accounts window.**

   That way, if you forget your password, and your hint isn't helping you remember it, you can insert your Password Reset Disk as a key. Windows XP will let you in to choose a new password, and all will be joyous. (But if you lose the Password Reset Disk, you have to beg for mercy from the administrator.) Hide your Password Reset Disk in a safe place because it lets *anybody* into your account.

Making your folders *really* private

Administrator *and* Limited account holders have the option of keeping *everybody* out of their My Documents folders — even other Administrator account owners. Follow these steps to make your My Documents folder private:

1. **Open My Computer and right-click on your My Documents folder.**
2. **Choose Sharing and Security, click the Make This Folder Private box, and click OK.**

Windows tags that folder as private, meaning it can be opened only when you're logged on under your own user account and with your own user account password. This protects your My Documents folder and anything inside it from probing eyes.

Technically, Administrator account holders can *still* peek into a Limited Account's private files, but that requires disabling Windows XP's normal Simple File Sharing system. Then Administrator account holders can set NTFS permissions and security settings for individual accounts and folders, a process which is much too complicated to discuss in this book.

Here are some tips that help you create a better password:

- When creating a password, use a word or combination of letters, numbers, and symbols of at least 7 to 14 letters. Don't *ever* use your name or user name. (That's the first thing that thieves try when breaking in.)
- Don't choose a common word or name. Try to think of something that wouldn't appear in a dictionary. Combine two words, for instance, to make a third. No grammar teachers will chide you this time.
- Uppercase and lowercase letters are treated differently. *PopCorn* is a different password than *popcorn*.

Chapter 14

Connecting Two or More Computers with a Network

In This Chapter

- Understanding a network's parts
- Choosing between a wired or wireless network
- Buying and installing parts for a network
- Setting up a small network
- Linking two computers quickly and easily
- Sharing files, printers, and an Internet connection on a network
- Locating other computers on a network

A network is simply a way for computers to share things. By connecting two or more computers, Windows XP conveniently turns them into a network, ready to pipe information to one another. Just link two computers with the right cable, and Windows XP can move your files and settings from an old computer to a new one, solving an age-old problem.

If your computers live too far apart to extend a cable, go *wireless:* Let your computers chatter through the airwaves like radio stations that broadcast and take requests.

This chapter explains several ways to link a handful of computers so they can share information (as well as their printers and Internet connection). Be forewarned, however: This chapter contains some pretty advanced stuff; don't tread here unless you're running an Administrator account on your computer and you don't mind doing a little head-scratching as you wade from conceptualization to actualization to, "Hey, it works!"

Understanding a Network's Parts

A *network* is simply two or more computers that have been connected so they can share things. Although computer networks range from pleasingly simple to agonizingly complicated, they all have three things in common:

- **A network port or adapter:** Every computer on your network needs its own network port or adapter. Adapters come in several forms. A *wired* network adapter, for instance, is simply a special jack where you plug in a cable to connect one computer with the other computers. A *wireless* network adapter translates your computer's information into radio signals and broadcasts them to the other computers.
- **A switch or router:** When you connect two computers with a single cable or with wireless connections, each computer is smart enough to swap messages with the other computer — there's no other place to send the messages. But connecting three or more computers requires a traffic cop in the form of a *switch* or *router*. Each computer connects to the boxlike switch or router, which sends the right message to the right computer.
- **Cables:** Wireless networks don't require cables. But wired networks need cables to connect the computers' network adapters to each other or to the router/switch.

After you connect your computers to each other through cables, wirelessly, or by using a combination of both, Windows XP's Network Setup Wizard jumps in. The wizard flips the right switches, letting everything communicate with each other. Your network resembles a spider, as shown in Figure 14-1, with each computer's cable connecting to the router or switch in the center.

A wireless network looks identical but without the cables. (The wireless switch or router coordinates the messages' paths.) Or, you can mix wired and wireless adapters to create a network resembling Figure 14-2. Some switches and routers come with built-in wireless access, sparing you the cost of adding an external wireless access point.

- Windows XP divides its attention between networked computers quite well. It lets every networked computer share a single Internet connection, for instance, so all users can surf the Internet or check their e-mail simultaneously. Everyone can share a single printer, too. If two people try to print something simultaneously, Windows stashes one person's files until the printer is free and then prints them when the printer's ready.
- TIP: Don't know if you're connected to a network or what other computers may be connected? Click the Start button and choose Search. Choose to search for Computers or People and then choose A Computer on the Network. (Don't enter a name to search for.) Click the Search button, and Windows XP searches for a network and then shows the names of every computer connected to your own.

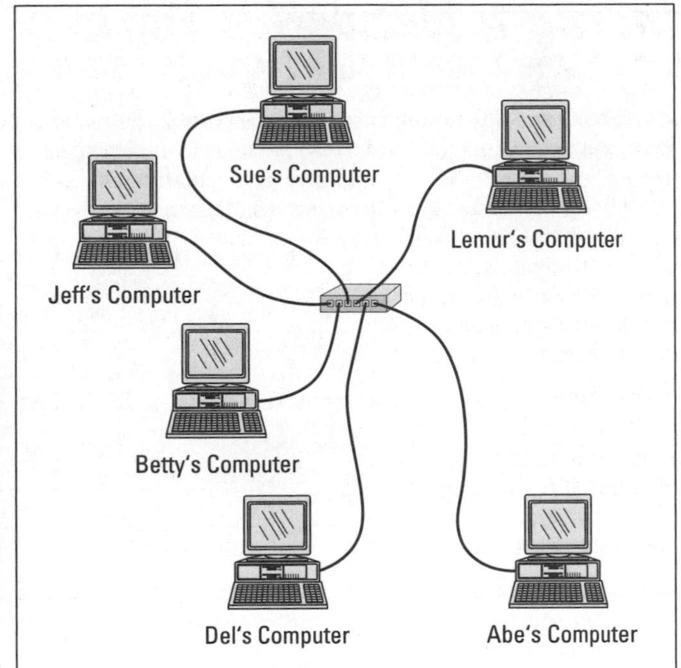

Figure 14-1: A network resembles a spider, with each computer's cable connecting to a router or switch in the center.

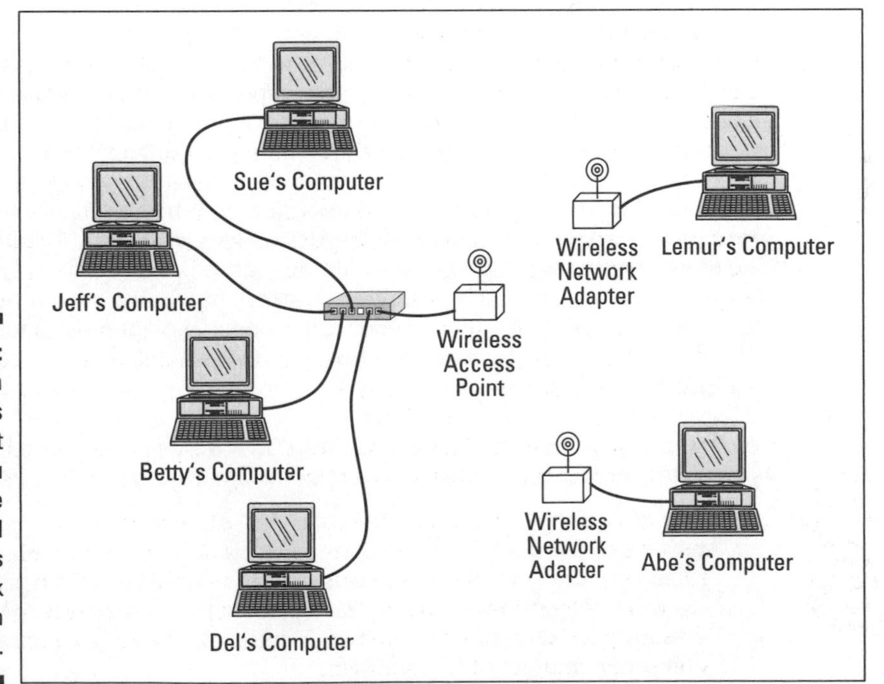

Figure 14-2: Adding a wireless access point lets you combine wired and wireless network adapters in one network.

Choosing between a wired or wireless network

Today, *wireless* is the buzzword, and it's easy to see why. It's easy to string cables between computers sitting on a single desk or even in the same room. But cables quickly become messy if the computers live in separate rooms. The solution comes with *wireless* network adapters, which convert the information to radio waves and broadcast the waves to the other computers on the network. The wireless adapters on the other computers catch the waves and convert them back into information.

But just as radio broadcasts fade as you drive out of the city, wireless signals fade as they travel through walls. The more they fade, the slower the connection becomes. If your wireless signals pass through more than two walls, your computers may not be able to communicate. Wireless networks take longer to set up because they have many more settings to tweak.

Wired connections work more quickly, efficiently, and inexpensively than wireless. But if your interior decorator says to remove the cables from the hallways, wireless may be your best option. Finally, you can set up adjacent computers with cables and use wireless for the rest.

To use wireless with broadband Internet access, buy a router with a built-in wireless access point. If you're using dial-up, buy a switch and a separate wireless access point to plug into it.

Setting Up a Small Network

If you're trying to set up a lot of computers — more than five or ten — you probably need a more advanced book; networks are fairly easy to set up, but sharing their resources can be scary stuff, especially if the computers contain sensitive material. But if you're just trying to set up a handful of computers in your home or home office, this information may be all you need.

So without further blabbing, here's a low-carb, step-by-step list of how to set up your own small and inexpensive network to work with Windows XP. The following sections show how to buy the three parts of a network — network adapters, cables (or wireless connections), and a switch or router for moving information between each computer. I explain how to install the parts and, finally, how to make Windows XP create a network out of your handiwork.

You find much more detailed instructions about home networking in my book *Upgrading & Fixing PCs For Dummies,* 6th Edition (Wiley).

Buying parts for a network

Walk into the computer store, walk out with this stuff, and you're well on your way to setting up your network:

Fast Ethernet or 100BaseT cable: Most networks connect PCs with *Ethernet* cable, which resembles phone cable but with slightly thicker jacks. Ethernet cable is sometimes called Ethernet RJ-45, Cat 5, or TPE (Twisted Pair Ethernet). The names usually include a number relating to the cable's speed rating: 10, 100, or 1,000. (Big numbers are faster.) When in doubt, buy Fast Ethernet or 100BaseT cable.

Some of today's newer homes come conveniently prewired with network jacks in the wall, sparing their owners the bother of buying and stringing cables from room to room. If your computers are too far apart for cables, buy a wireless network adapter, described next.

Network adapters: Each computer on the network needs its own network adapter, and those gadgets come in many varieties. Many computers come with a built-in network adapter, sparing you the cost. Many newer laptops come with *wireless* adapters preinstalled, which save you the cost of an adapter *and* cables.

When shopping for adapters, keep these factors in mind:

- An adapter should have a 10/100 Ethernet connector. Adapters can plug into a USB port, plug inside one of your computer's unused slots, or even piggyback on your home's power or telephone lines.
- The adapter's box should say that it's *Plug and Play* and supports Windows XP.

Router or switch: This choice depends on your Internet connection and network adapters:

- Broadband Internet users should purchase a *router* with a built-in switch that has enough ports for each networked computer. Dial-up users should purchase a *switch* with enough ports for each computer. The router or switch resembles the one shown in Figure 14-3.
- If you're using some or all wireless network adapters, make sure your router has built-in wireless capabilities. If you're using a switch, buy a wireless access point to plug into it. (Don't worry about available ports with wireless gear because wireless access points can usually accommodate dozens of wireless computers.)

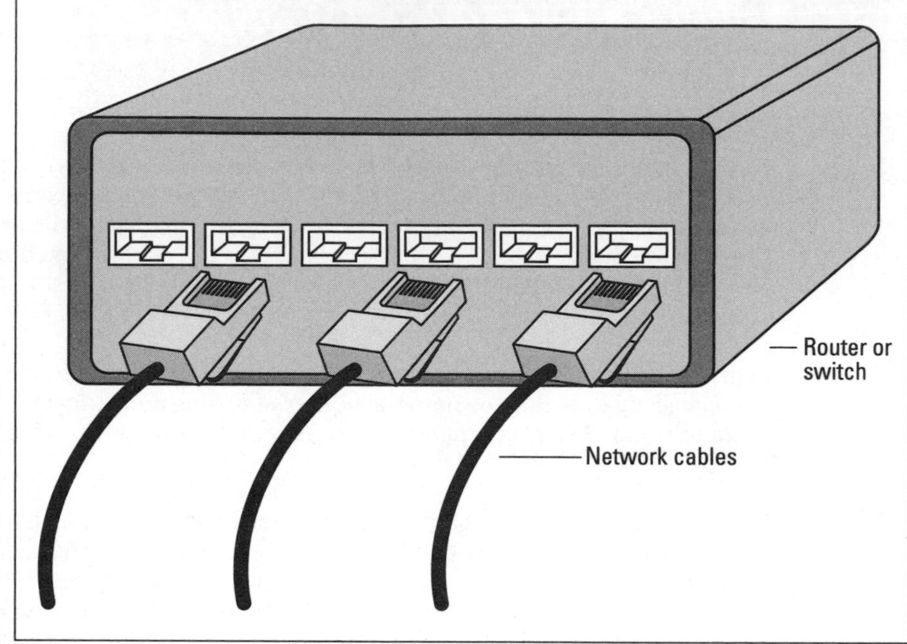

Figure 14-3: The router or switch needs a port for every computer's cable.

That's the shopping list. Drop this list onto the copy machine at the office and take it to the computer store.

Installing a network

After you've bought your network's parts, you need to plug everything into the right place. Windows XP should automatically recognize the newly installed network adapters and embrace them gleefully.

1. **Find your original Windows XP CD — you may need it.**
2. **Turn off and unplug all the computers on your soon-to-be network.**

   Turn 'em all off; unplug them as well.
3. **Turn off all the computers' peripherals — printers, monitors, modems, and anything else that's attached.**

4. **Install the network adapters.**

   Plug the USB adapters into your computers' USB ports. If you're using adapter cards, remove each computer's case and push the card into the proper size of slot. (If you live in a static-prone environment, ground yourself first by touching the side of the computer's case.)

   If a card doesn't seem to fit into a slot, don't force it. Different types of cards fit into different types of slots, and you may be trying to push the wrong type of card into the wrong type of slot. See if it fits into another slot more easily.

5. **Replace the computers' cases, if necessary, and connect each network cable between the computer's adapter and the router or switch box.**

   Unless you're using wireless adapters, you may need to route cables under carpets or around doorways. (Most routers and switch boxes have power cords that need to be plugged into a wall outlet as well.)

6. **Broadband Internet users should plug the cable modem into the router's modem port.**

   My Linksys router (with built-in wireless access and four-port switch) says *WAN* on its cable modem port. The computer's four ports are numbered, and an *Uplink* port is for plugging in an optional switch to expand my network.

   Dial-up modem users can keep the modem plugged into the computer. When that computer's turned on and connected to the Internet, Windows XP allows each networked computer to share its Internet connection.

7. **Turn on the computers and their peripherals.**

   Turn on the computers and their monitors, printers, modems, and whatever else happens to be connected to them.

- If all goes well, Windows XP wakes up, notices its newly installed network adapter, and begins installing its appropriate software automatically. Or, if the network adapter came with an installation CD, insert it now. (If the setup program doesn't run automatically, double-click the disc's Setup file to install the software.)
- If all *doesn't* go well, click Windows XP's Start button, choose the Control Panel, and double-click the Add Hardware icon. (You may need to click Switch to Classic View to see the icon.) Click the Next button to make Windows try to autodetect the new network adapter.

The easiest way to connect two computers

Sometimes you simply need to link two computers, quickly and easily, to move information from one to another. (From an old computer to a new one, for instance.) If both computers have FireWire ports, found on many laptops, the setup is very simple. Connect a FireWire cable between the two FireWire ports and run Windows XP's Network Setup Wizard, and you've created a quick-and-dirty network. You're done!

No FireWire ports? Then buy two network adapters (they come preinstalled on many new computers) and a *crossed cable,* which is a special breed of Ethernet cable. Be sure to emphasize "crossed cable" when shopping at the computer store and tell the folks there that it's for connecting two computers. (A regular Ethernet cable won't work; it must be crossed.) Connect the crossed cable between the two computers' network adapters and run Windows XP's Network Setup Wizard, and you've created a quick network between the two computers. If one computer connects to the Internet, the other computer should be able to share its Internet connection.

To connect two computers that each have wireless adapters, use the Network Setup Wizard to set them both up using "ad-hoc" mode rather than "peer-to-peer" mode. Also, set them both to the same channel, the same workgroup, and the same encryption key.

Running Windows' Network Setup Wizard

After you install the network adapters, cables (if necessary), and a router or switch, Windows' Network Setup Wizard handles the chores of coordinating their conversations.

Dial-up users should first run the wizard on the computer that connects to the Internet, as described in Chapter 8. (That wizard then lets all your networked computers share that computer's Internet connection.) After that computer is set up, run the wizard on the other networked computers.

If you're using broadband Internet access, you can use any order when running the wizard on each computer.

1. **Start the Network Setup Wizard and click the Next button.**

   Click the Start button, choose My Network Places, and choose Set Up a Home or Small Office Network from the Network Tasks area along the left. The Network Setup Wizard rises to the screen, as shown in Figure 14-4, ready for you to click Next.

Figure 14-4: The Network Setup Wizard automatically takes inventory of your networking equipment and sets up Windows XP to use it.

Don't see My Network Places on the Start menu? Then choose the Control Panel, select Network and Internet Connections, and choose Set Up or Change Your Home or Small Office Network.

2. **Read the screen and click Next.**

   The Network Setup Wizard takes inventory of your installed network adapters and Internet connection. Then it sets up the software to bring your network to life, placing appropriate network icons on your computer. That's why turning on everything is important, as the wizard requests. After you click Next, the wizard looks for your Internet connection.

3. **Tell the wizard about your Internet connection and click Next.**

   Specifically, the wizard needs to know whether your computer connects directly to the Internet or through a different computer on the network. If you're running this wizard on the computer that connects to the Internet, choose the first option, This Computer Connects Directly through the Internet.

   If your network connects to the Internet through a router or through another computer, choose the second option, This Computer Connects to the Internet through a Residential Gateway or through Another Computer on My Network.

4. **Choose your Internet connection from the list, if asked, and click Next.**

5. **Type a name and description for your computer and click Next.**

   When people search for your computer on the network, the name you choose here will be listed.

6. **If the settings look correct, click Next.**

   Windows XP lists the settings that it uses and asks for your okay. If you click Next, Windows XP checks out the Internet connection and lets other networked computers share it. It automatically installs a *protective* firewall, described in Chapter 10. And it starts setting up the network. (Give it a few minutes.)

7. **If your network includes Windows 98 or Windows 95 computers, create a Home Networking Setup disk by clicking the Create Disk button and click Next.**

   You need a floppy to create the disk.

   Ignore this step if you're networking all Windows XP computers. Just repeat these steps on those computers.

8. **Click Finish.**

   That should do the trick.

- The wizard does a reasonably good job of casting its spells on your computers. If the computers are all connected correctly and restarted, chances are they wake up in bondage with each other. If they don't, try restarting them all again.
- Click your Start menu and choose My Network Places, and you see your computer's shared folders as well as shared folders from other computers on your network.
- Windows XP automatically shares one folder on every networked computer: the Shared Documents folder, as well as any folders inside it, including Shared Music and Shared Pictures. Any files you place inside those folders are available to anybody on the network.
- To run the wizard on Windows 95 or 98 computers, insert the Network Setup disk you made in Step 7. Open My Computer, double-click your floppy drive, and double-click the `netsetup` file. The computer asks a few questions, tweaks itself, and reboots. (Just run the Network Wizard on networked Windows Me computers if Windows XP didn't already set them up.)
- All your networked computers are now able to share any shared files, your modem connection, and any printers. (I explain how to share things on the network in this chapter's next section.)

- If everything doesn't proceed as merrily as I describe here, don't worry. Networking *will* work. However, you need to make some more advanced tweaks that lay beyond this book's scope. Pick up a copy of Curt Simmons's *Windows XP Secrets* (Wiley). It's around 700 pages.

Setting Up a Wireless Connection

Although most wireless network adapters come with their own software, Windows XP comes with its own built-in wireless software, too. (Don't try to use both Windows' and the adapter's software simultaneously because they may quarrel. If Windows XP's doesn't work right, try the adapter's bundled software.) Although setting up and securing a wireless network is beyond the scope of this book, these tips help get you up and running with Windows XP's built-in software.

First, configure your wireless access point, whether it's built into your router or plugged into a switch. Different brands of wireless equipment use different software, but they all have these same basic settings:

- **Network name (SSID):** Enter a short, easy-to-remember name here to identify your particular wireless network. Later, when connecting to the wireless network with your computer, you'll select this same name to avoid accidentally connecting with your neighbor's wireless network.
- **Infrastructure:** Choose Infrastructure. (Ad Hoc mode creates on-the-fly networks with adjacent laptops for playing games during boring board meetings.)
- **Wireless Equivalent Privacy (WEP):** This encrypts your data as it flies through the air. Turn it on using the recommended settings. Write down all your chosen settings and passwords or passphrases here because you also need to enter them on your wireless computer before it can connect to the Internet.

When your wireless access point is up and running correctly, your computer notices it automatically. Windows XP notifies you with a little pop-up window from a wireless icon in the taskbar. If you're lucky, the window lists the wireless network's name and an Excellent signal strength, as shown in Figure 14-5.

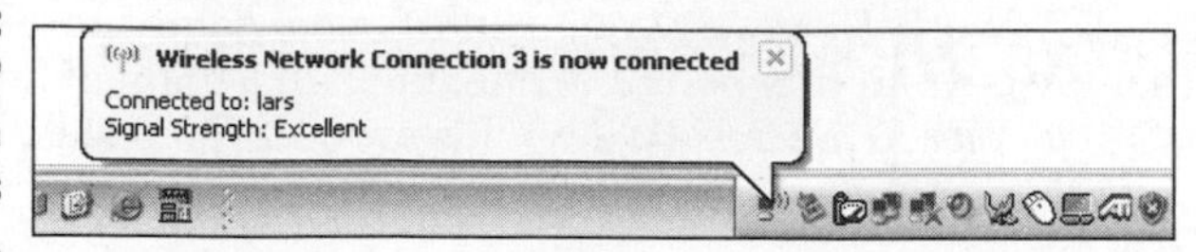

Figure 14-5: Windows XP finds a wireless connection.

To locate any other networks within range, double-click the taskbar's wireless network icon. Windows lists all the nearby wireless networks, as shown in Figure 14-6. (It automatically connects to the strongest one it can find.) Double-click a different one on the list, and Windows XP tries to connect with it.

- Signal strength is the biggest issue when trying to connect to a wireless network. Try to stay within a line of sight to the wireless access point's antenna, if possible. If your computer's wireless network adapter has an antenna, try pointing it in different directions while you watch Windows XP's little green signal strength meter rise or fall.
- If you're setting up a wireless access point, keep the WEP (Wireless Encryption Protocol) turned off until your wireless network is up and running. (The Unsecured wireless network shown in Figure 14-6 has WEP turned off.) That makes it easier for your computers to locate the network. When your network is working correctly, turn WEP back on. (That keeps your neighbors *off* your network.)

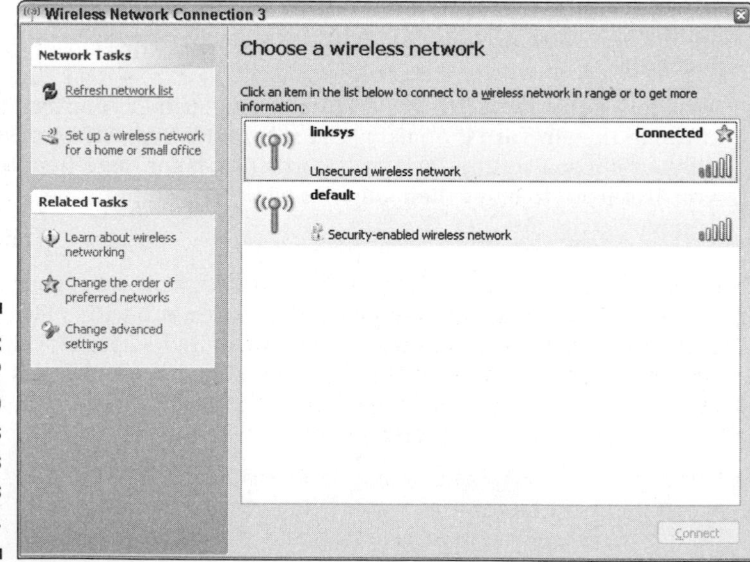

Figure 14-6: Windows XP located two wireless networks within its range.

Connecting wirelessly with a laptop

Many laptops come with built-in wireless network adapters for linking to *hotspots* (wireless networks) found in coffee shops, airports, and other public places. Windows XP can usually ferret them out and connect automatically, as shown in Figure 14-6. To connect, make sure your laptop's wireless adapter is turned on. Many stay turned off to save electricity when not in use. Look for your laptop's power settings on the taskbar, near the clock. If not there, try the Control Panel's Power Options settings.

Select the wireless network with the strongest signal and connect to it. If no password is required, you can start Web surfing right away. If a hotspot requires a password — like the "security-enabled" one listed in Figure 14-6 — you have to head for the cashier. Some places charge for wireless access, and some require you to install special wireless access software on your computer.

To avoid paying for wireless, try sitting on the patio. Many people don't turn on security for their wireless networks. If you can connect to a wireless network at an adjacent office building, you can Web surf for free (just don't say you heard it here).

Troubleshooting a Network

Setting up a network is the hardest part of networking. After the computers recognize each other (and connect to the Internet, either themselves or through the network), the network usually runs fine. But when it's not, here are some things to try:

- Turn off every computer (using the Start menu's Turn Off Computer option, of course). Check their cables to make sure everything's connected. If you're not using a router, turn on the computer with the Internet connection. When it's up, running, and connected to the Internet, turn on another one. When it's connected, move to the next computer, and repeat.
- If one computer doesn't connect, rerun the Network Setup Wizard on the problem computer. Restart the computer again, if necessary, and then try running the Network Setup Wizard again.

- Try making Windows XP check and repair the connection, if necessary. Choose Control Panel from the Start menu and select Network and Internet Connections. Click the Network Connections icon to see all your computer's network connections. Right-click on each network connection on each computer and choose Repair.
- If your network shares one computer's dial-up Internet connection, that computer must be turned on *and* connected to the Internet before the other computers can use that Internet connection.

- Choose Help and Support from the Start menu, choose Networking and the Web, and choose Fixing Networking or Web problems from the menu. Windows XP offers many built-in troubleshooting tools to diagnose and repair network problems.

Sharing and Accessing Your Computer's Files and Folders

To share any file or folder with your fellow computer users, move the file into your Shared Documents folder. (You find it listed in your My Computer window.) You must *move* or *copy* a file into the Shared Documents folder before it's accessible; shortcuts don't always work.

After you place a file or folder into your Shared Documents folder (or any folder inside that folder), that data is accessible to anybody who logs on to your network.

As a special perk, administrators can share folders without having to move them into the Shared Documents folder. The trick is to follow these steps:

1. **Open My Computer, right-click on a folder you'd like to share, and choose Sharing and Security from the pop-up menu.**

   A window appears, showing that folder's properties. It opens to the Sharing tab, shown in Figure 14-7.

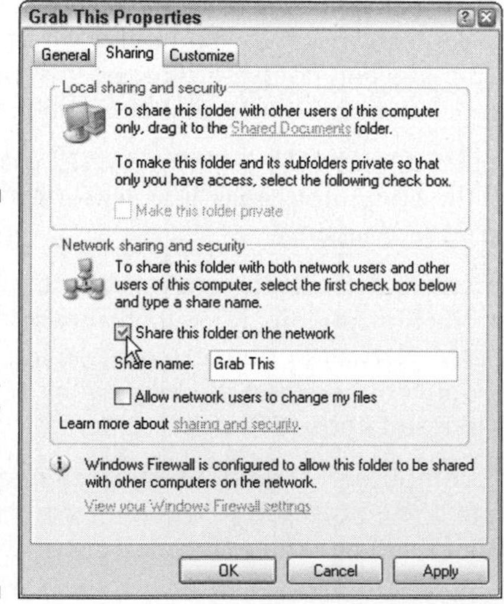

Figure 14-7: Click the Share This Folder on the Network box to allow anyone on the network to access that folder.

2. **Click the Share This Folder on the Network box.**

   A check mark in that box lets everybody peek at, grab, steal, change, or delete any of the files in that folder. This includes other user accounts on your computer as well as people on your network.

   To let visitors look inside the files but *not* change or delete them, remove the check mark from the Allow Network Users to Change My Files box.

3. **Click OK.**

   Windows makes that folder and all its contents available to anybody on your network.

To view all the accessible folders on the network (including your own shared folders), choose My Network Places from the Start menu. Your computer lists all the folders shared on your computer and on other networked computers, as shown in Figure 14-8.

- Think twice before sharing a lot of your folders. Even if you trust people, they might accidentally mess something up. To be the safest, share files only by physically placing them inside your Shared Documents folder.
- Icons for shared folders have a little hand beneath them, like the one shown in the margin.
- Inside the Shared Documents folder live two more folders: Shared Music and Shared Pictures. (Network users can access them, too.) Place *documents* you'd like to share in the Shared Documents folder. When you make MP3s from your CDs, store them in the Shared Music folder, too, so that everybody can enjoy them. Similarly place photos in the Shared Pictures folder.

Making folders private

Keeping your folders private and off the network is easy: Don't choose to share them. To remove any inadvertently shared folders from the network, right-click on their icon, choose Sharing and Security, and remove the check mark from the Share This Folder on the Network box.

To make doubly sure items in your My Documents folder stay private, make sure your hard drive is formatted with NTFS, described in Chapter 13. Then right-click on your My Documents folder, choose Sharing and Security, and click the Make This Folder Private button.

One more thing: Folders that you share on your network are accessible only to people using your computer network. People on the *Internet* can't access them. To be sure you're keeping out viruses, and worms that may encroach your privacy, be sure to purchase an antivirus program and keep it up-to-date. I cover computer security in Chapter 10.

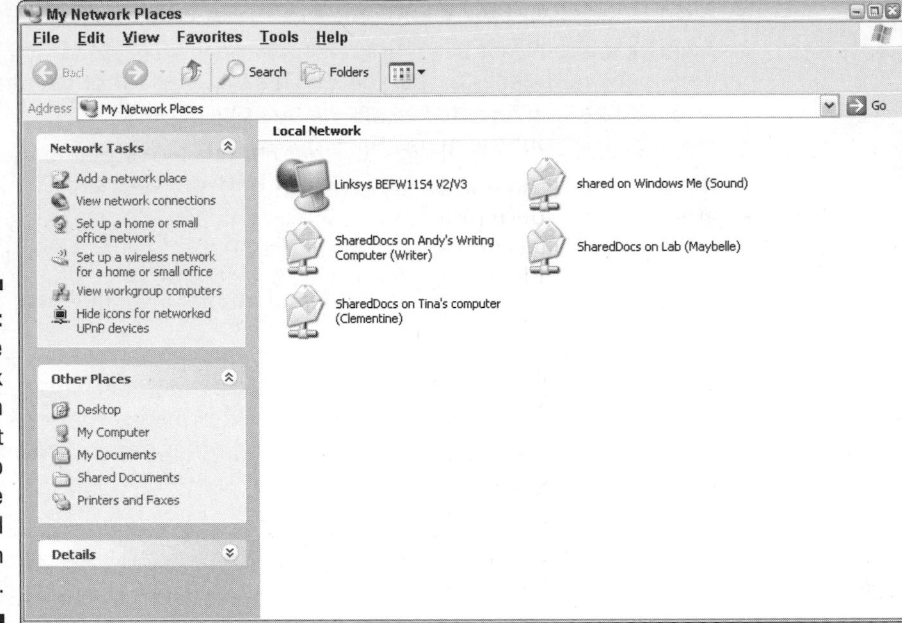

Figure 14-8: Choose My Network Places from the Start menu to see all the shared folders on the network.

Sharing a Printer on the Network

Many households or offices have several computers but only one printer. To let everybody on the network print on that printer, share it by following these steps on the computer connected to the printer:

1. **Turn on your printer, click Windows XP's Start button, and choose Printers and Faxes.**

2. **If you see an icon for your computer's printer, right-click on the icon and choose Sharing.**

   Sharing a printer works almost like sharing a folder. (If you *don't* spot an icon listed for your printer, move ahead to Step 4.)

3. **Click the Share This Printer button and, if desired, type in a name for your printer. Click OK.**

   Although Windows XP usually suggests a name for your printer, feel free to just name it *Printer.*

   If you're running computers with older versions of Windows on your network, click the Additional Drivers button. Click in the boxes next to the versions used by the other computers and click OK. Click OK to close the window, and you're through.

4. **If no icon is listed for your computer's printer, choose Add Printer from the File menu.**

   You should see an icon listed for the printers connected to your computer. If not, you have to install one by choosing Add Printer from the File menu. Fill out the questions Windows XP asks about your printer.

   If your printer came with an installation CD, use that. Windows XP recognizes many modern printers as soon as you plug them into the USB port. If the printer plugs into a printer port (also called the *LPT* port), you might have to tell Windows the printer's make and model.

   Finally, tell Windows XP to use that printer as the default printer if you want Windows XP to use that printer all the time. (This option comes in handy for people who have more than one printer.) You find more information about installing printers in Chapter 7.

   The new printer's icon now appears in your Printers and Faxes window; you also find its name listed in your software programs as an option for printing. Now go back to Step 3 to share the printer with the network.

   That's it. Any computer on your network can send information to any of the printers listed in the window.

If no printer is directly plugged into your computer, you can easily find out what networked printers are available. Click the Start button, choose the Control Panel, and select Printers and Other Hardware. Choose View Installed Printers or Fax Printers. (Or click the Printers and Faxes icon, depending on your setup.)

Can I get in trouble for looking into the wrong computer?

People usually *tell* you where to find files and things on your computers attached to the network. But if nobody's dropped you a hint, feel free to grab a torch and go spelunking on your own with My Network Places. If you're worried about getting into trouble, the rule is simple: Windows XP rarely lets you peek into networked areas where you're not supposed to be. In fact, Windows XP is so security conscious that it may keep you from seeing things that you *should* be able to see. (That's when you call on the office administrator or the computer's owner and ask him or her to share the appropriate folders.) If you try to peek inside a forbidden computer, you simply see an access denied message. No embarrassing sirens or harm done.

If you find yourself in a folder where you obviously don't belong — for example, the folder of employee evaluations on your supervisor's computer — quietly bring it to the administrator's attention.

Windows XP shows you the printers connected to your computer, as shown in Figure 14-9, as well as any being shared on the network.

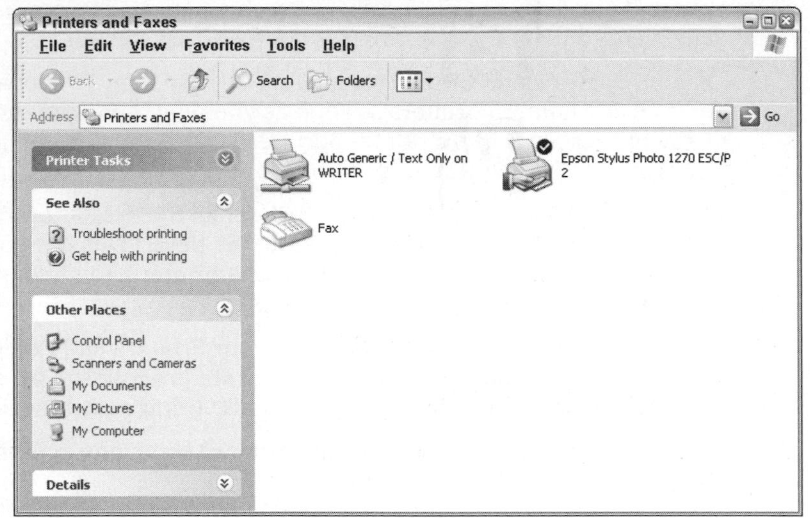

Figure 14-9: Windows XP lists any printers attached to your computer or available on the network.

If you don't see any printers listed in the Printers and Faxes window, yet you know that one is attached to the network, choose Add Printer in Step 4. This time tell Windows you're installing a *network* printer. Windows XP browses for any connected network printers and displays their names.

Shared printers (as well as folders) attached to *your* computer have a little hand beneath them, like the one in the margin.

Shared printers attached to *other* networked computers have a little cable beneath them, like the one in the margin.

Part V

Music, Movies, Memories (And Photos, Too)

"It's bad enough he fell asleep waiting for a huge music file to download into his music folder, but wait until he finds out he hit the 'SEND' button instead of selecting 'DOWNLOAD'."

In this part . . .

Up until now, the book has covered the boring-but-necessary stuff: adjusting your computer so you can get your work done. This part of the book lets you turn your computer into an entertainment center:

- Watch DVDs on your laptop.
- Create greatest hits CDs for your car stereo.
- Organize a digital photo album from your digital camera.
- Edit camcorder videos into something people *want* to watch.

When you're ready to play for a while, flip to this part of the book for a helping hand.

Chapter 15

Playing and Copying Music in Media Player

In This Chapter

- Playing CDs, DVDs, TV shows, MP3 and WMA music files, and Internet radio
- Creating, saving, and editing playlists
- Copying CDs to your hard drive, another CD, or portable music player
- Buying music and movies from online stores

Windows XP's Media Player 10 is a big bundle of buttons that reveals how much money you've spent on your computer. On expensive computers, Media Player rumbles like a home theater. On cheap ones, it sounds like a cell phone's ring tone.

Now on its tenth version, Media Player still sticks to the basics. It's fine for playing CDs and DVDs, organizing your music and movie files, and sending digital music to your portable MP3 player (as long as it's not an iPod, created by one of Microsoft's rivals). Media Player 10 also adds online music shopping, if you're hankering to download tunes directly to your computer.

Depending on its age, your computer may not have Media Player 10, the latest version. To see your player's version number, choose About from its Help menu. If you're not using Media Player 10, download it from Microsoft's Web site (`www.microsoft.com`).

Load up Media Player from the Start menu's All Programs area. Then check out this chapter for help on using Media Player's built-in features, as well as for tips on making Media Player do the things you *really* want it to do.

Stocking Media Player's Library

When first run, Media Player asks if it can sort through your computer's stash of digital music and videos, automatically stuffing everything into its neatly organized library. But if Media Player hasn't placed your computer's files into its library, tell it to by following these steps:

1. **Choose Search for Media Files from the Tools menu. (Or, just press F3.)**
2. **Tell Media Player where to search for your files.**

   Click the Search button to search only your My Music folder.

   To include another folder or drive in your search, click Browse and navigate to the folder or drive. To search your *entire* computer for media goodies, click the downward-pointing arrow in the Search On box and choose All Drives.
3. **Click the Search button to start searching.**

After searching, Media Player lists everything it finds in its library, shown in Figure 15-1, categorizing files by title, artist, album, genre, and other trivia. It separates your goodies into four main categories:

- **Music:** All your digital music appears here. Media Player recognizes three major music formats: MP3, WMA, and MIDI.
- **TV:** Here, Media Player lists TV shows recorded on special Windows XP Media Center Edition computers. Without that fancy version of Windows XP, you probably won't see any TV shows listed here.
- **Video:** Video you've recorded on a digital camera or camcorder as well as some video downloaded from the Internet appear here.
- **Playlists:** Covered later in this chapter, playlists are simply lists of songs that play in a certain order. You can create your own, and Media Player helps out by automatically creating playlists based on your listening habits. Whenever you tell Media Player to play a bunch of songs, it creates a playlist called Now Playing List, which you can save for quick, one-click listening.

To keep your library up-to-date automatically, choose Options from Media Player's Tools menu, click the Player tab, and add a check mark to the Add Music Files to Library When Played box. Whenever you double-click a song or video file, Media Player not only plays it but also adds it to its library.

You can use the steps in this section to search for files whenever you want; Media Player ignores the ones it has already cataloged and adds any new ones.

Figure 15-1: Media Player's Library sorts your music and videos into easy-to-browse categories.

Media Player offers zillions of options when creating its library. To see or change them, choose Options from Media Player's Tools menu and click the Library tab. There, you can make Media Player update your songs' tags (explained in the sidebar), correct your song's filenames, and perform other maintenance chores while stocking its library.

What are a song's *tags?*

Inside every music file lives a form containing the song's title, artist, album, and similar information. When deciding how to sort, display, and categorize your music, Windows Media Player reads those tags — *not* the songs' filenames. Most portable music players, including the iPod and Dell DJ, also rely on tags, so it's important to keep them filled out properly.

It's so important, in fact, that Media Player normally fills in the tags for you when it adds files to its library.

Many people don't bother filling out their song's tags; other people keep them meticulously updated. If your tags are filled out the way you prefer, stop Media Player from messing with them. Just click Options from the Tools menu, click the Library tab, and clear *every* box in the Automatic Media Information Updates for Files category. If your tags are a mess, leave those boxes checked so Media Player will clean up the tags for you.

To edit a song's tag manually in Media Player, right-click on it in the library and choose Advanced Tag Editor.

Understanding Media Player's Controls

Media Player uses the same basic controls when playing any type of file, be it a song, video, CD, or DVD. Figure 15-2 shows Media Player open to its Now Playing page as it plays an album in the background. The figure's labels explain each button's function; rest your mouse pointer over a mysterious button to see a pop-up explanation.

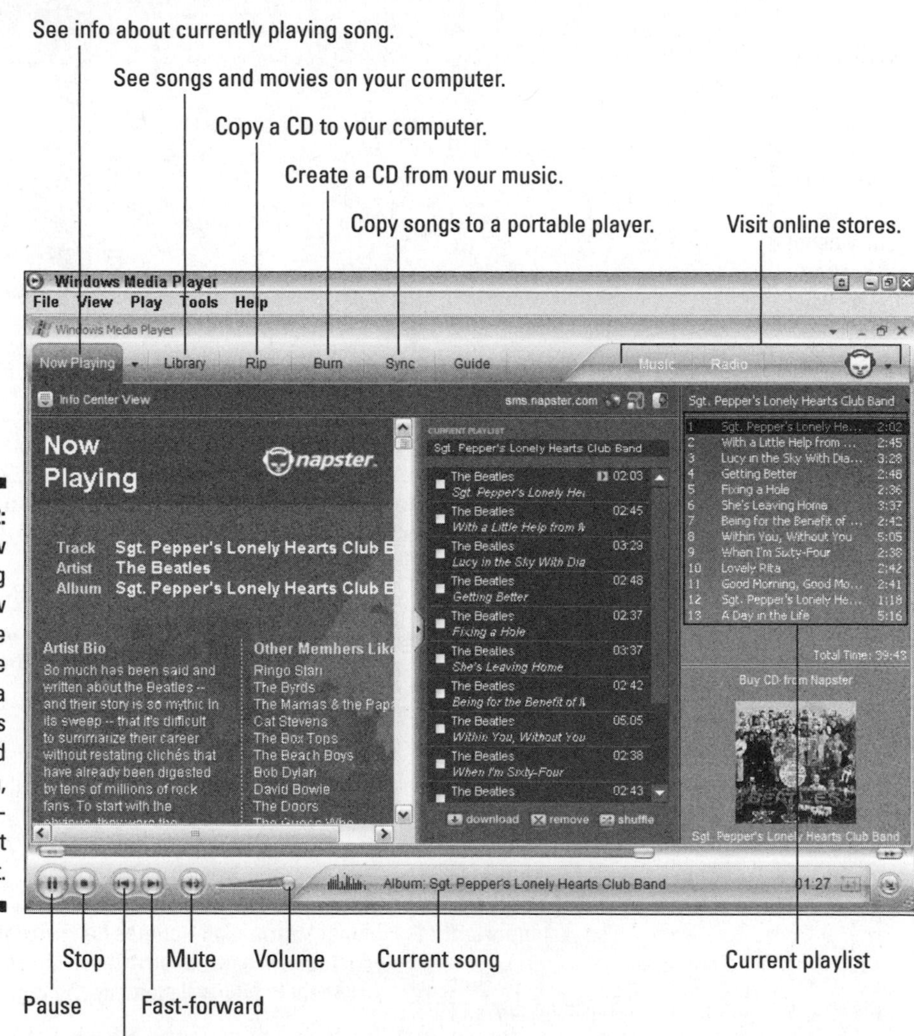

Figure 15-2: The Now Playing window displays the album you're hearing, a list of its songs and their length, and information about the artist.

The buttons along the bottom work like any tape or CD player, letting you play, stop, rewind, fast-forward, and mute the current song or movie. Click the large square blue buttons along the player's top to perform these common tasks:

- **Now Playing:** Click here to view information about what you're currently hearing.
- **Library:** Media Player organizes your music, movies, and playlists here. To play anything listed in the library, right-click on the item and choose Play. (Or double-click it.)
- **Rip:** Copy a CD or some of its files to your hard drive. (Choose Options from the Tools menu to customize how it's copied.)
- **Burn:** Copy music from your hard drive to a CD.
- **Sync:** Copy your current Now Playing list or other files to your portable music player.
- **Guide:** Browse Microsoft's Web site (`www.windowsmedia.com`) to hear songs, watch movies, or tune into Internet radio stations.
- **Online Stores:** New to Media Player 10, the top area along the far right lets you buy songs and movies online instead of trading them with your friends for free.

Playing CDs

As long as you insert the CD in the CD drive correctly (usually label-side up), playing a music CD is one of Media Player's easiest tasks. The biggest stumbling block comes with the pop-up form, shown in Figure 15-3, that appears when you insert the CD.

Turn off the copy protection, *quickly*

Many of Media Player's options and settings are simply cosmetic. But be sure to turn off the copy protection to avoid serious problems later. Choose Options from the Tools menu and click the Rip Music tab.

Then remove the check mark from Copy Protect My Music. That prevents Microsoft from adding *Digital Rights Management,* a fancy term meaning you won't be able to play your copied music on other computers or your portable music player.

Although it's important to protect the artist's rights, make sure you protect your *own* rights to CDs you've purchased.

Figure 15-3: When you insert a CD, Windows XP asks you what to do with it.

Eager to please, Windows XP begs to know how to handle your newly inserted CD. Should it *play* the CD? *Copy* its music onto your hard drive? *Open it* in My Computer and display its files and folders? Or do nothing at all?

Choose the action you want it to take — Play Audio CD, for instance — and then click the OK button. Media Player dutifully follows your instructions. (To bypass the form in the future and automatically play any inserted audio CDs, select the adjacent Always Do the Selected Action check box before clicking OK.)

- Too flustered for quick decisions? Pressing the Esc key kicks the question box off your screen (until the next time you insert a CD, that is).
- Don't choose the Open Folder to View Files option when you insert a music CD, or you'll just see a pointless list of numbered files named Track. Windows XP won't let you copy songs that way; you must use Media Player's Rip button, instead.

- Windows XP automatically highlights your last choice, so pressing Enter makes the form perform the same action that you chose last time.
- To change the way Windows XP automatically acts when you insert a CD, open My Computer, right-click on your CD drive, and choose Properties. Click the AutoPlay tab to customize how XP reacts depending on the inserted CD's content, be it music files, pictures, video, mixed, or a standard music CD.

- When playing a CD or anything else in Media Player, press F8 to mute the sound and pick up that phone call.

Playing DVDs

Media Player plays DVDs as well, letting a laptop do double-duty as a portable DVD player. Grab your favorite DVD, some headphones, and watch what *you* like during that next long flight.

Although Media Player plays, burns, and copies CDs, it can't do *anything* fancy with DVDs. It can't record movies to your hard drive or burn any of your files to a DVD. But when you insert a DVD into your DVD drive, Media Player immediately begins playing it, as shown in Figure 15-4. (If it doesn't start playing, choose DVD from the Play menu and select your DVD drive.)

Yes, Media Player spies on you

Just like your bank, credit card company, and grocery store club card, Media Player spies on you. Media Player's 5,806-word online Privacy Statement boils down to this: Media Player tells Microsoft every song, file, or movie that you play, and some people find that creepy. But if Microsoft doesn't know what you're playing, Media Player can't connect to the Internet and retrieve applicable artist information and artwork.

If you don't care that Microsoft hums along to your CDs, don't bother reading any further. If you *do* care, choose your surveillance level by selecting Options from Media Player's Tools menu and clicking the Privacy tab. Here's the rundown on the Privacy tab options that cause the biggest ruckus:

Display Media Information from the Internet: If checked, Media Player tells Microsoft what CD or DVD you're playing and retrieves doodads to display on your screen: CD covers, song titles, artist names, and similar information.

Update My Music Files: Microsoft examines your files, and if it recognizes any, it fills in the songs' tags with the correct information. On the sly, Microsoft also helps itself to any tags you fill out using Media Player's Tag Editor. (See the "What are a song's tags?" sidebar for more information on tags.)

Send Unique Player ID to Content Providers: Known in the biz as *data mining,* this option lets other corporations track how you use Media Player. To leave yourself out of their databases, leave this blank.

Cookies: Like several other Windows XP programs, Media Player tracks your activity with little files called *cookies.* I cover cookies in Chapter 8 because Media Player's cookies are controlled through Internet Explorer.

Save File and URL History in the Player: Media Player lists the names of your recently played files on its File menu for your convenience — and the possible guffaws of your coworkers or family. Remove this check mark to keep people from seeing the names of files you've played recently.

Figure 15-4: Hold down Alt and press Enter to see the full-screen movie; press those keys again to return to normal view.

www.kittyfeet.com

Media Player works very much like your TV's DVD player, with the mouse acting as the remote. Click your mouse on on-screen words or buttons to make the DVD do your bidding.

- To play the DVD full-screen, hold down the Alt key and press Enter. Media Player fills the screen with the movie. (Hold down Alt and press Enter to revert to normal mode.) Move your mouse off-screen, and the movie's controls go away; jiggle the mouse to bring the controls back in view.
- Whenever you insert a DVD, Windows XP bugs you with a pop-up window (refer to Figure 15-3), asking how it should handle the situation. For answers, read the "Playing CDs" section, earlier in this chapter; that information applies to DVDs as well as CDs.

- Media Player might refuse to play your DVD, complaining about needing a compatible *decoder.* That's because Media Player borrows the decoder software that came with your computer's *other* DVD playing program. If your computer didn't come with a third-party DVD viewer, Media Player won't play any DVDs. (Click the error message's Web Help button to visit a Web site where you can download a decoder for about $15.)

Playing Videos and TV Shows

Many digital cameras can capture short videos as well as photos, so don't be surprised if Media Player places several videos in its library's Video section. In fact, Media Player also finds any videos you've created in Windows XP's Movie Maker program, covered in Chapter 16.

Playing videos works much like playing a digital song: Double-click the file's name in the library's Video section and start enjoying the action, as shown in Figure 15-5.

Media Player lets you watch videos in several sizes. Hold down Alt and press Enter to make it fill the screen, just as when watching a DVD. (Repeat those keystrokes to return to the original size.)

As for watching or recording TV shows, Media Player only plays TV shows recorded in a special format called *DVR-MS,* and many TV tuner cards don't record in that format. That format is used mainly by Windows XP's Media Center Edition PCs, a special breed of computer covered in *Windows XP Media Center Edition 2004 PC For Dummies,* by Danny Briere and Pat Hurley (Wiley).

- To make the video adjust itself automatically to the size of your Media Player window, choose Video Size from the View menu and select Fit Video to Player on Resize.
- When downloading video from the Internet, make sure it's stored in Windows Media format. Media Player can't play QuickTime or RealVideo. Those two formats require free players available from Apple (`www.apple.com/quicktime`) or Real (`www.real.com`). Make sure you download the *free* versions — sometimes the sites try to sucker you into buying their pay versions.

- Some Web sites only *stream* their video to your computer — you can't save the video to play later. But you can try: After watching a streaming Web video, choose Save from Media Player's File menu. If that option is *grayed out,* the Web site has forbidden you from saving the video.
- When choosing video to watch on the Internet, your connection speed is your guide. If you have a dial-up connection, watch the video's 56K version. Broadband users can watch either the 100K or 300K. You can't damage your computer by choosing the wrong one; the video just won't look right.

Figure 15-5: Double-click a video file's name to watch it in Media Player.

Playing Music Files (MP3s and WMAs)

Media Player plays several types of digital music files, but they all have one thing in common: When you tell Media Player to play a song or album, Media Player immediately places that item on your *Now Playing List* — a list of items queued up for playing one after the other.

If you want to play a song listed in Media Player's library (or a music file in any folder, for that matter), double-click its name. Media Player begins playing it immediately, and the song appears in the Now Playing list. (If this doesn't work as described, click the Library Options button and choose Play Selected Item on Double-Click.)

- To play an entire album in Media Player's library, right-click on the album from the library's Album Artist category and choose Play.
- Want to hear several files or albums, one after the other? Right-click on the first one and choose Play. Right-click on the next and choose Add to Now Playing List. Repeat until you're done. Media Player queues them all up in the Now Playing List.

- Although Media Player can't *create* MP3s unless you purchase an extra piece of software known as an *encoder* or *codec,* it can *play* MP3s without trouble.

Playing Internet Radio Stations

Now that Media Player's partnership with Napster lets you pay to hear Internet radio, Media Player's latest version makes it more difficult to listen to *free* Internet Radio stations. No Radio button appears along the top, and you can't save favorite stations in the library.

But if you're willing to search for the Internet's free stations, click Media Player's Guide button. The Windows Media Web site (`www.windowsmedia.com`) appears in Media Player.

Click the word Radio from near the top of the Web site's page. The Web site, which changes daily, offers things to hear. Click Radio Tuner to search a list of stations by keyword: the artist or station's name, for instance. Or, browse by genre: Alternative Rock, Jazz, Rock, and others.

Many of the stations found on this site, unfortunately, want you to pay for the privilege of listening.

- To find free stations, head to Google (`www.google.com`) and search for the words `Internet Radio Station` to see what turns up. When you find a station broadcasting in Windows Media Audio format, click the Web site's Tune In button to load Media Player and start listening.
- I downloaded a copy of Winamp (`www.winamp.com`), an MP3 player that lets me listen to the thousands of radio stations available through Shoutcast (`www.shoutcast.com`).
- If you prefer to pay for customized Internet radio, check out this chapter's "Buying Music and Movies from Online Stores" section, later in this chapter, and check out Napster's subscription plan.

Creating, Saving, and Editing Playlists

A *playlist* is simply a list of songs (and/or videos) that play in a certain order. So what? Well, their beauty comes with what you can *do* with them. Save a playlist of your favorite songs, for instance, and they're always available for play back with a single click.

To save your *current* Now Playing List as a playlist, click the playlist's current name along its top, choose Save Playlist as, and type in its new name.

To create a *new* playlist, follow these steps:

1. **Choose New Now Playing List from Media Player's File menu.**
2. **Click the words Now Playing List (located just above the current playlist) and choose Edit using Playlist Editor from the drop-down menu.**

   Media Player's Edit Playlist window appears, as shown in Figure 15-6. See how Artist\Album appears in the drop-down list at the top? That tells the window to list all the artists' names, with their albums beneath them. For instance, I've double-clicked Jimi Hendrix's name to see his albums.

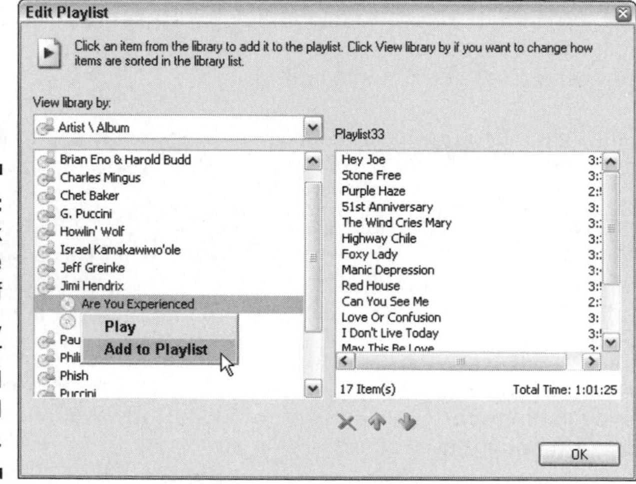

Figure 15-6: Right-click on the names of songs, albums, or artists and choose Add to Playlist.

3. **To view your library by individual songs instead, choose Artist from the View Library By drop-down list. Then double-click an artist's name to reveal all of that artist's songs — not albums.**
4. **Right-click on the album or song you want and choose Add to Playlist.**

   Your choice pops up in the list box on the right.
5. **Added something you don't want? Right-click on that item from the right window and choose Remove from List. Rearrange your playlist by dragging and dropping items further up or down the list.**

   Whenever you add or remove items from a playlist, the window updates the playing time from the bottom of the right side. That lets you know how long your playlist takes to play.

6. **When you're happy with your playlist, click the OK button.**
7. **To save your newly edited playlist, click its current name atop the playlist window, choose Save Playlist As, and type in its new name.**

Make your own Desert Island Disc or Greatest Hits playlists; you can then burn them to a CD to play in your car. After you create a playlist, insert a blank CD into your CD burner and click the Start Burn button along the Playlist's bottom. Try listening to the CD before taking it on a long trip; sometimes CDs don't burn well, and you want to make sure it burned correctly before taking it on the road. I explain how to copy and create CDs in more detail later in this chapter.

To edit a previously created playlist, begin playing it. Then click its name at the top of the playlist window and choose Edit using Playlist Editor.

Copying CDs to Your Hard Disk

First, the bad news. Media Player can't always create MP3s, the industry standard for digital music. Instead, it tries to create copy-protected WMA files that don't work in many portable players and won't play on other computers — your laptop, for instance.

To remove the copy protection from WMA files, choose Options from Media Player's Tools menu and click the Rip Music tab. Then *remove* the check mark from the Copy Protect Music box and click OK. After all, you own the CD; you should be able to take that music wherever you go.

To copy CDs to your hard drive, follow these instructions:

1. **Open Media Player and insert the CD into your computer.**

   If the CD starts playing, click the Stop button on the Play controls.

2. **Click CDs and Devices from Media Player's File menu, choose Rip Audio CD, and select the CD drive with the CD.**

   Sometimes Media Player immediately fills in the album's artist and song titles. If it doesn't, click the Find Album Info button near the player's top-right corner. Media Player connects to the Internet, tries to identify your CD, and fills in the information. (Media Player's library relies on tag information.)

If it doesn't find the information, click the Artist Not Found button and use the forms to manually fill in the song titles, artist name, and CD name. Done? Move to Step 3.

3. **Make sure the songs you want to copy are checked.**

   Normally Media Player copies every song on the CD. To leave Tiny Tim off your ukulele compilation, for example, remove the check mark from Tiny Tim's name.

4. **Click the Rip Music button.**

   If you're ripping your first CD, Media Player asks what quality level you prefer when saving your songs. Normally, click Keep My Current Format Settings. If you have questions, read the "Media Player's ripping quality settings" sidebar.

   Media Player begins copying your songs from your CD to your My Music folder, using the artist's name as a folder, with the album name as a folder inside it. The process takes about 10 to 20 minutes, depending on your computer's power.

Here are some tips for ripping CDs to your computer:

- Some record companies add copy protection to their CDs to keep you from copying them to your computer. If you buy a copy-protected CD, try holding down the Shift key when inserting it into your computer. Sometimes that keeps the copy-protection software from working.
- Don't fiddle around on your computer while it's ripping songs — just let it sit there and churn away. Running other programs might distract it, leaving gaps in your music.
- To rip your music as MP3 files, you need to buy an MP3 encoder. (Microsoft didn't include one.) Choose Options from Media Player's Tools menu, click the Rip Music tab, and choose Learn More about MP3 Formats. Internet Explorer opens to a page where you can download the MP3 encoder for about ten bucks.
- Music stored in your My Music folder is easier to find later.
- View your My Music folder in Thumbnail view (choose Thumbnail from the folder's View menu) to see the album's artwork on the folder. If you don't see the artwork, add your own: Locate the album's artwork on the Internet, right-click on the image, and choose Save Picture As. Save the image with the name *folder* inside the album's folder. (Windows looks for files named "folder" and uses them for thumbnails.)

Media Player's ripping quality settings

Musical CDs contain a *huge* amount of information — so much, in fact, that the complete Rolling Stones catalog probably wouldn't fit on most hard drives. To keep music files manageably small, ripping programs, such as Media Player, *compress* songs to about one-tenth of their normal size. Compressing the songs lessens their quality, so the big question becomes, how much quality loss is acceptable?

The answer is when you can hear the difference, a much-debated point among listeners. Many people can't tell the difference between a CD and a WMA song ripped at 64 Kbps (kilobits per second), so Media Player defaults to that standard. Also, *ripped* songs are usually played on computers or portable players — not high-fidelity stereos — so 64 Kbps WMA files sound fine.

If you'd rather sacrifice more disk space for better quality, kick up the quality a notch by choosing Options from the Tools menu and clicking the Rip Music tab. Slide the bar to the left (Best Quality) to rip at a higher quality. (For music files that don't lose *any* fidelity, choose Windows Media Audio Lossless from the drop-down list, and prepare for huge files.)

For the most versatility, consider dumping Media Player's WMA format and switching to MP3. If MP3 isn't an option listed in the Format drop-down list, click Learn More about MP3 Formats. You have to download an MP3 encoder for about $10. Unlike WMA, the MP3 format doesn't have copy protection, and it works with many more music players. (Most people use 128 Kbps rather than 64 Kbps when ripping with MP3, but let your own ears be your guide.)

Duplicating Music CDs

Ever wanted a disposable copy of your favorite CD to play in their car? No sense scratching up your original. You'll want to make copies of CDs for your kids, too, before they create pizzas out of them. Media Player makes it fairly easy to copy a music CD:

1. **Rip the CD to your hard drive.**
2. **Insert a blank CD into your writable CD drive.**
3. **Click the Library button to see your saved music.**
4. **Right-click on the album in your library and choose Add to Burn List.**
5. **Click the Burn button and click the Start Burn button.**

Media Player copies your songs to your blank CD to create a copy of the CD. It might be all you need.

Now, for the fine print. This isn't really *duplicating* a CD, and here's why: Media Player compresses each song when copying it to your hard drive, dropping the quality a notch in the process. Copying the songs back to CD drops a little more quality. Some listeners can't tell the difference. Others can.

To make the best duplicate possible in Media Player, rip your CD using Windows Media Audio Lossless, as described in the "Media Player's ripping quality settings" sidebar. Then copy those same songs back to a blank CD. (Erase the ripped "lossless" songs because those files are *huge.*)

Copying Songs to Your Portable Player

Media Player 10 doesn't work with all portable music players, including the bestselling iPod. And it's clearly optimized for transferring WMA files — not the MP3 files used by most portable players. Most people stick with the transfer software that came with their portable player. But if you're willing to give Media Player a go, follow these steps:

1. **Connect your player to your computer.**

   This usually involves connecting a USB cord between your device and a port in the back of your computer.

2. **Load Media Player and click the Sync button.**

   Media Player is fairly quick to list the files on players holding only a few hundred songs, but if your player holds thousands, you may be twiddling your thumbs for several minutes.

3. **Click Edit Playlist and create a playlist of songs you'd like to add.**

   I describe the Playlist Editor earlier in this chapter.

4. **Click the Start Sync button.**

   The Start Sync button lives just above the playlist window.

Media Player sends your playlist to your player, as shown in Figure 15-7.

- To change how Media Player sends files to your portable media player, choose Options from the Tools menu and click the Devices tab. Double-click your player's name to see its current options. Different players have different options, and some require firmware upgrades to work with Media Player 10.
- For best results, visit your portable music player's Web site and make sure you're using your player's latest version of downloadable firmware. (You'll have to read the player's manual for updating instructions.)

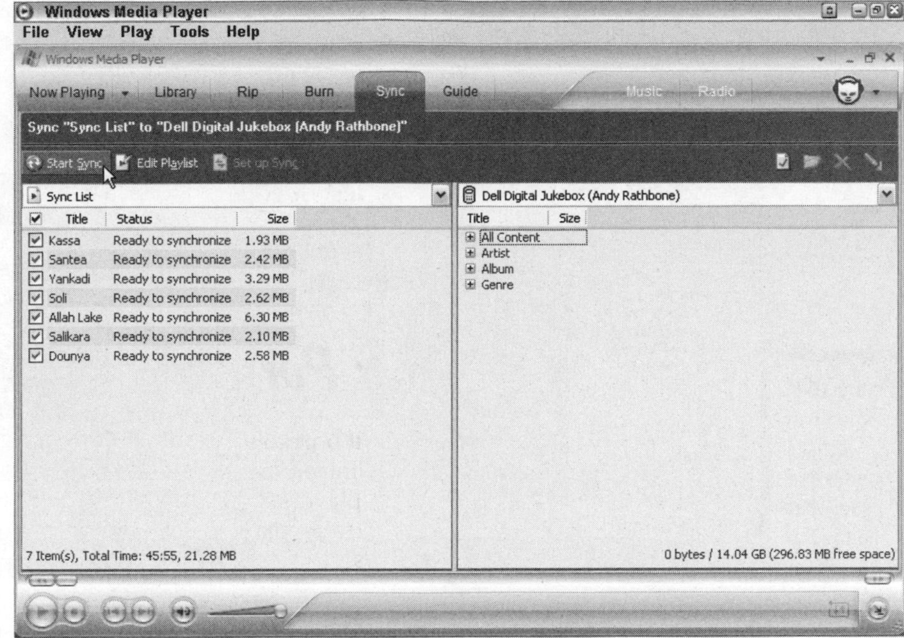

Figure 15-7: Media Player 10 works well when sending WMA files to your portable player — *if* your portable player can accept them.

Buying Music and Movies from Online Stores

Media Player 10's biggest new feature could be the online store. There, you can pay to download songs and movies or listen to a customized radio station. To start shopping, follow these steps:

1. **Choose Online Stores from the View menu, and select an online store.**

   Media Player's line-up of online stores includes Napster, CinemaNow, and Wal-Mart, but don't be surprised if the stores change as the online market matures.

   Choosing a store usually requires you to download a *plug-in* — a piece of software that embeds itself inside Media Player to add its own brand of copy protection and other features. After you download and install the plug-in, you're ready to shop, as shown in Figure 15-8.

Figure 15-8: Type in an artist's name and see what songs are available for purchase.

2. **Simply browse the menus, or head straight for what you want: Type the artist's or album's name in the Search box.**

   Napster shows you what it has to offer.

3. **When you're ready to buy a song, double-click it and fill out the paperwork.**

   Be sure to read the fine print before typing in your credit card number. Stores offer different copy-protection plans, song selections, portable player compatibility, and pricing models.

- Some stores charge a monthly subscription fee to listen to anything you want. Others charge $0.99 per song. Some stores let you copy songs to a limited number of devices; others have songs that expire after a set time.
- Media Player's Now Playing window (refer to Figure 15-2) now integrates with the online store. Whenever you play something from your own computer's library, the Now Playing window connects to the online store to show similar songs you might be interested in hearing — or buying.
- CinemaNow, the online movie store, isn't nearly as integrated with Media as Napster. Choosing CinemaNow simply displays the online store's Web site in Media Player, just as it does in Internet Explorer.

Another player keeps opening my files!

You'd never hear Microsoft say it, but Media Player isn't the only Windows program for playing songs or viewing movies. In fact, you need QuickTime (`www.quicktime.com`) to view lots of Internet videos stored in Apple's competing QuickTime movie format. Many Internet sounds and videos come stored in Real's (`www.real.com`) competing RealAudio or RealVideo formats, which Media Player can't handle, either.

And some people use Winamp (`www.winamp.com`) for playing their music as well as a wide variety of Internet radio stations. With all the competing formats available, many people install several different media players — one for each format. Unfortunately, this leads to bickering among each player because they all fight to become your default player. To pick and choose which player opens which format, look on the player's Options page and select only the formats you want it to handle.

In Media Player, for instance, choose Options from the Tools menu and click the File Types tab to select which types of files it should and shouldn't open.

Chapter 16

Fiddling with Photos and Movies

In This Chapter

- Copying digital camera photos into your computer
- Viewing photos in your My Pictures folder
- Saving digital photos to a CD
- E-mailing photos
- Printing photos
- Copying camcorder footage into your computer
- Editing your clips into a movie
- Adding transitions between clips
- Saving your completed movie and sharing it with others

Film is free with digital cameras, so snap all the photos you want. Actually, take *twice* as many. That professional photographer's trick increases your odds of capturing a good one.

Here's another tip — this one is for camcorder owners who have a stack of videotapes sitting in a cupboard: Windows Movie Maker's AutoMovie program automatically scans your footage, weeds out the bad shots, and saves the highlights as a single movie that's much easier on the eyes of your friends and relatives. (And it's a lot more accessible than those videotapes in the cupboard.)

This chapter introduces you to the growing relationship among Windows, digital cameras, and camcorders — both digital and analog. It explains how to move your digital photos and movies onto your computer, display them to the family, e-mail them to distant relatives, and save them in easy-to-find locations on your computer.

One final note: After you've started creating your family album on a computer, please take steps to back it up properly. (This chapter explains how to copy them to a CD.) Your family memories can't be replaced.

Using Your Computer as a Digital Shoebox

With an eye on the digital camera boom, Microsoft's programmers have transformed Windows' built-in My Pictures folder into a computerized family album. After you've dumped your digital camera photos into that folder, Windows XP makes it easy to create on-the-fly slide shows, screen savers, wallpaper, and a host of other tricks.

This section walks you through connecting your camera to your computer and copying the photos to the computer.

Every time you change your digital camera's battery, make sure the camera's clock shows the current time and date. If it doesn't, please take the time to set it correctly. Digital photos don't come with a "date developed" date stamped on the back. If your camera's clock is set correctly, it hides the current time and date inside each photo, letting your grandkids know when you snapped it. (In Windows, right-click on a photo and choose Properties to see when it was taken.)

Dumping the camera's photos into your computer

Most digital cameras come with software that grabs your camera's photos and places them into your computer. You don't have to install it, however, or even bother trying to figure it out. Windows XP's built-in software easily fetches photos from nearly any make and model of digital camera when you follow these steps:

1. **Plug the camera into your computer.**

   Find your camera's special transfer cable. One end plugs into your camera, and the other into your computer's *USB port,* a rectangular-looking hole about a half-inch long and an eighth-inch high. (Most USB ports live on the back of the computer, but newer computers sport them up front.)

   Some high-end digital cameras expect to plug into a *FireWire* port, which isn't found on most PCs. I explain how to add a FireWire port to your computer in *Upgrading & Fixing PCs For Dummies,* 6th Edition (Wiley).

2. **Turn on your camera and wait for Windows XP to recognize it.**

If you're plugging in the camera for the first time, Windows XP usually heralds its presence with a small pop-up window above your taskbar by the clock. The Microsoft Scanner and Camera Wizard then announces *its* presence, as shown in Figure 16-1.

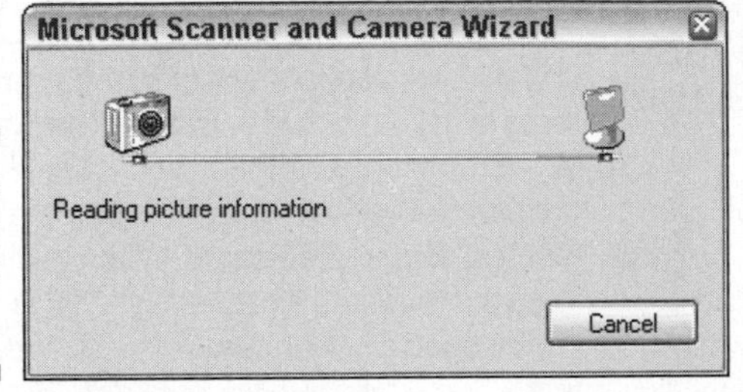

Figure 16-1: The wizard connects to the camera.

If Windows XP doesn't recognize your camera, make sure the camera is set to Display mode rather than Shoot mode.

3. **When the Scanner and Camera Wizard appears, click Next.**
4. **Make sure a check mark appears next to all the pictures and then click Next, as shown in Figure 16-2.**

   If any pictures don't have check marks in their boxes, click the words Select All to select them all. That lets you dump *all* your camera's pictures into your computer, where they're easier to work with.

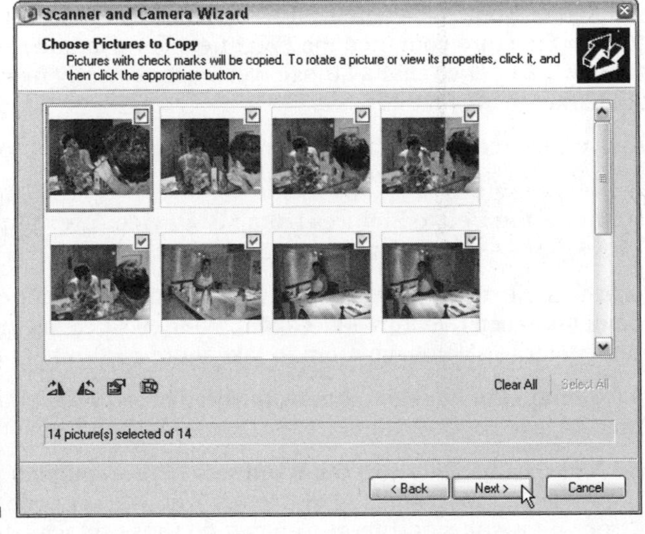

Figure 16-2: Click Select All to place a check mark next to all the pictures and then click Next.

Grabbing your camera's photos with a card reader

Windows XP's Scanner and Camera Wizard grabs photos from your camera fairly easily. But a *digital card reader* does a much better job. A digital card reader is a little box with a cable that plugs into your computer's USB port, just like your camera does.

To dump your camera's pictures into your computer, just remove the camera's memory card and slide it into your card reader. Windows XP notices that you've inserted the card and assigns it a drive letter. At that point, Windows treats your card like any other disk drive, be it a CD or your hard drive.

Select all the photos on your card (they're usually in a folder called DCIM) and cut and paste them to a folder in your My Pictures folder.

Digital card readers are cheap (less than $25), easy to set up, fast at copying images, and much more convenient. Plus, you can leave your camera turned off while dumping the vacation photos, saving the battery. When buying a card reader, make sure it can read the type of memory cards used by your camera — as well as several other types of memory cards. (That ensures it will work with any new computer-related gadgets you might acquire around the holidays.)

5. **Type a name for the group of pictures in the first text box.**

   Type a descriptive word into the Name box for Windows to use for the filenames. Type the word Hawaii, for instance, and Windows XP names the photos as Hawaii 001, Hawaii 002, Hawaii 003, and so on.

6. **Click the Browse button and either choose Create New Folder or find an existing folder where you want to save your pictures.**

   Windows XP lets you create a new folder in your My Pictures folder (or any other) to store your incoming pictures. For example, you could create a Hawaii folder so that all those pictures are neatly filed away and easy to find in My Pictures.

   After you've selected a name and folder for storing your photos, the window should look like Figure 16-3.

7. **Make sure that the Delete Pictures from My Device After Copying Them check box is selected and then click Next.**

   When you click Next, Windows copies the pictures from your camera to your computer. When they're safely copied, Windows deletes the pictures from your camera so you have room to take more pictures.

8. **Choose Nothing - I'm Finished Working with These Pictures and click Next.**

   Windows XP actually offers two other options here — publish your pictures to a Web site (Microsoft's MSN Groups Web site) or order prints online (from Microsoft's partners). You can do those things later, after you've examined and edited your pictures. I explain edits and printing later in this chapter.

9. **Click Finish.**

   Windows XP lists where your pictures are stored and lets you click the link to see the pictures immediately. (Clicking the Finish button does the same thing.)

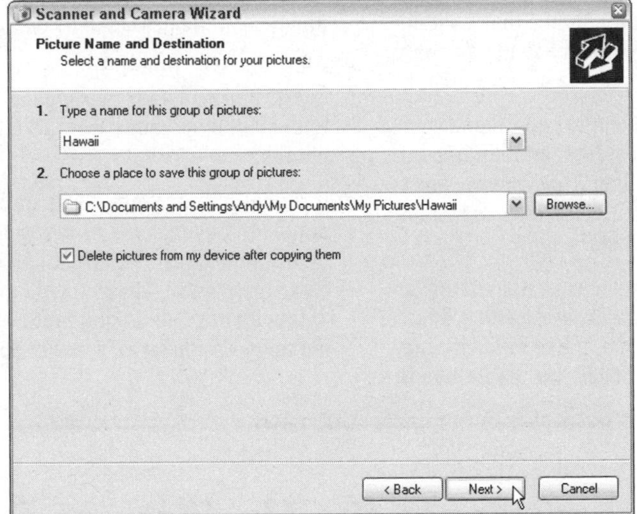

Figure 16-3: Type a name for Windows to name the photos and create a folder for Windows to store them in.

Windows XP doesn't recognize my camera!

Although Windows XP usually greets cameras as soon as they're plugged into the computer, sometimes the two don't become friends immediately. To let them share the same vibe, follow these steps:

1. **Open Printers and Other Hardware from the Control Panel.**
2. **Click the Scanners and Cameras icon.**
3. **Choose Add an Imaging Device (hidden at the top of the window's left side).**

   The Installation Wizard appears to greet the two.

4. **Choose the manufacturer, model, and port.**

   Click your camera manufacturer's name on the window's left side and choose the camera model on the right. Click Next and choose Automatic Port Detection. If your camera is turned on and plugged in correctly, Windows should place an icon for it in both your My Computer area and your Control Panel's Scanners and Camera area.

If Windows XP *still* doesn't recognize your camera, Windows XP needs a translator to understand its language. Unfortunately, that translator will have to be the camera's bundled software.

Keeping digital photos organized

It's tempting to create a folder called New Camera in your My Pictures folder and start dumping new pictures into it. But when it comes time to find a particular photo, that system breaks down quickly. Follow these tips to keep your pictures organized and easy to retrieve:

- After each photo-taking session, dump your digital camera's pictures into their own folder on your computer. That way you don't have to sort through unrelated photos when trying to find a particular image.
- Create a few main folders like Home, Family, Friends, Holidays, Travel, and Parties. Then create folders within those folders and name them specifically for each event you've photographed. (To create a folder, right-click on a blank spot inside the My Pictures folder, choose New, select Folder, and type in the new folder's name.)
- After you've created folders, the Browse button makes it easy to navigate to the right folder to dump your camera's latest set of photos.
- If digital photography turns into a hobby, consider buying one of many third-party photo programs like ThumbsPlus (`www.cerious.com`). They provide more photo management and editing features, improving upon Windows XP's basic tools.

Viewing photos in the My Pictures folder

Your My Pictures folder, conveniently located in your My Documents folder, easily earns kudos as the best spot to store your digital photos. That folder offers all the file-viewing tools found in your regular folders but adds several new tricks for displaying, editing, e-mailing, and printing your photos.

Here's the rundown on viewing your photos (or any other graphic file, for that matter) in the My Pictures folders.

Viewing photos in Thumbnail or Filmstrip mode

Old-time photographers often printed their slides or photos as a *contact sheet* — a single piece of paper showing rows of postage-stamp-sized pictures. Windows XP's Thumbnail view, shown in Figure 16-4, displays the computerized equivalent. Choose Thumbnails from the folder's View menu, and the My Pictures folder quickly displays rows of miniature photos across the screen.

Thumbnail mode comes in handiest when looking for a particular photo in a folder stuffed with images.

For a larger look at your pictures, choose Filmstrip from the View menu. The My Pictures folder displays one row of thumbnails across the screen's bottom, with a larger image of one photo above it, as shown in Figure 16-5. Click any picture along the bottom to see a larger view along the top.

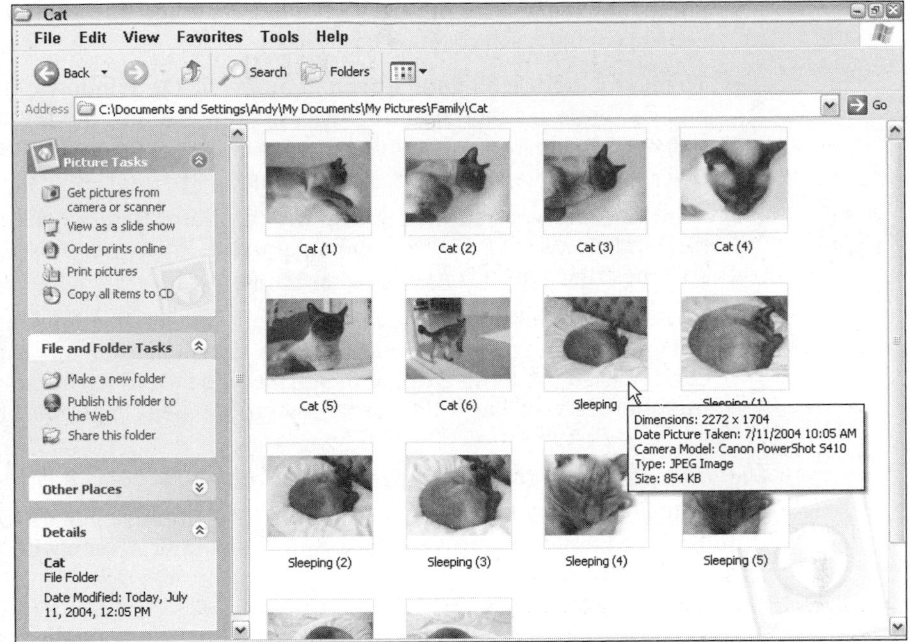

Figure 16-4: Choose Thumbnails from the View menu to display your photos in small rows.

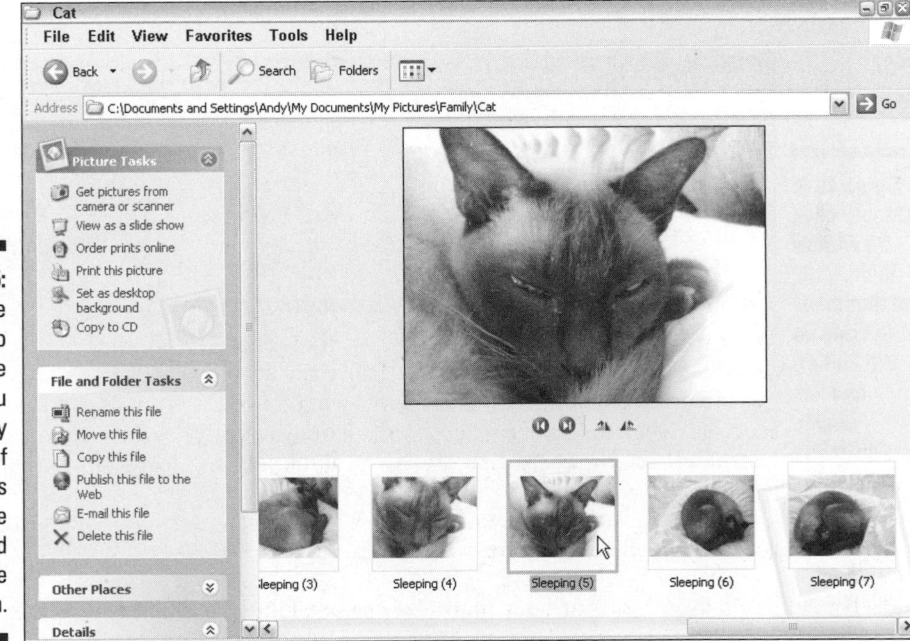

Figure 16-5: Choose Filmstrip from the View menu to display a row of photos with one enlarged picture above them.

- Spot a blurred or ugly photo? Right-click on it and choose Delete. No sense keeping trash on your hard disk.
- To make a picture fill your screen, double-click it. Windows XP's Picture and Fax Viewer, covered in the next section, displays the picture. (If it doesn't pop up, right-click the file, choose Open With, and select Windows Picture and Fax Viewer.)

- Want to cover your entire desktop with a photo? Right-click on the picture and choose Set as Desktop Background. Windows immediately splashes that photo across your desktop.
- Hover your mouse pointer over any photo for detailed information (refer to Figure 16-4). You see the photo's size, date snapped, and model of camera used, plus the graphic file format it's stored in (in this instance, the photo is saved as a JPG, pronounced "jay-peg," a popular format).

Viewing photos in the Picture and Fax Viewer

For a full-screen peek at an individual photo, just double-click its icon or thumbnail. Windows' Picture and Fax Viewer fills your screen with the photo, as shown in Figure 16-6.

Table 16-1 provides a handy explanation of the buttons beneath each picture in the Picture and Fax Viewer. (If this book is not close by, hover your mouse pointer over a button for a brief description.)

Figure 16-6: Double-click a photo's name, icon, or thumbnail to bring up the Picture and Fax Viewer, which lets you print, rotate, enlarge, shrink, delete, or edit the photo.

Table 16-1 Buttons in the Windows Picture and Fax Viewer

Click This Button . . .	*. . . To Do This*
	View the previous image in the folder.
	Move to the next image in the folder.
	Resize the image to fit in the window.
	Show the image at actual size. (Given the immensity of today's digital photos, this usually shows a subject's single pore rather than his or her face.)
	Start a slide show of all pictures in the folder.
	Magnify the current image.
	Shrink the current image.
	Rotate the image clockwise.
	Rotate the image counterclockwise.
	Delete the image and show the next one in the folder.
	Send the image to the printer. (A dialog box lets you adjust the printing options.)
	Copy the image to a different folder. (It *doesn't* mean Save.)
	Open the image in Paint for very basic editing. Instead, buy an easy-to-use photo-editing program like Adobe Photoshop Elements.
	See the Viewer's Help program.

Fixing rotated pictures

In the old days, it never mattered how you tilted your camera when taking the photo; you simply turned the picture to view it. Most of today's computer monitors don't swivel, so Windows XP rotates the photo for you — if you figure out how.

The trick is to right-click on any photo as Windows displays it in Thumbnail mode. Choose Rotate Clockwise or Rotate Counter Clockwise to turn your green cliffs into grassy meadows.

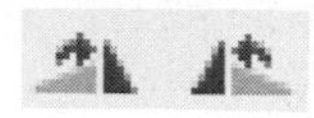

- If you're viewing a turned photo in Filmstrip mode, click one of the two Rotate icons along the picture's bottom (as shown in the margin) to rotate the photo to the left or right.

- Windows XP normally rotates photos *losslessly* — without losing any photo quality. The bizarre exception is if the photo's length or width isn't evenly divided by 16. (Four-megapixel photos measuring 2272 x 1704 pixels, for instance, have this problem.) If Windows XP sends you a message saying "rotating it might permanently reduce its quality," you're better off using the camera's menus to rotate the picture or rotating the picture in a more professional photo-editing program.

Creating a slide show

Thumbnail mode makes it easy to find a single photo from a folder, and Filmstrip mode lets you page quickly through all the pictures in a folder. But when the family is gathered around the computer to view the vacation photos, nothing beats the slide show. Windows XP's built-in slide show fills your entire screen with each photo, one after the other.

To start the slide show, open the folder of pictures you'd like to display. Then choose View as a Slide Show from the task pane along the window's left edge. Windows immediately darkens the monitor and then fills the screen with the folder's first picture, waits a few seconds, and then moves onto the next and repeats.

- Before starting the slide show, rotate pictures as needed so they're all right side up. If you miss one and Windows displays it sideways, hold down Ctrl and press K to quickly rotate the picture clockwise (or press L to rotate the picture counterclockwise).
- The slide show includes all the photos in the folder as well as any photos in folders that live in that folder.
- Select just a few of a folder's pictures and click the slide show button to limit the show to just those pictures. (I explain how to select photos and other items in Chapter 4.)

- When selecting a screen saver (described in Chapter 11), choose My Pictures Slideshow from the list. Windows creates a repeating slide show of every photo in your My Pictures folder.
- Feel free to add music to your slide show by playing a song in Media Player, described in Chapter 15. Or, if you picked up a Hawaiian CD while vacationing on the islands, insert that in your CD player for a soundtrack.

Viewing details about photos

Digital cameras place a surprising amount of information known as *EXIF* data inside every photo they take. To see the notes your camera automatically jots down into your files, right-click on a photo and choose Properties. Click the Summary tab and, if necessary, click the Advanced button to see the information shown in Figure 16-7.

Inside each photo that it takes, the camera stuffs detailed information about the image's size, resolution, camera make and model, shutter speed, lens aperture, focal length, exposure time, date and time, and other tidbits. The amount of information varies according to your camera's make and model.

Microsoft realized that most amateur photographers don't really need or care about this information, so Windows — and some photo editors — don't always preserve it when saving an edited file. If you care about these details, stick to a photo editor that lists Preserves EXIF Data as a feature.

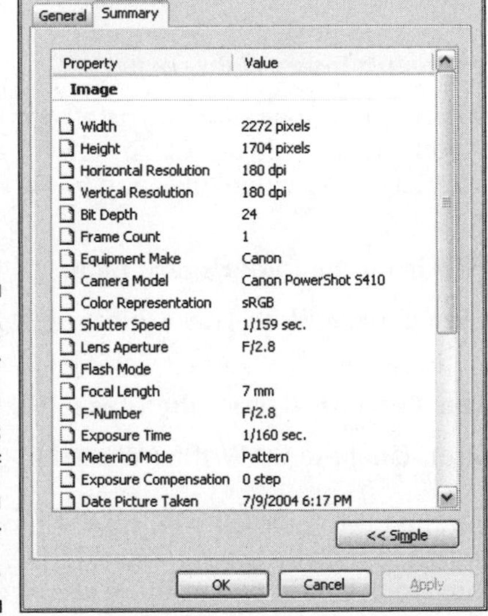

Figure 16-7: Your camera inserts this type of information into your photos.

Copying your digital photos to a CD

Shoeboxes full of family photos hang around in closets for generations because, compared to computers, they're almost indestructible. Even a few bug nibbles won't ruin the whole collection. Your computer, on the other hand, doesn't usually last a decade, and more than a few people have lost all their hard drive's contents because of a failure or malfunction.

The point? Don't lose all your photos because you were too lazy to back them up. Head to the computer or office supply store and pick up a stack of blank CDs. (Pick up a writable CD drive, too, if you don't have one.) Here's how to copy every item in your My Pictures folder to a CD:

1. **Insert a blank CD into your writable CD drive.**

   If Windows asks you what to do with your CD, choose Take No Action.

2. **Open your My Pictures folder and click Copy All Items to CD in the task pane.**

   Don't see the task pane along your folder's left edge? Then select all the items in your My Pictures folder, right-click on the selected items, choose Send To, and select your writable CD drive.

   Windows XP gathers your files and folders of photos and gets ready to write them to your CD drive.

   If Windows displays some weird message about copying Thumbs, click the Repeat My Answer Each Time This Occurs box and click the Skip button.

3. **Click the balloon by your screen's lower-right corner.**

   Windows XP's balloon announces that it's ready to write your files. Click the balloon to see the files; you should see your CD drive with a shortcut to either your My Pictures folder or individual files and folders you've selected within that folder.

4. **Click Write These files to CD from the folder's task pane.**

   Don't see the task pane? Then choose Write These Files to CD from the folder's File menu.

5. **Follow the CD Writing Wizard's steps to write the files to CD.**

   I give detailed instructions for using the CD Writing Wizard in Chapter 4.

- Don't have enough space on the CD to hold all your files? Unfortunately, Windows XP isn't smart enough to tell you when to insert the second CD. That means you have to copy your files in two or more steps, copying files and folders to the CD in smaller batches. (Most third-party CD writing programs handle this situation more gracefully than Windows XP.)

- If Windows runs out of disk space while it gathers your photos, that means your hard drive is running low on space. Run Disk Cleanup, covered in Chapter 12. If your computer *still* runs out of disk space, your computer needs a new hard drive. Until you buy one, try copying files and folders to the CD in small batches.

E-mailing photos

The problem boils down to this: Digital cameras create *huge* files that look nice when printed. But e-mail requires small files to squeeze through the Internet's pipelines; if the files are too big, they'll bounce back to your Inbox or take up too much space in others' e-mail accounts. To solve this technical conundrum, Windows XP conveniently offers to resize your digital photos when you e-mail them. Here's how to take advantage of its kind offer:

1. **Right-click on the desired photo or photos, choose Send To from the menu, and choose Mail Recipient.**

   Windows XP offers to make your e-mailed pictures smaller, as shown in Figure 16-8. Take it up on its offer.

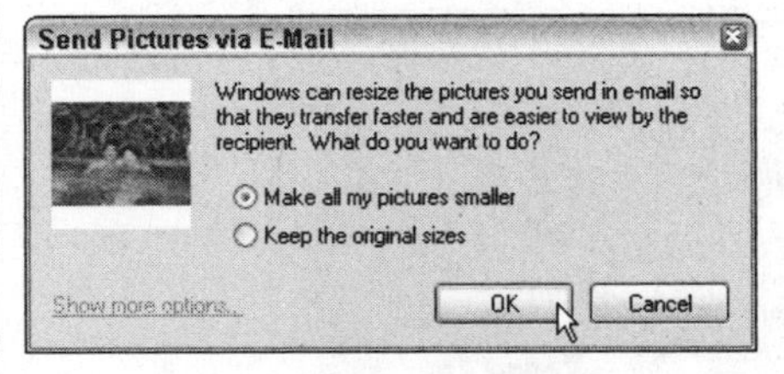

Figure 16-8: E-mail a photo with Outlook Express.

2. **Choose Make All My Pictures Smaller.**

   Windows resizes the photos you've selected. (Windows doesn't remember your choice and shows this box whenever you e-mail any photo.)

3. **Choose the recipient's name in your Outlook Express Address Book and click Send.**

   I cover Outlook Express in Chapter 9.

Windows XP normally shrinks photos to 640 x 480, which appears larger than a printed photograph on nearly any monitor. If you want the recipient to use it for a desktop background, click Show More Options, shown in Figure 16-8, and choose Large (Fits in a 1024 x 768 Window).

Cropping photos with Paint

A very basic graphics program, Paint creates simple drawings. If it's the only graphics program you have, you'll probably use it mostly for cropping photos to remove extraneous elements. Here's the procedure:

1. **Open the photo with Paint.**

   Right-click on your digital photo, choose Open With, and select Paint. (Selecting Edit from the menu does the same thing.)

2. **Click the Select tool.**

   Shown in the margin, it's the little square box near Paint's top-left corner.

3. **Point at the top-left corner of the portion you'd like to crop.**

   For instance, if you're looking for a head shot, point just over the top-left corner of the person's head.

4. **While holding down the mouse button, point at the opposite corner of what you'd like to crop.**

   Shown in Figure 16-9, I've selected my wife's face from a vacation photo.

Figure 16-9: Paint works well for cropping vacation photos.

5. **Choose Copy from Paint's Edit menu.**

   That copies her face to the Clipboard.

6. **Choose New from Paint's File menu.**

   That loads Paint again to accept the newly cropped image. (Paint can display only one image at a time.)

7. **Choose Paste from Paint's Edit menu and save the photo.**

   The newly cropped photo appears in Paint.

8. **Choose Save from the File menu to save the new image.**

   After you've saved a spouse's head, head to the Control Panel's User Accounts area and use it for his or her user account picture. (I explain user accounts in Chapter 13.)

Printing pictures

Windows XP's Photo Printing Wizard offers nearly as many options as the drugstore's photo counter, printing full-page glossies, wallet prints, and nearly anything in between.

The key to printing nice photos is buying nice photo paper and using a photo-quality printer. Be sure to see printed samples before buying a printer and use that printer's recommended printer paper.

Here's how to move what you saw in your camera's viewfinder to the printed page:

1. **Right-click on any photo, choose Print, and click Next.**

   The Photo and Printing Wizard announces its presence; click Next to proceed.

2. **Click to place a check mark next to pictures you'd like to print and then click Next.**

   The wizard shows every photo in your folder but places a check mark next to only the picture you've clicked. Feel free to click any others, if you wish, before clicking Next.

3. **Choose your desired printing options and click Next.**

   If you have more than one printer, select the desired printer in the top box. Click the Printing Preferences button and choose the type of photo paper you'll be printing on.

   Follow the instructions for inserting your photo paper into your printer. It must face the correct direction and print on the correct side. Some paper requires backing sheets, as well.

4. **Choose your photo layout and the number of times to use each picture and then click Next.**

   Each time you choose an option, the wizard displays a preview of the printed page, as shown in Figure 16-10.

   The wizard shuttles your photo off to the printer to be applied to paper.

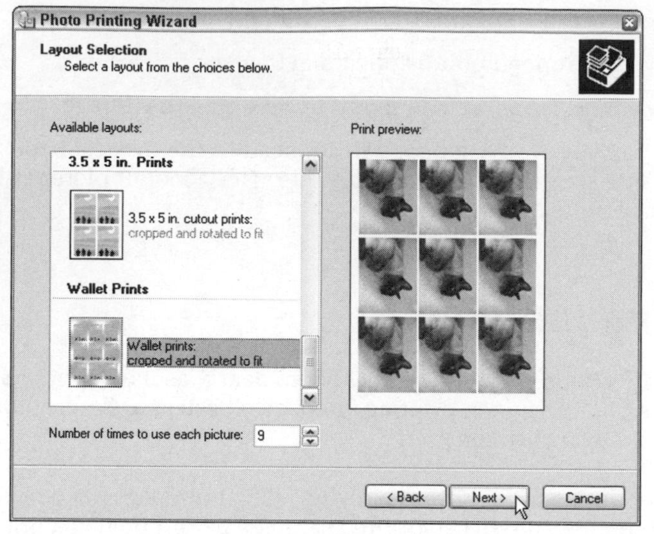

Figure 16-10: Choose a layout and the number of photos to see a preview of the printed page.

- Many photo printers and some digital cameras come with Adobe Photoshop Elements. If yours did, print from it instead of Windows XP. Photoshop Elements lets you touch up, sharpen, and adjust colors of photos, printing them at their best.
- Many photo developers now print digital photos using better quality paper and ink than your own printer. Check their pricing and ask how they like their photos delivered — by CD or memory card. Also, save money by doing any editing or color adjusting yourself. (They charge extra for this.)
- Don't leave photo paper in your printer tray; it's expensive, and you don't want to waste it accidentally printing out a letter.
- Keep printed photos out of sunlight because they fade easily.

Creating, Editing, and Viewing Digital Movies

The shelves of most camcorder owners weigh heavy with tapes filled with vacation footage, sporting events, and mud-bathing children. Windows XP's built-in Movie Maker helps you turn that pile of tapes into complete, edited movies.

If you've suffered through Windows XP's first Movie Maker program, you'll appreciate the huge improvements in Movie Maker's newest version. Instead of leaving you with a stark opening screen, Movie Maker now takes a task-oriented approach. Shown in Figure 16-11, Movie Maker's task pane gently guides you through the three steps of creating a movie: capture, edit, and save.

The newest version of Movie Maker 2 comes with Service Pack 2, and you can also download it through Windows Update. To see what version of Movie Maker you have, choose About from its Help menu. (The current version at this time is Version 5.)

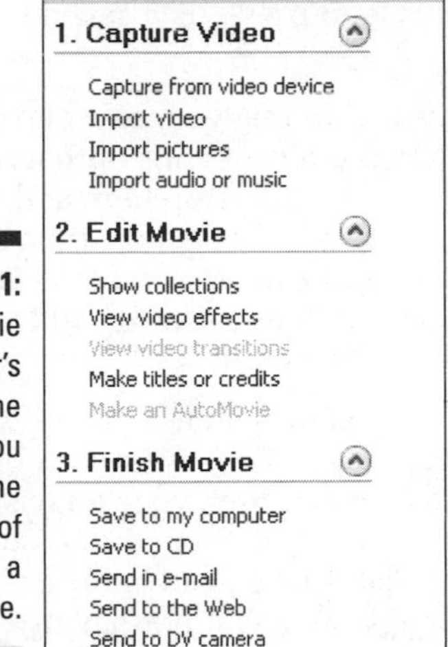

Figure 16-11: Movie Maker's task pane guides you through the steps of creating a movie.

Letting Movie Maker's robot build an AutoMovie

If you're not up to learning Movie Maker's controls and simply want a movie — *fast* — then let Movie Maker's AutoMovie function do it all automatically. After you've imported your video footage and/or photos, choose Make an AutoMovie from the Edit Movie section. Select the movie style you're after, be it a page-turning photo album, clean-and-simple cuts and fades, a flashy music video, a vintage "aged" movie, or a sports flick that narrows in on your fast pans and zooms.

Movie Maker takes over from there, robotically assembling a movie from your footage and/or photos. It spends some time analyzing your work, looking for the interesting pans and zooms, leaving out the jigglies and dark shots, and assembling the highlights into a complete flick. Although not perfect, AutoMovie is a surprisingly quick way to turn that tall stack of videotapes into short, easily accessible movies.

Pressed for time? Try out Movie Maker's new AutoMovie mode, described in the nearby sidebar, "Letting Movie Maker's robot build an AutoMovie." The program automatically analyzes your footage and creates a quick, on-the-fly movie. The robotically assembled movie works well as a starting point for your own movie or simply for learning Movie Maker's controls.

If you're editing movies manually, the rest of this section explains these three steps:

- **Capture Video:** Step one gathers your raw materials. You'll copy your camcorder's footage onto the hard drive, watching as Movie Maker breaks each camcorder shot into a separate *clip.* (That makes it easy to weed out any bad shots: Just click one and press Delete.) You can also bring in music files, digital photos, and previously saved footage to enhance your movie.
- **Edit Movie:** The second step involves combining your raw clips, music, and pictures into a movie. Drag and drop the best clips onto a line, creating an order that tells the movie's story. You can stop here and simply combine your clips into a movie. Budding producers take time to edit each clip down to its best few seconds. You can also add *transitions* between the clips — the way one clip fades into the next. Add a musical soundtrack, if you wish, and opening/closing credits.
- **Finish Movie:** In the third step, Movie Maker combines your edited batch of clips into a complete movie, ready to be played back on your computer or, if dumped back onto your camcorder, your television.

Creating movies requires a *lot* of free hard disk space. A 15-minute movie can consume 2.5 gigabytes. If Movie Maker complains about not having enough space, you have two choices: Create smaller videos one chunk at a time or upgrade your computer with a second hard drive. Also, use the defragment and disk cleanup tools I cover in Chapter 12 before making or editing a movie. Those tools help keep your hard disk in good shape.

Step one: Importing pictures from your video camera

Before Movie Maker can edit your camcorder's video, you must copy it onto your computer through a cable. Most digital camcorders connect to a computer's FireWire or USB 2.0 port. (Regular USB ports are too slow.) Because many older computers lack these ports, you can install them by plugging special cards inside your computer. (I describe the process in *Upgrading & Fixing PCs For Dummies,* 6th Edition (Wiley).

Sill using an *analog* rather than digital camcorder? You can still dump your movies into Windows XP by installing a *video capture* card in your computer.

To copy digital video into your computer, follow these steps:

1. **Connect your digital camcorder to your computer.**

   When Windows XP recognizes your digital camcorder, as shown in Figure 16-12, it offers to record video. Unless you're already familiar with Movie Maker, choose Take No Action. That gives you time to load Movie Maker and import the video yourself.

Figure 16-12: You likely want to choose Take No Action.

2. **Open Movie Maker.**

   Choose All Programs from the Start menu, select Accessories, and choose Windows Movie Maker to summon the program, shown in Figure 16-13. (Note the Movie Tasks pane in the top-left corner, which leads you through each step of creating a movie.)

   If Windows XP recommends that you set your screen resolution to 1024 x 768 or higher, do so now. (I explain how in Chapter 11.) That gives you more on-screen elbow room for editing your video.

3. **Choose Capture from Video Device.**

   Although Movie Maker calls this step Capture Video, it really allows you to import all the raw materials you need to create your movie: video, sound, and digital photos. Here's the rundown:

   - **Capture from Video Device:** The most common choice for digital camcorders, this copies your camcorder's entire tape to your computer's hard drive.
   - **Import Video:** Choose this to incorporate video already stored on your computer.
   - **Import Pictures:** This lets you add digital photos to your work area, ready to be sprinkled into your movies.

- **Import Audio or Music:** Many movies work best if you ignore the camcorder's wind-blown soundtrack and add your own sounds: recorded narration or music files. (Movie Maker even lets you mix several sound sources, layering the camcorder's recorded sounds with your own voice *and* music.)

Start by choosing Capture from Video Device to bring your video into the program. Wait until your video is safely on your computer before importing any photos or music files.

4. **Choose your camcorder from the list, if asked, and click Next.**

   Windows lists all the video gadgetry hooked up to your computer, including webcams and digital cameras. Choose your digital camcorder from the list.

5. **Create a name and designate a folder for your video and then click Next.**

   Name your incoming video after the event you've filmed, be it a vacation, wedding, or visit to a skateboard park.

   Choose or create a folder on your *second* hard drive, if your computer has two. Only have one hard drive? Then choose your My Videos folder.

6. **Choose your video setting and click Next.**

   These video settings dictate the quality of your imported video:

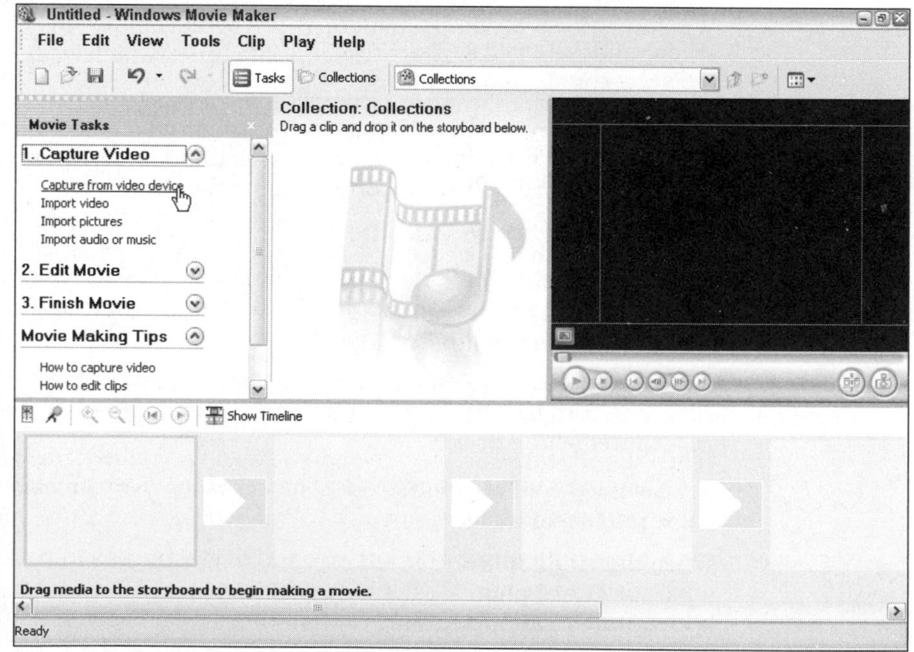

Figure 16-13: Windows Movie Maker walks you through the three steps for creating a movie.

- **Best Quality for Playback on My Computer:** Choose this if your movie will only be viewed on your computer, posted on a Web site, or e-mailed to others. This option creates smaller, lower-quality movies that play well on computers.
- **Digital Device Format:** Choose this only when editing a movie that will be dumped back onto your camcorder or written to a DVD. This consumes a *huge* amount of space, so if you're serious about editing movies, install a second hard drive of 120GB or more and devote it entirely to movie editing.

7. **Choose your capture method and click Next.**

   Again, here are the choices:

   - **Capture the Entire Tape Automatically:** This dumps the entire tape onto your computer. Although it's the most versatile option, it requires *lots* of free hard disk space.
   - **Capture Parts of the Tape Manually:** Choose this to copy short portions of the tape to your computer for editing. This works best for people with smaller hard drives who must edit in brief segments.

   Click the Show Preview During Capture check box to watch the movie as it's dumped to your computer's hard drive. If the captured footage stutters when played back, erase it and recapture the video with this box *un*checked.

8. **Wait for Windows to capture the tape.**

   Depending on the capture method you chose in Step 7, Windows XP either automatically grabs your video or lets you dump parts of it to your computer.

   Let your computer work uninterrupted while it's grabbing video because it needs lots of processing power for smooth captures. Don't listen to digital music in the background, for example, or browse the Web.

   If you're capturing only part of the tape, you'll control your digital camcorder with Movie Maker's on-screen controls — you don't even need to touch the camcorder. Fast forward to the section you want, click the Record button, and record the part you want. Grab a little more than you need because you can always edit it later.

   With an analog camcorder, you'll push the camcorder's Play button and click Movie Maker's Record button to grab the sections you want.

   When the capture completed window appears, you're done — the video now lives on your computer. Movie Maker takes over, breaking your shots into separate clips so you can easily delete the awful ones.

When the video is finally saved on your computer, feel free to import any music or digital photos. (The task pane's Capture Video section offers both options.) Imported songs and photos appear as icons at the top of your list of clips.

Step two: Editing your movie

After you've imported the video, songs, and photos, you're ready to assemble everything into a movie, weeding out the bad shots and splicing together the good stuff. If you're not picky, you can finish in a few minutes. If you're a budding Lucas, Coppola, or Kurosawa, you can spend days here, lining up the shots, adding transitions, and coordinating breaks with a soundtrack that holds everything together.

Don't worry that your edits will harm the original video you've saved onto your computer. You're only working with a copy.

As you work, feel free to play back your work at any time. Just click the Play button on the preview window.

These steps walk through the edits you can make:

1. **Familiarize yourself with the clips Movie Maker has left on your workspace.**

   Shown in Figure 16-14, Movie Maker's left side lists the steps required to create the movie. The middle strip shows all the shots you took during your movie, lined up in order from first to last. The right side shows a little movie playback window. (Double-click any clip to see it play in the window.)

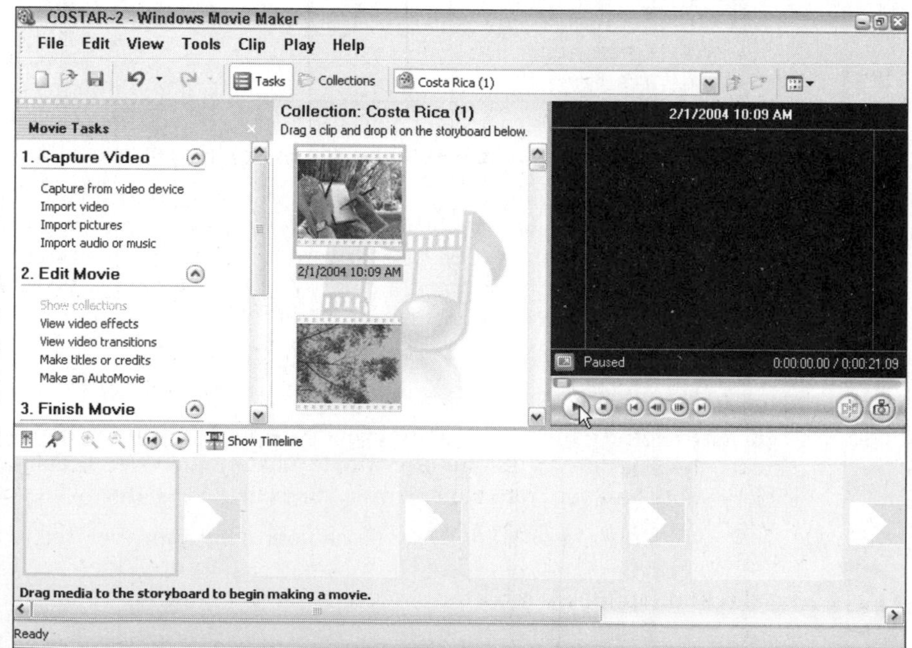

Figure 16-14: Look through your captured clips for interesting footage and double-click any clip to view it.

Along the bottom lies the storyboard — your workspace for linking clips in an order that tells a story, be it a vacation narrative or a science-fiction thriller.

2. **Drag and drop shots from the middle pane onto the storyboard in the order you'd like them played back.**

   When you spot some clips that would look good spliced together in a certain order, drag and drop them, one after another, onto the storyboard along the bottom. Place them in the order you'd like them played back, and Movie Maker begins to look like Figure 16-15. (When you drag a clip onto the storyboard, it doesn't disappear from your clip collection; you can reuse the same clip as many times as you want.)

   If you feel like you're done, jump ahead to the next section, "Step three: Saving your edited movie." If you'd like to trim your clips a bit or, perhaps, add a soundtrack or fades between clips, move to the next step.

3. **Click Show Timeline to edit your clips and add music, if desired.**

   The Show Timeline button, located at the top of the storyboard area, changes the storyboard's look. Instead of displaying each clip as a square block, Movie Maker expands the clips in proportion to their length, providing a quick visual reference, as shown in Figure 16-16. The first clip on the timeline, for instance, is much longer than the others and could use some trimming.

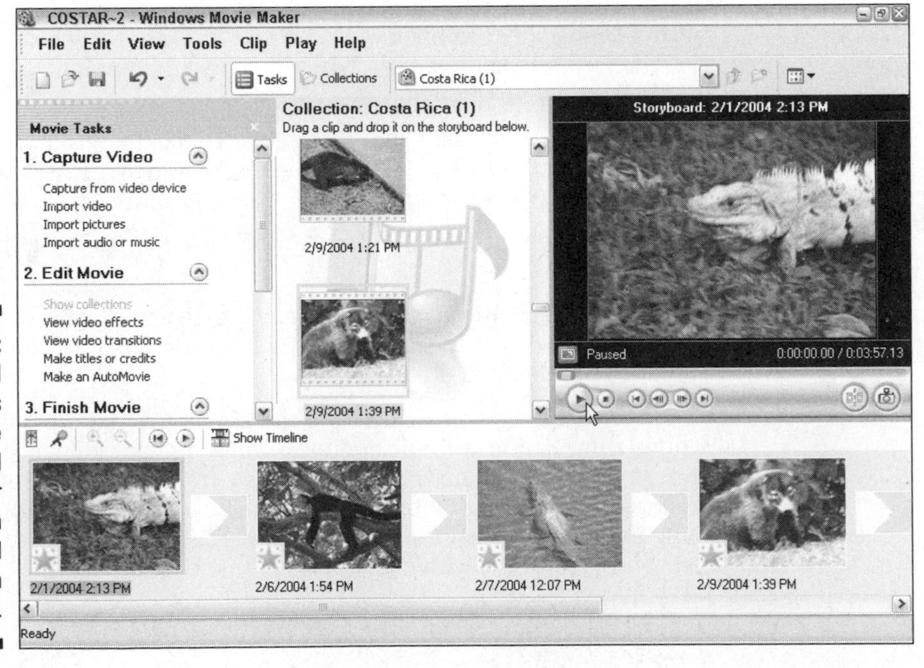

Figure 16-15: Drag and drop clips onto the storyboard in the order in which they should appear in your movie.

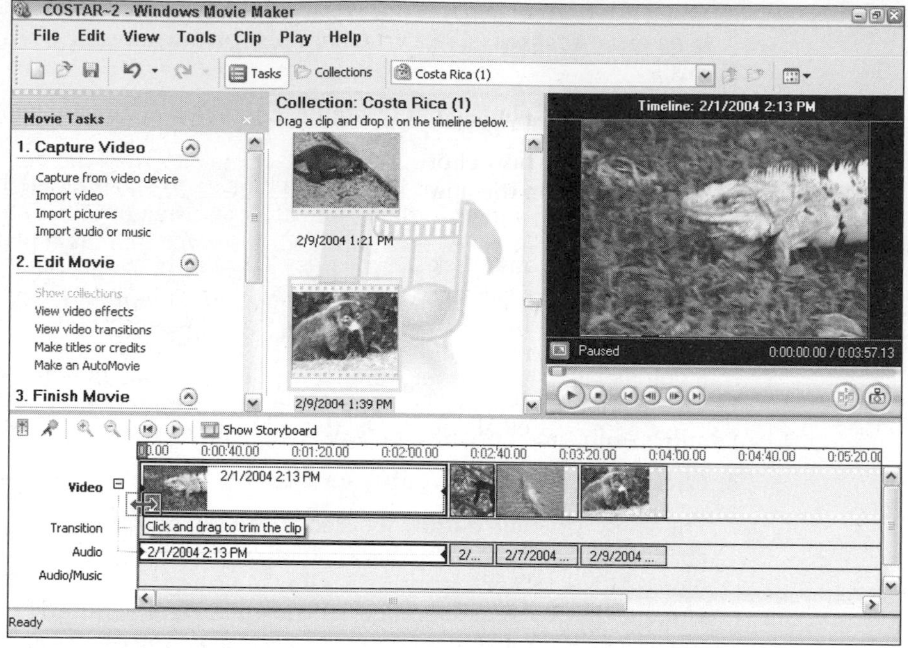

Figure 16-16: The timeline view shows the length of your clips and lets you slide in their edges to edit them.

To trim the clip's beginning, click on the horizontal line where the clip starts. (The mouse turns into two red arrows.) As you slide the line inward, keep an eye on the movie preview window; the window updates to show your current position. When you reach the point where the clip should start, let go of the mouse.

Movie Maker quickly trims the clip to its new beginning. Similarly, sliding the line at a clip's end will trim the clip's end. Repeat for each clip until you've kept only the good parts.

Made a mistake and trimmed too much? Choose Undo Trim Clip from the Edit menu.

Click the little magnifying glasses to toggle between close-up and faraway views of your editing. Close-up views let you edit a clip to start at the crack of a baseball bat, for instance.

To add music, drag a music file onto the timeline's Audio/Music area. Windows mixes it in with the audio captured by your camcorder. (Right-click on either the audio track or the music track to change its volume.) Similarly, drag any digital photos onto the timeline to incorporate them into your movie. Adjust the length of movies and photos by dragging in their borders, just as with clips.

If you're satisfied with your work, jump to the next section, "Step three: Saving your edited movie." If you're ready for more fine-tuning, move to the next step.

4. **Click Show Storyboard and add transitions.**

   Transitions are how clips join together. One clip can fade into another, for instance. Or, the new clip can slide the old clip off the side of the screen.

   To add transitions, click View Video Transitions in the Edit Movie area of the Movie Tasks section. Double-click any transitions, and the preview window shows how they work. When you find one you like, drag and drop it between two adjoining clips.

   When you're satisfied with your clips, transitions, and sounds, move to the next step: Tell Movie Maker to assemble your movie, described in the next section.

- Movie Maker offers a huge bag of tricks. Click Make Titles or Credits in the Movie task pane's Edit Movie section, for instance, to type in an opening title and the ending credits where you're the producer, director, cinematographer, and key grip.
- Although Movie Maker provides dozens of transitions, don't get carried away. Wild transitions look like somebody has been playing with effects, not making a movie.

Step three: Saving your edited movie

When you've finished editing your clips into a movie, choose Save Movie File from Movie Maker's File menu. The program offers to save your work into a single file using several options: Save the file on your computer, a CD, e-mail, a Web site, or a digital camcorder. Your choice dictates the size and quality Movie Maker uses when saving the file.

After you choose an option, Windows lets you choose a filename and location for the finished movie. Finally, Windows creates your movie, choosing the appropriate file size and quality for your implementation:

- Creating movies can take a *long* time. Windows needs to arrange all your clips, add the transitions and soundtracks, and compress everything into a single small file.
- Movies saved back onto your digital camcorder receive the best size and quality because the camcorder can record the huge file on tape.

- Movies saved for e-mail and a Web site have the lowest quality; otherwise, they'd take too long for most people to download.
- If your movies are *very* short, Windows can save a high-quality copy to a CD. But most high-quality movies consume much more space than a CD can hold.
- Although it's handy with a CD, Windows XP doesn't know how to write files to a DVD, unfortunately. You'll need a third-party program for this task, and most DVD drives include a DVD-burning program.

Part VI
Help!

The 5th Wave
By Rich Tennant
©RICHTENNANT
Oh come on-
how fatal
can it be?
FATAL
ERROR

In this part . . .

Windows XP can do hundreds of tasks in dozens of ways. This means several thousand things can fail at any given time.

Some problems are easy to fix. For example, one misplaced click on the desktop makes all your icons suddenly vanish. One more click in the right place puts them all back.

Other problems are far more complex, requiring teams of computer surgeons to diagnose, remedy, and bill accordingly.

This part helps you separate the big problems from the little ones. You'll know whether you can fix it yourself with a few clicks and a kick. If your situation is worse, you'll know when it's time to call in the surgeons.

Chapter 17

The Case of the Broken Window

In This Chapter

- Keeping a new computer from shutting down
- Restoring calm with System Restore
- Repairing a mouse
- Creating and using a password reset disk
- Making older programs run under Windows XP
- Fixing vanishing icons, stuck menus, and frozen screens
- Fixing a malfunctioning printer

Sometimes you just have a sense that something's wrong. The computer makes quiet grumbling noises, or Windows XP starts running more slowly than Congress. Other times, something's obviously gone haywire. Programs freeze, menus keep shooting at you, or Windows XP greets you with a cheery error message when you turn on your computer.

Many of the biggest-looking problems are solved by the smallest-looking solutions. This chapter may be able to point you to the right one.

My New Computer Keeps Getting Shut Down!

If you see a pop-up message like the one shown in Figure 17-1 whenever you go online, and your computer subsequently shuts down, you're dealing with the Blaster worm, an Internet nuisance since August 2003. (It has infected more than 16 million computers worldwide.)

First, stop your computer from immediately shutting down by choosing Run from the Start menu and typing this into the box:

```
shutdown -a
```

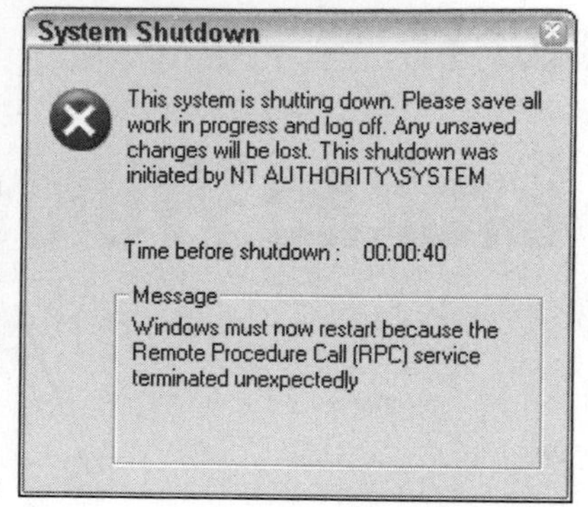

Figure 17-1: Messages like this are a sign of the Blaster worm.

Clicking the OK button stops the shutdown, giving you time to turn on Windows Firewall:

1. **Open the Control Panel from the Start menu and choose Network and Internet Connections.**
2. **Click the Network Connections icon.**
3. **Right-click on your Internet connection and choose Properties.**

   To protect your dial-up connection, right-click on the icon in the Dial-up section. To protect your DSL or cable modem connection, right-click on the Local Area Connection icon.
4. **Click the Advanced tab and click the little box in the Internet Connection Firewall section.**
5. **Visit Windows Update and install all patches marked Critical.**
6. **Finally, update your antivirus program and scan your computer to make sure it's not carrying the Blaster worm.**

These instructions are meant solely for people who don't use Windows Update, haven't kept their antivirus programs up-to-date, or haven't installed any of Windows XP's service packs. Using any one or all of those things will protect you from the Blaster worm. I explain how to update your computer with Service Pack 2 in Chapter 1. I offer all the details on Windows Update and antivirus programs in Chapter 10.

Restoring Calm with System Restore

When your computer is a disaster, wouldn't you love to go back in time to when Windows worked *right?* Windows XP's built-in time traveling program, System Restore, lets you turn back the clock with a few clicks.

It works like this: Every day or so, Windows takes a snapshot of Windows' most important settings and saves them by date, known as a *restore point.* When your computer begins acting up, tell System Restore to return to a restore point created when everything worked fine.

System Restore won't erase any of your files or e-mail, but programs installed after a restore point's date may need to be reinstalled. System Restore is also reversible; you can undo your last restore point or try a different one.

To send your computer back to a restore point, when it was working much better, follow these steps:

1. **Save any open files, close any loaded programs, and load System Restore.**

   Choose Start, click All Programs, and begin weaving your way through the menus: Choose Accessories, select System Tools, and click System Restore.

2. **Click Restore My Computer to an Earlier Time and then choose Next.**
3. **Click a calendar date when your computer worked well and then choose Next.**

   If the symptoms appeared today, choose a restore point from yesterday. But if the symptoms have been going on for longer, choose a day *before* your computer began having its problems.

4. **Make *sure* you've saved any open files and then click Next.**

   Your computer grumbles a bit and then restarts, using those earlier settings that worked fine.

Removing infected restore points

If your computer has a virus, erase all your restore points before disinfecting your computer with an antivirus program. Here's what to do:

1. **Click Start, right-click on My Computer, and choose Properties.**
2. **Click the System Restore tab and select the Turn Off System Restore check box.**
3. **Click Apply and then click OK.**
4. **Restart the computer.**
5. **After updating your antivirus program with the latest virus definitions, scan and disinfect your entire computer.**
6. **When the computer is disinfected, repeat Steps 1 through 4, except that in Step 2, uncheck Turn Off System Restore.**

When you're through, create a new restore point named after the virus you just disinfected. That leaves you with a safe restore point for future use.

- If your system is *already* working fine, feel free to create your own restore point: In Step 2, click the Create a Restore Point button. Name the restore point something descriptive, such as *Before Letting the Babysitter Play with the Computer.* (That way you know which restore point to use if things go awry.)
- Before installing a program or any new computer toys, load System Restore and create a restore point in case the installation is a disaster. Create a restore point *after* successfully installing something, too. Returning to that restore point won't undo your installation.
- You can save quite a few restore points, depending on your hard drive's size. My 20GB hard drive, for instance, currently contains 22 restore points. (Windows XP deletes the oldest restore points to make room for the newer ones.)

- If you restore your computer to a time *before* you installed some new hardware or software, those items may not work correctly. If they're not working correctly, reinstall them. Also, as described in the "Removing infected restore points" sidebar, be sure to erase your restore points if your computer contracted a virus. Using an infected restore point can reinfect your computer.

My Mouse Doesn't Work Right

Sometimes, the mouse doesn't work at all; other times, the mouse pointer hops across the screen like a flea. Here are a few things to look for:

- If no mouse arrow is on the screen after you start Windows, make sure that the mouse's tail is plugged snugly into the computer's rump. Then exit and restart Windows XP.
- If the mouse arrow is on-screen but won't move, Windows may be mistaking your brand of mouse for a different brand. You can make sure that Windows XP recognizes the correct type of mouse by following the steps on adding new hardware in Chapter 11.

- A mouse pointer can jump around on-screen when the mouse's innards become dirty. Follow the cleaning instructions I give in Chapter 12.
- If the mouse was working fine and now the buttons seem to be reversed, you've probably changed the right- or left-handed button configuration setting in the Control Panel. Double-click the Control Panel's Mouse icon and make sure that the configuration is set up to match your needs. (I cover this in Chapter 11.)

My Double-Clicks Are Now Single Clicks!

In an effort to make things easier, Windows XP lets people choose whether a single click or a double-click should open a file or folder.

But if you're not satisfied with the click method Windows XP uses, here's how to change it:

1. **Open any folder — the Start menu's My Documents folder will do.**
2. **Choose Folder Options from the Tools menu.**
3. **Choose your click preference in the Click Items as Follows section.**
4. **Click OK to save your preferences.**

Don't like to follow steps? Just click the Restore Defaults button in Folder Options, and Windows brings back double-clicking and other standard Windows XP folder behaviors.

Making and Using a Password Reset Disk

A *password reset disk* works like a key to your user account. Should you forget your password down the road, inserting the disk lets you back into your computer. You might want to leave a password reset disk in your safety deposit box for when you've, uh, moved on. Family members of deceased computer owners often find themselves locked out of the family photos as well as other important documents.

Creating a password reset disk

Follow these steps to create the disk:

1. **Choose Control Panel from the Start menu and choose User Accounts.**

   If you're an administrator, click the user account you want to protect. (Limited accounts can password-protect only their own accounts.)

2. **In the Related Tasks area along the left side, click Prevent a Forgotten Password.**

3. **When the Password Protect Wizard emerges, click Next.**
4. **Insert a blank, formatted floppy disk into drive A and then click Next.**

   Your computer needs a floppy drive to create a password reset disk. (You can't use a CD.)
5. **Type your password in the Current User Account Password box and then click Next.**

   The Forgotten Password Wizard creates your reset disk.
6. **Click Next and then click Finish.**

Label it *Password Reset Disk* if it's going into your safety deposit box. If it's going to sit where others can find it, label it something innocuous like *1993 Tax Records.*

Using a password reset disk to enter a user account

If you've forgotten your password — and you have a password reset disk, described in the previous section — here's how to enter your user account:

1. **At the Welcome screen, click the user account name and press Enter.**

   Because you've pressed Enter instead of entering the password, Windows gives you several options, including using a password reset disk.
2. **Choose Use Your Password Reset Disk.**

   The Password Reset Wizard materializes. If you don't see the Use Your Password Reset Disk option, however, that account doesn't have a working Password Reset Disk. You're out of luck.
3. **Click Next, insert the password reset disk into your floppy drive, and click Next.**
4. **Type a new password into the Type a New Password box. Repeat the password in the second box.**
5. **Type a hint in the Password Hint box to remind you of your password.**
6. **Click Next and then click Finish.**
7. **Type your new password into the Type Your Password box and press Enter.**

   Windows XP lets you back into your user account.

Whenever you use the password reset disk, Windows XP automatically updates the disk with your new password. That way the disk stays updated in case you forget the new password, too.

My program is frozen!

Eventually one of your programs will freeze up solid, leaving no way to reach its normal Close command. These three steps will extricate the frozen program from your computer's memory (and the screen, as well):

1. **Hold down the Ctrl, Alt, and Del keys simultaneously to fetch the Task Manager.**
2. **Click the Applications tab, if necessary, and then click the frozen program's name.**
3. **Click the End Task button, and Windows XP whisks away the frozen program.**

If your computer acts a little strangely afterward, play it safe by restarting your computer from the Start menu.

If you're locked out of a user account and don't have a password reset disk, your best bet is to open the phone book's business listings to Computer Repair and look for the words *Data Recovery.* A specialist can usually retrieve just about anything for the right price.

Making Older Programs Run under Windows XP

Many programmers design their software to run on a specific version of Windows. When a new Windows version appears a few years later, some programs feel threatened by their new environment and refuse to work.

If an older game or other program refuses to run under Windows XP, there's still hope because of Windows XP's secret *Compatibility mode.* This trick fools programs into thinking that they're running under their favorite older version of Windows so everything works well.

If your old program has problems with Windows XP, follow these steps:

1. **Right-click on the program's icon and choose Properties.**
2. **When the Properties dialog box appears, click the Compatibility tab.**
3. **After checking the program's box or installation disks to see its required Windows version, select that version from the Compatibility mode's drop-down menu, as shown in Figure 17-2.**

   For more information as well as a list of compatible programs, click Learn More about Program Compatibility (near the bottom of Figure 17-2).
4. **Click OK and then try running your program again to see if it's working better.**

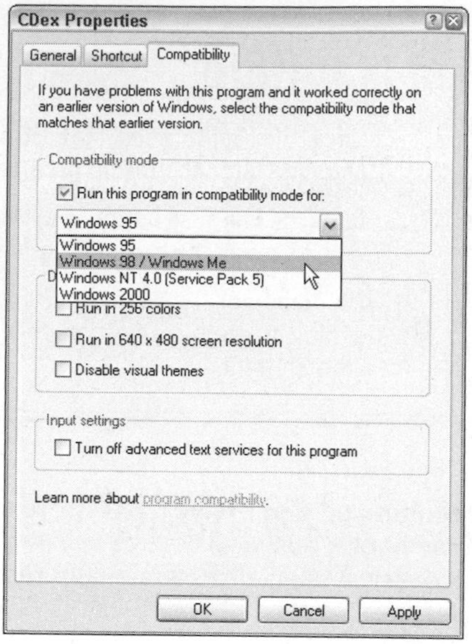

Figure 17-2: Compatibility mode lets you trick programs into thinking they're running on older Windows versions.

It Says I Need to Be an Administrator!

You *do* need to be an administrator to perform most of the best stuff on Windows XP. (Somebody has to be in charge of installing new software, changing network settings, and adding new computer parts.) Usually the computer's owner has the Administrator account, so if you see a message that says you need to be an administrator to do something on the computer, you need to find the computer's owner and ask for help. I cover different types of user accounts in Chapter 13.

I'm Stuck in Menu Land

If your keystrokes don't appear inside your program but instead make a bunch of menus shoot out from the top of the window, you're stuck in Menu Land. Somehow, you've pressed and released Alt, an innocent-looking key that's easy to hit accidentally. If you press and release Alt, Windows turns its attention away from your work and toward the menus along the top of the window.

To get back to work, press and release Alt one more time. Alternatively, press Esc twice. One or the other is your ticket out of Menu Land.

All My Desktop Icons Vanished

When you place a file or shortcut on your desktop, you can usually see it easily. But what if all the icons suddenly vanish from your desktop? That scary scenario can happen because Windows XP offers an odd option to make your desktop icons invisible.

Sure, invisible icons make your desktop look impeccably clean, but it's awfully hard to click invisible icons. To make them reappear, right-click on the desktop, choose Arrange Icons By, and then select Show Desktop Icons. That toggles the option back on, and your icons all reappear.

My Computer Is Frozen Up Solid

Every once in a while, Windows just drops the ball and wanders off somewhere to sit under a tree. You're left looking at a computer that just looks back. None of the computer's lights blink. Panicked clicks don't do anything. Pressing every key on the keyboard doesn't do anything, or worse yet, the computer starts to beep at every key press.

When nothing on-screen moves (except sometimes the mouse pointer), the computer is frozen up solid. Try the following approaches, in the following order, to correct the problem:

- **Approach 1:** Press Esc twice.

  This action usually doesn't work but give it a shot anyway.

- **Approach 2:** Press Ctrl, Alt, and Delete all at the same time.

  If you're lucky, the Task Manager appears with the message that you discovered an unresponsive application. The Task Manager lists the names of currently running programs, including the one that's not responding. Click the name of the program that's causing the mess and then click the End Process button. You lose any unsaved work in that program, of course, but you should be used to that. (If you somehow stumbled onto the Ctrl+Alt+Delete combination by accident, press Esc to quit Task Manager and return to Windows.)

  If that still doesn't do the trick, try clicking the Task Manager's Shut Down menu and choosing Restart. Your computer should shut down and restart, hopefully returning in a better mood.

- **Approach 3:** If the preceding approaches don't work, push the computer's reset button. When the Turn Off Computer box appears, choose Restart.

- **Approach 4:** If not even the reset button works (and some computers don't even have reset buttons anymore), turn the computer off by pushing its power button. (If that merely brings up the Turn Off the Computer menu, choose Restart, and your computer should restart.)
- **Approach 5:** If you press in the computer's off button long enough, it will eventually stop resisting and turn off.

The Printer Isn't Working Right

If the printer isn't working right, start with the simplest solution first: Make sure that it's plugged into the wall and turned on. Surprisingly, this step fixes about half the problems with printers. Next, make sure that the printer cable is snugly nestled in the ports on both the printer and the computer. Then check to make sure that it has enough paper and that the paper isn't jammed in the mechanism.

Then try printing from different programs, such as WordPad and Notepad, to see whether the problem is with the printer, Windows XP, or a particular Windows program. These tests help pinpoint the culprit.

For a quick test of a printer, click the Start button, choose the Control Panel, and select Printers and Other Hardware. Click Printers and Faxes to see the printers connected to your computer. Right-click on your printer's icon, choose Properties, and click the Print Test Page button. If your printer sends you a nicely printed page, the problem is probably with the software, not the printer or Windows XP.

While you're still at the Printers and Faxes window, press the F1 key to bring up the Printing Help window. Try the printer's troubleshooting program — Fixing a Printing Problem — to figure out why the printer is goofing off.

You'll find more information about printing, including troubleshooting information, in Chapter 7.

Chapter 18

Strange Messages: What You Did Does Not Compute

In This Chapter

- Understanding taskbar messages
- Deciphering messages in Internet Explorer
- Responding to messages on the desktop

Most error messages in life are fairly easy to understand. A VCR's flashing clock means you haven't set its clock yet. A car's pleasant beeping tone means that you've left your keys in the ignition. A spouse's stern glance means you've forgotten something important.

But Windows XP's error messages could have been written by a Senate subcommittee, if only they weren't so brief. The error messages rarely describe what you did to cause the event and, even worse, what to do about it.

In this chapter, I've collected some of Windows XP's most common messages. Match up an error message's subject or picture with the ones here and then read your appropriate response and the chapter covering that particular problem.

Access Is Denied

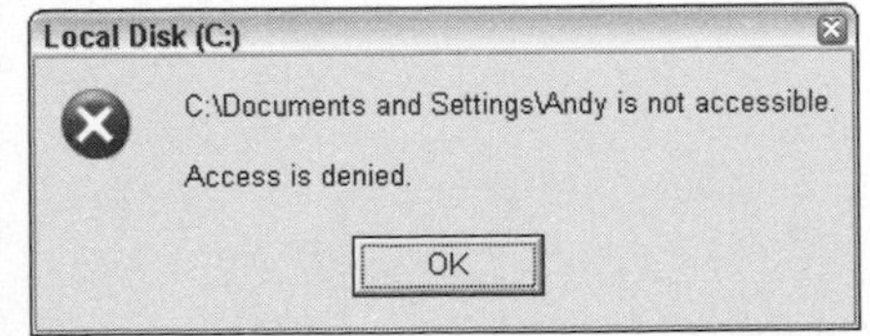

Figure 18-1: Ask the owner to open the folder or file.

Meaning: You're not allowed to see inside this folder.

Probable cause: The computer's owner hasn't given you permission.

Solutions: Only a person with an Administrator account — usually the computer's owner — can grant permission to open certain folders, so you need to track down that person. (If you're the administrator, you may grant access by choosing either to share that folder or to move its contents into the Shared Documents folder, actions both described in Chapter 13.)

Allow This Page to Install ActiveX Controls

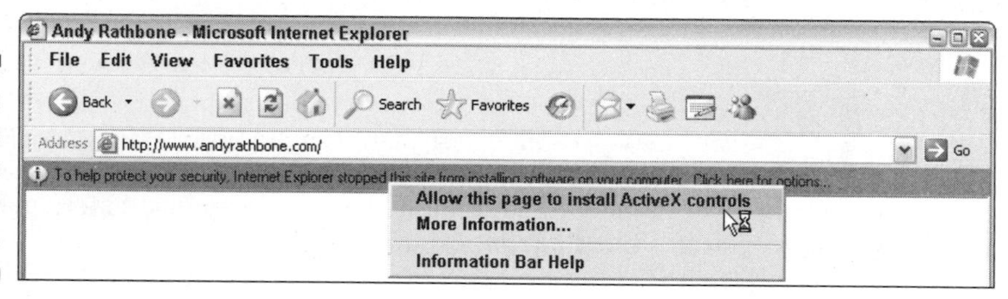

Figure 18-2: Choose Allow if you trust the site.

Meaning: This page wants to install extra software on your computer.

Probable cause: The Web site wants to enhance its appearance on your screen.

Solutions: If you trust the site, choose Allow This Page to Install ActiveX Controls. If you don't trust the site, don't choose anything. (Many sites still work fine.) Some ActiveX software enhances Internet Explorer or the Web site. But some sites abuse the technology and install offensive software. Service Pack 2, covered in Chapter 10, blocks all ActiveX software unless you specifically allow it to be installed.

AutoComplete

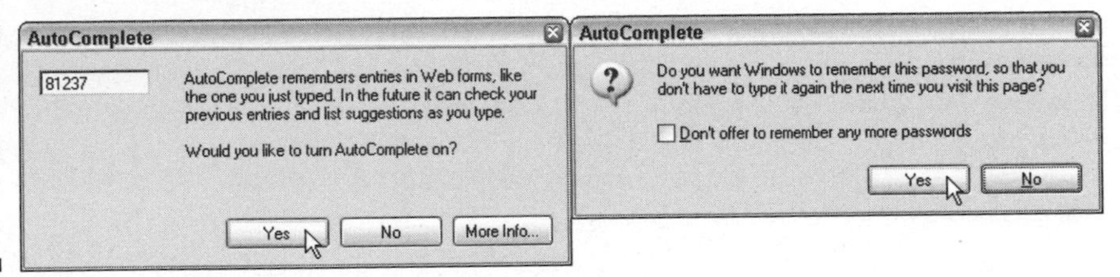

Figure 18-3: AutoComplete fills in words.

Meaning: When turned on, Internet Explorer's AutoComplete guesses what you're about to type and tries to fill it in for you.

Probable cause: Every Windows user is eventually asked to make this decision.

Solutions: Covered in Chapter 10, AutoComplete handily fills in some online forms with words you've used previously. Although a timesaver, AutoComplete poses a potential security problem for some people.

Click Here to Activate Now

Figure 18-4: The activation balloon.

Meaning: If you don't activate Windows by clicking here, Windows will stop working.

Probable cause: Windows XP's copy-protection scheme requires every user to activate his or her copy so that nobody else — including you — can use that copy on another computer.

Solutions: Click the message and let Windows connect to the Internet to activate itself. No Internet connection? Then dial the activation phone number and talk to the Microsoft people personally. ***Note:*** If you never see this message, then your copy of Windows has already been activated by the manufacturer. (I cover activation in Chapter 2.)

Did You Notice the Information Bar?

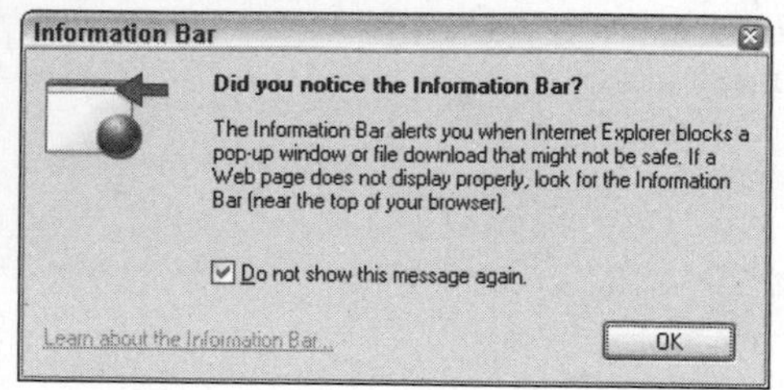

Figure 18-5: Internet Explorer blocked something.

Meaning: Proud of its new security measures, Internet Explorer tells you to examine the little top-edge strip that says something has been blocked from your currently viewed Web site.

Probable cause: You've just installed Service Pack 2, and Windows XP is calling attention to its new safety features.

Solutions: Look at the new Information Bar (refer to Figure 18-2), make sure the Do Not Show This Message Again check box is selected, and click OK. (I cover the Information Bar in Chapter 10.) Don't check that box if you *prefer* to know when Internet Explorer blocks something from your currently viewed site.

Do You Want to Run This File?

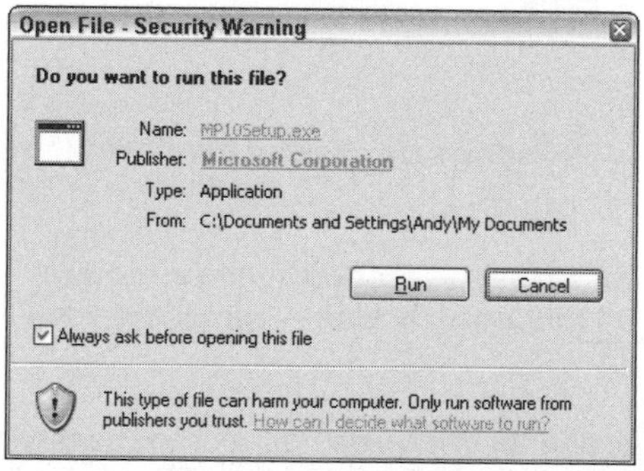

Figure 18-6: To run or install a program, click Yes.

Meaning: Because some programs try to install themselves on the sly, Windows asks you to confirm that you really *do* want to run that file that's starting to load.

Probable cause: You've downloaded a new program from the Internet, and you're trying to install it or run it for the first time.

Solutions: If this message pops up out of the blue, click Cancel. If you're trying to run a program, click Run. (If you don't want to see this question again, remove the check mark from the Always Ask Before Opening This File box and then click either Run or Cancel.)

Error Renaming File or Folder

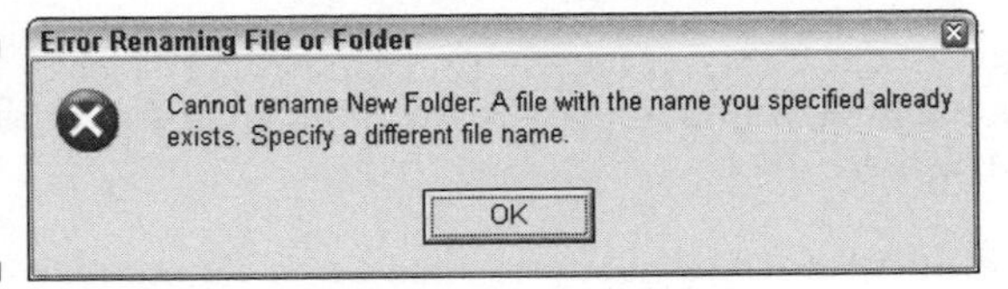

Figure 18-7: This name won't work.

Meaning: Another file or folder in your folder already has that name.

Probable cause: You're naming or renaming a file or folder to a name that's already been chosen.

Solutions: Name the file or folder something different. If one folder in your My Pictures folder is called *Mouse,* name the new folder *Mouse1,* or something similar. (I cover renaming files and folders in Chapter 4.)

Found New Hardware

Figure 18-8: Windows finds a new gadget.

Meaning: Windows recognizes a newly installed computer part and is installing it automatically.

Probable cause: This message usually occurs after you plug devices into your computer's USB port.

Solutions: Relax. Windows knows what's going on and will take charge.

Language Pack Installation

Language pack installation

To display language characters correctly you need to install the following language pack:

Japanese

Never install any language packs.

Install Cancel

Figure 18-9: You visited a site with Japanese.

Meaning: Internet Explorer wants to install new fonts so you can read a site with Japanese characters.

Probable cause: While planning that trip to Japan or shopping for imports, you've visited a Japanese Web site.

Solutions: Click the Install button. Windows XP installs the fonts automatically, and you'll be able to view the Web site. You'll encounter this message each time you visit a site containing characters Internet Explorer can't currently handle. (I cover Internet Explorer in Chapter 8.)

Hiding Your Inactive Notification Icons

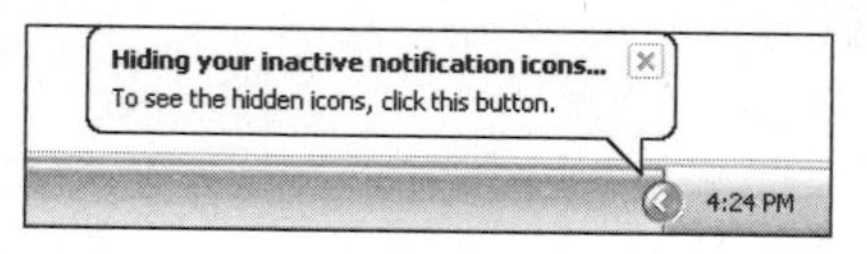

Figure 18-10: Hiding the little icons.

Meaning: Windows wants to hide the little icons that line up by your clock.

Probable cause: Windows likes to keep your desktop tidy, so instead of lining up icons by your clock, it offers to hide them every 60 days.

Solutions: Click the little arrow button by your clock to unveil the icons when you need them. If you want some or all of the icons to stay visible, right-click on a blank part of the taskbar, choose Properties, and click the Customize button at the bottom of the window. That lets you decide which icons are shown and which stay hidden.

If You Remove This File, You Will No Longer Be Able to Run This Program

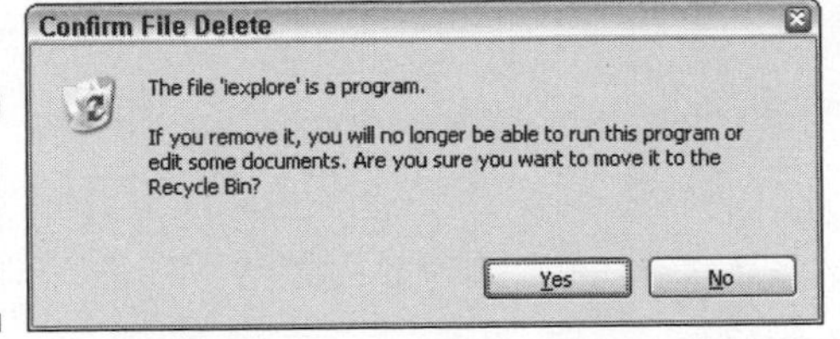

Figure 18-11: Deleting a program file.

Meaning: You're trying to delete a file needed by one or more programs.

Probable cause: You're clearing off some hard disk space to make room for incoming programs. You may have accidentally tried to delete something you shouldn't have.

Solutions: Click the No button to abort deleting the file. To avoid problems, remove programs with the Control Panel's Add or Remove Programs icon. If your program came with its own uninstall program, feel free to use that instead. (I cover the Control Panel in Chapter 11.)

New Fax Received

Figure 18-12: A fax has arrived.

Meaning: Windows XP's fax program just received a fax through your dial-up modem.

Probable cause: If you're expecting a fax, it has arrived; if you're not expecting a fax, it's probably a junk fax.

Solutions: Click the little icon that's sprouting the message, and Windows' Fax Console displays the new fax. (I cover sending and receiving faxes in Chapter 7.)

New Programs Installed

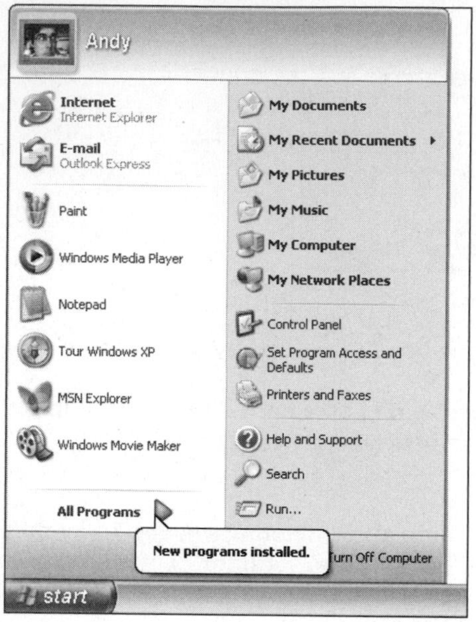

Figure 18-13: Windows announces that you've installed a new program and highlights its location on the Start menu.

Meaning: Windows is reminding you that the Start menu now contains your newly installed program.

Probable cause: Until you look at the newly installed program's icon on the Start menu, Windows keeps displaying this message.

Solutions: Either look at the program's icon on the Start menu or disable the message feature: Right-click on the Start button, choose Properties, and click the Customize button. Click the Advanced tab and remove the check mark from the Highlight Newly Installed Programs check box.

New Updates Are Ready to Install

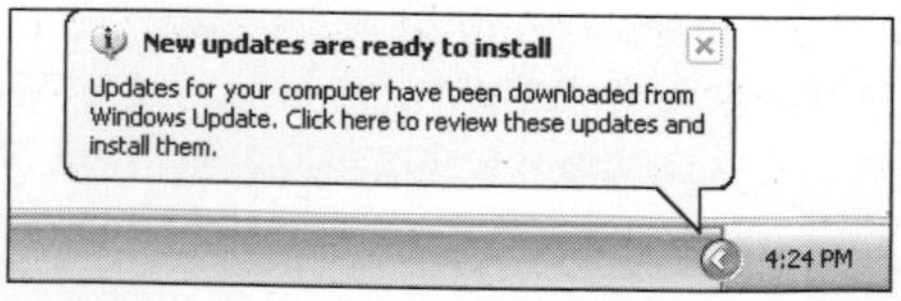

Figure 18-14: Microsoft is sending an update.

Meaning: Microsoft is sending you a software update to improve Windows or to fix a recently discovered problem.

Probable cause: Microsoft discovered a new problem with Windows, so it automatically sent you software to fix it.

Solutions: Click the pop-up message to accept and install the updates. You may need to save your work and let Windows restart to incorporate its changes. In Chapter 10, I explain how to make Windows install these problem fixers automatically, sparing you the trouble and keeping your copy of Windows up-to-date.

The Publisher Could Not Be Verified

Open File - Security Warning

The publisher could not be verified. Are you sure you want to run this software?

Name: DR8420E_PCFW_US_0054.EXE
Publisher: Unknown Publisher
Type: Application
From: C:\Documents and Settings\Andy\Desktop

Run Cancel

Always ask before opening this file

This file does not have a valid digital signature that verifies its publisher. You should only run software from publishers you trust.
How can I decide what software to run?

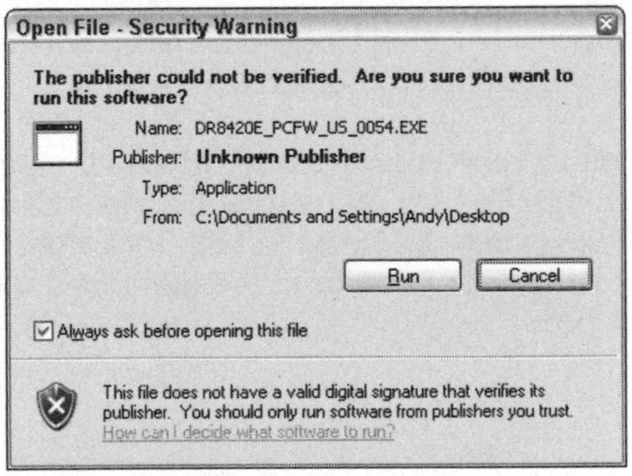

Figure 18-15: Windows doesn't recognize the software publisher.

Meaning: Windows can't verify that the software you're about to install was created by its claimed publisher.

Probable cause: Microsoft's *digital signature* program works like a name tag. Windows compares the digital signatures of both the software and its claimed publisher. If they match, everything's fine. If they *don't* match, beware: The software may be trying to trick you. But most often, you'll see messages like the one shown in Figure 18-15 because the publisher simply ignored Microsoft's digital signature system, leaving Windows in the dark.

Solutions: Many small companies skip the digital signature process, leading to these messages. If this message pops up from a small company, you're probably still safe. But if you see it when trying to run software from a large software company like Microsoft, don't run the software. It's probably trying to trick you.

There Are Unused Icons on Your Desktop

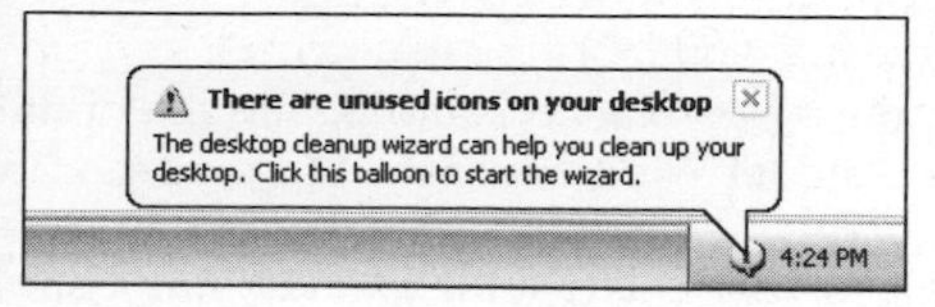

Figure 18-16: An offer to remove icons.

Meaning: In its incessant desire to keep your desktop tidy, Windows keeps track of how often you click the icons on your desktop. It tells you if you haven't clicked some for a while and asks if you want to get rid of them.

Probable cause: Every 60 days, Windows automatically runs its Desktop Cleanup Wizard, which offers to remove the icons you haven't clicked. It moves them to a new desktop folder called Unused Desktop Shortcuts. (You can always retrieve them from there, if desired.)

Solutions: Say No. If you want to keep your desktop tidy, do it yourself so that you can keep track of things. To turn off the feature, right-click on your desktop, choose Properties, and click the Desktop tab. Click the Customize Desktop button and remove the check mark from the Run Desktop Cleanup Wizard Every 60 Days check box.

To Help Protect Your Computer, Windows Firewall Has Blocked This Program . . .

Security Alert

To help protect your computer, Windows Firewall has blocked this program from receiving unsolicited information from the Internet or a network.

Name: Microsoft Fax Console

Publisher: Microsoft Corporation

Unblock this program

Keep blocking this program

Keep blocking this program, but ask me again later

Learn more about Windows Firewall

OK

Figure 18-17: Windows Firewall in action.

Meaning: Windows Firewall temporarily stopped this program from communicating through the Internet until you decide whether it should be allowed access.

Probable cause: A program tried to connect to the Internet, but Windows XP's built-in firewall program stopped it. That keeps viruses, worms, and other renegade programs from spreading and sharing information.

Solutions: If you think the program should be allowed to connect to the Internet, choose Unblock This Program. To let it connect *just this once,* choose Keep Blocking This Program, But Ask Me Again Later. To ban it from connecting, choose Keep Blocking This Program. (I cover Windows Firewall in Chapter 10.)

When You Send Information to the Internet . . .

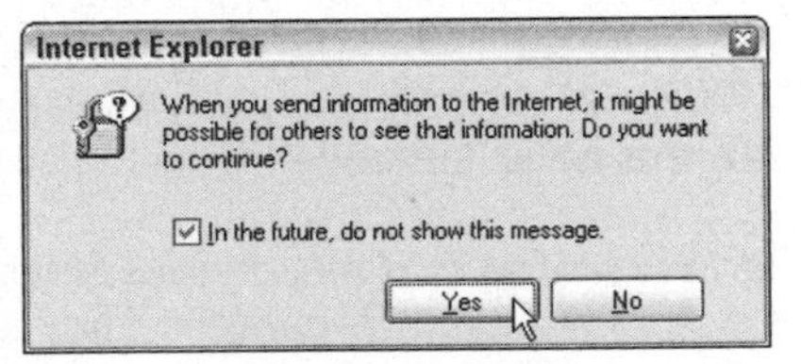

Figure 18-18: The Internet isn't completely secure.

Meaning: Windows is warning you that it's possible for people to read information as it's sent through the Internet.

Probable cause: Nothing is secure — not even the Internet. The employees who work at your Internet service provider can read the information you send, for instance. Hackers, too, sometimes run programs to read messages as they travel through the Internet. Law enforcement agencies can and do read your e-mail without warning. (Microsoft adds this warning so the company is not held liable if somebody reads your e-mail without your knowledge.)

Solutions: Don't worry about it too much. Postal service employees, for instance, can read your postcards if they want to. When I worked at a drugstore, one bored gal at the photo counter always peeked into people's photo envelopes. *Nothing* is secure while it moves from one place to another.

Windows Cannot Open This File

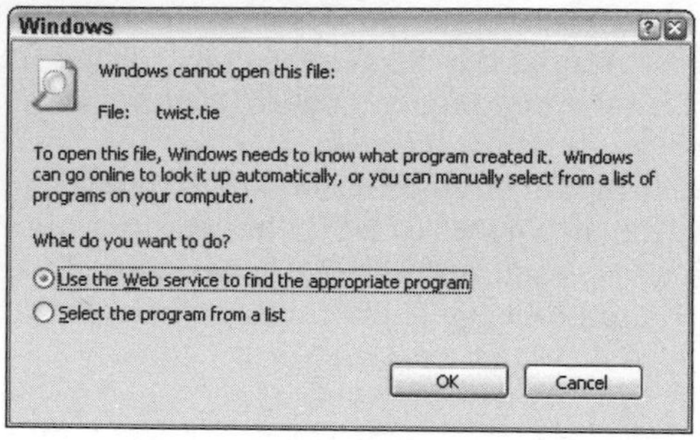

Figure 18-19: What program should open this file?

Meaning: Windows doesn't know which program created the file that you double-clicked, so it displays a list of programs and asks *you* to choose the right one.

Probable cause: Windows XP usually sticks secret hidden codes, known as *file extensions,* onto the ends of filenames. When you double-click a Notepad text file, for instance, Windows XP spots the secret, hidden file extension and uses Notepad to open the file. If Windows doesn't recognize the secret code letters, however, it complains with this error message.

Solutions: If you know what program created that file, choose Select the Program from a List and choose it from the list of programs. Then select the Always Use This Program to Open These Files check box. If you're stumped, choose Use the Web Service to Find the Appropriate Program. Windows examines the file and offers suggestions and links for downloading the right program.

You Have Files Waiting to Be Written to the CD

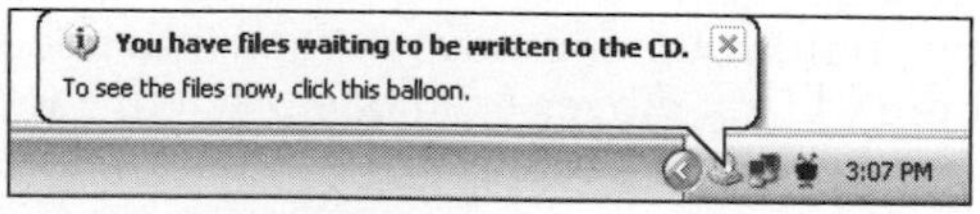

Figure 18-20: You said to copy files to a CD.

Meaning: Files are waiting to be copied to a CD in your computer's CD burning drive.

Probable cause: You told Windows to copy files to a CD recording drive.

Solutions: Click the message to see the waiting files. If the message disappeared too quickly, open My Computer from the Start menu and double-click the CD recording drive; Windows lists the files waiting to be copied. To copy the files, insert a writable CD into your recording drive and click Write These Files to CD. (Changed your mind and don't want to burn the files to a CD? Then just delete the listed files; they're only shortcuts, not the actual files.) I cover CD burning in Chapter 4.

Chapter 19

Moving from an Old Computer to a New One

In This Chapter

- Using the Files and Settings Transfer Wizard
- Copying files and settings with a home network or portable hard drive
- Copying files and settings through a direct cable connection
- Copying files and settings by using floppy disks
- Choosing what files and settings to copy
- Opening old files with other programs
- Disposing of the old computer

Even the most exciting new computer is missing one very important thing: all the files from your old computer. How do you move everything from one PC to another? How can you even *find* everything you want to move? To help solve the problem, Microsoft provided Windows XP with a virtual moving van called the Files and Settings Transfer Wizard.

When dropped in the driver's seat, the wizard not only grabs your old computer's data but also settings from many of your programs — your favorite Web sites, for instance, as well as your Outlook Express e-mail accounts and settings used by some other popular programs. After you approve a list of suggested files and settings, the wizard tracks it all down and copies it to your new computer.

This chapter introduces you to the wizard and explains how to copy your data as easily as possible between your two computers. Be a little wary of the wizard, though. The Bearded One offers so many options that it's perfectly normal to scratch your head several times while you stumble through each step of his wizardry.

Windows XP's original wizard had a few problems that have been corrected on newer computers and through Windows Update. If your version of Windows has Service Pack 1 or Service Pack 2, your wizard is fine. If not, install Service Pack 2 through Windows Update. You can find more about service packs in Chapter 1.

Using the File and Settings Transfer Wizard

Everybody knows that wizards work in mysterious ways. The Files and Settings Transfer Wizard breaks tradition by working in two clearly defined steps. First, you check items off a list, selecting the files and settings you'd like to transfer from your old computer. The wizard fetches your selected information and packs it up into a folder for easy travel.

Second, you tell the wizard how it should transport that bundle of files and settings to your new computer. Unfortunately, "magically" isn't an option; you must choose one of the following means of travel: direct cable, floppy drive, network, or other. (I explain these options in detail later in this section.)

After you've chosen both your transfer method and the items to transfer, the wizard carries out your commands, grabbing everything from one computer and stuffing it into the right places on your new computer.

- The wizard can transfer your files and settings from computers running Windows 95, Windows 98, Windows Me, Windows XP, Windows NT 4.0, or Windows 2000.
- Although the wizard gladly copies data and settings from many programs, it doesn't copy the *programs* themselves. You must install your old programs onto your new computer using their original installation CDs or disks. If you don't have those CDs or disks, you'll have to buy new copies.

- Be sure to install your programs onto your new computer *before* running the wizard. That way they're ready to accept the data from the old programs.

- If the Files and Settings Transfer Wizard seems too complicated or demanding, it's certainly not the only way to move the information. Most computer repair shops perform this task, and they offer a wider variety of options than Windows XP's wizard. Call for quotes.

Using the wizard *without* a Windows XP CD

The Files and Settings Transfer Wizard lives right on your Windows XP CD, making the program easy to move from one computer to another. However, not everybody *has* a Windows XP CD. (New computers, for instance, usually come with special OEM or Recovery CDs, which don't work like retail Windows XP CDs.) Adding to the problem, some older computers don't have a CD drive, rendering the portable-wizard-on-a-CD trick useless.

Users without a Windows XP CD or a CD drive can still use the wizard by stuffing it onto a floppy disk. To do that, follow these steps on any computer running Windows XP:

1. **Choose All Programs from the Start menu, choose Accessories, choose System Tools, and then click Files and Settings Transfer Wizard.**

   The wizard welcomes you.

2. **Click Next.**
3. **Choose New Computer and click Next.**

   If Windows Firewall appears, click the Unblock button to allow the wizard to peek at any computers connected to your own.

4. **Choose the I Want to Create a Wizard Disk in the Following Drive option and click Next.**

   This tells the wizard to stuff himself onto a floppy disk so you may insert him into your old computer.

5. **Insert a blank, formatted floppy disk into drive A and click OK.**

   The wizard places a copy of himself onto your floppy disk. If the wizard doesn't fit, try a different disk or reformat a new disk, as described in Chapter 4.

   Leave your new computer sitting at this step until you reach Step 10.

6. **Insert your new wizard floppy disk into your *old* Windows computer.**
7. **Click the old computer's Start menu and click Run.**
8. **Type `a:\fastwiz` and then click OK.**
9. **Collect your files and settings from your *old* computer.**

   Follow the wizard's instructions, as explained in Step 4 of the "Choosing things to move from your old computer" section.

10. **Return to your new computer and click Next.**

The wizard on your Windows XP computer then takes over. Creating the floppy adds a little time to the process, but it's a handy way to deal with CD-related problems.

Choosing things to move from your old computer

Before summoning the Files and Settings Transfer Wizard, close down any currently running programs. You should also choose the way you want to copy the files between the computers, which I explain later in this section.

Make sure you've installed your old programs onto your new computer *before* running the wizard. If the program isn't on your new computer to accept the incoming settings, the wizard's work will be wasted; you'll have to install the programs and repeat the wizard.

Choosing what files to copy from your old computer can be the most difficult part of the transfer process. After you've made those decisions, however, the wizard takes over and does all the grunt work. Don't get discouraged if this part seems difficult.

When you're ready, follow these steps to put the wizard to work:

1. **Insert your Windows XP CD or floppy into your *old* computer, choose Perform Additional Tasks, and choose Transfer Files and Settings.**

   The Files and Settings Transfer Wizard leaps to the screen, as shown in Figure 19-1.

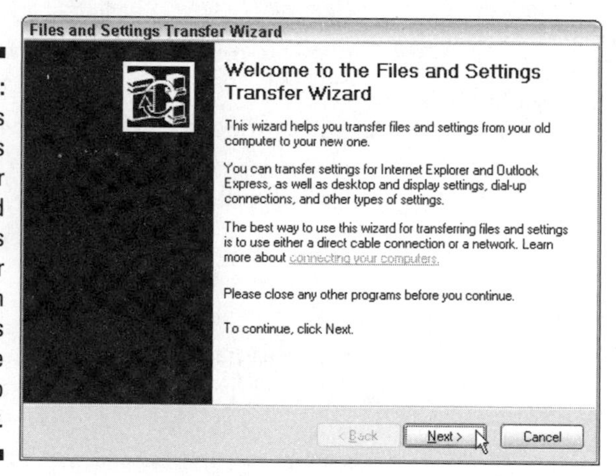

Figure 19-1: The Files and Settings Transfer Wizard copies files and popular program settings from one computer to another.

If your Windows XP CD doesn't include the wizard or if your old computer doesn't have a CD drive, put the wizard on a floppy as described in the nearby sidebar, "Using the wizard without a Windows XP CD."

2. **Click Next, select the Old Computer option (as shown in Figure 19-2), and click Next.**

   The wizard spends a little time examining the computer, its files, and its connections.

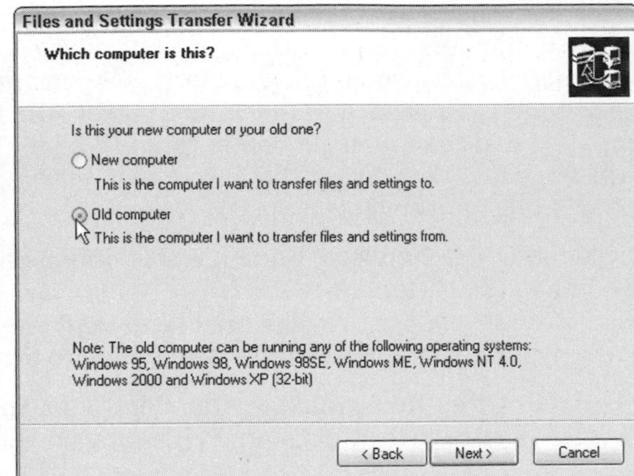

Figure 19-2: Choose the Old Computer option to tell the wizard to gather your computer's files and settings.

If Windows Firewall appears, click the Unblock button to allow the wizard to peek at any connected computers.

3. **Select a transfer method and then click Next.**

   Tell the wizard where to save your newly gathered files and settings, as shown in Figure 19-3, so they can be shuttled off to the new computer through a cable, network, or portable hard drive. Depending on your connection method, the wizard behaves a little differently. Here's the breakdown:

Figure 19-3: The wizard collects the old computer's files and settings and places them in your chosen location.

   - **Direct Cable:** If you choose this option, the wizard tells you to connect the two computers' serial ports with a special *file-transfer* or *null-modem* serial cable, which is available at most computer stores. Click the Autodetect button, and the wizard makes sure that the two computers can communicate before proceeding to the next step. If the wizard freezes during the Autodetect, you've probably bought the wrong type of cable.
   - **Home or Small Office Network:** Don't see this option on your networked computers? Then choose the Other option, instead. From there, click Browse, choose My Network Places, and select a folder anywhere on your network. The wizard then moves to the next step.
   - **Floppy Drive or Other Removable Media:** Click here, and the wizard quickly moves to the next step. Depending on your needs, keep a large stack of floppies on hand for feeding to the computers.
   - **Other:** Click Browse and use My Computer or My Network Places to create a new folder for your files and settings. You can create a folder on a connected portable hard drive, a folder on your existing hard disk, or any folder on your network. If you use a portable drive, you simply connect it to your new computer after you've finished copying files from your old computer.

For the quickest and easiest transfers, network the two computers, as I describe in Chapter 14. A portable hard drive works well, too. The serial cable and floppy methods are frustrating, especially when transferring lots of files.

The wizard must first create a temporary folder that holds all your chosen files and settings, and the folder can be huge. If you're creating that folder on your *old* computer — not a portable hard drive or network — you may run out of space.

4. **Choose the information you want to transfer and click Next.**

   As shown in Figure 19-4, the wizard gives you the following options:

   - **Settings Only:** The wizard skips your files but transfers the settings listed on the right.
   - **Files Only:** The wizard doesn't transfer settings, but it automatically transfers the folders and files listed on the right.
   - **Both Files and Settings:** The wizard transfers everything listed on both its Files and Settings lists.

   For each choice, the wizard tailors its lists to match the speed and capacity of your transfer method. (Floppy users, for instance, won't see as many large files on the list as network or hard drive users.)

For the best control over what the wizard transfers, choose Both Files and Settings and then select the Let Me Select a Custom List of Files and Settings When I Click Next check box.

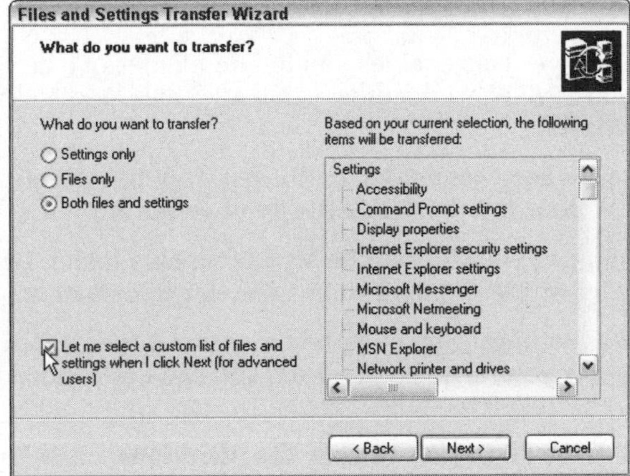

Figure 19-4: Click the Custom List check box to choose what files, folders, and settings the wizard should transfer.

5. **If you selected the Custom List check box, another window appears, as shown in Figure 19-5. Here, you add or remove settings, files, and folders from the transfer list.**

   Here's a rundown on the buttons shown in Figure 19-5:

Figure 19-5: Click the Add or Remove buttons to tailor the transfer list so that it meets your needs.

- **Add Setting:** Click here to add any settings the wizard didn't list in Figure 19-4.
- **Add Folder:** Similarly, click here to add unlisted folders.
- **Add File:** Click here to add specific *files* to the transfer list — your "Air Pressure inside Beer Foam" thesis, for instance.
- **Add File Type:** This enables you to add *all* files of a certain type: for example, all Word documents, all MP3 files, and all Excel spreadsheets.
- **Remove:** To keep something on the list from being transferred, select the item and then click the Remove button.

If you don't store all your files in the My Documents folder, be sure to select those files or their folders when selecting information.

The wizard lists settings from only the programs it recognizes. If it doesn't recognize your favorite program, you can't add its settings to the list.

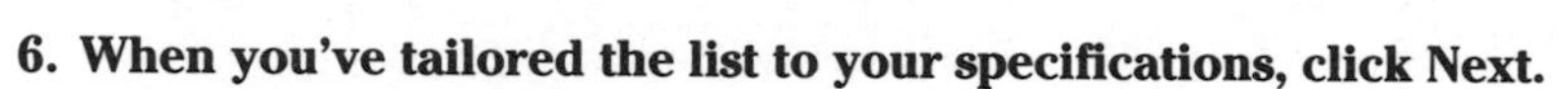

6. **When you've tailored the list to your specifications, click Next.**

   The wizard immediately begins copying your desired goods to a temporary folder.

7. **Click Finish.**

The wizard grabs everything on the list and stores it in a big folder. Congratulations; you've completed the first part of the wizard's task.

The next section explains how to run the wizard on your *new* computer and tell it to start grabbing that information.

Moving things to the new computer

After you've run the wizard on your old computer, telling it to grab all your files and/or settings, the rest is easy. Here's how to unleash the wizard on your new computer and make it grab all your carefully selected information:

1. **Start the Files and Settings Transfer Wizard on your new computer.**

   Depending on how you've chosen to transfer the information from your old computer, the wizard might already be running on your new computer and ready to grab your files. If it is, move to Step 4.

   If the wizard *isn't* already running on your new computer, click Start, click Accessories, click System Tools, stop to pant for breath, and then click Files and Settings Transfer Wizard.

2. **Choose the *New* Computer option and click Next.**

   This is the same window shown in Figure 19-2, by the way.

3. **Click the option button next to I Don't Need the Wizard Disk - I Have Already Collected My Files and Settings from My Old Computer; then click Next.**

   You already collected your files and settings in the previous section, so click the last option on the list, as shown in Figure 19-6.

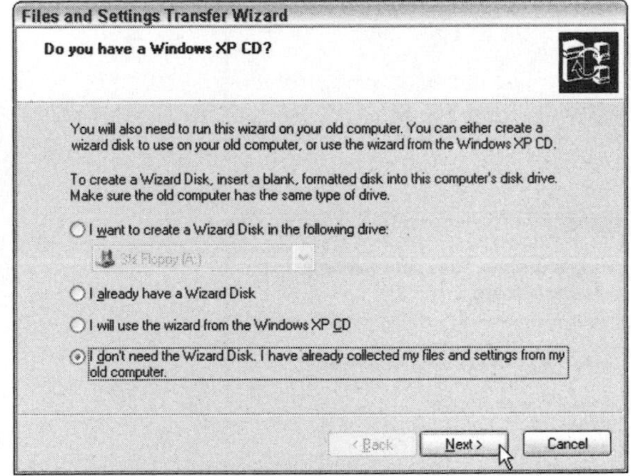

Figure 19-6: Because you already gathered the files in the previous section, click the last option.

4. **Tell the wizard where to find the collected information, as shown in Figure 19-7, and click Next.**

   The wizard may need to look through a cable, a stack of floppies, or a folder on a network or portable hard drive. After you click Next, the wizard gathers the collected information.

   If the wizard can't find your information for some reason, it's in a folder named `USMT2.UNC`. (If you can't seem to find it either, search for it using the Start menu's Search command, covered in Chapter 6.)

   The wizard copies your old computer's selected files and settings to your new computer. Depending on the amount of information and how you're moving it, this can take from minutes to hours. Feel free to go to sleep while the wizard works quietly in the background.

5. **Click the Finish button and restart your computer.**

   When the wizard finally finishes, as shown in Figure 19-8, click the Finish button and restart your computer. When your new computer wakes up, it should have much of the look and feel of your old computer. Your Outlook Express e-mail accounts should be able to collect your mail, for instance, and your My Documents folder should be filled with your old files.

Files and Settings Transfer Wizard

Where are the files and settings?

Where should the wizard look for the items you collected?

Direct cable (a cable that connects your computers' serial ports)

Floppy drive or other removable media

3½ Floppy (A:)

Other (for example, a removable drive or network drive)

D:\here

Browse...

< Back | Next > | Cancel

Figure 19-7: Tell the wizard where to find the information collected from the old computer.

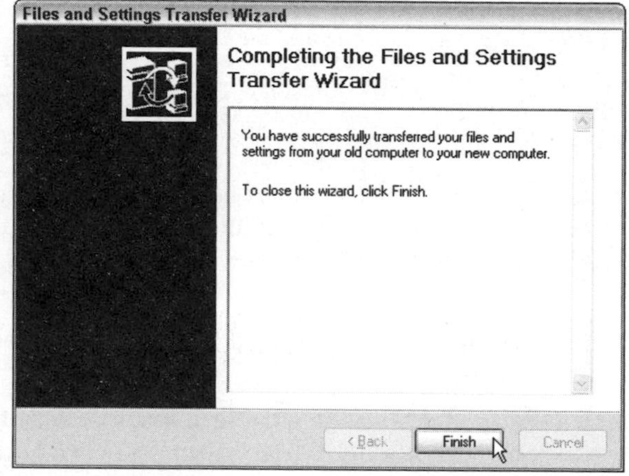

Figure 19-8: Click Finish and restart your computer, and it wakes up with your old settings, files, and folders.

My New Computer Won't Open My Old Computer's Files!

Just as tires from a Volvo don't always fit wheels from a Volkswagen, files created in one program can't always be opened by a different program. This problem has several solutions, described in the following list:

- **Open your files in your old program, use its Save As command, and see if it can save files in more than one format.** Some considerate programs will save files using other programs' formats. For instance, many competing word processors can all read files saved as RTF (Rich Text Format). Similarly, many spreadsheets can read files saved as Comma Delimited or Tab Delimited.

- **Purchase a file conversion program.** Some programs make their money entirely by translating files into formats understood by other programs. Ask at your computer store or look in the store's Utilities section. Most conversion programs specialize in certain types of files — graphics, for instance, or word processors. Others perform a variety of common conversions.
- **Call a computer repair shop.** Some offer data conversion services or can recommend a place that does.
- **Type in all your data again.** This last-resort option works, but it makes one question the value of a computer in the first place.

Disposing of the Old Computer

After you've transferred everything of value from the old computer to the new, what do you do with the old computer? You're left with several options.

Many people simply pass their old computers down to the kids, much like the oldest child's clothing moves down to the next oldest child. Kids don't need powerhouse computers for typing term papers.

Others donate them to charities, although many charities are picky about what they'll accept. Make sure the computer's still working and has a monitor.

Throw it in the trash. An increasing number of cities and states are outlawing this, however, because of the hazardous waste that enters the landfills. California, Texas, and other states ban some computer equipment from landfills.

Recycle it. Dell, for instance, will recycle your old computer when you buy a new Dell computer. Even if you're not buying Dell, visit the recycling page (`www.dell.com/recycling`) at Dell's Web site for lots of general recycling information. Ask your IBM dealer about its recycling plan as well.

It's wise to keep an old computer around for several weeks as you use your new computer. You might remember an important file or setting on the old computer that hasn't yet been transferred over.

Erasing the old computer's hard drive

A freshly donated hard drive can be a thief's delight. If it's like most hard drives, it contains passwords to Web sites, e-mail accounts, and programs; credit card numbers; identifying information; and possibly financial records. None of this should fall into the wrong hands.

If your hard drive contains particularly sensitive information, purchase a data destruction program, available in the Utilities section of most computer stores. These specially designed programs completely erase the hard drive and then fill it up again with random characters. (Many programs can repeat that process several times to reach the required government privacy specification.)

Chapter 20

Help on the Windows XP Help System

In This Chapter

- Finding helpful hints quickly
- Finding help for a particular problem
- Moving around in the Help system
- Searching the entire Help system
- Keeping helpful items handy
- Using the Windows XP Help and Support Center

Sometimes, if you raise your hand in just the right way, Windows XP walks over and offers you some help. Other times, Windows refuses to give you a straight answer. Instead, it shuffles you to another location: a horrible computerized answering machine sending you from one computerized dead end to another.

This chapter offers some help on digging the most information from Windows' frequently unhelpful Help and Support system.

Get Me Some Help, and Fast!

Don't bother plowing through this whole chapter if you don't need to: Here are the quickest ways to make Windows XP dish out helpful information when you're stumped.

Press F1

When you're confused in Windows XP, press the F1 key or choose Help and Support from the Start button's menu. The F1 key always stands for "Help!" Windows XP checks to see what program you're using and fetches some helpful information customized to your particular program or situation. Other times, pressing F1 brings up Windows' huge Help and Support Center, which gets its own section later in this chapter.

Right-click on the confusing part

Windows XP constantly flings confusing questions onto the screen, expecting you to come up with an answer. If you know where to tackle the program, however, you can often shake loose some helpful chunks of information.

When a particular button, setting, box, or menu item has your creativity stifled, right-click on it. A What's This box often appears, as shown in Figure 20-1, letting you know that Windows XP can offer help about that particular area. Click the What's This box, and Windows XP tosses extra information onto the screen, explaining the confusing area you clicked, as shown in Figure 20-2.

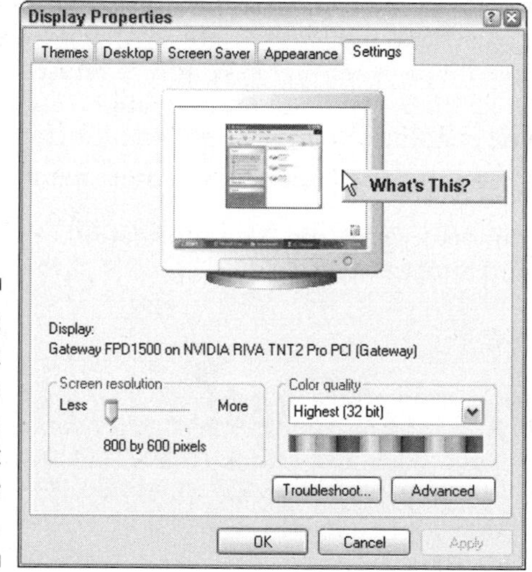

Figure 20-1: Right-click on a confusing object to get the *What's This* hint.

Another trick is to click the little question mark icon near the top-right corner of some windows. A question mark then attaches itself to your mouse pointer. Click any confusing object to see a pop-up explanation like the one in Figure 20-2.

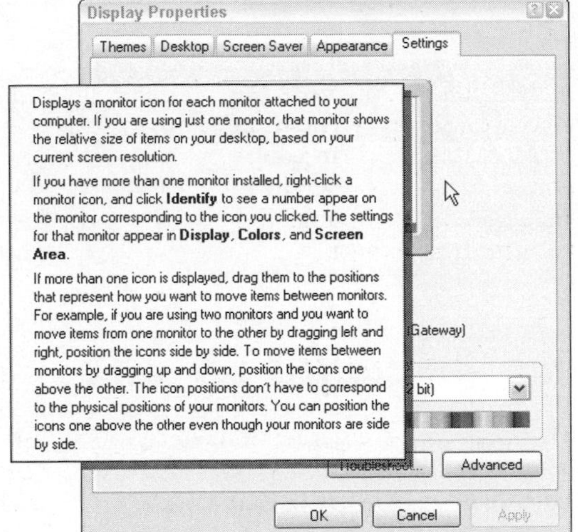

Figure 20-2: Clicking the pop-up What's This button to see pertinent information.

Sending in Windows XP's troubleshooting robots

Windows XP's Help and Support program comes with built-in robots designed to diagnose and solve your computer's problem. To summon the bots, follow these steps:

1. **Choose Help and Support from the Start menu.**

2. **Choose Fixing a Problem from the Pick a Help Topic menu.**

   Fixing a Problem hides near the Help screen's bottom-left corner. As you can see in Figure 20-3, it's ready to tackle a wide variety of problems, from general to specific.

3. **Click the subject that troubles you.**

   Click E-Mail and Messaging Problems, for example, if your e-mail isn't working correctly; Windows unveils the troubleshooter robots designed for different communication problems. Choose the E-Mail Troubleshooter if that's your problem, although the troubleshooters for Internet Explorer and modems are standing by if needed.

4. **Answer the troubleshooter's questions.**

   As you answer the questions, shown in Figure 20-4, Windows narrows down your problem until it decides whether it can fix the problem itself or whether the situation requires outside intervention (in which case, you need to beg assistance from the computer store or manufacturer, the computer guru at work, or a 12-year-old neighbor).

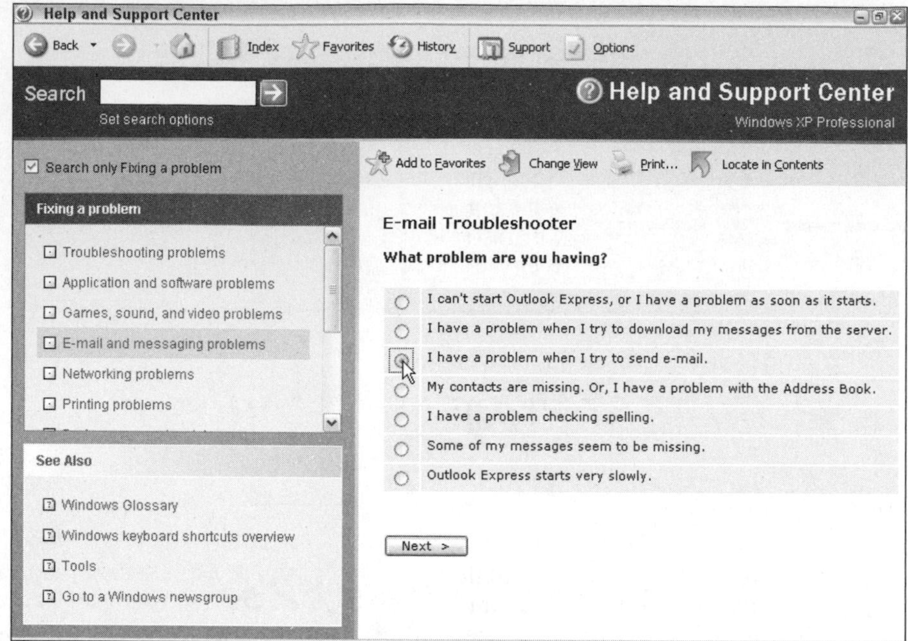

Figure 20-3: The Troubleshooter programs help to solve a wide variety of problems.

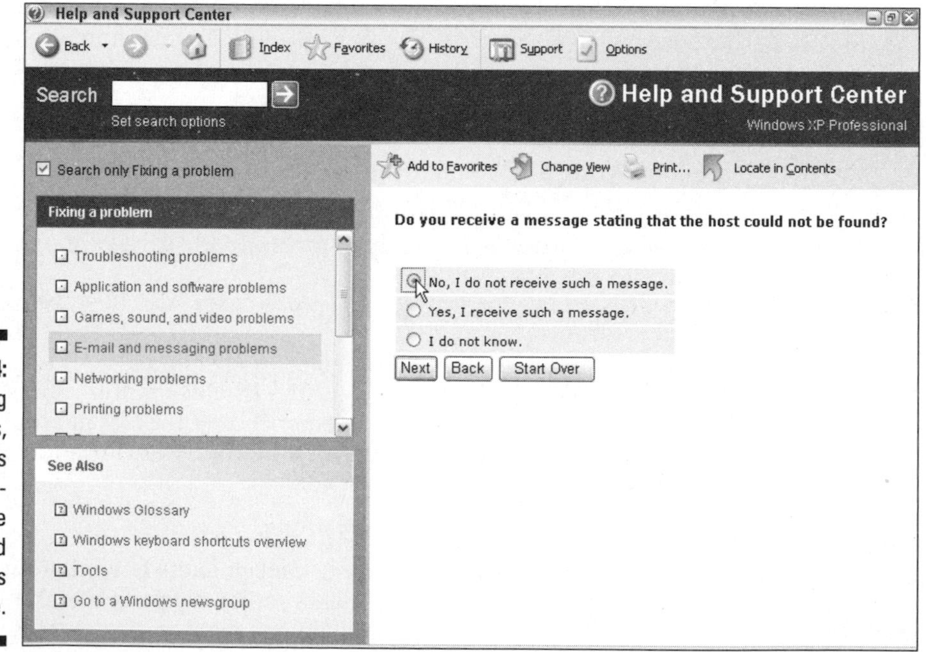

Figure 20-4: By asking questions, Windows often diagnoses the problem and suggests a cure.

Keeping helpful tips handy

Found a particularly helpful area? Save it for future reference by clicking the Add to Favorites button near the top of its page. Then when you click the Favorites button along the top of the Help and Support Center window, that list's name appears, ready to be displayed when you click it.

If you forget to place that particularly helpful page in your Favorites area, you still have a way to find it. Click the History button next to next to the Favorites button. It immediately displays a list of pages you've visited. Hopefully, you spot the one you're looking for.

Consulting a Program's Built-In Computer Guru

Almost every Windows program has the word Help in its top menu. Click Help to call that program's built-in computer guru to your aid. For example, click Help in the Paint program and choose Help Topics, as shown in Figure 20-5, and the Help program opens with a brief description of the program.

Figure 20-5: Choosing Help Topics in Paint.

To start picking the computer guru's brain, follow these steps:

1. **Click the word at the top (Paint, in this case), and Windows XP lists popular subjects.**
2. **Click a subtopic, such as Create Pictures, and the program lists tasks involved in creating pictures.**
3. **Click one of the tasks — Erase a Small Area, for example — to see an explanation, as shown in Figure 20-6.**

Confused about a term used in the Help window? If the term is underlined (like background color is in Figure 20-6), click it, and a new window pops up, defining the term.

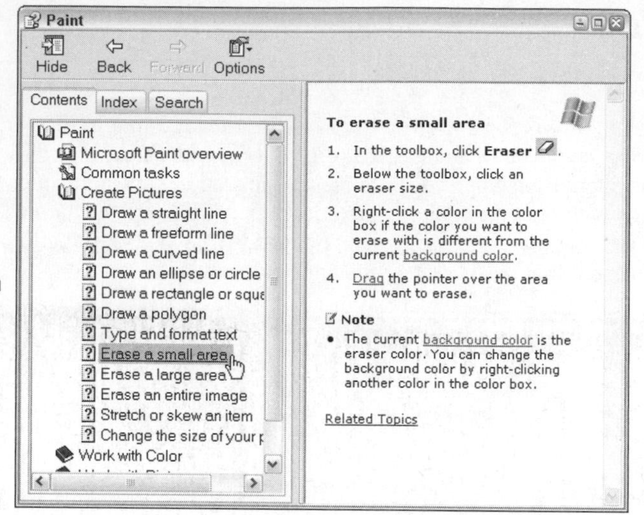

Figure 20-6: Choose a topic to see more specific help areas.

The Windows XP Help system is sometimes a lot of work, forcing you to wade through increasingly detailed menus to find specific information. Still, using Help offers a last resort when you can't find the information elsewhere. And it's often much less embarrassing than tracking down the neighbor's teenagers.

If you don't see your problem listed in the Help program's Table of Contents page, try the other two tabs:

- **Index tab:** A quick way to jump directly to the right subject is by clicking the Index tab. Just like a book's index, it presents an alphabetical list of everything the Help program is willing to discuss. If you see a subject that even remotely resembles what you're confused about, double-click it. Windows XP brings up that page of Help information. Windows indexes alphabetically and, unfortunately, isn't very smart. So, if you're looking for help on margins, for example, don't type **adding margins** or **changing margins**. Instead, type **margins** so that Windows jumps to the words beginning with *M.*
- **Search tab:** Type a few words describing your problem and click the List Topics button to see Help pages discussing that topic. Click any helpful-looking items to read their tips. (Click the Back button to return to the Search results.)

If you're impressed with a particularly helpful page, send it to the printer: Right-click on the page and choose Print from the menu that appears. Windows XP shoots that page to the printer so that you can keep it handy until you lose it.

Using the Windows Help and Support Center

Windows XP comes with a surprisingly good Help program. It even connects to the Internet to find the latest answers to your problems. To summon the program, choose Help and Support Center from the Start menu. The Help and Support Center rises to the screen, as shown in Figure 20-7.

The Help and Support Center offers assistance in these categories:

- **Pick a Help Topic:** Start here for the best results because you can browse Help topics organized by subject. Click Customizing Your Computer, for example, to find help with changing Windows XP's various components: its Start menu, desktop, backgrounds, screen savers, fonts, files, and similar subjects.
- **Ask for Assistance:** The Remote Assistance program lets you invite a savvier Windows XP user to connect to your computer through the Internet. Through a rather complicated process, the Geek connects to your computer and sees *your* desktop on his screen. If you're not into that kind of computer intimacy, click the Support link to get help from Microsoft or other Internet users.

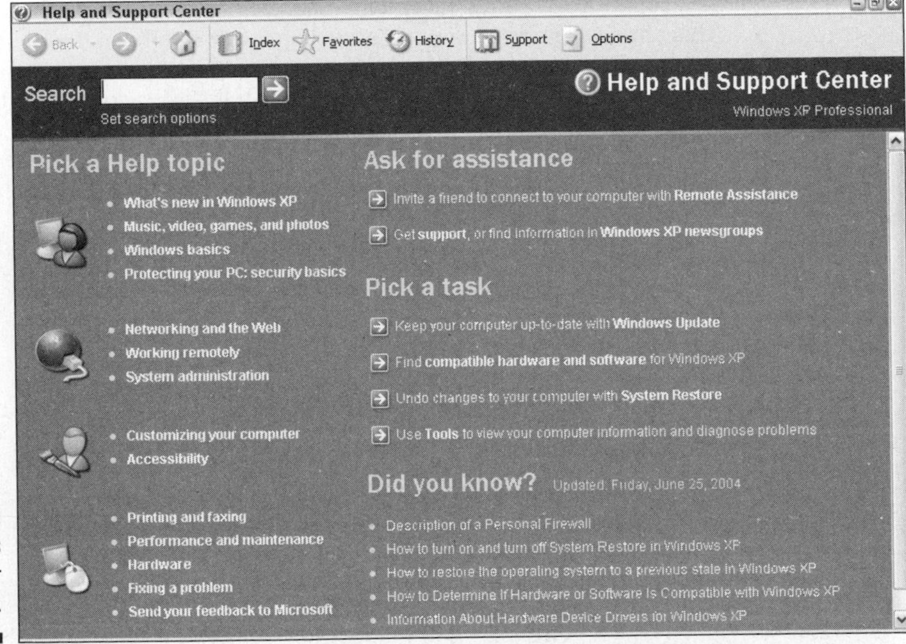

Figure 20-7: The Windows Help and Support Center offers assistance with Windows and your computer.

- **Pick a Task:** You'll find the most commonly used items here. One click enables you to keep your computer up-to-date, check the compatibility of hardware or software, restore your computer back to a time when it worked well, and run diagnostic tools to view information and test your computer.
- **Did You Know:** Windows XP connects to the Internet and pulls up answers to frequently asked questions and other updated information. You may just get lucky and spot something useful.

Start your quest for help at the Pick a Help Topic area. If your troublesome subject is listed here, click it and begin narrowing down the search for pertinent information.

If that doesn't help, use the Search command at the page's top. Type in a word or two describing your problem and click the green arrow next to the Search box. Type **e-mail**, for instance, to see every help topic dealing with e-mail. It lists the topics in three categories:

- **Suggested Topics:** The first and most valuable area, this lists troubleshooters, step-by-step tutorials, and general information about your subject.
- **Full-Text Search Matches:** This all-encompassing search lists every topic mentioning the search term you entered, no matter how briefly. It often brings up too much general information to be useful.
- **Microsoft Knowledge Base:** Quite helpful for more advanced users, this shows results found in a huge Microsoft database listing problems, bugs, and solutions for every Microsoft product. Because it connects to Microsoft's online database, it requires an Internet connection.

The Windows Help and Support Center works much like a Web site. To move back one page, click the little green Back arrow in the upper-left corner. That arrow helps you out if you've backed into a corner.

Part VII

The Part of Tens

"IT'S INCREDIBLE! I'M SEEING LIFE FORMS NEVER BEFORE IMAGINED!! BIZARRE, COLORFUL, ALMOST WHIMSICAL!!!"

In this part . . .

Everybody likes to read Top Ten lists in magazines — especially in the grocery store checkout aisle when you're stuck behind someone who's just pulled a rubber band off a thick stack of double coupons and the cashier can't find the right validation stamp.

Unlike the reading material at the grocery store, the chapters in this part of the book are actually useful. You find lists of ways to make Windows XP more efficient — or at least less hostile. Another thankfully short list contains important things to remember about Windows. Finally, check out the list of things to look forward to in the *next* version of Windows.

Some lists have more than ten items; others have fewer, but who's counting, besides the poor cashier wading through all those double coupons?

Chapter 21

Ten Aggravating Things about Windows XP (And How to Fix Them)

In This Chapter

- Getting rid of the Welcome screen
- Changing the volume quickly and easily
- Managing taskbars and button bars
- Keeping track of multiple windows
- Lining up two windows on the desktop
- Understanding what activities only an administrator can do
- Putting the right task panes on folders
- Finding out your version of Windows
- Understanding the Print Screen key

Windows XP would be great if only . . . (insert your pet peeve here). If you find yourself thinking (or saying) those words frequently, read this chapter. Here, you find not only a list of the most aggravating things about Windows XP but also ways you can fix them.

Windows Makes Me Log On All the Time!

Windows offers two ways to return to life from its swirling and churning screen saver. Windows can return you to the Welcome screen, where you must log back on to your user account. Alternatively, Windows XP can simply return you to the program you were using when the screen saver kicked in.

Some people prefer the security of the Welcome screen. If the screen saver kicks in when they're spending too much time at the water cooler, they're protected: Nobody can walk over and start reading their e-mail.

Other people don't need that extra security, and they simply want to return to work quickly. Here's how to accommodate either camp:

1. **Right-click on a blank part of your desktop and choose Properties.**
2. **Click the Screen Saver tab.**

   Windows XP shows the screen saver options, including whether or not Windows should wake up at the Welcome screen.
3. **Depending on your preference, remove or add the check mark from the On Resume Display Welcome Screen box.**

   If the box *is checked,* Windows XP is more secure. The screen saver wakes up at the Welcome screen, and users must log on to their user accounts before using the computer.

   If the box *isn't checked,* Windows XP is more easygoing, waking up from the screen saver in the same place where you stopped working.
4. **Click the OK button to save your changes.**

If you don't *ever* want to see the Welcome screen, then use a single user account without a password. That defeats all the security offered by Windows XP's User Account system, but it's more convenient if you live alone.

Turning Down (Or Up) the Volume

Nearly any electronic gadget that makes noise — a radio, a TV, or an electric guitar — comes with an easy-to-reach volume knob. Not XP.

To rectify matters, here's how to put Windows XP's volume control where it belongs — right next to the little clock in the bottom-right corner of your screen:

1. **Click the Start button, open the Control Panel, and click the Sounds, Speech, and Audio Devices icon.**
2. **Click the Sounds and Audio Devices icon and select the Place Volume Icon in the Taskbar check box.**

   A little speaker appears next to your clock.
3. **Click OK to close the window.**

   Whenever you need to adjust the sound level in a hurry, click the little speaker by your clock. A sliding volume control appears, letting you turn the sound up or down by sliding the control up or down. Click the Mute button to turn the sound off completely. Whew!

The Taskbar Keeps Disappearing!

The taskbar is a handy Windows XP feature that usually squats along the bottom of your screen. Sometimes, unfortunately, it up and wanders off into the woods. Here are a few ways to track it down and bring it home.

If you can spot only a slim edge of the taskbar — the rest of it hangs off the screen's edge, for example — place the mouse pointer on the edge you *can* see. After the mouse pointer turns into a two-headed arrow, hold down your mouse button and move the mouse toward the screen's center to drag the taskbar back into view.

Keep dragging the taskbar until you've positioned it in the right place and then let go of the mouse button.

- If your taskbar drops from sight whenever the mouse pointer doesn't hover nearby, turn off the taskbar's Auto Hide feature: Right-click on a blank part of the taskbar and choose Properties from the pop-up menu. When the Taskbar and Start Menu Properties dialog box appears, click to remove the check mark from the Auto Hide box. (Or, to turn on the Auto Hide feature, add the check mark.)
- While you're in the Taskbar and Start Menu Properties dialog box, make sure that a check mark appears in the Keep the Taskbar on Top of Other Windows check box. That way, the taskbar always rides visibly on the desktop, making it much easier to spot.
- To keep the taskbar locked into place so that it won't move, right-click on the taskbar, choose Properties, and select Lock the Taskbar. Remember, though, that before you can make any changes to the taskbar, you must first unlock it.

My Bar Full of Buttons Just Fell Off!

It's happened to the best of us. We try to click a single button amid a row of other buttons in a program or the taskbar, and the entire row of buttons falls off and lands onto the desktop. Or it simply moves off kilter.

What did you do wrong? Nothing, it turns out. Microsoft figures that some people enjoy the versatility of moving their buttons around. So, Windows lets people drag the bar off the program and place it someplace else. Those little toolbars are *portable*.

To place the bar back where it started, place the mouse pointer on the bar, hold down your mouse button, and drag the bar back where it belongs. Release the mouse button, and the bar reattaches itself. Or, if that's not working right, try double-clicking the bar. The bar often reattaches itself automatically.

Sometimes it takes a long time to reattach a toolbar, with lots of dragging and dropping until it's in just the right place. Keep trying, and you'll eventually reposition it. (***Hint:*** Look for a little vertical line on the bar because it often serves as a makeshift handle.)

Keeping Track of Open Windows

You don't *have* to keep track of all those open windows. Windows XP does it for you with a secret key combination: Hold the Alt key and press the Tab key, and the little bar appears, displaying the icons for all your open windows. Keep pressing Tab; when Windows highlights the icon of the window you're after, release the keys. The window pops up.

Or, use the taskbar, that long strip along the bottom of your screen. Covered in Chapter 2, the taskbar lists the name of every open window. Click the name of the window you want, and that window hops to the top of the pile.

In Chapter 6, you find more soldiers to enlist in the battle against misplaced windows, files, and programs.

Lining Up Two Windows on the Screen

With all its cut-and-paste stuff, Windows XP makes it easy for you to grab information from one program and slap it into another. With its drag-and-drop stuff, you can grab an address from a database and drag it into a letter in your word processor.

The hardest part of Windows XP is lining up two windows on the screen, side by side, to make for easy dragging. *That's* when you need to call in the taskbar. First, open the two windows and place them anywhere on the screen. Then turn all the other windows into icons (minimize them) by clicking the button with the little line that lives in the top-right corners of those windows.

Now, right-click on a blank area of the taskbar and then click one of the two Tile commands listed on the menu. The two windows line up on the screen perfectly.

It Won't Let Me Do Something Unless I'm an Administrator!

Windows XP gets really picky about who gets to do what on your computer. The computer's owner gets the Administrator account. And the administrator usually gives everybody else a Limited account. What does that mean? Well, only the administrator can do these things on the computer:

- Install programs and hardware.
- Create or change accounts for other users.
- Install Plug and Play–type hardware, such as some digital cameras and MP3 players.
- Turn off the Guest account.
- Read everybody else's files.

People with limited accounts, by nature, are limited to fairly basic activities. They can do these things:

- Run installed programs.
- Change their account's picture and password.

Guest accounts are meant for the baby sitter or visitors who don't permanently use the computer. If you have a broadband or other "always on" Internet account, guests can browse the Internet, run programs, or check their e-mail. (As described in Chapter 13, Guest accounts aren't allowed to *start* an Internet session, but they can use an existing one.)

My Folders List the Wrong Task Panes!

Windows XP places a customized *task pane* along every folder's left edge listing shortcuts related to that folder. The task pane shortcuts in your My Documents folder, for instance, let you create new folders, share folders, or quickly jump to your desktop or other handy places.

Shortcuts listed on the My Pictures task pane, by contrast, let you grab pictures from a camera, view your photos as a slide show, print photos, and perform other photo-related activities.

Occasionally, however, Windows XP places the wrong task pane in a folder. The My Music task pane might show up in your My Pictures folder, for instance.

To fix the problem, close the folder. Then right-click on it, choose Properties, and click the Customize tab. Select the folder's contents in the drop-down list and click the OK button. Windows usually adjusts the task pane accordingly to match the folder's contents.

But if that still doesn't fix the problem, follow these steps:

1. **Open any folder.**
2. **Choose Folder Options from the Tools menu.**
3. **Click the View tab and click the Reset All Folders button.**

   Windows XP displays all its folders with their original look, restoring misplaced task panes in the process. The changes take place the next time the folders are opened.

What Version of Windows Do I Have?

Windows has been sold in more than a dozen flavors since its debut in November 1985. How can you tell what version the store really installed on your computer?

Open the Start menu, right-click on My Computer, and choose Properties. Click the General tab if that page isn't already showing.

Under the word *System,* Windows displays its version, version number, and the latest service pack installed.

My Print Screen Key Doesn't Work

Windows XP takes over the Print Screen key (labeled PrtSc, PrtScr, or something even more supernatural on some keyboards). Instead of sending the stuff on the screen to the printer, the Print Screen key sends it to Windows XP's memory, where you can paste it into other windows.

- If you hold the Alt key while pressing the Print Screen key, Windows XP sends a picture of the current *window* — not the entire screen — to the Clipboard for pasting.
- If you *really* want a printout of the screen, press the Print Screen button to send a picture of the screen to its memory. (It won't look like anything has happened.) Then open Paint or WordPad, choose Paste from the Edit menu, and when your picture appears, print from that program.

Chapter 22

Ten Things to Remember about Windows XP

In This Chapter

- Poking windows and icons so they do what you want
- Keeping Windows secure and happy
- Customizing the way Windows looks

With so many things in Windows XP to remember, how can you possibly keep track of them all? Don't bother trying. I've whittled them down to the dozen of the most important things and dropped them into this chapter for easy reference. Memorize at will or simply dog-ear this page and keep the book handy by your computer.

When in Doubt, Right-Click

Mysterious icons, menu items, and programs live throughout Windows, leaving you with the nagging question, just what am I supposed to do with this thing? When something in Windows leaves you scratching your head, try this easy-to-remember trick:

When in doubt, right-click.

When you right-click on something, Windows brings up a handy menu listing everything you're able to do with that item. This trick works on icons, your desktop, Web sites, songs in Media Player, your taskbar, words in a word processor, and nearly any other right-clickable item.

Feel free to hover your mouse pointer over confusing menus options as well. When Windows XP senses an unsure mouse, it often provides a helpful pop-up explanation.

Create Restore Points

When everything's going particularly well with your computing day, you don't usually think about System Restore. But you should. While smiling blissfully, capture that happy moment in time by creating your own restore point, as described in Chapter 12. Then when things *aren't* going particularly well, return to happier times by using that restore point. The more good restore points you've created, the easier it will be to return to good times.

Make Windows Update Automatic

Being more than three years old in the computer world means Windows XP is an old-timer. And like an aging house, it has developed plenty of leaks. So many, in fact, that Microsoft has released dozens of patches to fix all the problems.

Most people prefer *working* on their computers rather than installing patches. So, Windows XP's Service Pack 2 tells Windows Update to perform its duties automatically. When you connect to the Internet, your computer automatically downloads any new patches and installs them in the background. For details on automating updates, flip to Chapter 10.

Show the Quick Launch Toolbar

Instead of wading through the Start menu to find a program, you can simply click the program's icon on the Quick Launch toolbar, which resides on the taskbar. Microsoft removed the Quick Launch toolbar in Windows XP Home, but this secret switch puts it back in place:

Right-click on an unused part of your taskbar. (The clock will do.) Point at the word Toolbars on the pop-up menu and choose Quick Launch.

Add Your Favorite Goodies to the Quick Launch Toolbar

Quick Launch icons, described in the preceding section, are merely *shortcuts* — pointers to programs and places. That means you can add Quick Launch icons for nearly anything: folders, programs, Web sites, or even frequently used icons from your Control Panel. To add your own frequently used icons, drag and drop them onto the toolbar. For more about customizing the taskbar, see Chapter 2.

Use the Show Desktop Icon

The Quick Launch toolbar sports the obvious icons for Internet Explorer and Media Player. But the Show Desktop icon (shown in the margin) comes in handy, especially when you're faced with a desktop covered with windows. Click this icon to minimize everything on your desktop immediately. (Click it again to put everything back the way it was.)

Use BCC When Forwarding E-Mails

E-mails get forwarded from person to person more often than the flu. When you succumb to the urge to keep an e-mail "going" by forwarding it to all your friends, don't simply place all their names in the To box and click Send. Use your e-mail's blind carbon copy feature instead. That still forwards the message to everybody but keeps their names and addresses private. I explain the blind carbon copy feature and how to use it in Chapter 9.

Add Your Own User Account Picture

Windows XP automatically assigns a generic photo to your user account; that picture graces your Welcome screen and sits atop your Start menu. But you can choose any picture you want, even something just snapped from your digital camera.

To personalize your user account photo, double-click the photo at the top of your Start menu. When the Pick a New Picture for Your Account window appears, choose Browse for More Pictures. Navigate to the folder containing the picture you want and double-click it to assign it to your user account.

Windows XP automatically shrinks the photo to fit and assigns it to your user account.

Share Files with Other User Accounts

Windows XP keeps everybody's user accounts private. But every user account has access to the *Shared Documents* folder and every folder inside it. You find shortcuts to the Shared Documents folder in My Computer as well as the task pane for your My Documents folder.

To share a file with everybody on your computer, copy or move it to your Shared Documents folder.

Make Windows Open to the Size You Want

When you open a new window, whether in a folder, in a program, or on the Internet, it's often hard to guess what size you'll see. Sometimes the window fills the screen; other times it's only half size.

But Windows has a method to this seeming randomness, and it works like this: Windows always open to the same size they were when *last closed.* Drag and drop a window's corners or edges until it's the size you want. Then close it. The next time you open the window, it opens to that same size. I explain more window tricks in Chapter 3.

Lock Your PC before Leaving

After you walk away from your computer at work, anybody can sit down and start fiddling with your files. Logging off from your user account stops intruders, but that takes lots of time. Instead, lock your computer before walking away by holding down the Windows key and pressing the L key. Windows XP quickly jumps to the Welcome screen.

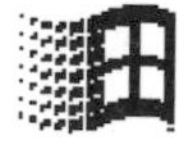

To log back in, just click your user account name and type in your password. Windows quickly jumps back to your desktop, just the way you left it. (The Windows key, which bears the little Microsoft Windows logo, sits between the Ctrl and Alt keys of most keyboards.)

Chapter 23

Ten Things to Look Forward to in the Next Version of Windows

In This Chapter

- Buying a new computer
- Enjoying the pretty visuals
- Keeping your computer more secure
- Using new tools for photos, searches, and DVD burning

By the looks of things, the Microsoft folks have *finally* read the *Windows For Dummies* books. They've realized people don't want to work with their computers; they simply want to get their work *done.* The next version of Windows, dubbed Longhorn, promises to do just that.

It Won't Run Well on Older Computers

Windows XP cruises along just fine on my 500 MHz Gateway Pentium III. Simply loading Longhorn, by contrast, took more than an hour. After finally installing itself, Longhorn crawled across my screen and preened its stylish feathers. In short, when it's time to upgrade to Longhorn, it's probably time to buy that new computer you've been putting off. Longhorn is built for cutting-edge computer parts.

Longhorn Looks Much Prettier

Longhorn is full of new 3-D effects — if your computer's video card is powerful (expensive) enough to handle the extra load. The taskbar's trusty clock, for instance, sports stylish hands that tick along as you work. Icons like the Recycle Bin are *transparent.* When you move them to different places on your desktop, the background shows through. Windows similarly blend into your background when you're not working on them, making your current program easier to spot. The desktop also has a new Sidebar with little add-on sections called *trays* that slide in and out. Among the things you'll find there are a clock, a contact list, and a photo slide show.

New Improved Digital Photo Viewer

Microsoft assumes everybody now owns a digital camera, so Longhorn's My Pictures folder boasts a few extra tricks. It offers to tweak your photos automatically while sucking them from your camera, applying filters to correct obvious problems. Instead of struggling with Windows' lowly Paint program, you'll get built-in tools to crop a photo, fix red-eye, and adjust exposure problems. You can even add a few key words to describe your photos, making them easier to locate again.

Improved Security

Tired of being the butt of jokes, Microsoft is working hard to make Windows more secure and less vulnerable to viruses and worms. And Microsoft is obviously serious because it has discovered a way to make more money at the same time: Longhorn includes new antivirus technology, and Microsoft's Next Generation Secure Computing Base (NGSCB) teams up with security features built in to upcoming computer parts. For example, microprocessors will help protect users from evil forces like spam and Internet break-ins. (I'll believe the spam killer when I see it.)

Improved Filing System

Ever noticed how a search engine can dig up the most esoteric information on the vast Internet before you have time to locate a commonly used file on your own hard drive? Longhorn now employs similar search-engine technology so that you can find that crucial missing piece of information quickly and easily. Microsoft also makes the Search program more visual and easier to use. Looking for the item you played with yesterday is a snap.

Longhorn Supports DVD Burning

Better late than never. Longhorn finally lets you burn DVDs as easily as Windows XP burns CDs. To solve the DVD format wars currently going on among manufacturers, Longhorn decided to support *all* the formats. It also supports the new HD-DVD standard, which lets a DVD store a full-length, high-definition movie.

Appendix A

Upgrading to Windows XP

In This Appendix

- Preparing to install Windows XP
- Deciding between Windows XP Home and Professional
- Upgrading to Windows XP
- Activating Windows XP
- Returning to your old version of Windows

New computers today come with Windows XP preinstalled — it's practically unavoidable. If you're reading this chapter, then your computer is probably still running Windows 98 or Windows Me.

To upgrade that old workhorse to Windows XP, pick up a copy of Windows XP Home, Upgrade Edition. Be sure to buy the *Upgrade* edition. The *Full* edition (which costs twice as much) is for people installing Windows XP onto a new computer or one they've built themselves.

Upgrading to Windows XP

Windows XP usually runs well on computers purchased within the past three or four years. Before upgrading, make sure you've run through the following checklist:

- **Computer power:** Make sure that your computer is strong enough to run Windows XP. Windows XP lists its requirements on the side of its software box, but here's a briefer: a 233 MHz or faster processor from the Pentium/Celeron family (or AMD's K6/Athlon/Duron family); 128MB or more RAM; 1.5GB of available hard drive space; a SuperVGA video card and monitor; and a CD-ROM drive.
- **Compatibility:** Before upgrading or installing, download and run Microsoft's *Upgrade Advisor.* It alerts you beforehand what parts of your computer may not run well under Windows XP. You'll find the Upgrade

Deciding between Windows XP Home and Professional

Windows XP Professional and Windows XP Home look and act almost exactly the same. Most consumers save money by purchasing Windows XP Home, which can do everything I've described in this book. (Windows XP Professional usually costs about $100 more.)

The people buying Windows XP Professional are usually computer nerds. Others need to connect to their office computers in a more advanced way (specifically, through a *Windows server domain*). Windows XP Home can still connect to most office networks just fine, and it handles most needs.

Microsoft explains the differences between the two operating systems in more detail at the Windows XP Web site (`www.microsoft.com/windowsxp`).

Advisor on Microsoft's Web site at `www.microsoft.com/windowsxp/home/upgrading/advisor.mspx`. Beware: It's almost 50MB, so you need a speedy broadband Internet connection.

- **Security:** Before upgrading to Windows XP, turn off your antivirus software and other security programs. They might innocently try to protect you from Windows XP's upgrade process.
- **Backup:** Back up all your important data. I discuss backups in Chapter 10.

Installing the Windows XP Upgrade

Follow these steps to upgrade your existing Windows operating system to Windows XP.

To be safe, unplug your computer from its modem or the phone line while installing Windows XP. When Windows XP is fully installed, make sure you've turned on its firewall before letting it connect to the Internet.

1. **Insert the Windows XP CD into your CD drive and choose Install Windows XP, as shown in Figure A-1.**
2. **In the Installation Type drop-down list, choose Upgrade (Recommended) and click Next, as shown in Figure A-2.**
3. **Read the License Agreement, click the button next to the I Accept This Agreement option, and click Next.**

   Take an hour or so to read Microsoft's 53-page License Agreement carefully. You need to select the I Accept This Agreement option before Microsoft allows you to install the software.

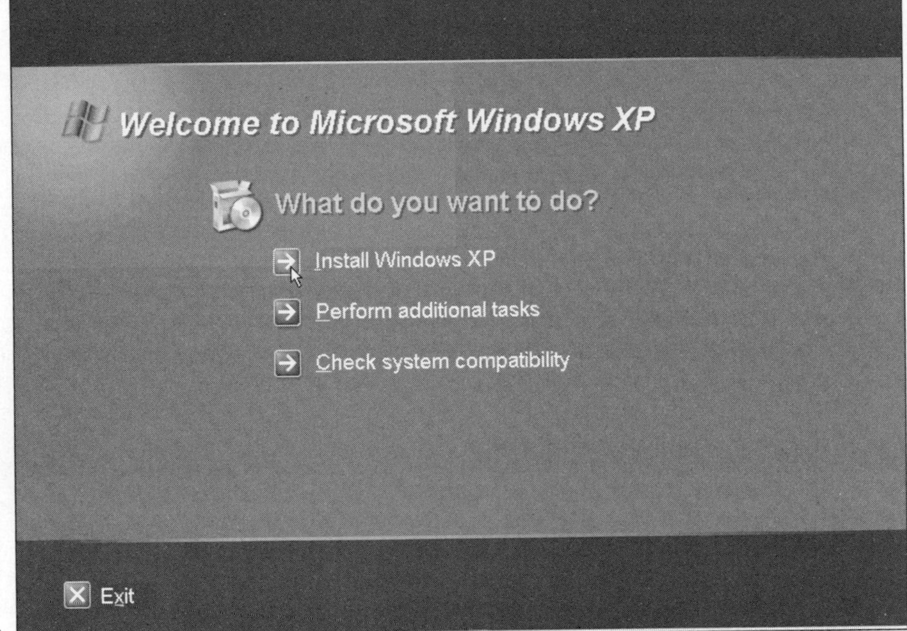

Figure A-1: Choose Install Windows XP from the Windows XP CD.

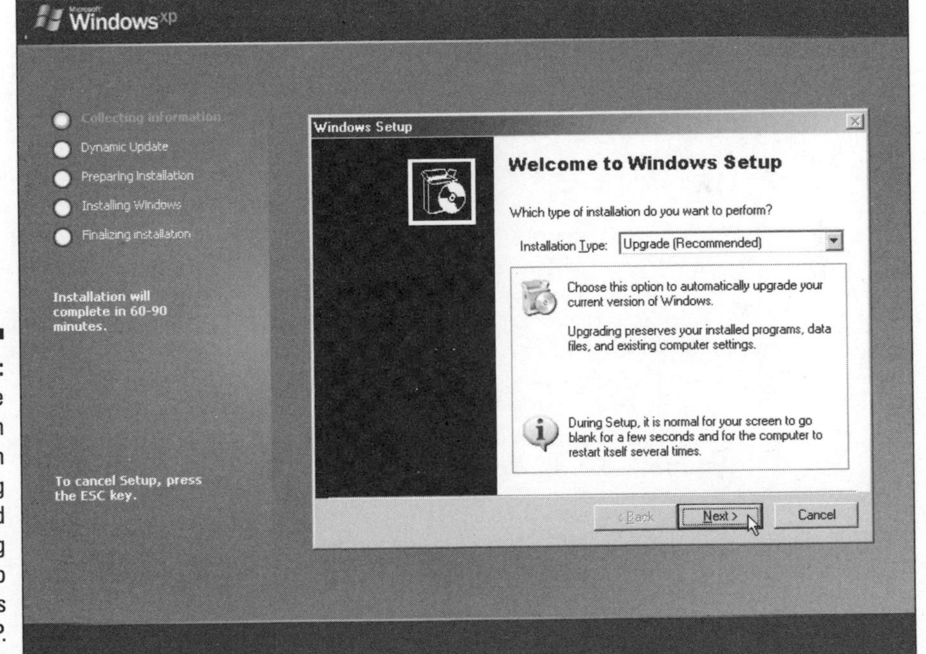

Figure A-2: Click the Next button to begin upgrading your old operating system to Windows XP.

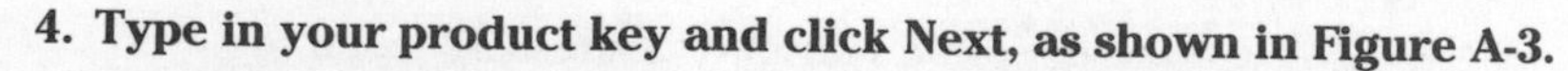

4. **Type in your product key and click Next, as shown in Figure A-3.**

   The *product key* usually lives on a little sticker affixed to the CD's case. No product key? You're stuck. You can't install Windows XP without a product key.

   Write your product key on top of your Windows XP CD with a felt-tip pen. (Write on the side of the CD that's *printed.*) That way you'll always have your valid product key with your CD.

5. **Create the Upgrade Report by selecting the options Show Me Hardware Issues and Limited Set of Software Issues. Then click Next.**

   Even if you've already run the Upgrade Wizard, tell Windows XP to create the Upgrade Report. It's better to be informed than caught off guard at the last minute.

6. **View the report and click Next.**

   Click the Full Report button to see details of Windows findings. If it looks like you may need to buy some new parts or software, click the Save As button or Print button. That way you have something to take to the store when shopping.

   When you click Next, Windows XP starts its *real* installation. Your drives churn away as Windows copies files to your hard disk, restarts itself, and then copies some more files. Windows XP eventually rests, leaving a question mark dancing on-screen.

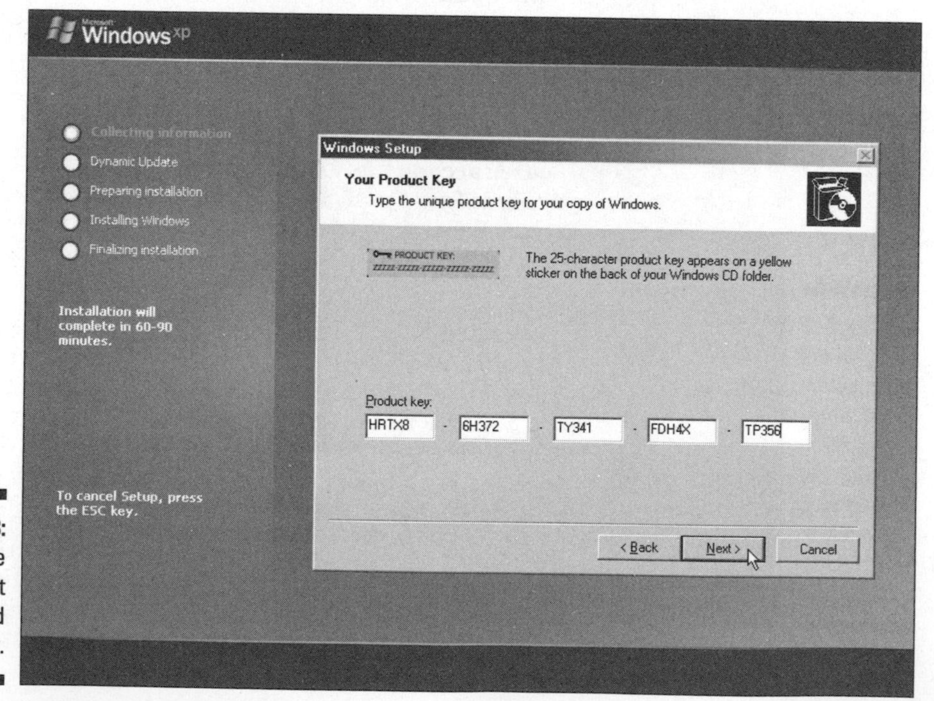

Figure A-3: Type in the product key and click Next.

7. **When the question mark stops dancing, click the Next button in the screen's bottom-right corner.**
8. **Decide whether to Activate Windows XP now or in 30 days and click Next.**

   Choose the 30-day option. That gives you time to make sure everything works correctly before the Activation process locks your computer to that copy of Windows XP.

   Windows XP's Activation feature takes a snapshot of your computer's parts and assigns it to Windows XP's serial number. That prevents you from installing that same copy onto another computer. Unfortunately, the Activation feature may also hassle you if you change a lot of parts in your computer. (It's particularly sensitive when you add or replace network cards.)

9. **Create user accounts for everybody using the computer.**

   Type your name into the first box, followed by the names of other people who will be using your computer. (You can do this later, if you wish, using the steps I describe in Chapter 13.)

10. **Click the Finish button.**

    Windows XP's grassy knoll appears on the screen, announcing that you've finished. But don't rest too much. Run through the following steps to complete the process:

    - **Use Windows Update.** Connect to the Internet, described in Chapter 8, and visit Windows Update to download any security patches and updated drivers issued by Microsoft.
    - **Make sure that Windows XP recognizes your software.** Run all your old programs to make sure they still work.
    - **Check the user accounts.** Windows XP often doesn't keep any logon passwords from your older version of Windows, so head for the Control Panel's User Accounts area and edit the user accounts for your computer's users. Add any new accounts, while you're at it.

    - **Convert your hard drive to NTFS.** Some older computers use the FAT32 file system, which doesn't provide Windows XP with much security. Choose Help and Support from Windows XP's Start menu and look up *NTFS* for more detailed information. Convert to NTFS only if you're sure you'll be keeping Windows XP; after you've converted, you can't uninstall Windows XP and revert to your old Windows version.
    - **Return to your old operating system or get rid of it to free up hard drive space, if needed.** Did Windows XP mess up everything? The "Returning to your old version of Windows" sidebar explains what to do. If all is well, you can use Add/Remove programs to delete the old system instead.

Returning to your *old* version of Windows

When you upgrade to Windows XP, the program graciously packs away your old operating system into a huge file and stashes it away onto your hard drive. If Windows XP isn't treating your computer very nicely — things just aren't working the way you planned — it's fairly easy to return to the days of your faithful old operating system. Here's how.

1. **Open the Control Panel from the Start menu.**
2. **Double-click the Add or Remove Programs icon.**
3. **Choose Windows XP Uninstall and click the Change/Remove button.**
4. **Choose Uninstall Windows XP and click Continue.**
5. **Click Yes.**

Windows XP closes down, reboots your computer, and reappears, but still as Windows XP. Finally, Windows XP puts itself to sleep and closes down one more time, eventually reappearing as your old operating system.

Index

• A •

• B •

• C •

• D •

• F •

• G •

• H •

• I •

• J •

• K •

• L •

• M •

• N •

• O •

• P •

• R •

• S •

• U •

• V •

• W •

• Y •

• Z •